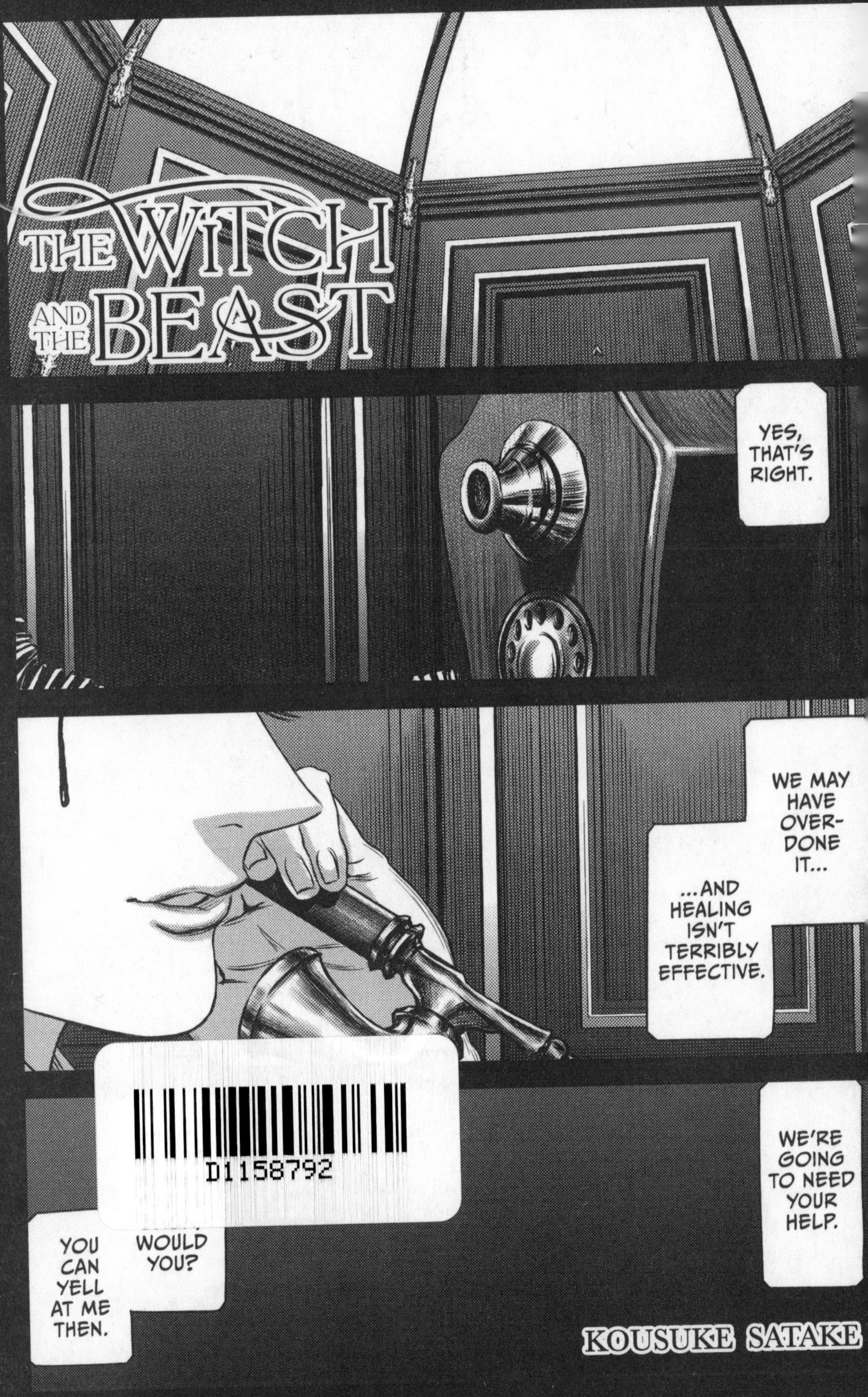
THE WITCH AND THE BEAST
YES, THAT'S RIGHT.
WE MAY HAVE OVER-DONE IT...
...AND HEALING ISN'T TERRIBLY EFFECTIVE.
WE'RE GOING TO NEED YOUR HELP.
WOULD YOU?
YOU CAN YELL AT ME THEN.
KOUSUKE SATAKE

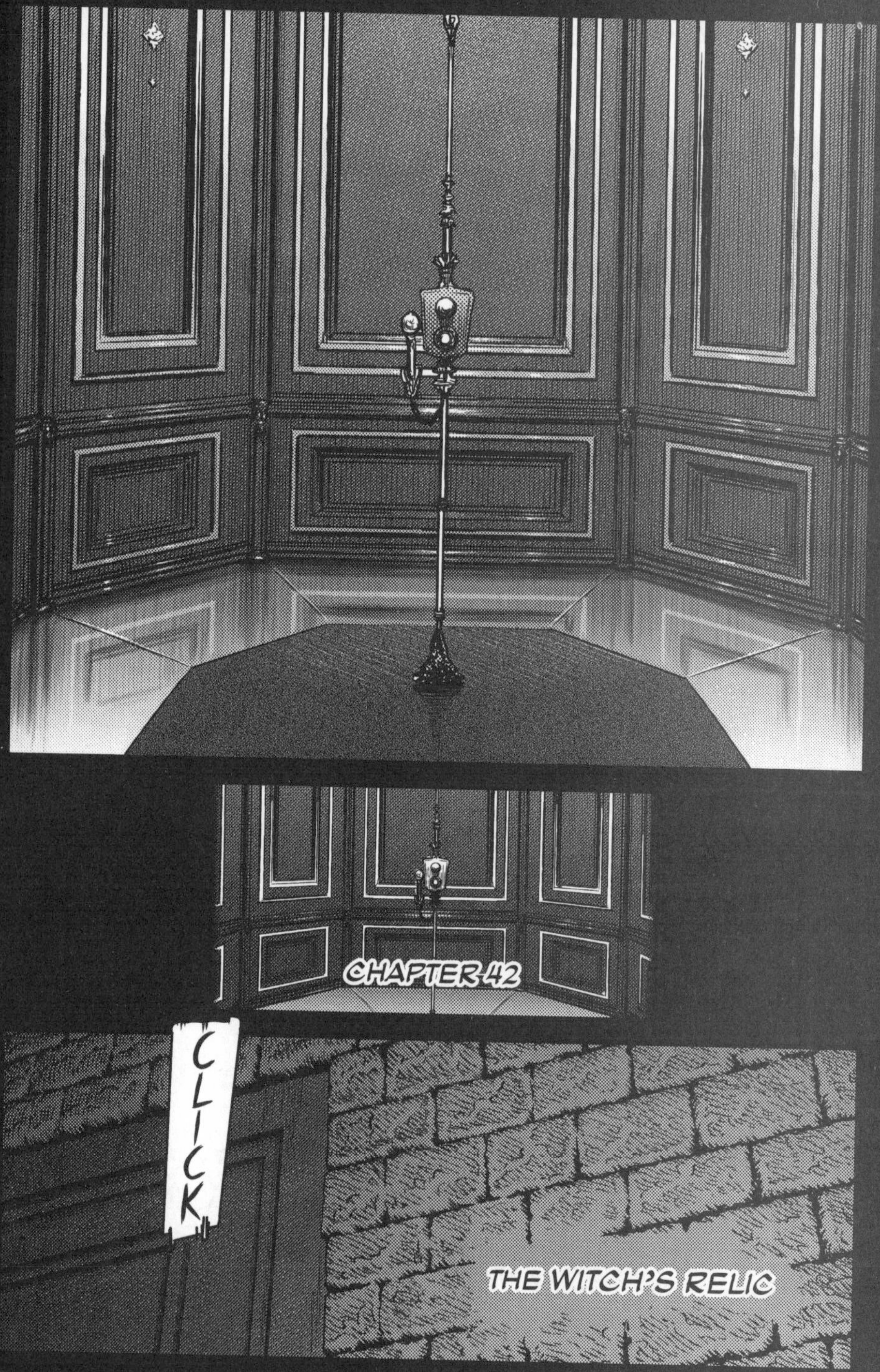
CHAPTER 42
CLICK
THE WITCH'S RELIC

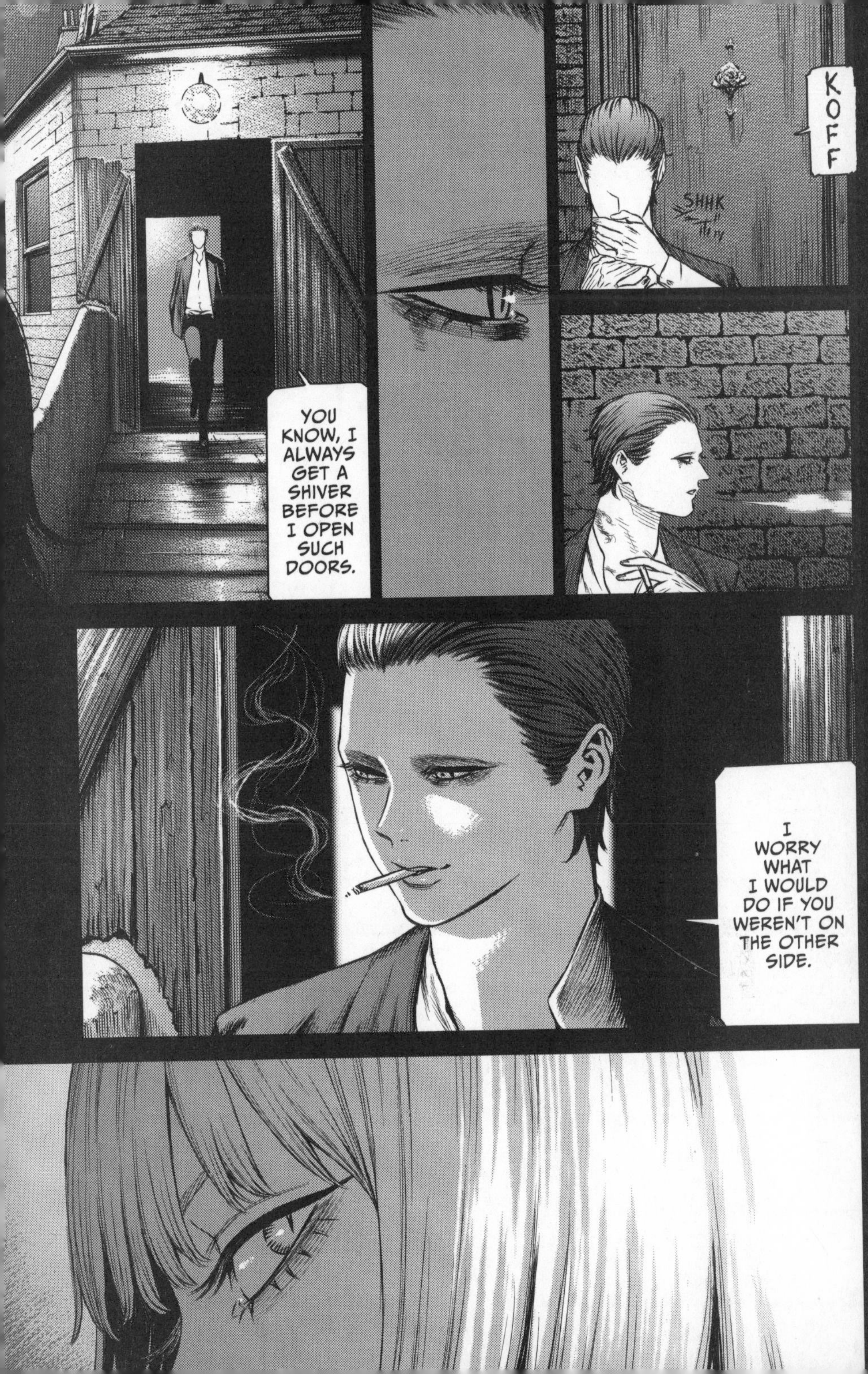
KOFF
SHHK
YOU KNOW, I ALWAYS GET A SHIVER BEFORE I OPEN SUCH DOORS.
I WORRY WHAT I WOULD DO IF YOU WEREN'T ON THE OTHER SIDE.

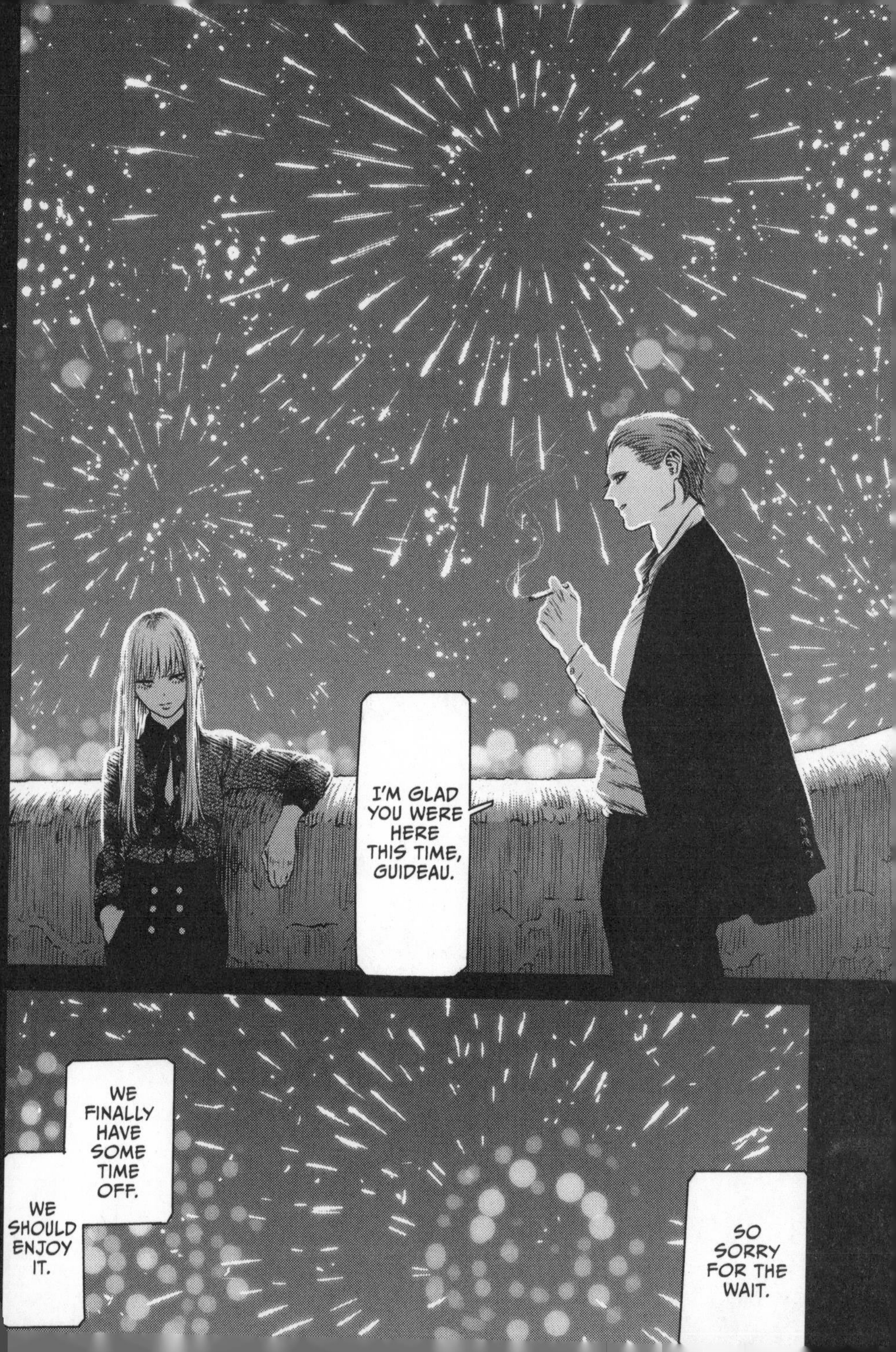
I'M GLAD YOU WERE HERE THIS TIME, GUIDEAU.
SO SORRY FOR THE WAIT.
WE FINALLY HAVE SOME TIME OFF.
WE SHOULD ENJOY IT.

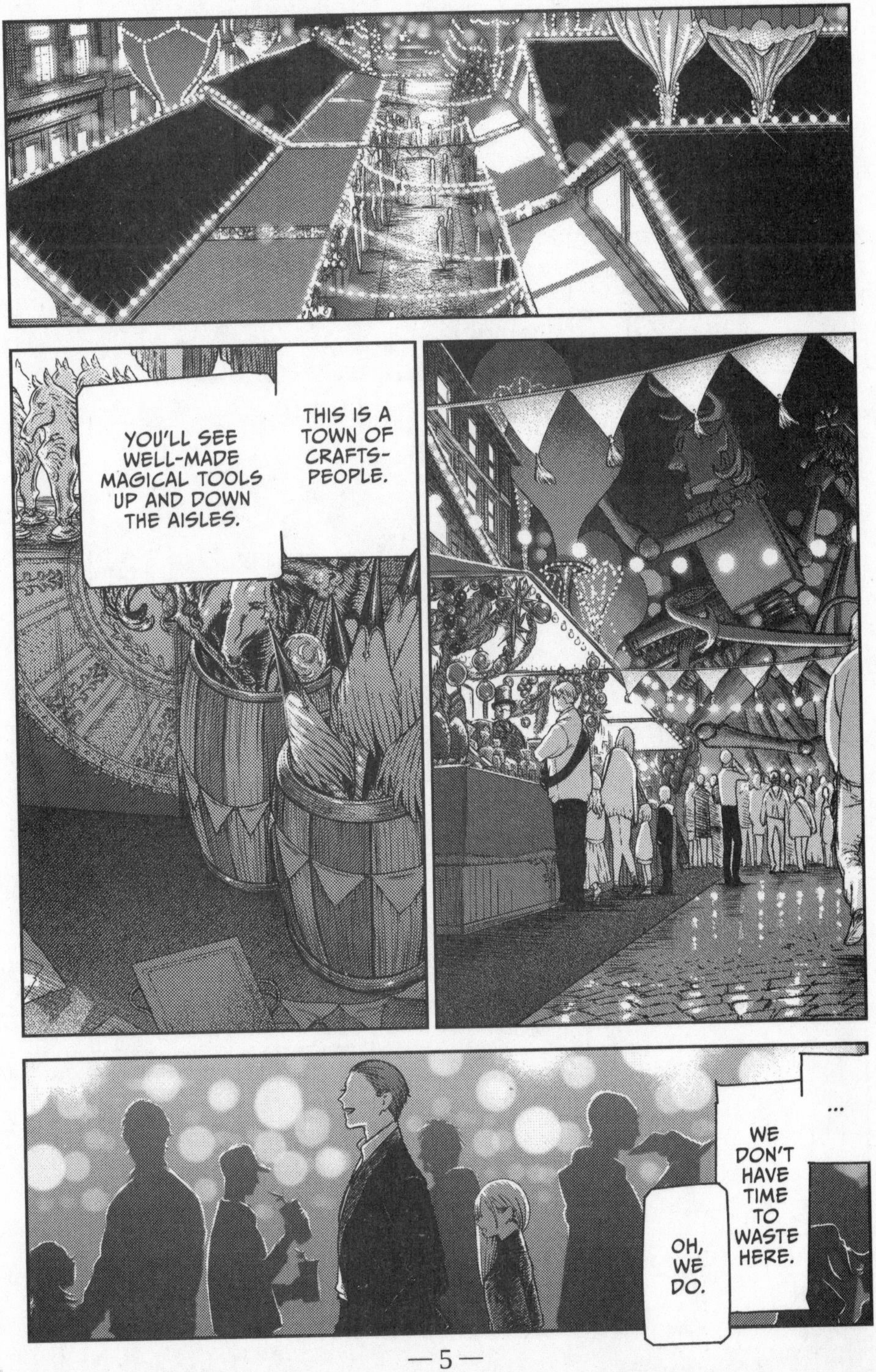
THIS IS A TOWN OF CRAFTS-PEOPLE.
YOU'LL SEE WELL-MADE MAGICAL TOOLS UP AND DOWN THE AISLES.
...
WE DON'T HAVE TIME TO WASTE HERE.
OH, WE DO.

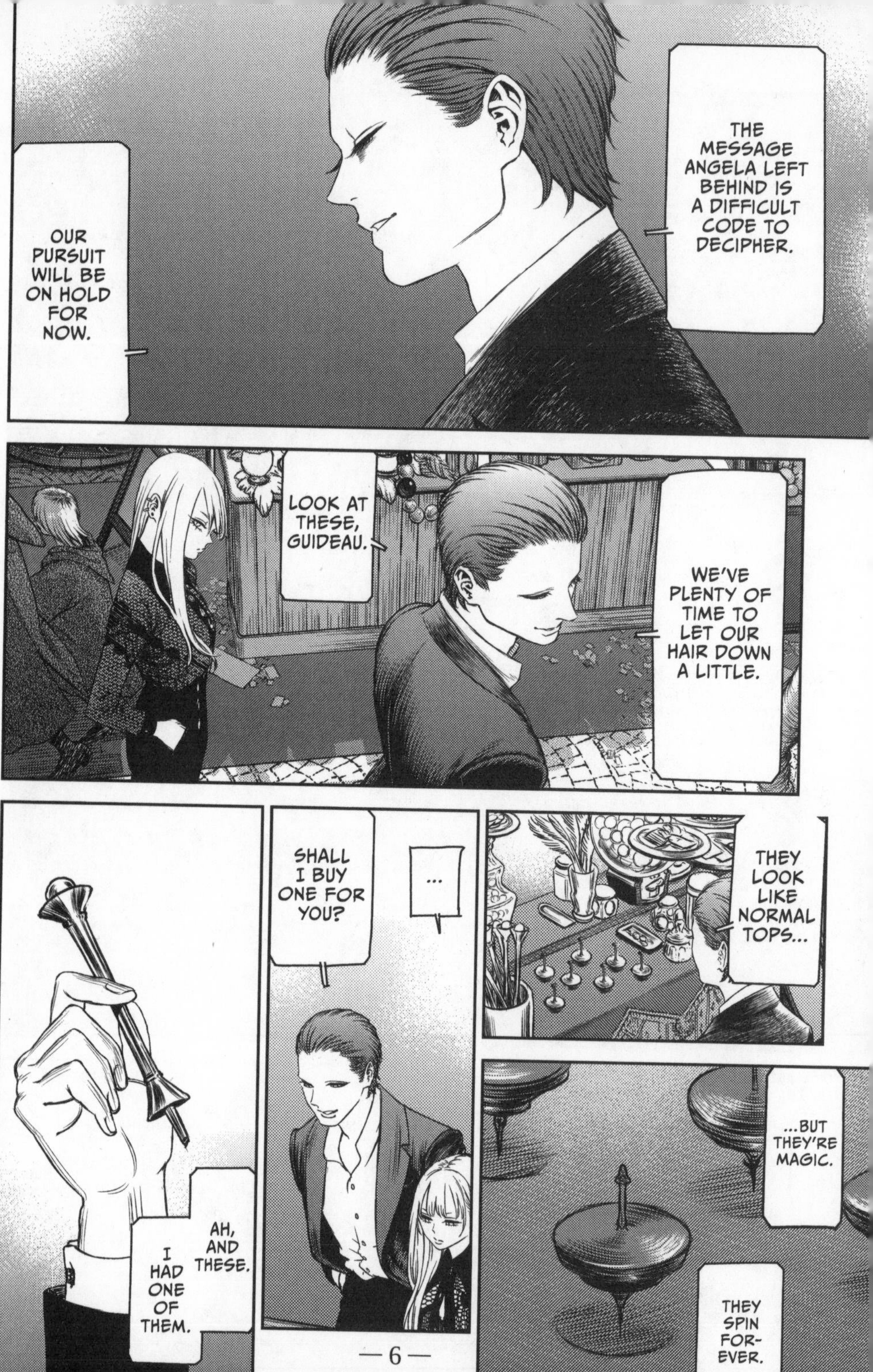

THE MESSAGE ANGELA LEFT BEHIND IS A DIFFICULT CODE TO DECIPHER.
OUR PURSUIT WILL BE ON HOLD FOR NOW.
WE'VE PLENTY OF TIME TO LET OUR HAIR DOWN A LITTLE.
LOOK AT THESE, GUIDEAU.
THEY LOOK LIKE NORMAL TOPS...
...BUT THEY'RE MAGIC.
THEY SPIN FOREVER.
...
SHALL I BUY ONE FOR YOU?
AH, AND THESE.
I HAD ONE OF THEM.

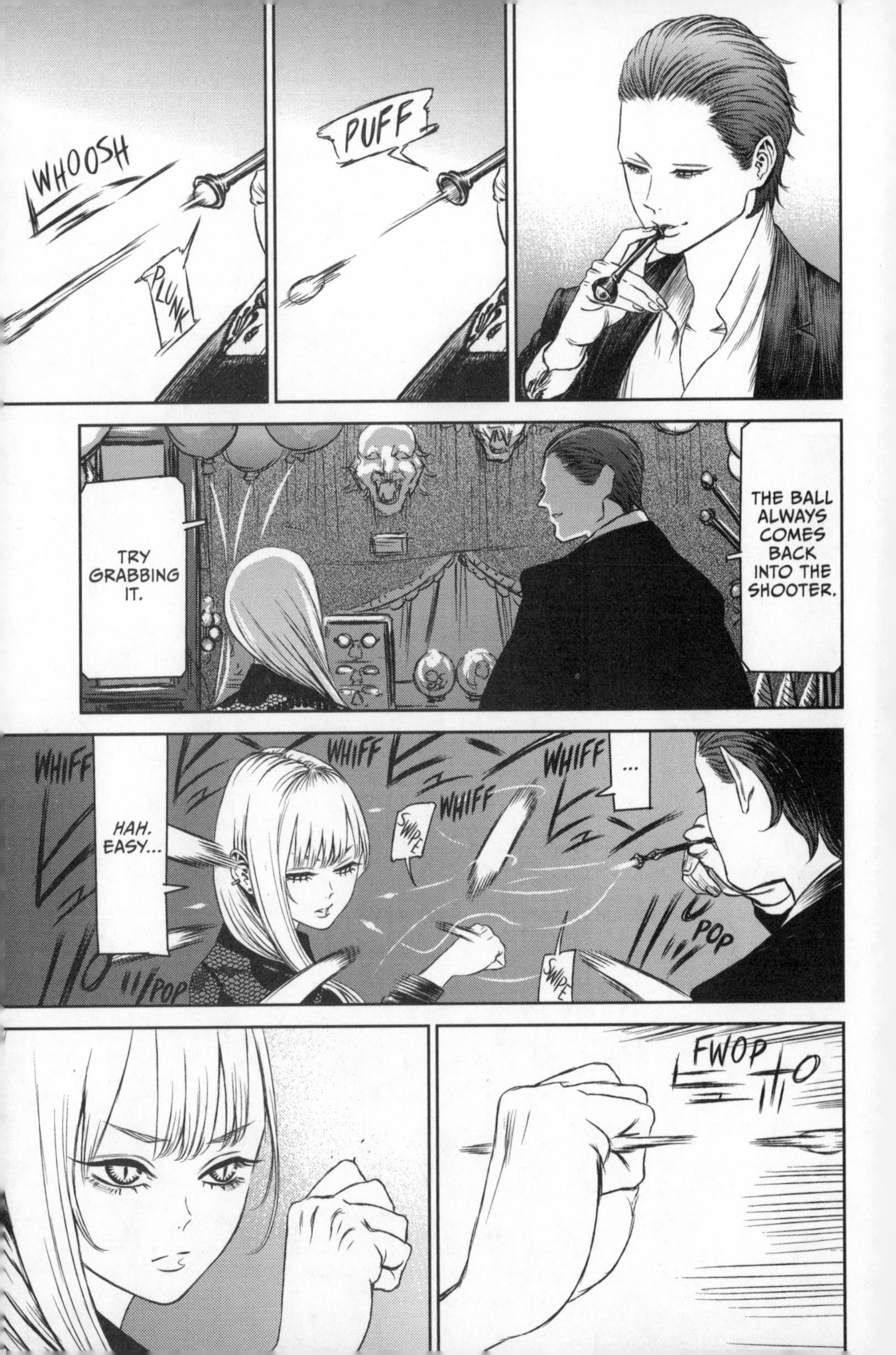
PUFF
WHOOSH
PLUNK
THE BALL ALWAYS COMES BACK INTO THE SHOOTER.
TRY GRABBING IT.
WHIFF
...
POP
WHIFF
WHIFF
SWIPE
HAH. EASY...
WHIFF
SWIPE
POP
FWOP

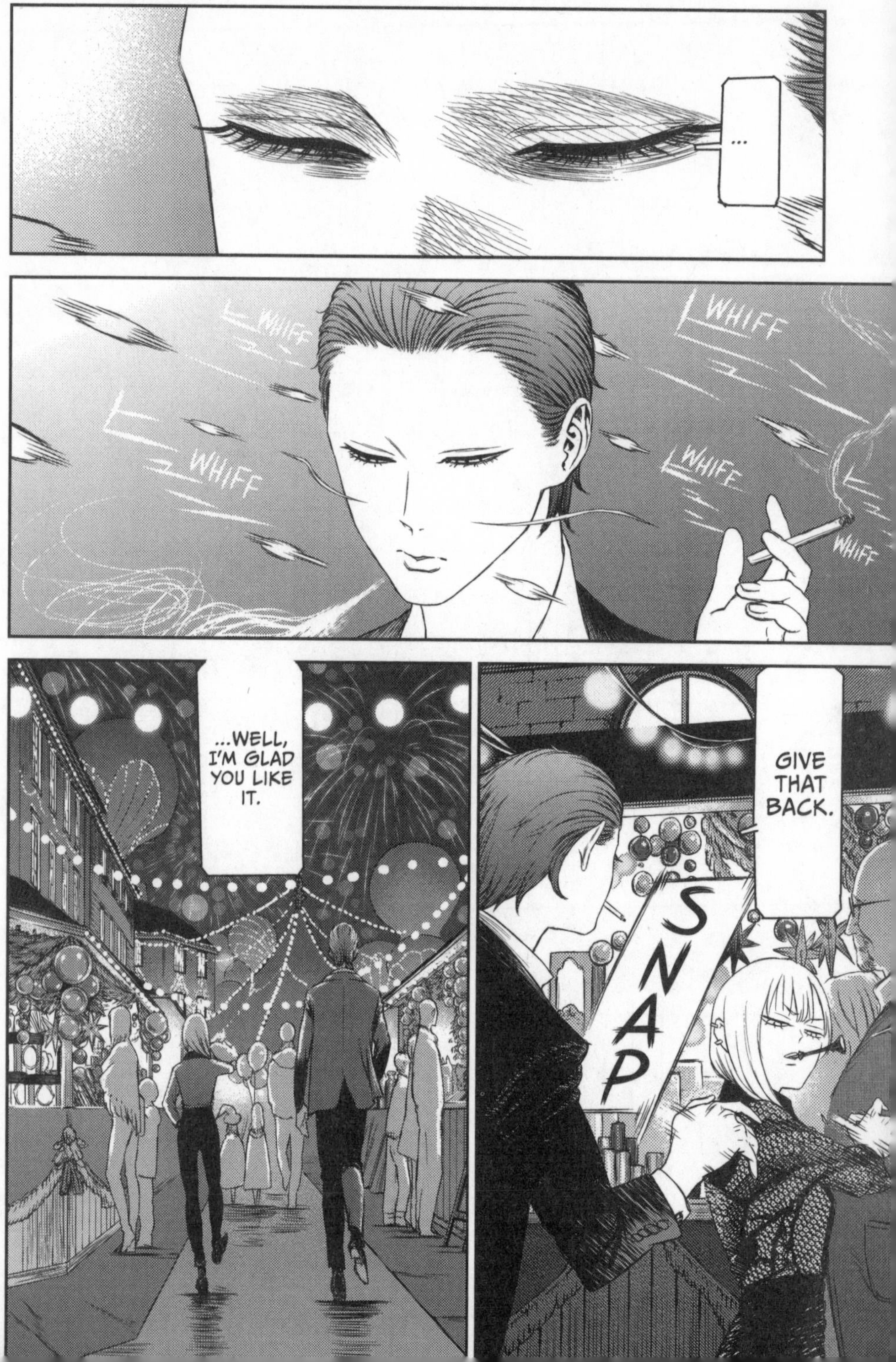
...
WHIFF
WHIFF
WHIFF
WHIFF
WHIFF
GIVE THAT BACK.
SNAP
...WELL, I'M GLAD YOU LIKE IT.

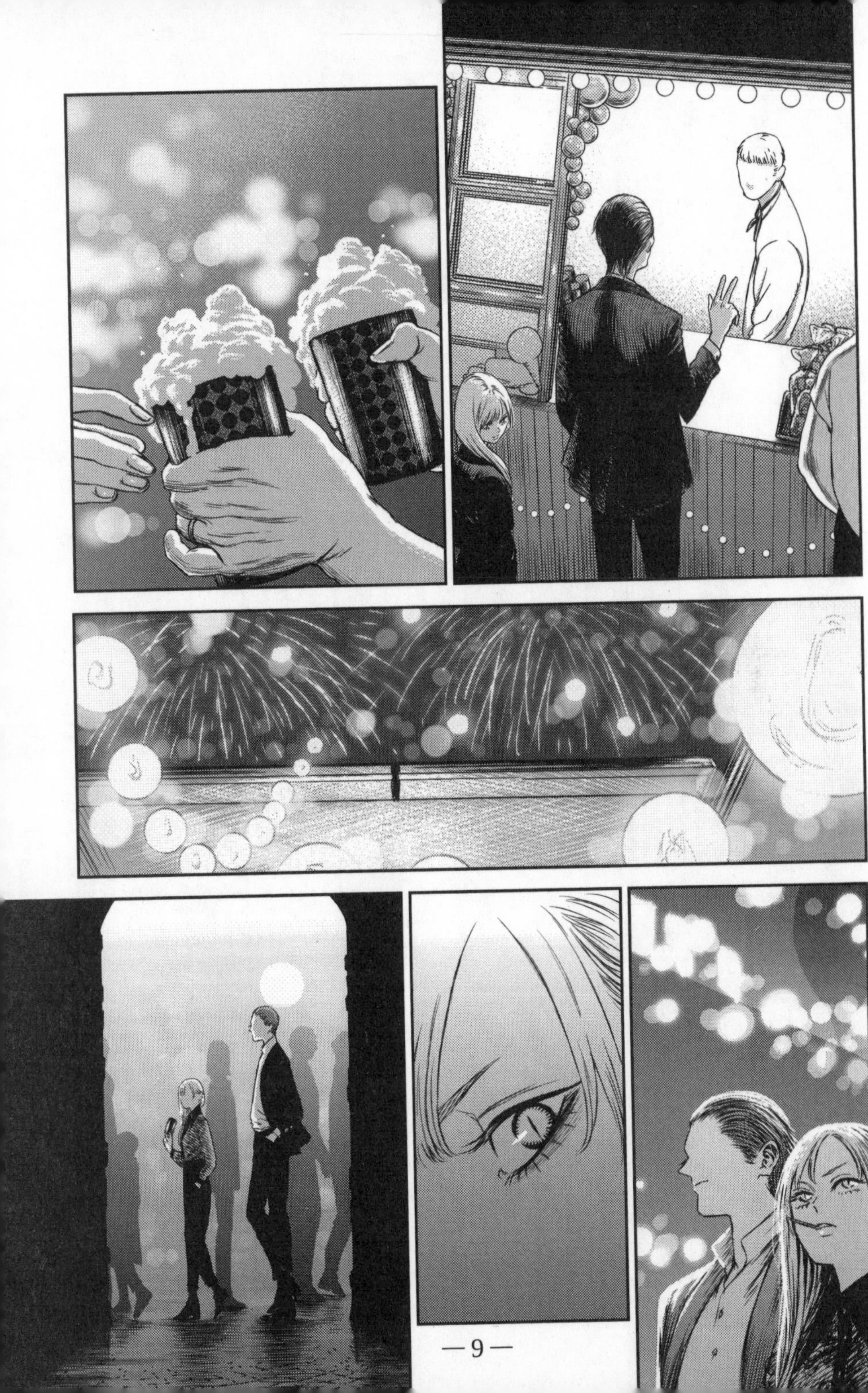

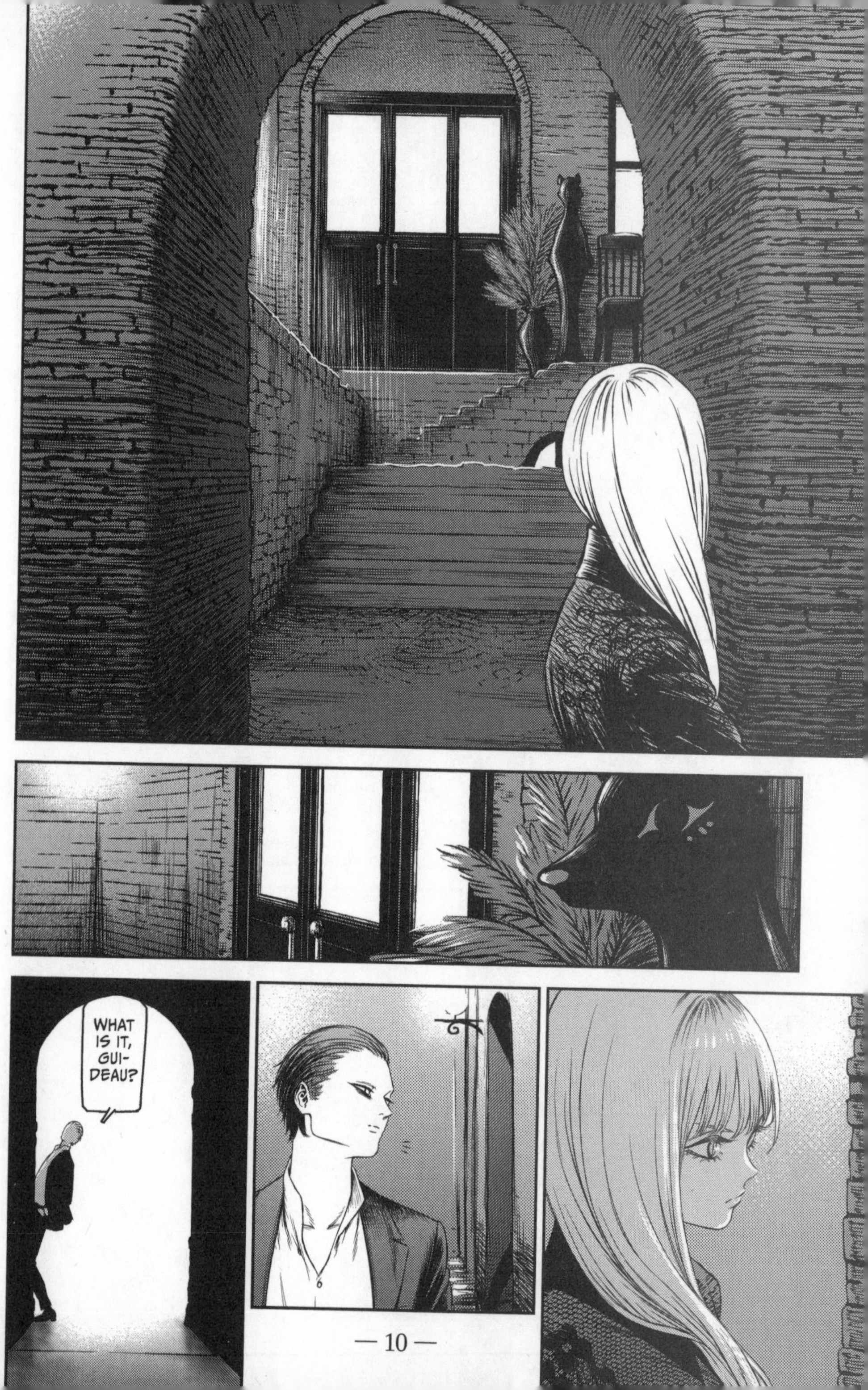
WHAT IS IT, GUI-DEAU?

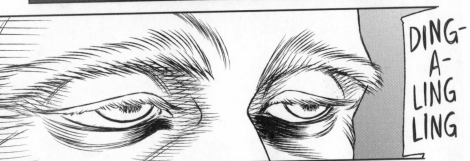

DING-
A-
LING
LING

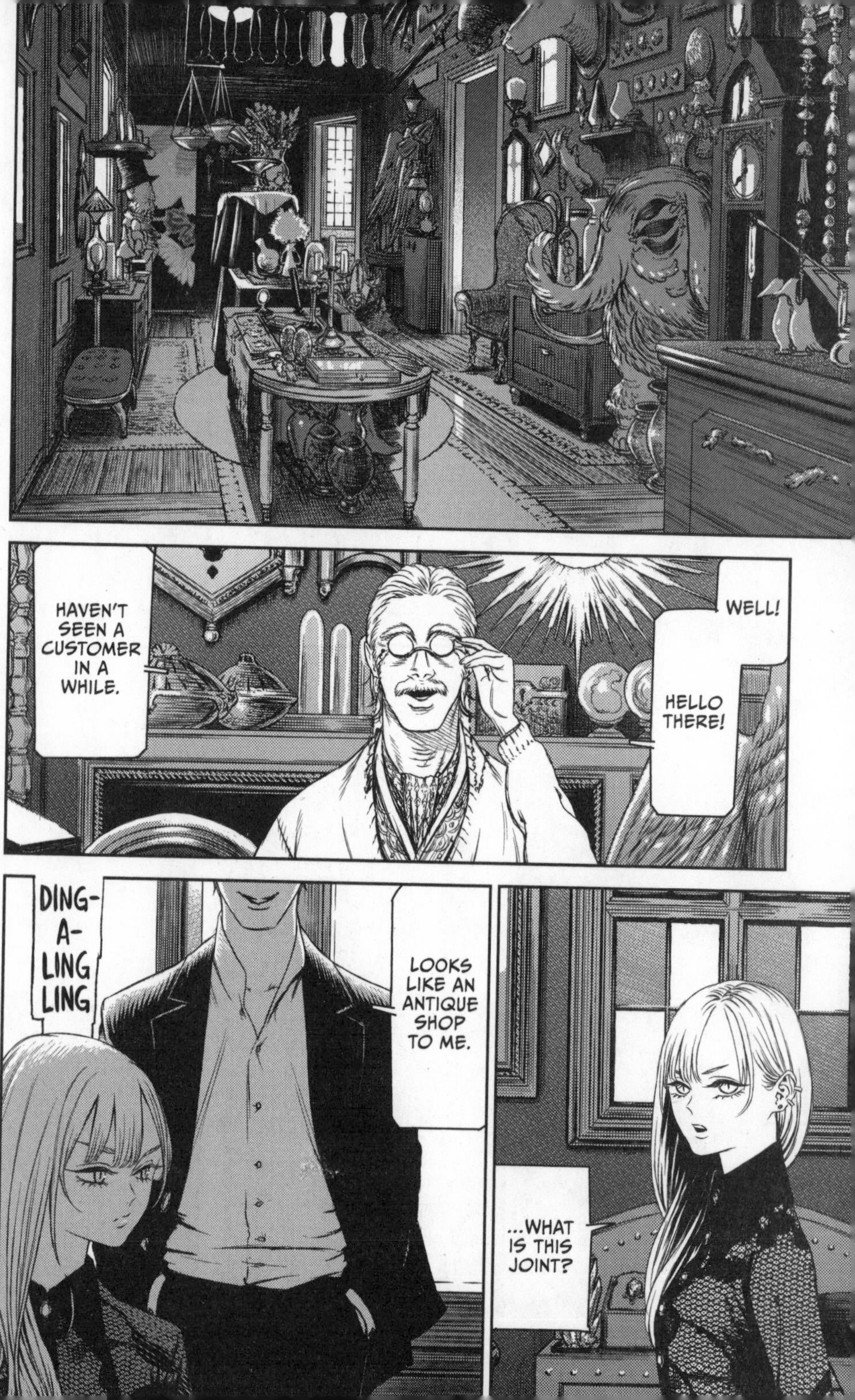
WELL!
HELLO THERE!
HAVEN'T SEEN A CUSTOMER IN A WHILE.
...WHAT IS THIS JOINT?
LOOKS LIKE AN ANTIQUE SHOP TO ME.
DING-A-LING LING

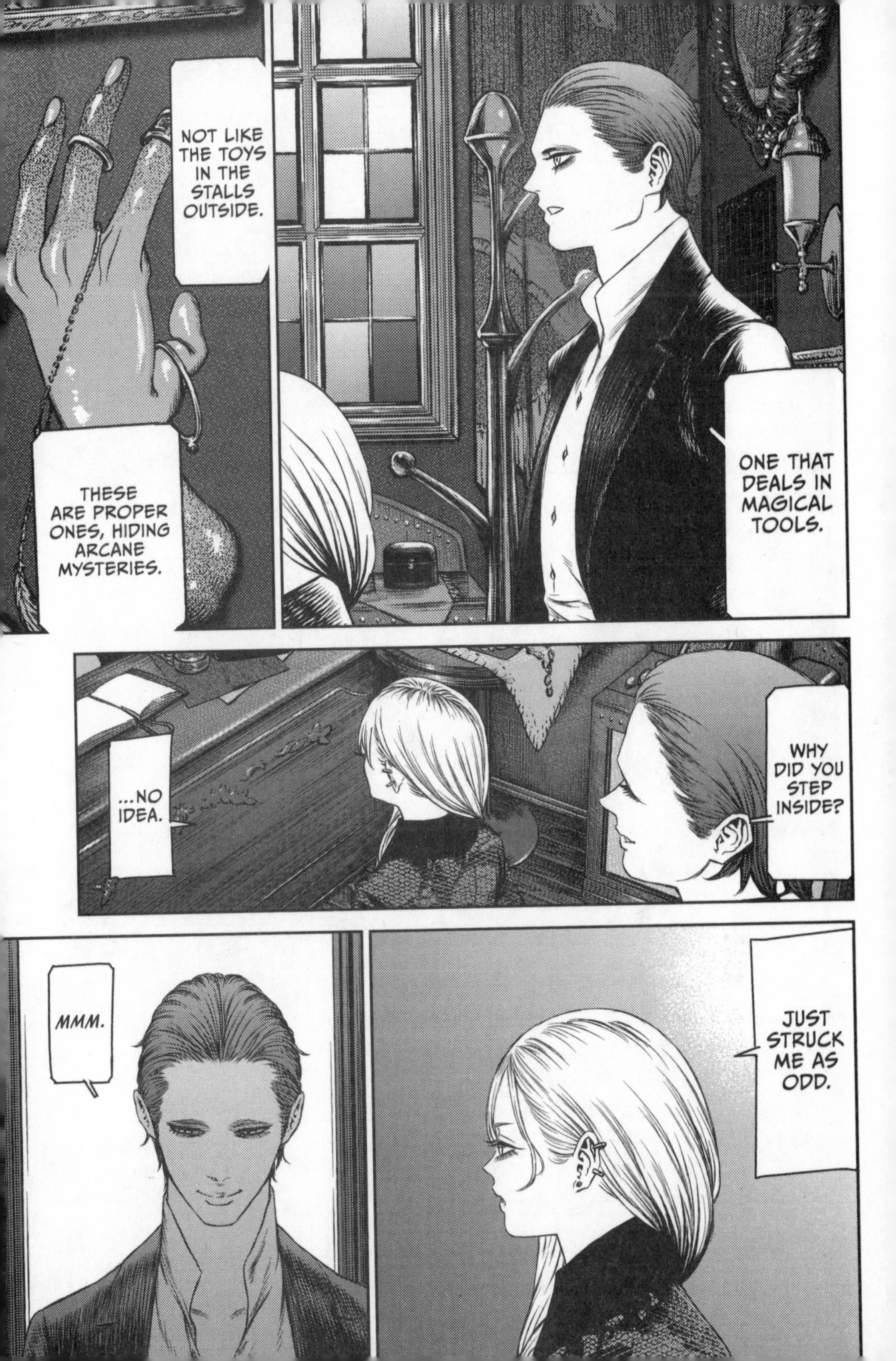
ONE THAT DEALS IN MAGICAL TOOLS.
NOT LIKE THE TOYS IN THE STALLS OUTSIDE.
THESE ARE PROPER ONES, HIDING ARCANE MYSTERIES.
WHY DID YOU STEP INSIDE?
...NO IDEA.
JUST STRUCK ME AS ODD.
MMM.

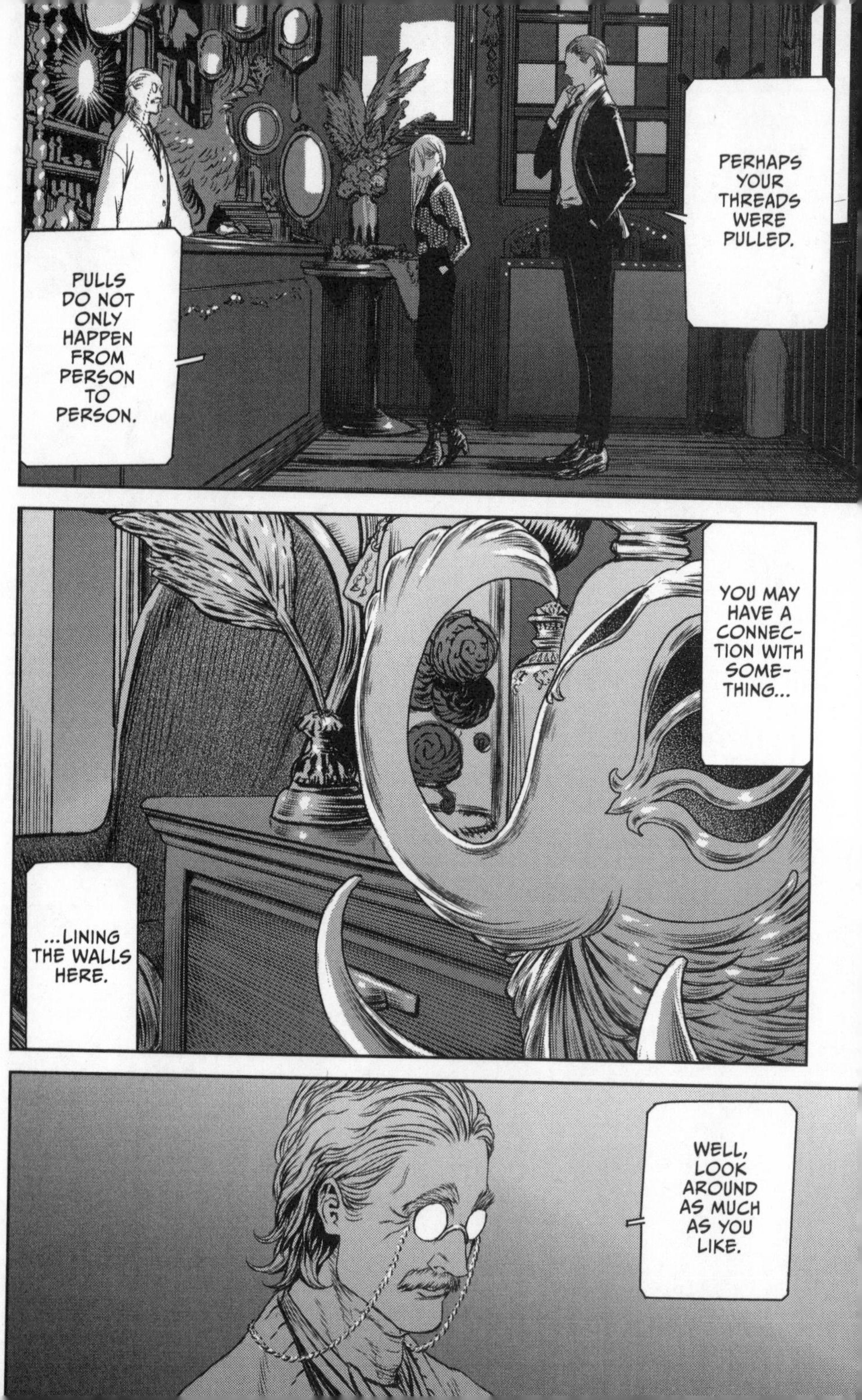
PERHAPS YOUR THREADS WERE PULLED.
PULLS DO NOT ONLY HAPPEN FROM PERSON TO PERSON.
YOU MAY HAVE A CONNECTION WITH SOMETHING...
...LINING THE WALLS HERE.
WELL, LOOK AROUND AS MUCH AS YOU LIKE.

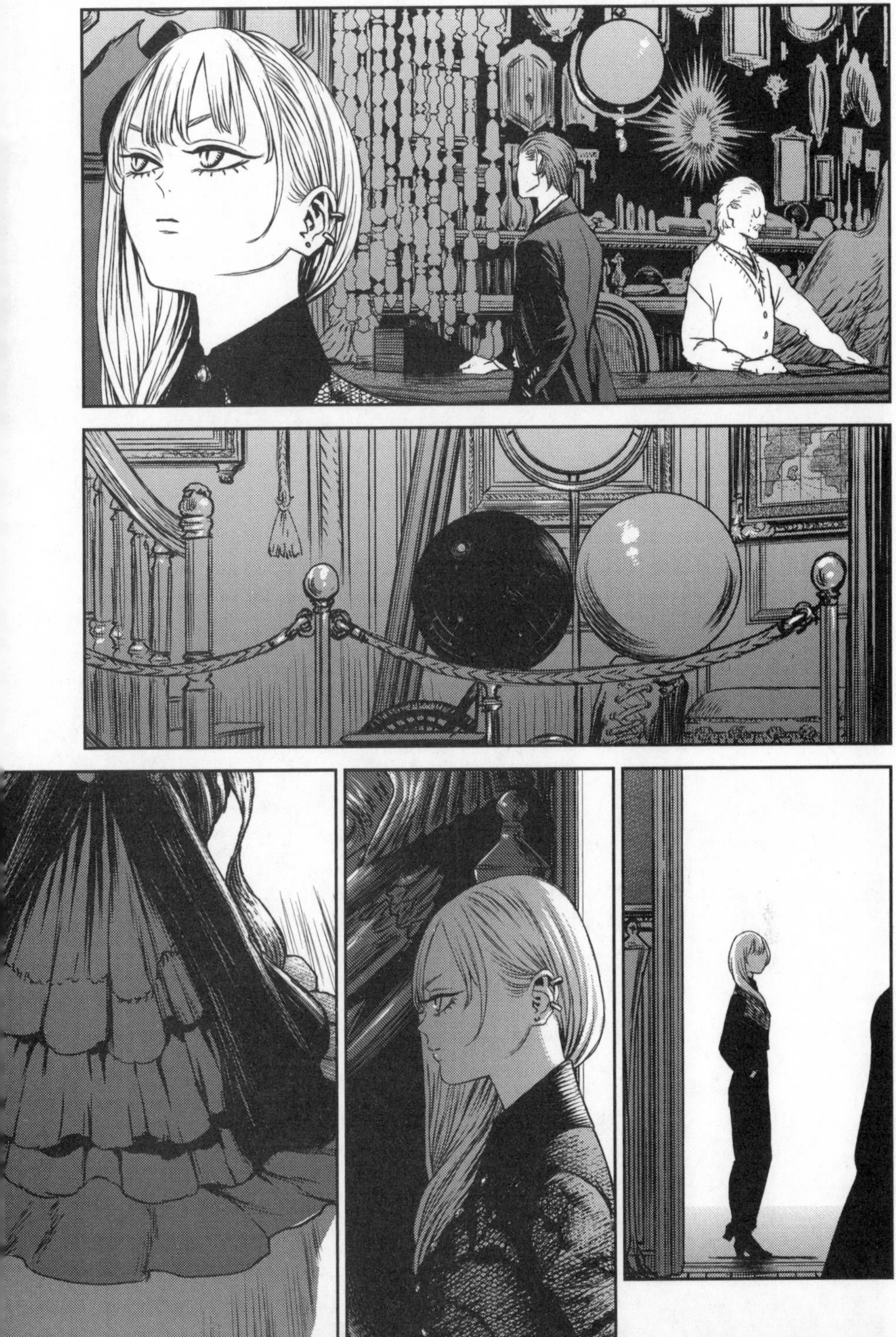

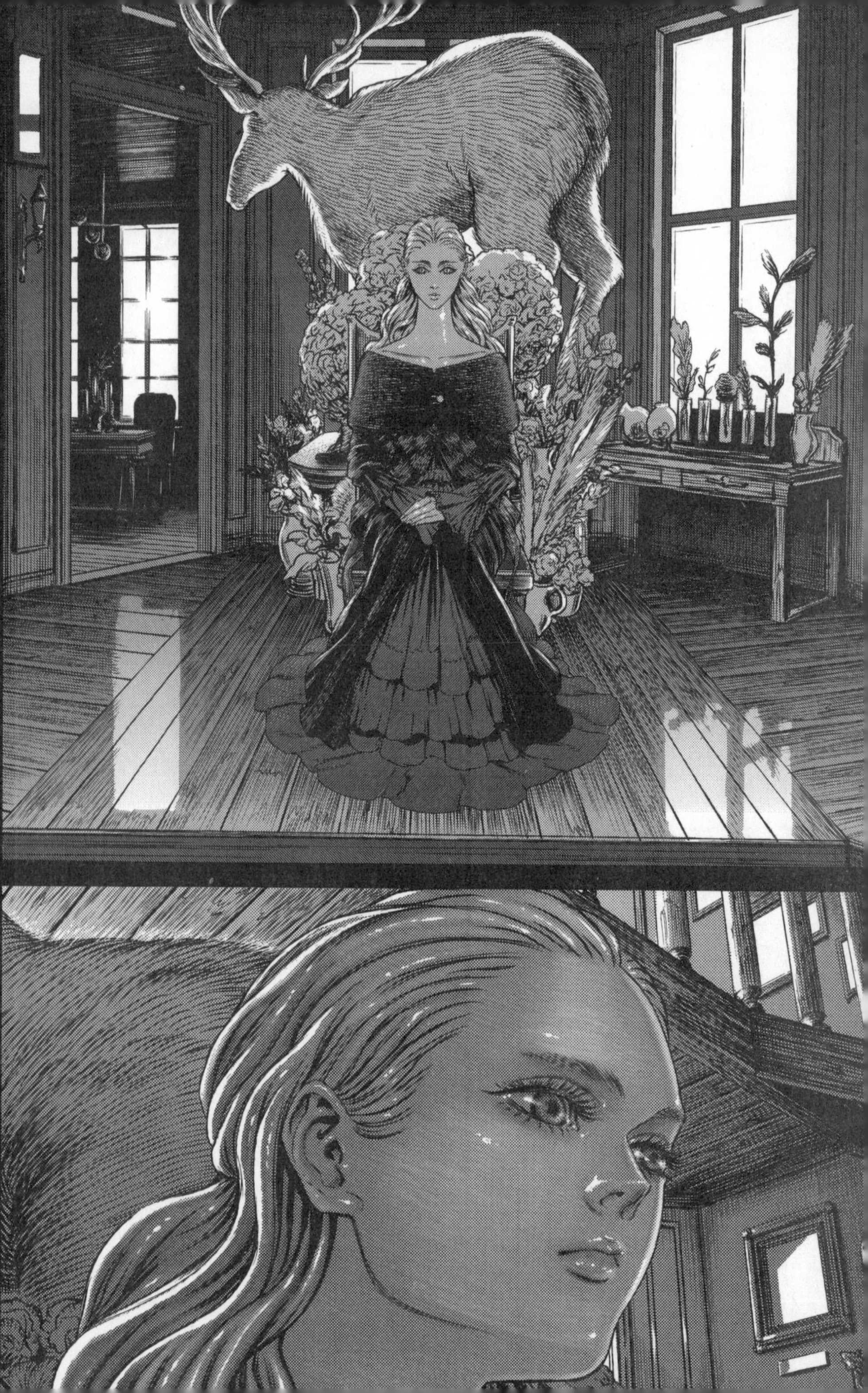

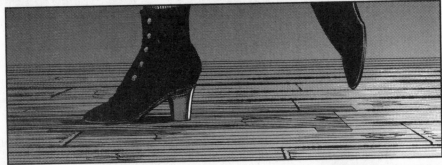

A DOLL
...?

IS IT
YOU?

NOK

NOK

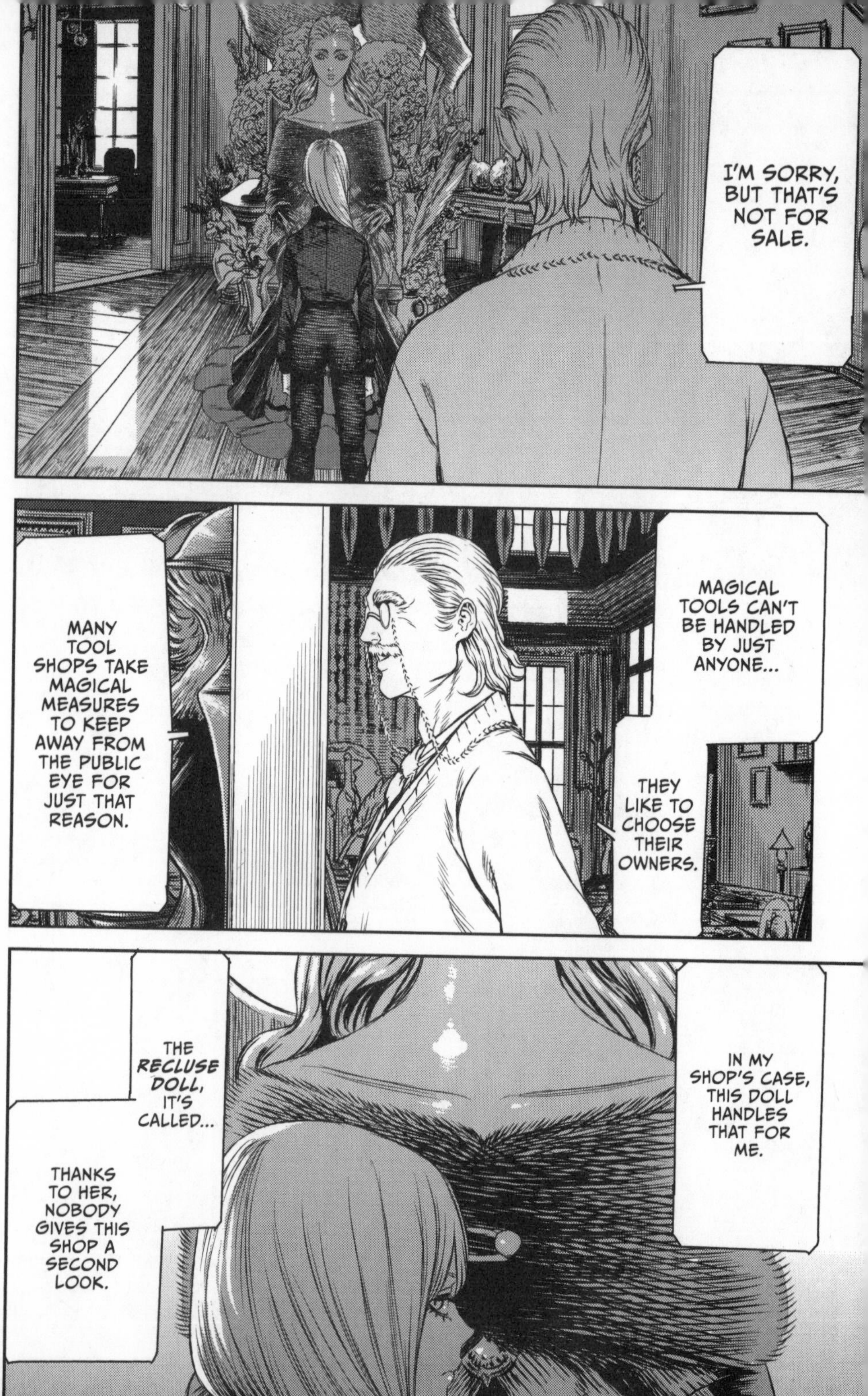
I'M SORRY, BUT THAT'S NOT FOR SALE.
MAGICAL TOOLS CAN'T BE HANDLED BY JUST ANYONE...
THEY LIKE TO CHOOSE THEIR OWNERS.
MANY TOOL SHOPS TAKE MAGICAL MEASURES TO KEEP AWAY FROM THE PUBLIC EYE FOR JUST THAT REASON.
IN MY SHOP'S CASE, THIS DOLL HANDLES THAT FOR ME.
THE *RECLUSE DOLL*, IT'S CALLED...
THANKS TO HER, NOBODY GIVES THIS SHOP A SECOND LOOK.

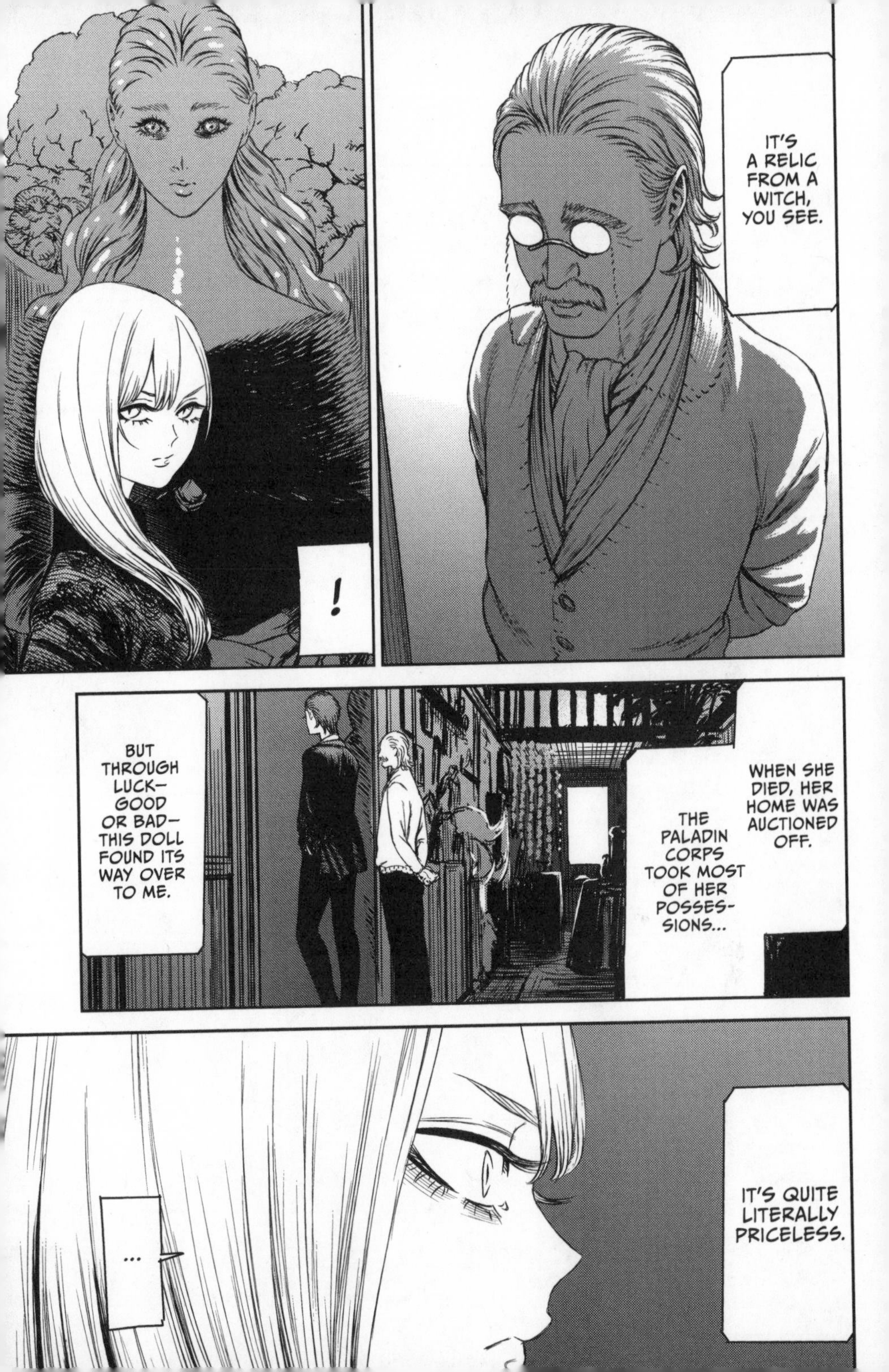
IT'S A RELIC FROM A WITCH, YOU SEE.
!
WHEN SHE DIED, HER HOME WAS AUCTIONED OFF.
THE PALADIN CORPS TOOK MOST OF HER POSSESSIONS...
BUT THROUGH LUCK—GOOD OR BAD—THIS DOLL FOUND ITS WAY OVER TO ME.
IT'S QUITE LITERALLY PRICELESS.
...

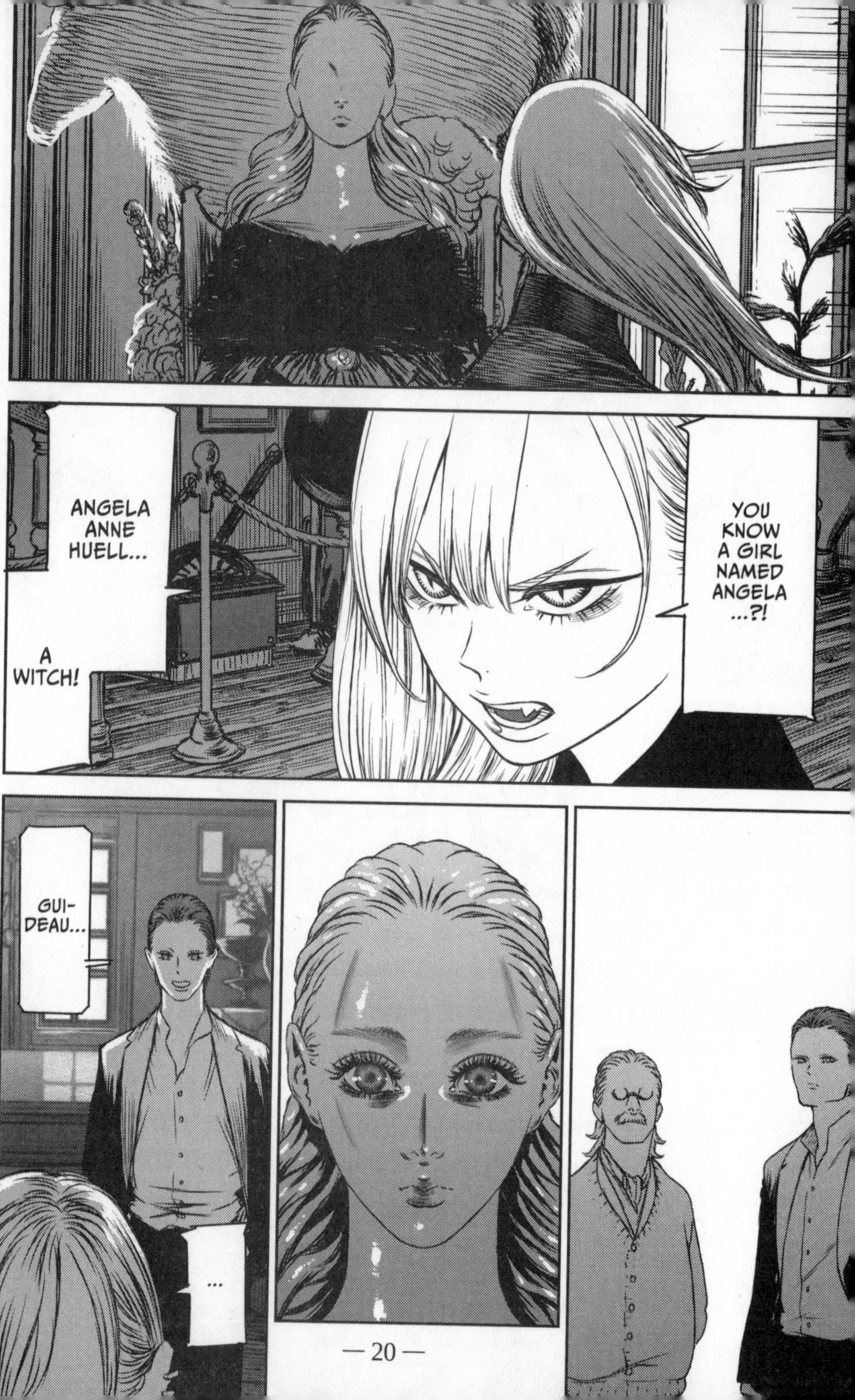
YOU KNOW A GIRL NAMED ANGELA ...?!
ANGELA ANNE HUELL...
A WITCH!
GUI-DEAU...
...

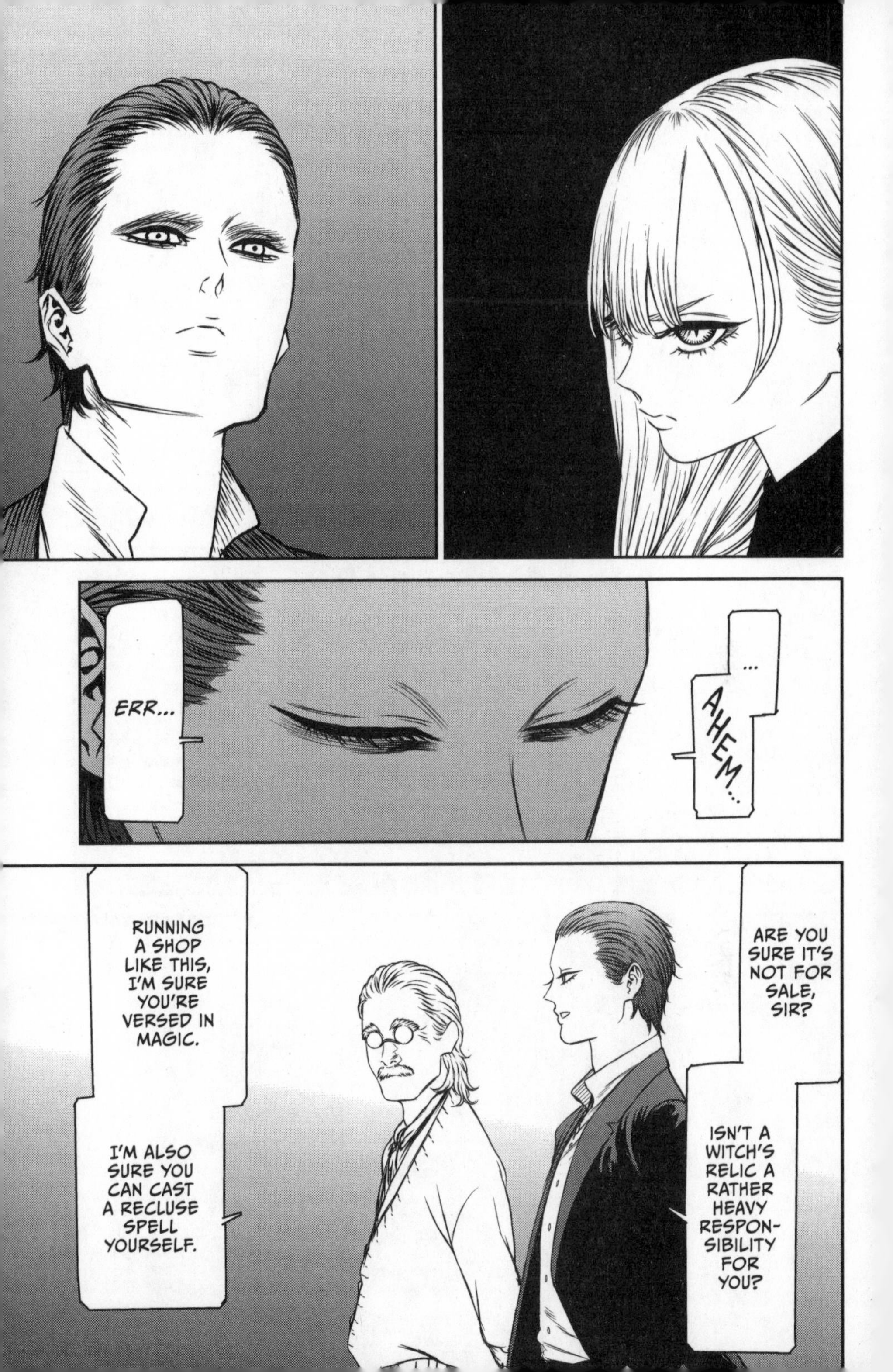
...
AHEM...
ERR...
ARE YOU SURE IT'S NOT FOR SALE, SIR?
RUNNING A SHOP LIKE THIS, I'M SURE YOU'RE VERSED IN MAGIC.
ISN'T A WITCH'S RELIC A RATHER HEAVY RESPON-SIBILITY FOR YOU?
I'M ALSO SURE YOU CAN CAST A RECLUSE SPELL YOURSELF.

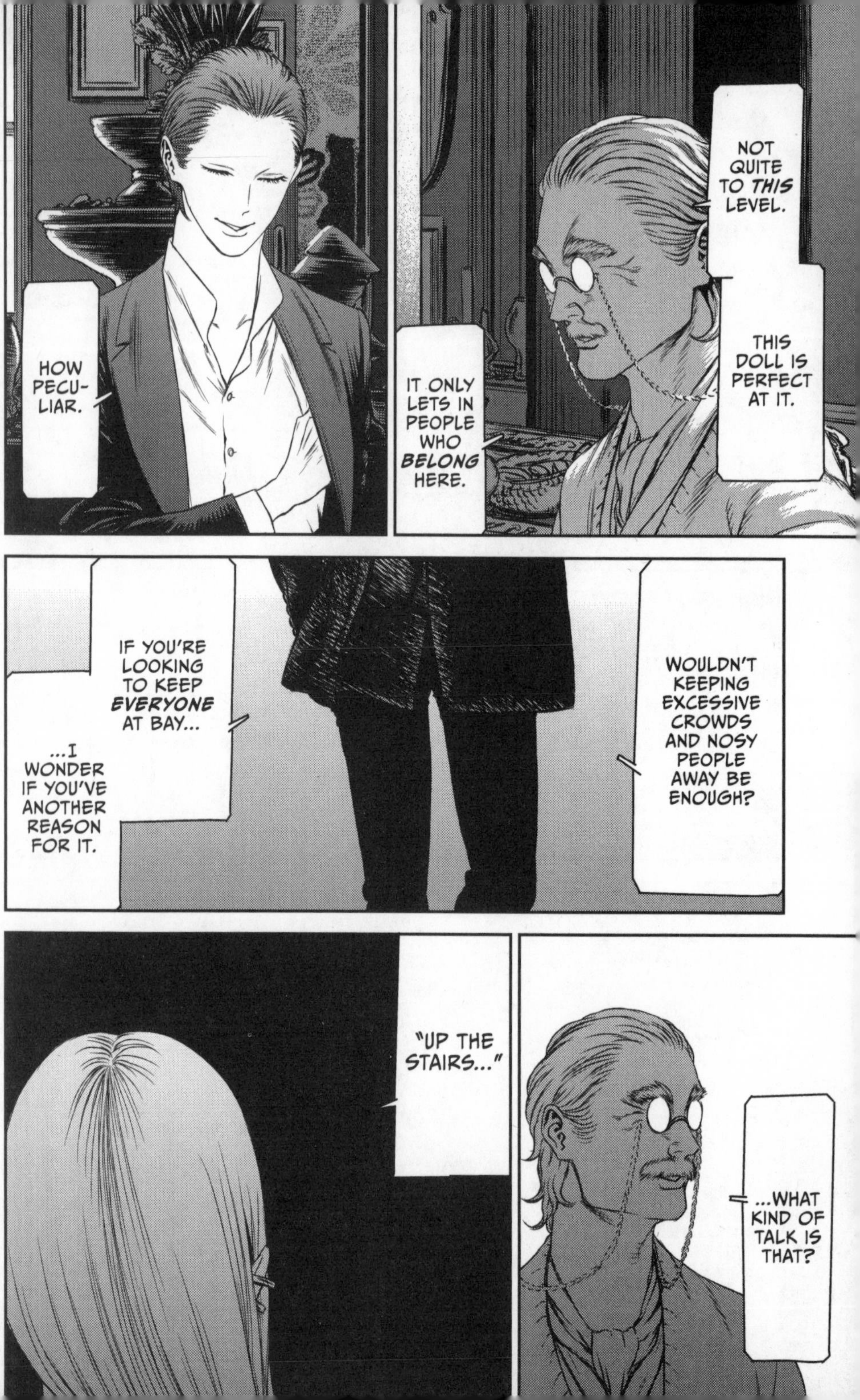
NOT QUITE TO *THIS* LEVEL.
THIS DOLL IS PERFECT AT IT.
IT ONLY LETS IN PEOPLE WHO *BELONG* HERE.
HOW PECU-LIAR.
WOULDN'T KEEPING EXCESSIVE CROWDS AND NOSY PEOPLE AWAY BE ENOUGH?
IF YOU'RE LOOKING TO KEEP *EVERYONE* AT BAY...
...I WONDER IF YOU'VE ANOTHER REASON FOR IT.
...WHAT KIND OF TALK IS THAT?
"UP THE STAIRS..."

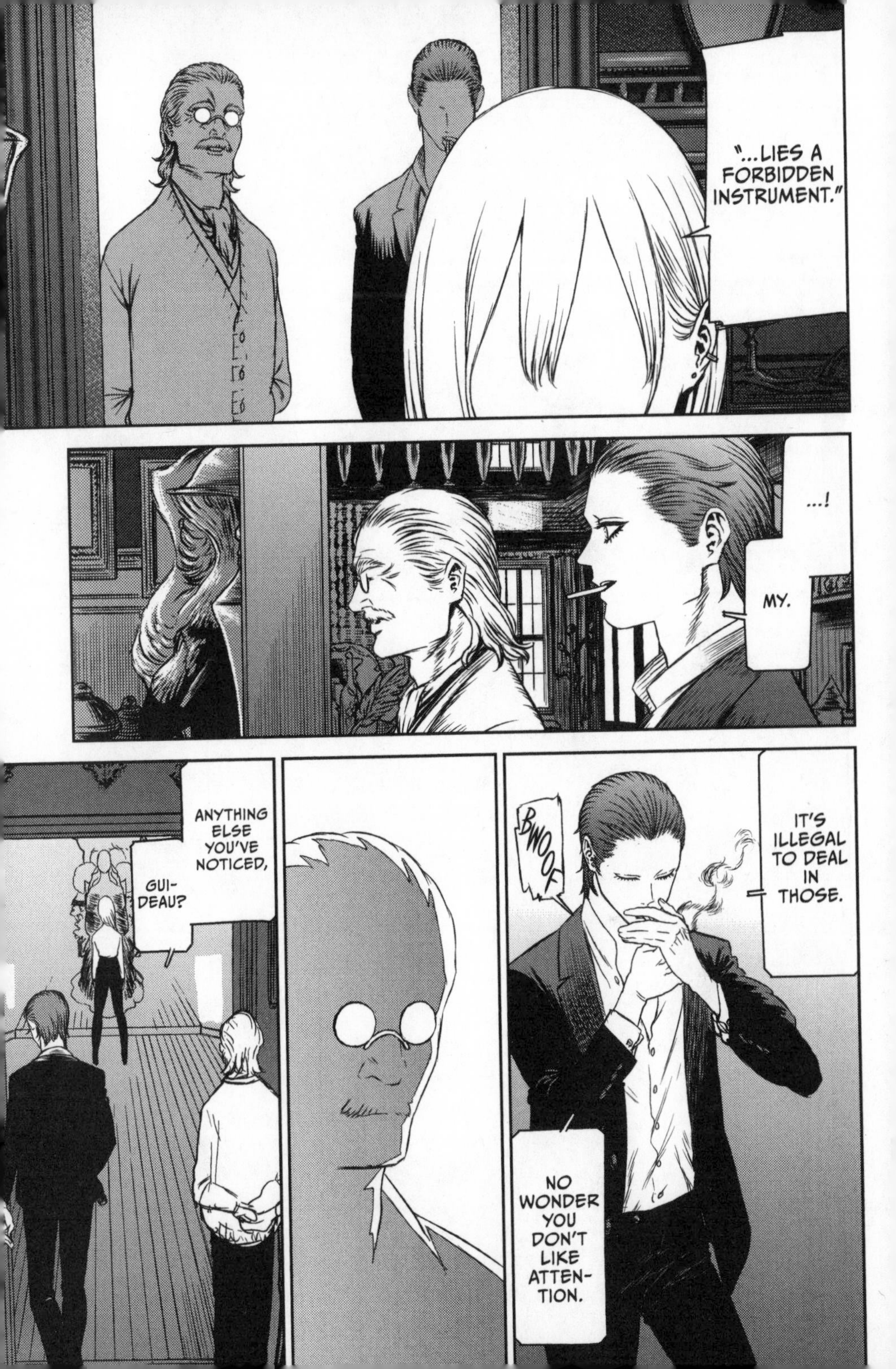
"...LIES A FORBIDDEN INSTRUMENT."
...!
MY.
IT'S ILLEGAL TO DEAL IN THOSE.
BWOOF
NO WONDER YOU DON'T LIKE ATTEN-TION.
ANYTHING ELSE YOU'VE NOTICED,
GUI-DEAU?

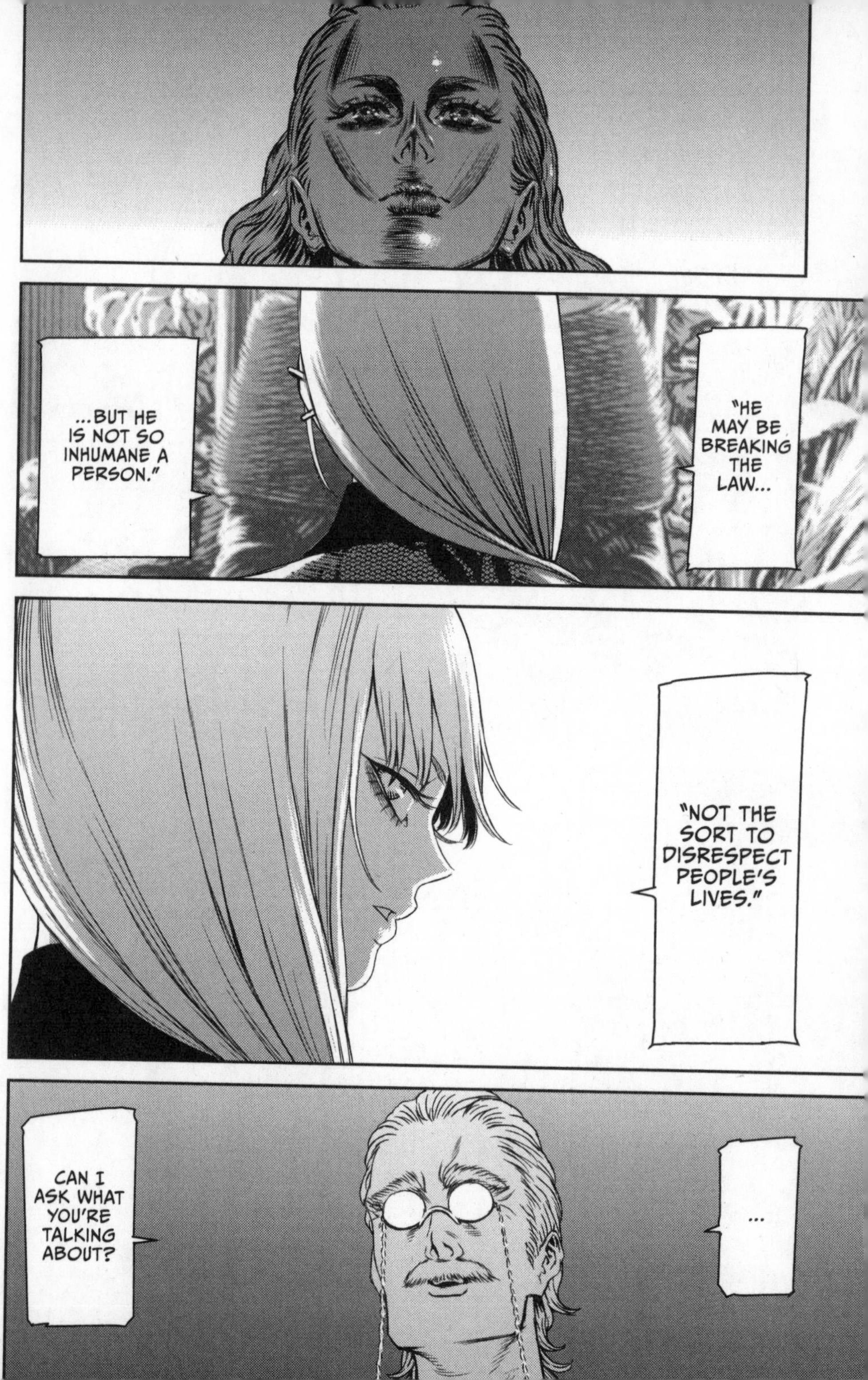
"HE MAY BE BREAKING THE LAW...
...BUT HE IS NOT SO INHUMANE A PERSON."
"NOT THE SORT TO DISRESPECT PEOPLE'S LIVES."
...
CAN I ASK WHAT YOU'RE TALKING ABOUT?

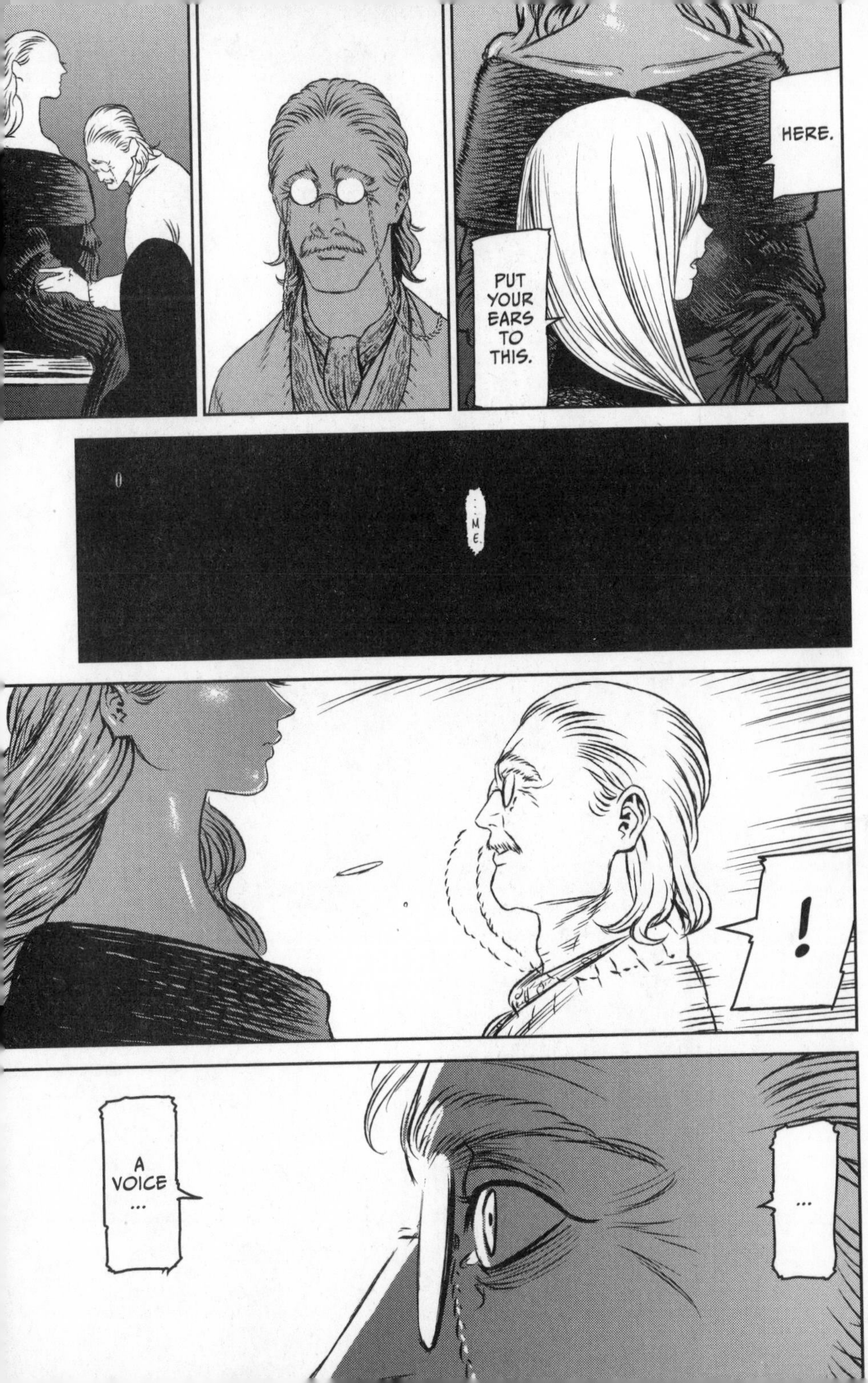
HERE.
PUT YOUR EARS TO THIS.
...ME.
!
...
A VOICE ...

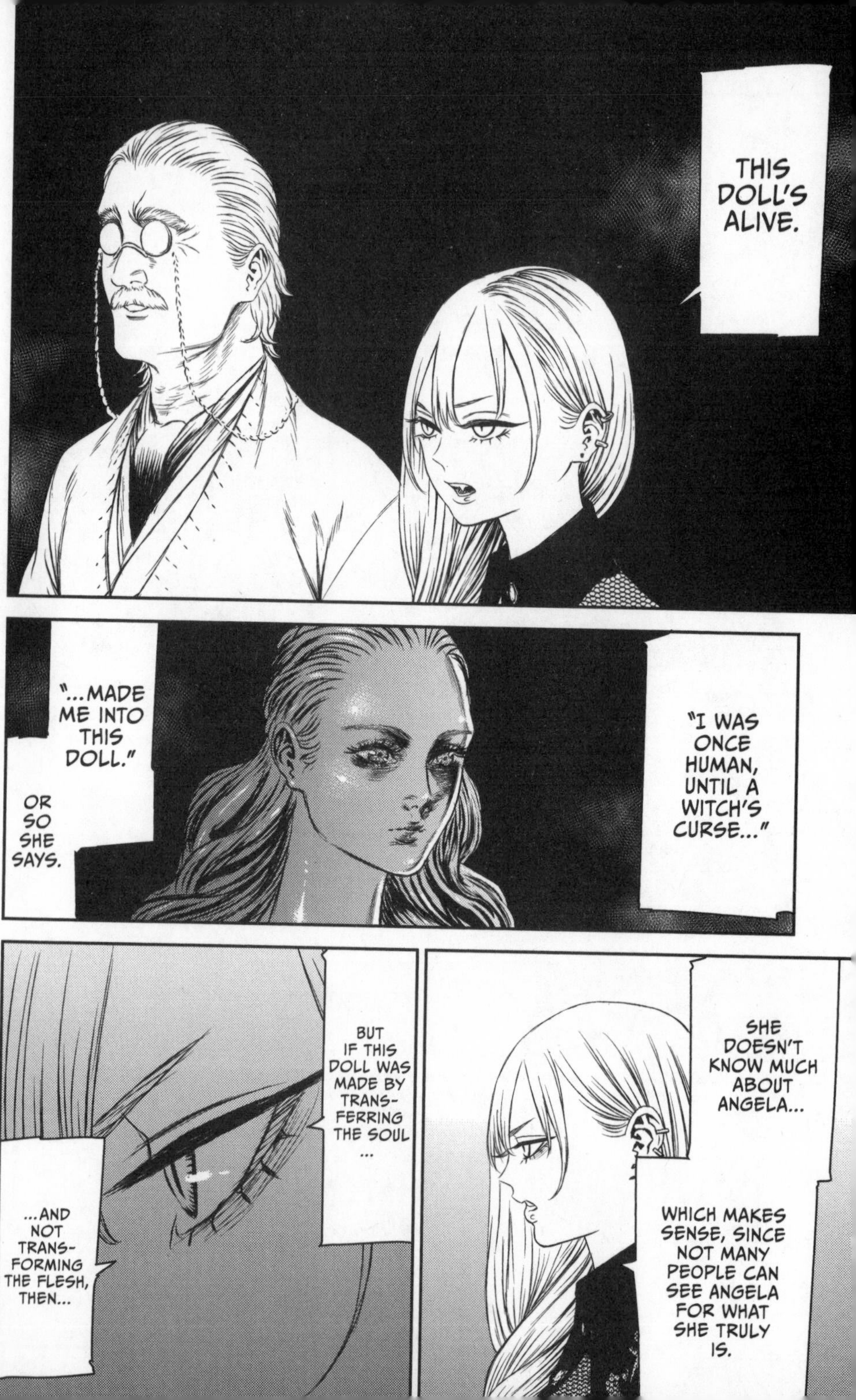
THIS DOLL'S ALIVE.
"I WAS ONCE HUMAN, UNTIL A WITCH'S CURSE..."
"...MADE ME INTO THIS DOLL."
OR SO SHE SAYS.
SHE DOESN'T KNOW MUCH ABOUT ANGELA...
WHICH MAKES SENSE, SINCE NOT MANY PEOPLE CAN SEE ANGELA FOR WHAT SHE TRULY IS.
BUT IF THIS DOLL WAS MADE BY TRANS-FERRING THE SOUL...
...AND NOT TRANS-FORMING THE FLESH, THEN...

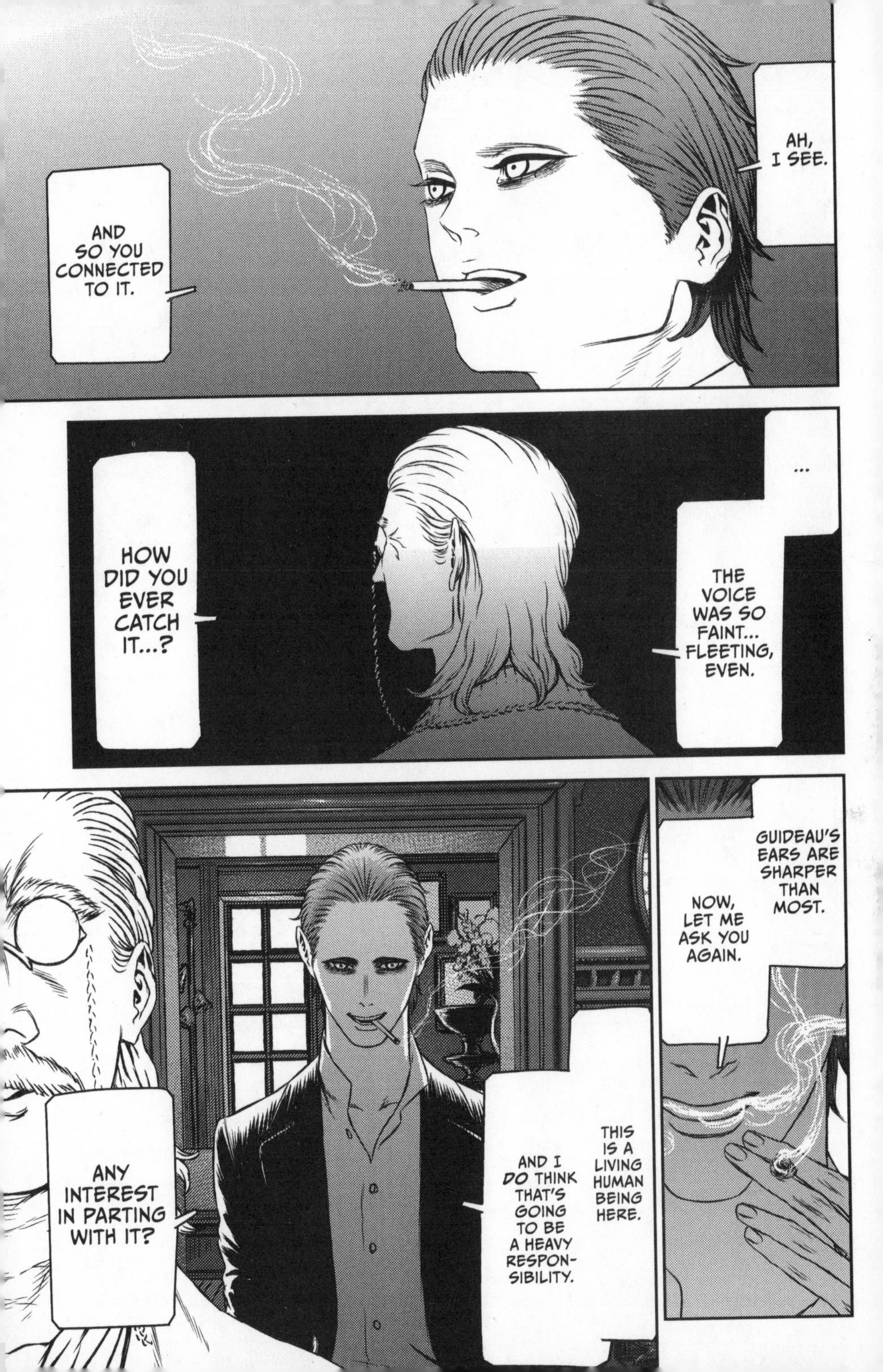
AH, I SEE.
AND SO YOU CONNECTED TO IT.
...
THE VOICE WAS SO FAINT... FLEETING, EVEN.
HOW DID YOU EVER CATCH IT...?
GUIDEAU'S EARS ARE SHARPER THAN MOST.
NOW, LET ME ASK YOU AGAIN.
THIS IS A LIVING HUMAN BEING HERE.
AND I *DO* THINK THAT'S GOING TO BE A HEAVY RESPON-SIBILITY.
ANY INTEREST IN PARTING WITH IT?

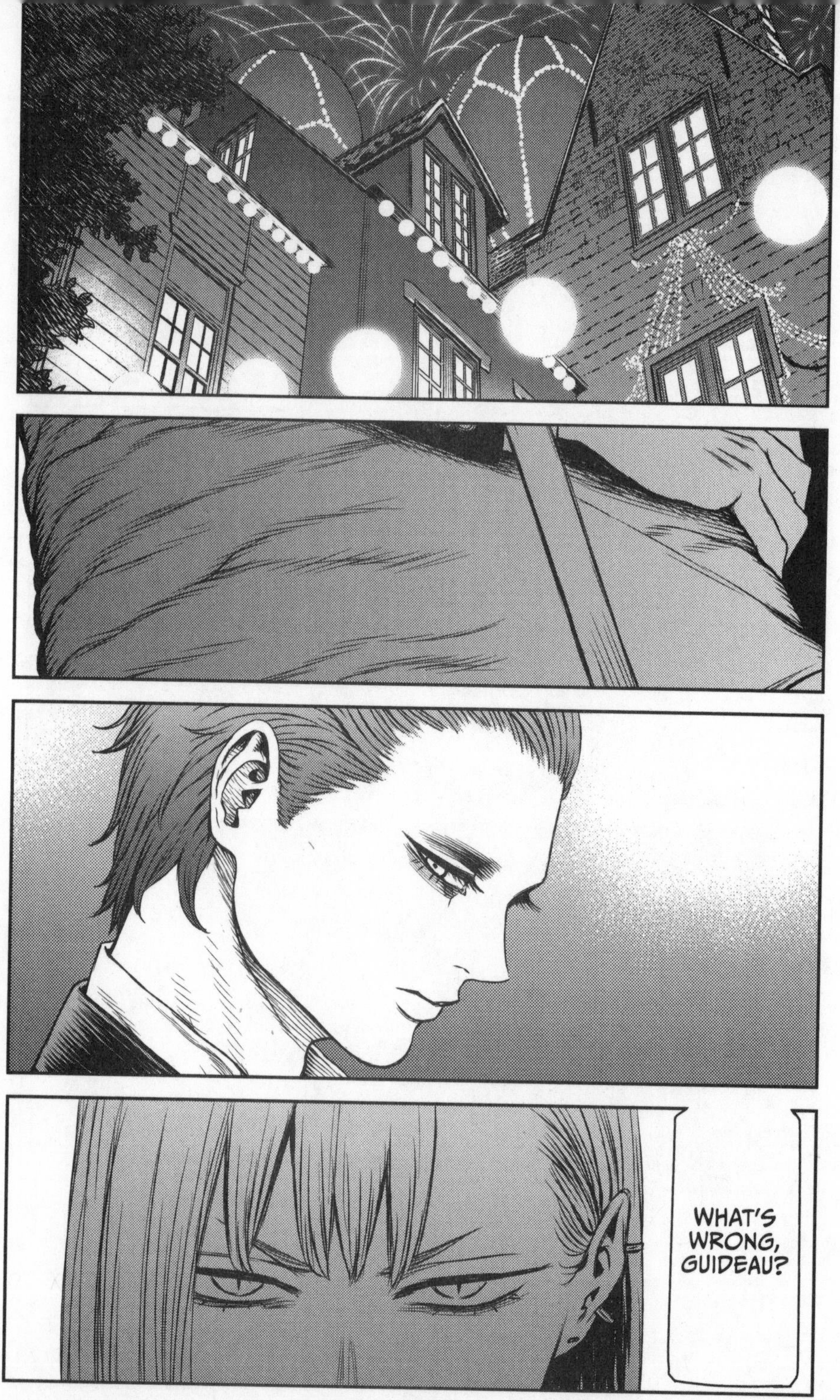
WHAT'S WRONG, GUIDEAU?

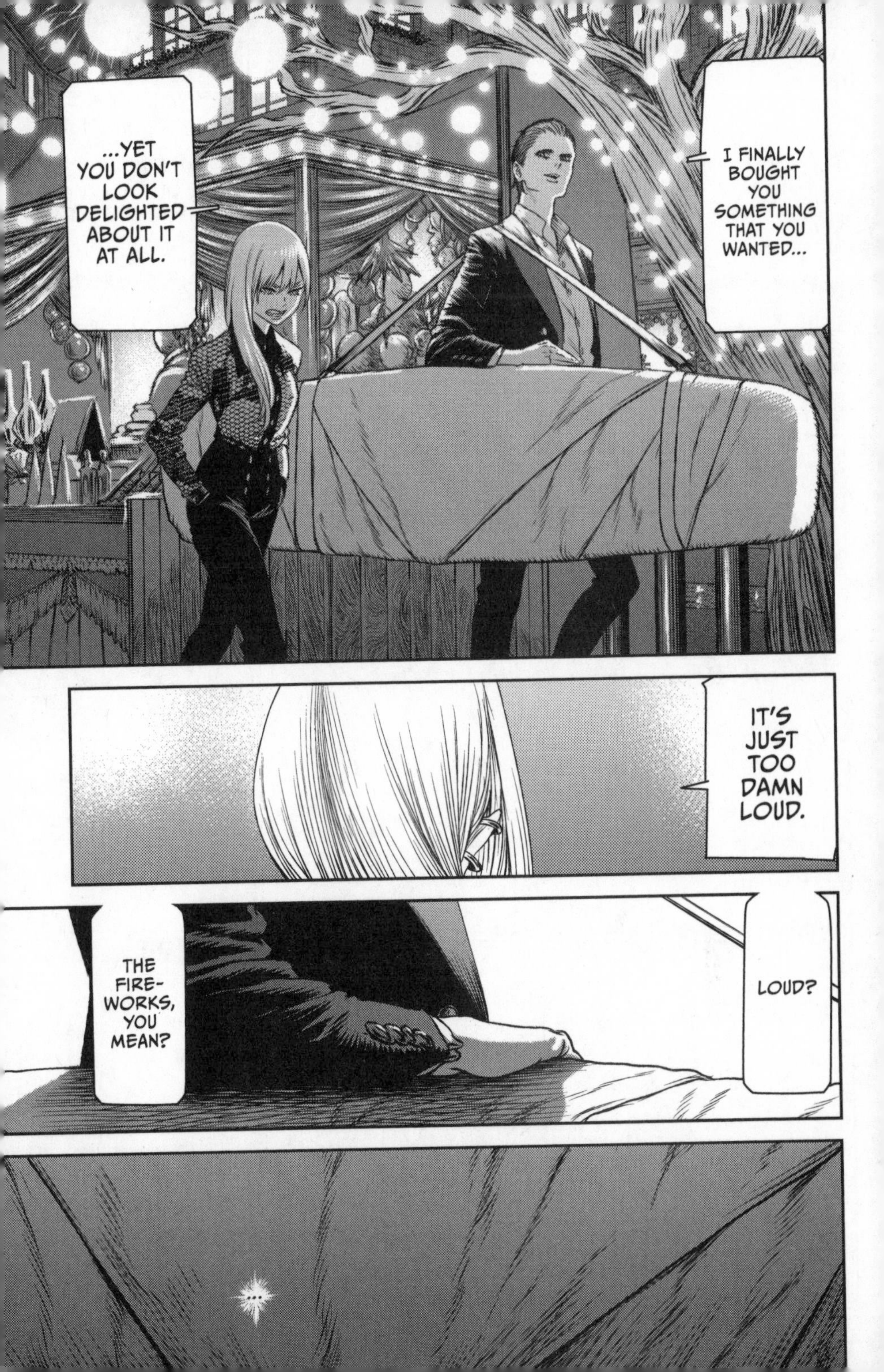
I FINALLY BOUGHT YOU SOMETHING THAT YOU WANTED...
...YET YOU DON'T LOOK DELIGHTED ABOUT IT AT ALL.
IT'S JUST TOO DAMN LOUD.
LOUD?
THE FIRE-WORKS, YOU MEAN?
...

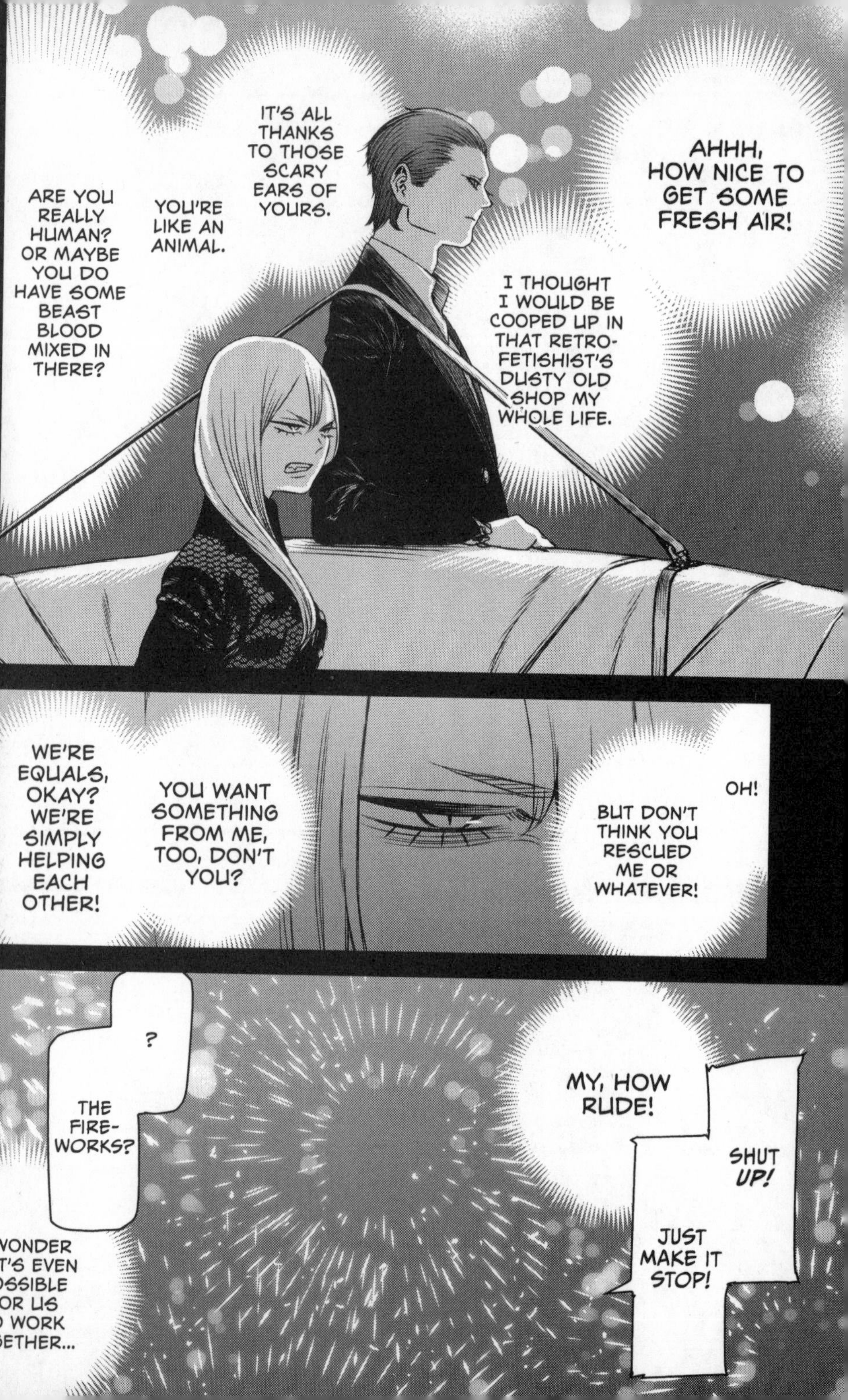
AHHH, HOW NICE TO GET SOME FRESH AIR!
I THOUGHT I WOULD BE COOPED UP IN THAT RETRO-FETISHIST'S DUSTY OLD SHOP MY WHOLE LIFE.
IT'S ALL THANKS TO THOSE SCARY EARS OF YOURS.
YOU'RE LIKE AN ANIMAL.
ARE YOU REALLY HUMAN? OR MAYBE YOU DO HAVE SOME BEAST BLOOD MIXED IN THERE?
OH!
BUT DON'T THINK YOU RESCUED ME OR WHATEVER!
YOU WANT SOMETHING FROM ME, TOO, DON'T YOU?
WE'RE EQUALS, OKAY? WE'RE SIMPLY HELPING EACH OTHER!
MY, HOW RUDE!
SHUT *UP!*
JUST MAKE IT STOP!
?
THE FIRE-WORKS?
I WONDER IF IT'S EVEN POSSIBLE FOR US TO WORK TOGETHER...

THE WITCH AND THE BEAST

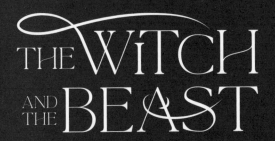

THE WITCH AND THE BEAST

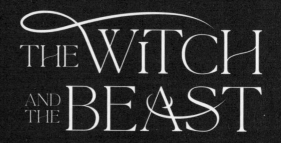

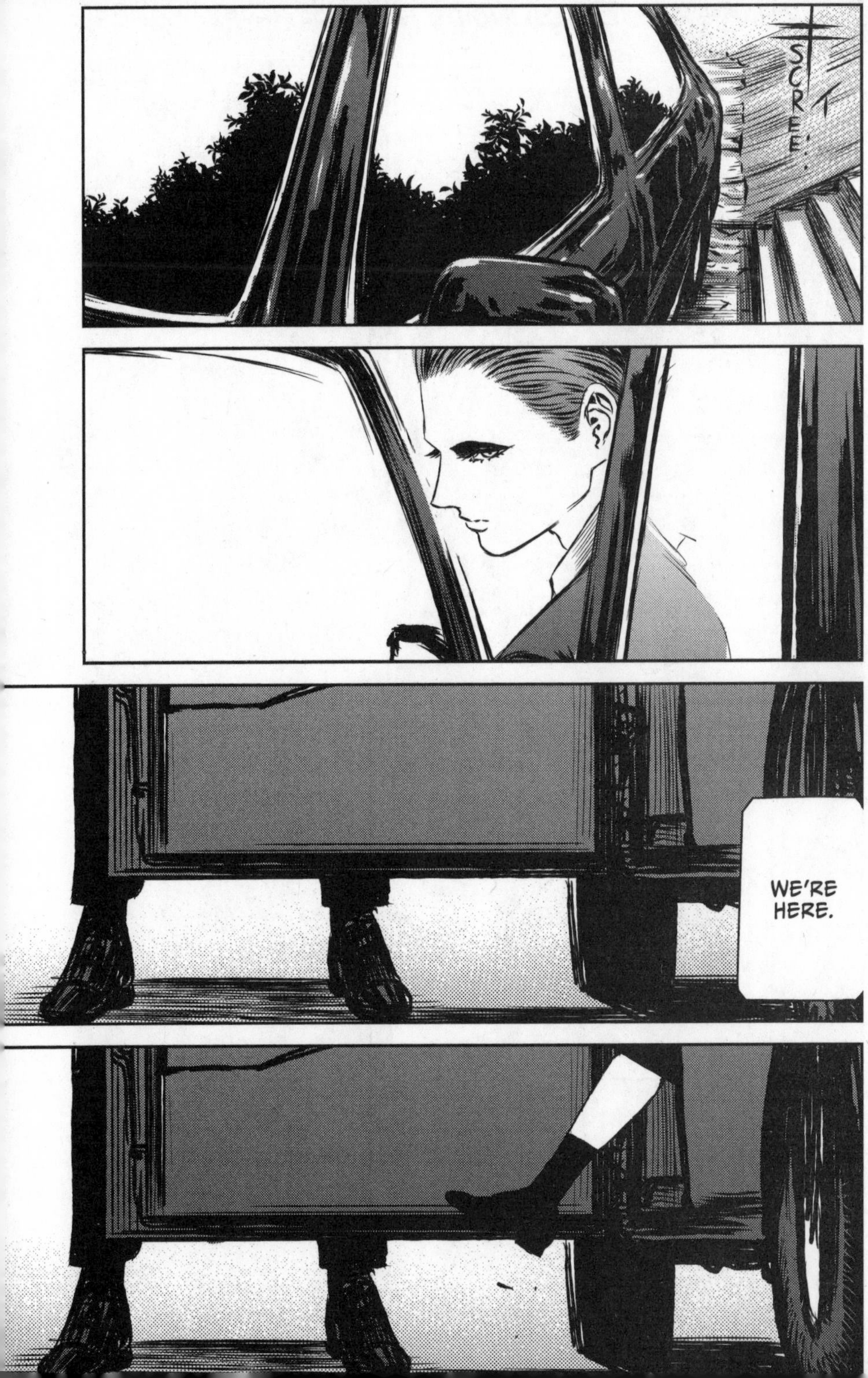
SCREE!
WE'RE HERE.

CHAPTER 43: CHAOS INSIDE THE STORM—PROLOGUE

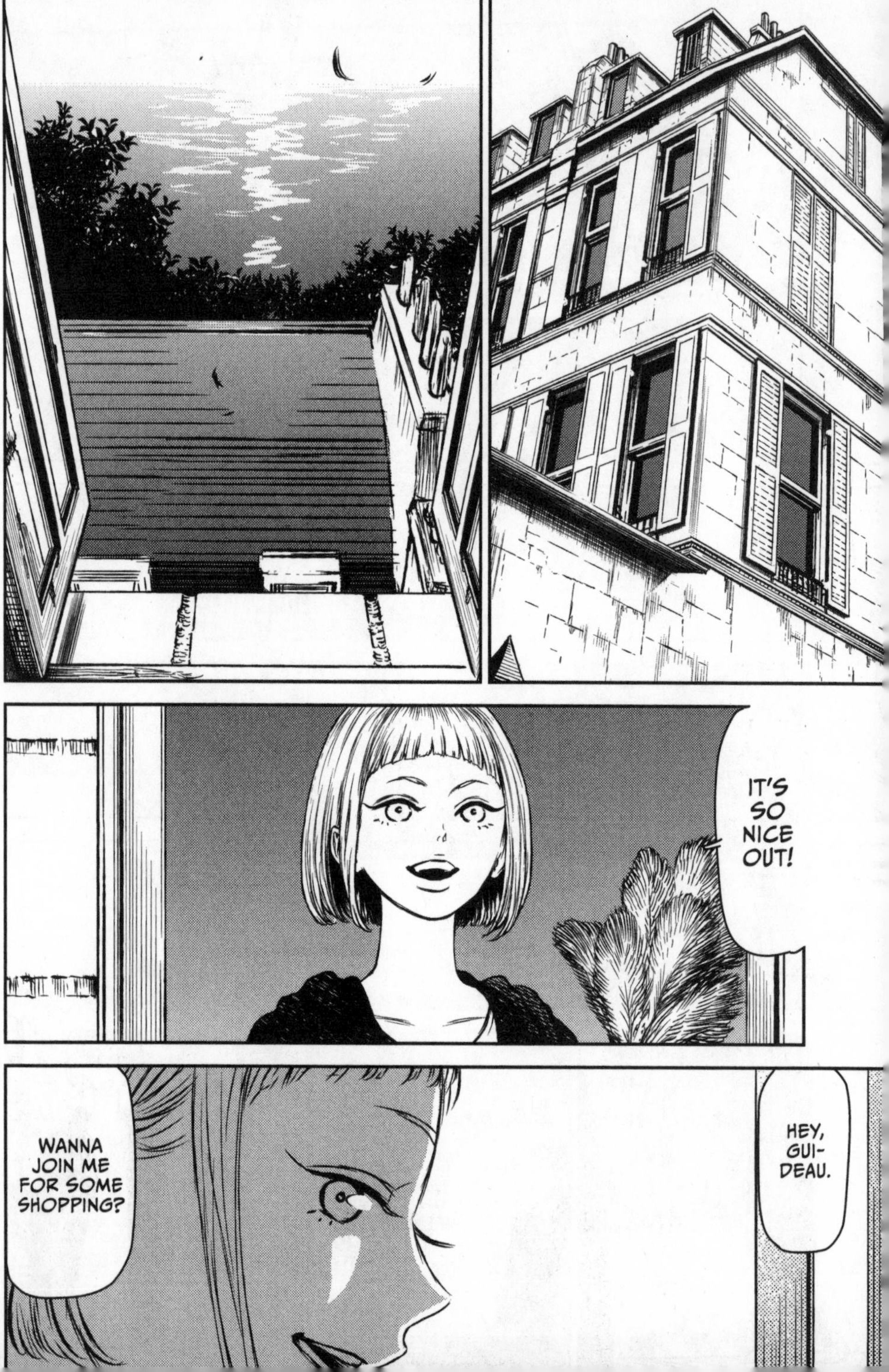
IT'S SO NICE OUT!
HEY, GUI-DEAU.
WANNA JOIN ME FOR SOME SHOPPING?

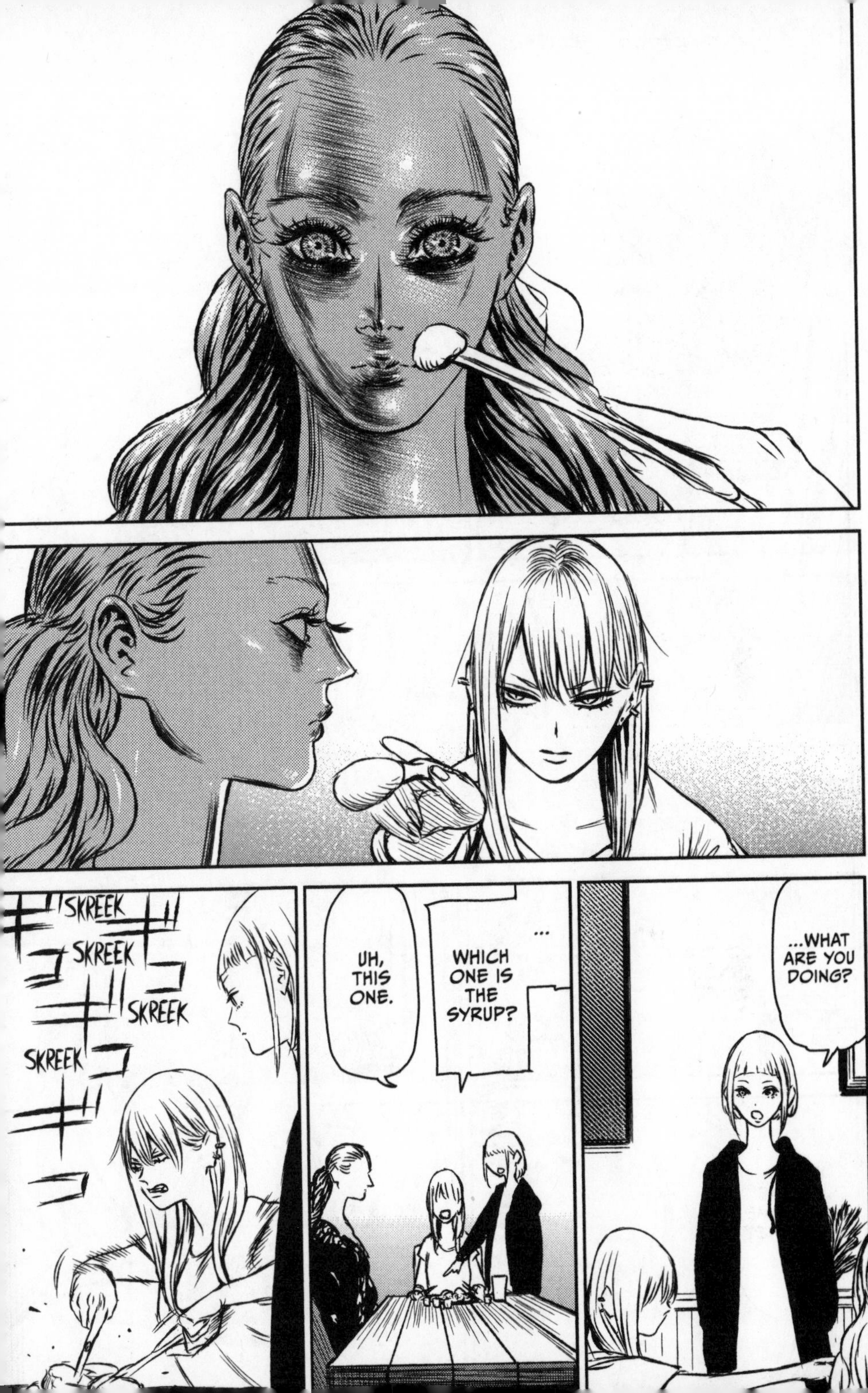
...WHAT ARE YOU DOING?
...
WHICH ONE IS THE SYRUP?
UH, THIS ONE.
SKREEK
SKREEK
SKREEK
SKREEK

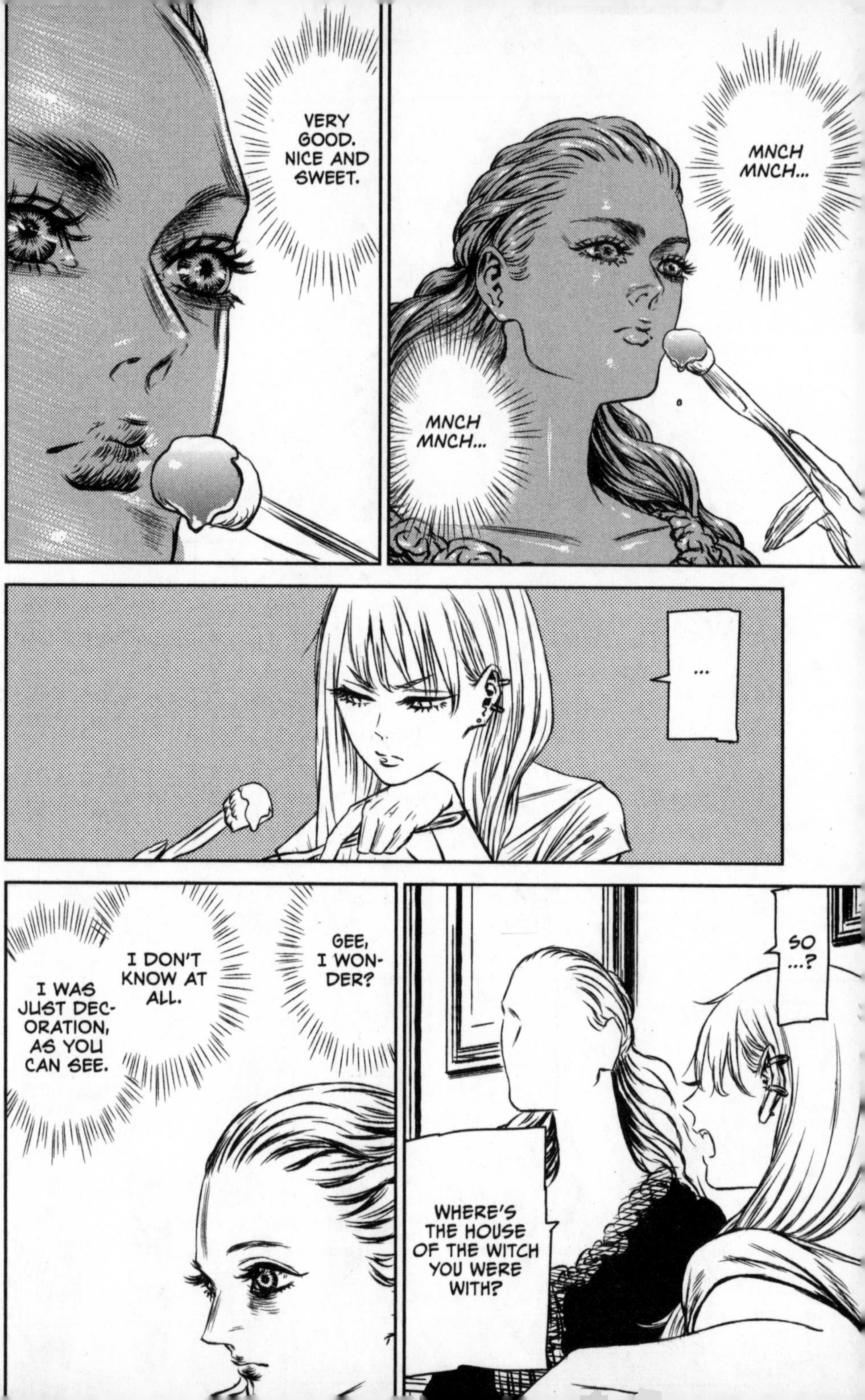
MNCH MNCH...
MNCH MNCH...
VERY GOOD. NICE AND SWEET.
...
SO ...?
WHERE'S THE HOUSE OF THE WITCH YOU WERE WITH?
GEE, I WONDER?
I DON'T KNOW AT ALL.
I WAS JUST DECORATION, AS YOU CAN SEE.

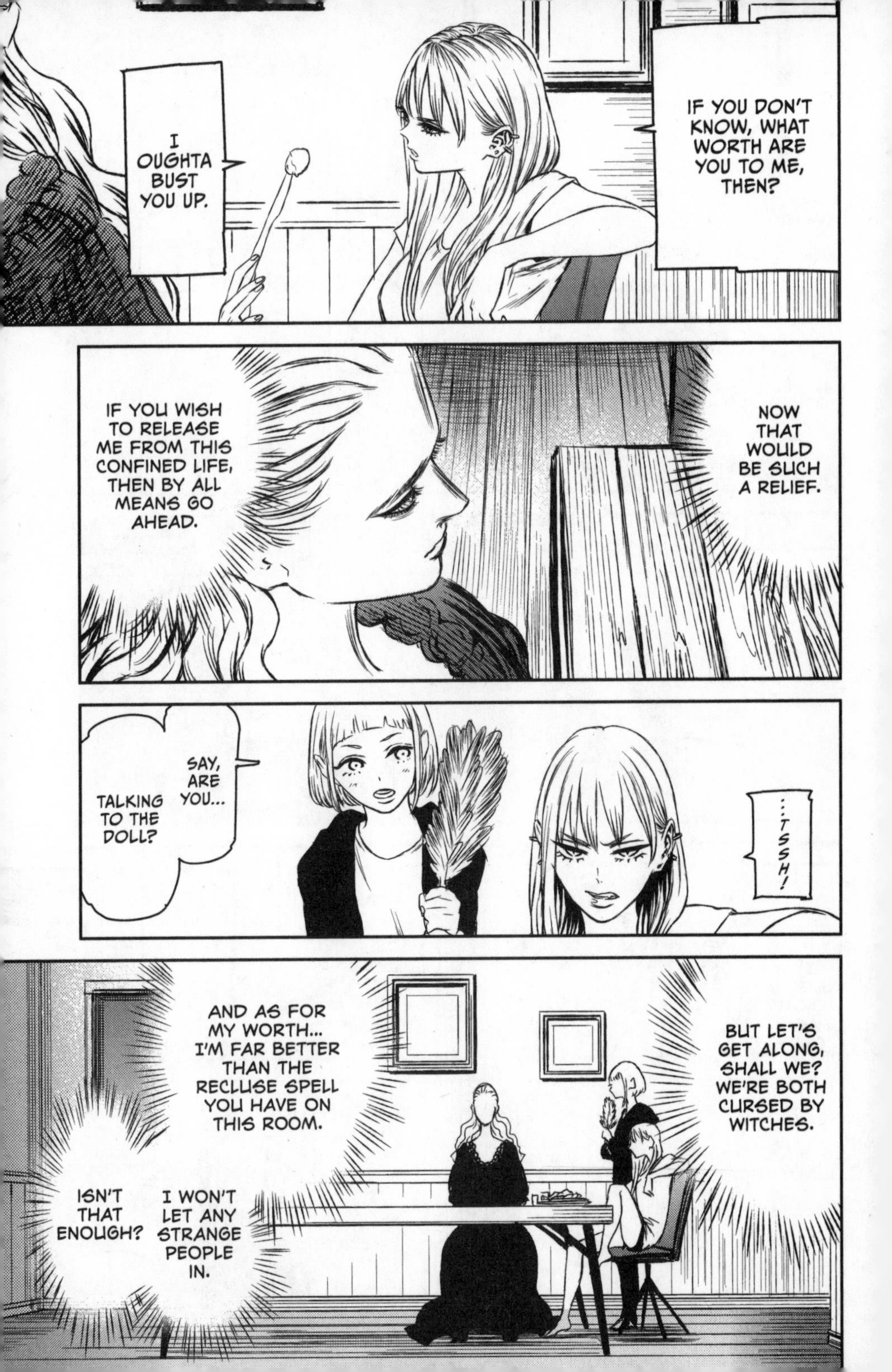
IF YOU DON'T KNOW, WHAT WORTH ARE YOU TO ME, THEN?
I OUGHTA BUST YOU UP.
NOW THAT WOULD BE SUCH A RELIEF.
IF YOU WISH TO RELEASE ME FROM THIS CONFINED LIFE, THEN BY ALL MEANS GO AHEAD.
...TSSH!
SAY, ARE YOU...
TALKING TO THE DOLL?
BUT LET'S GET ALONG, SHALL WE? WE'RE BOTH CURSED BY WITCHES.
AND AS FOR MY WORTH... I'M FAR BETTER THAN THE RECLUSE SPELL YOU HAVE ON THIS ROOM.
I WON'T LET ANY STRANGE PEOPLE IN.
ISN'T THAT ENOUGH?

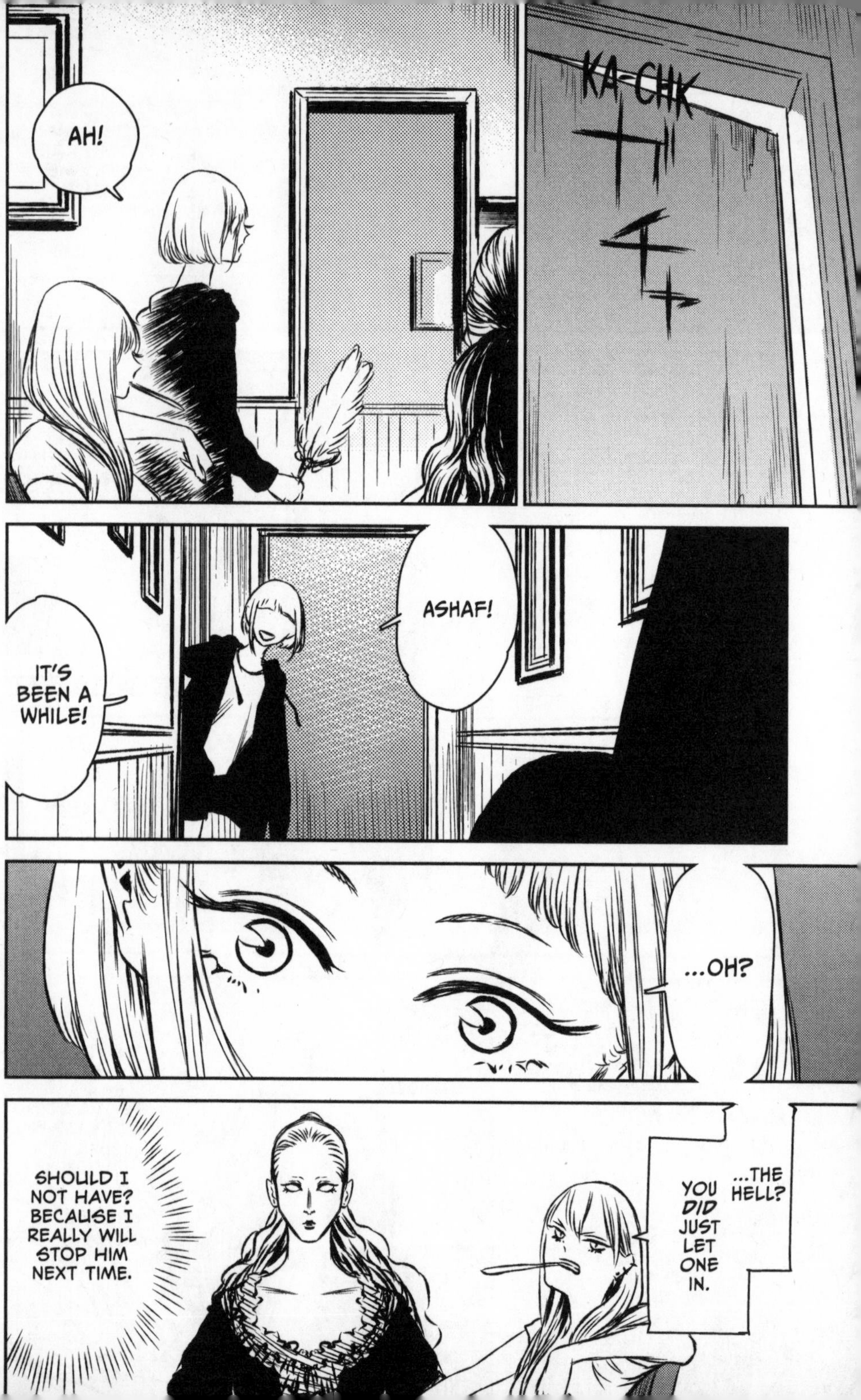
KA-CHK
AH!
ASHAF!
IT'S BEEN A WHILE!
...OH?
...THE HELL?
YOU *DID* JUST LET ONE IN.
SHOULD I NOT HAVE? BECAUSE I REALLY WILL STOP HIM NEXT TIME.

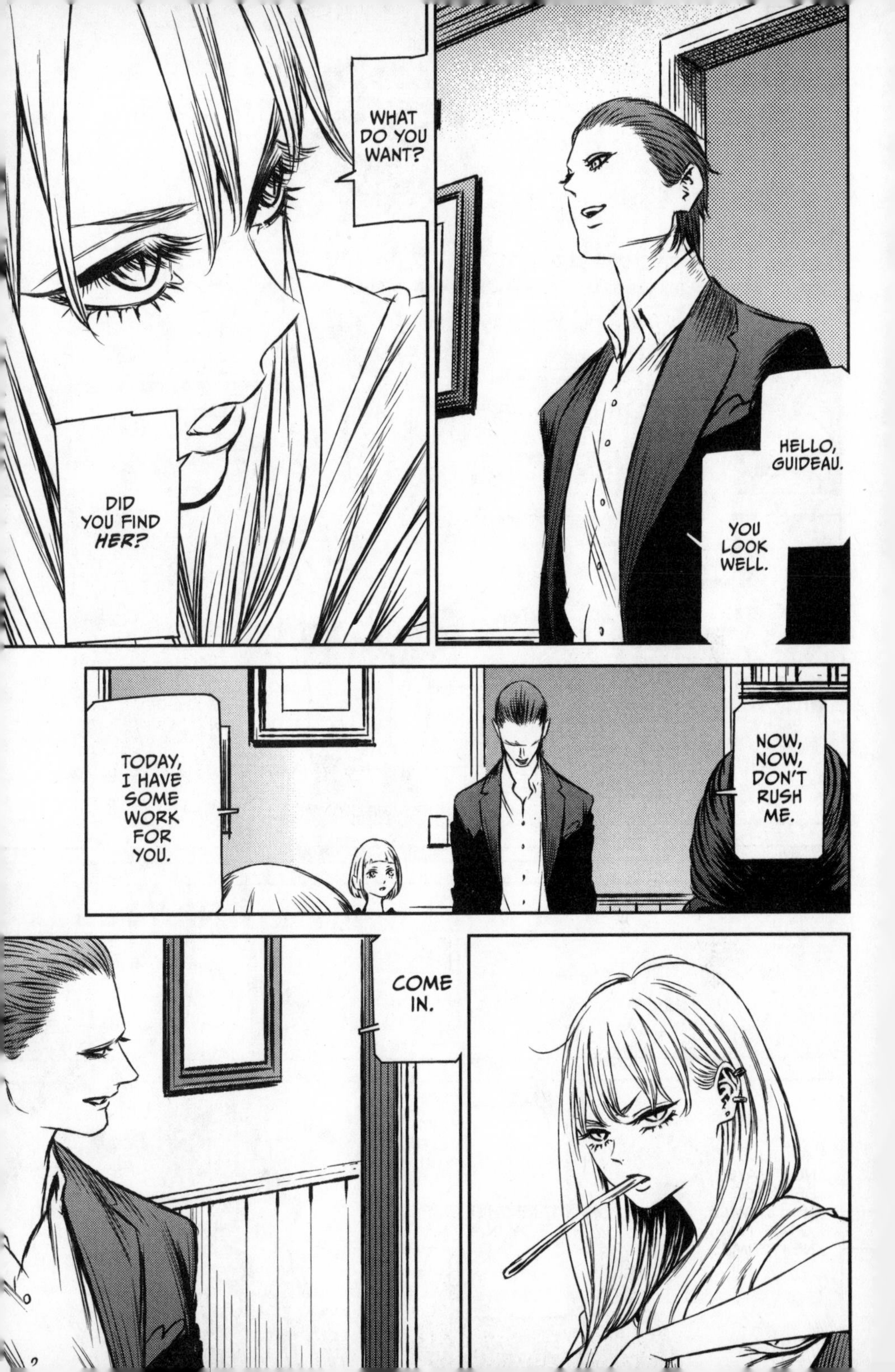
HELLO, GUIDEAU.
YOU LOOK WELL.
WHAT DO YOU WANT?
DID YOU FIND *HER?*
NOW, NOW, DON'T RUSH ME.
TODAY, I HAVE SOME WORK FOR YOU.
COME IN.

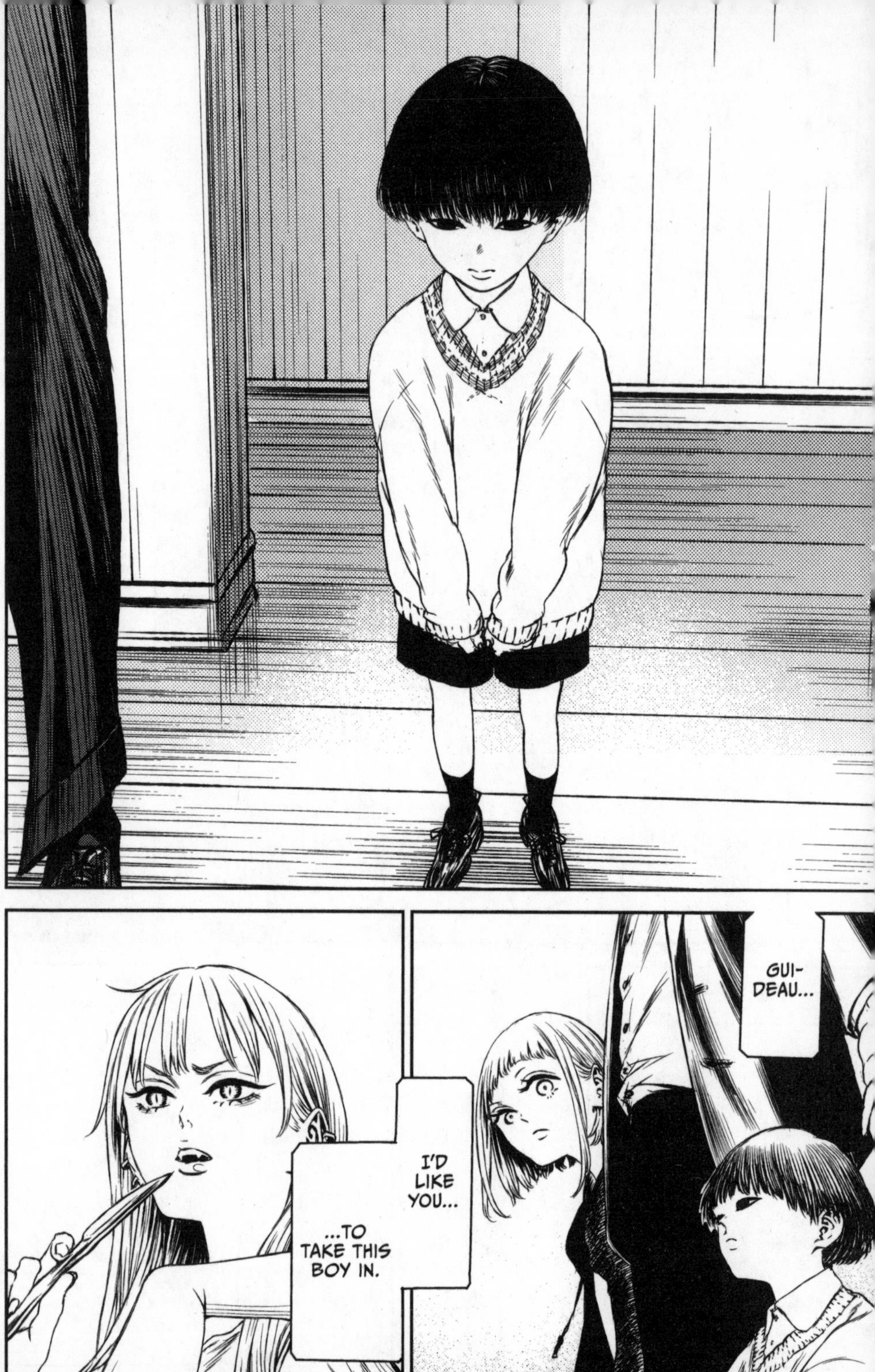
GUI-DEAU...
I'D LIKE YOU...
...TO TAKE THIS BOY IN.

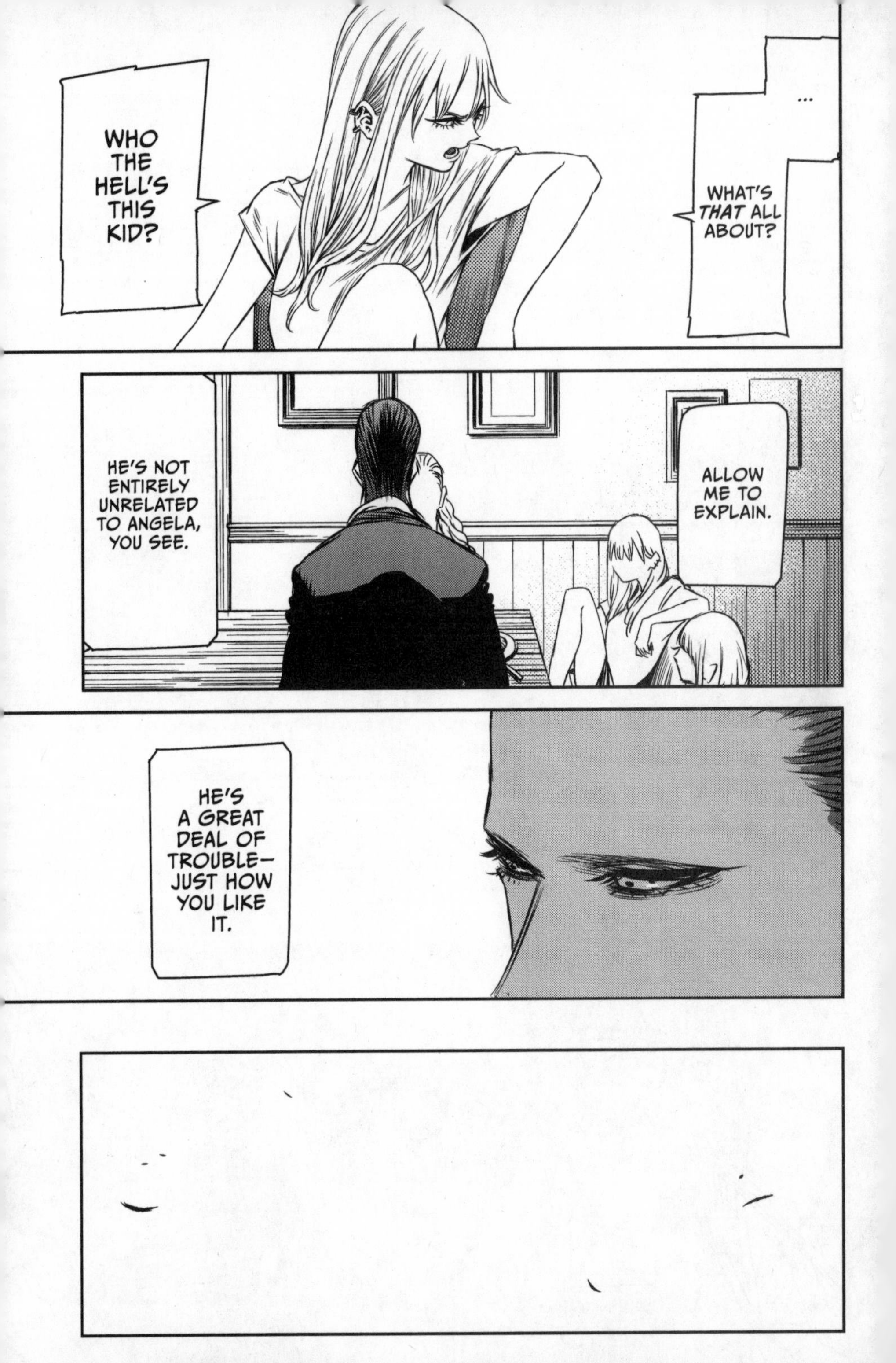
...
WHAT'S *THAT* ALL ABOUT?
WHO THE HELL'S THIS KID?
ALLOW ME TO EXPLAIN.
HE'S NOT ENTIRELY UNRELATED TO ANGELA, YOU SEE.
HE'S A GREAT DEAL OF TROUBLE—JUST HOW YOU LIKE IT.

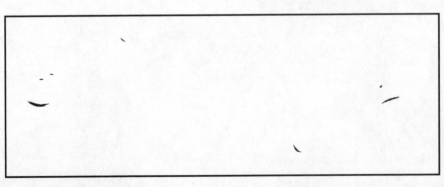

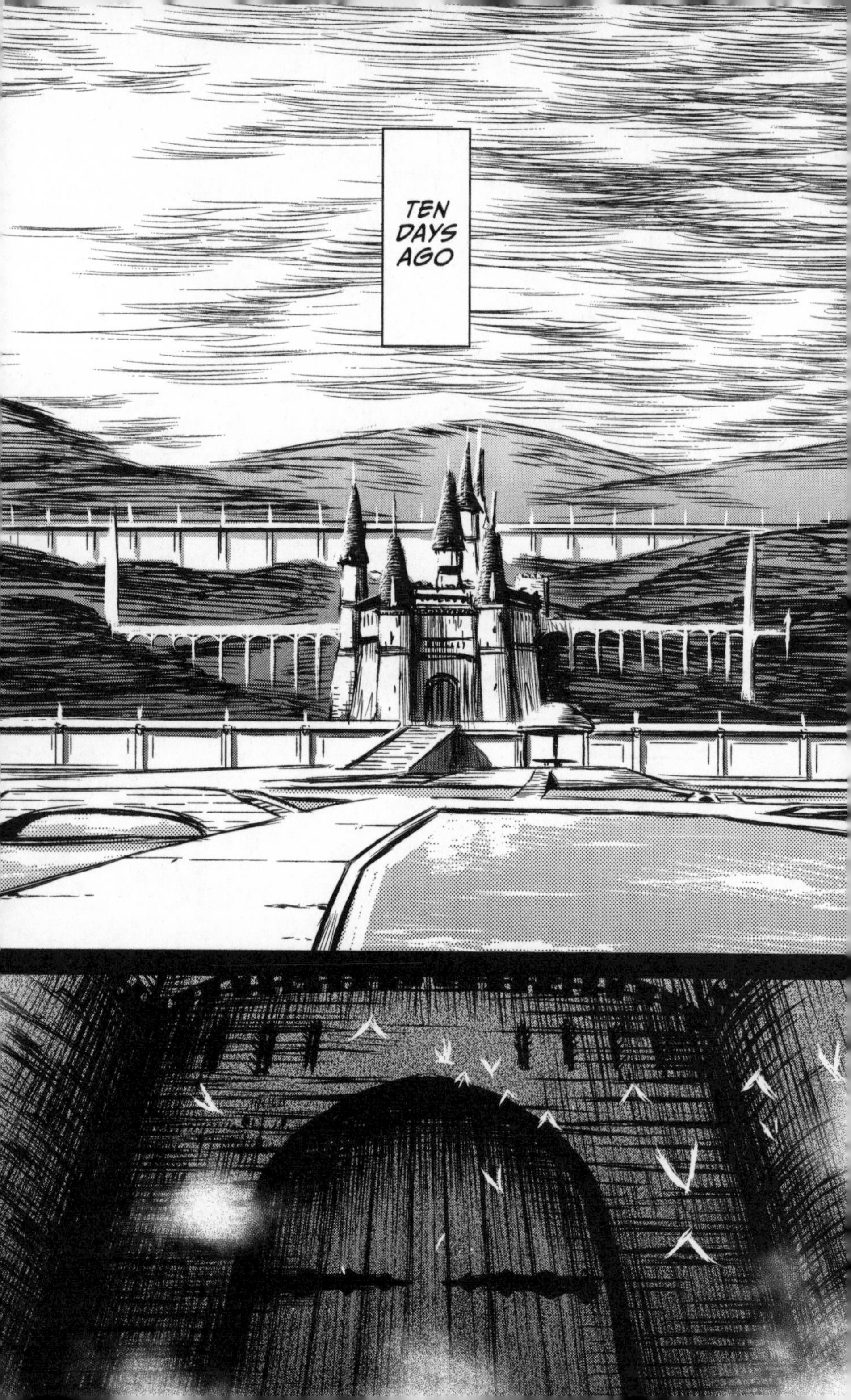
TEN DAYS AGO

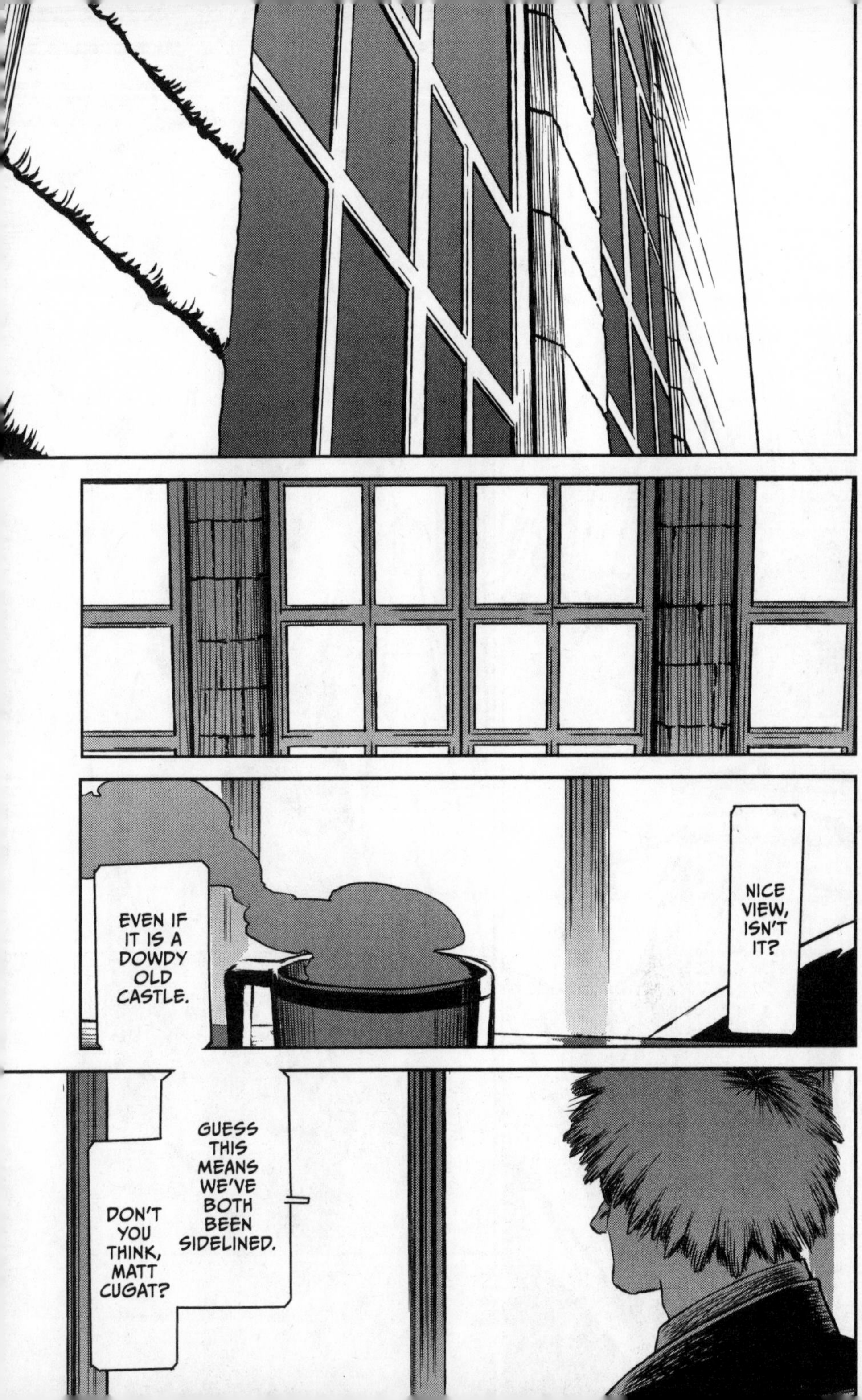
NICE VIEW, ISN'T IT?
EVEN IF IT IS A DOWDY OLD CASTLE.
GUESS THIS MEANS WE'VE BOTH BEEN SIDELINED.
DON'T YOU THINK, MATT CUGAT?

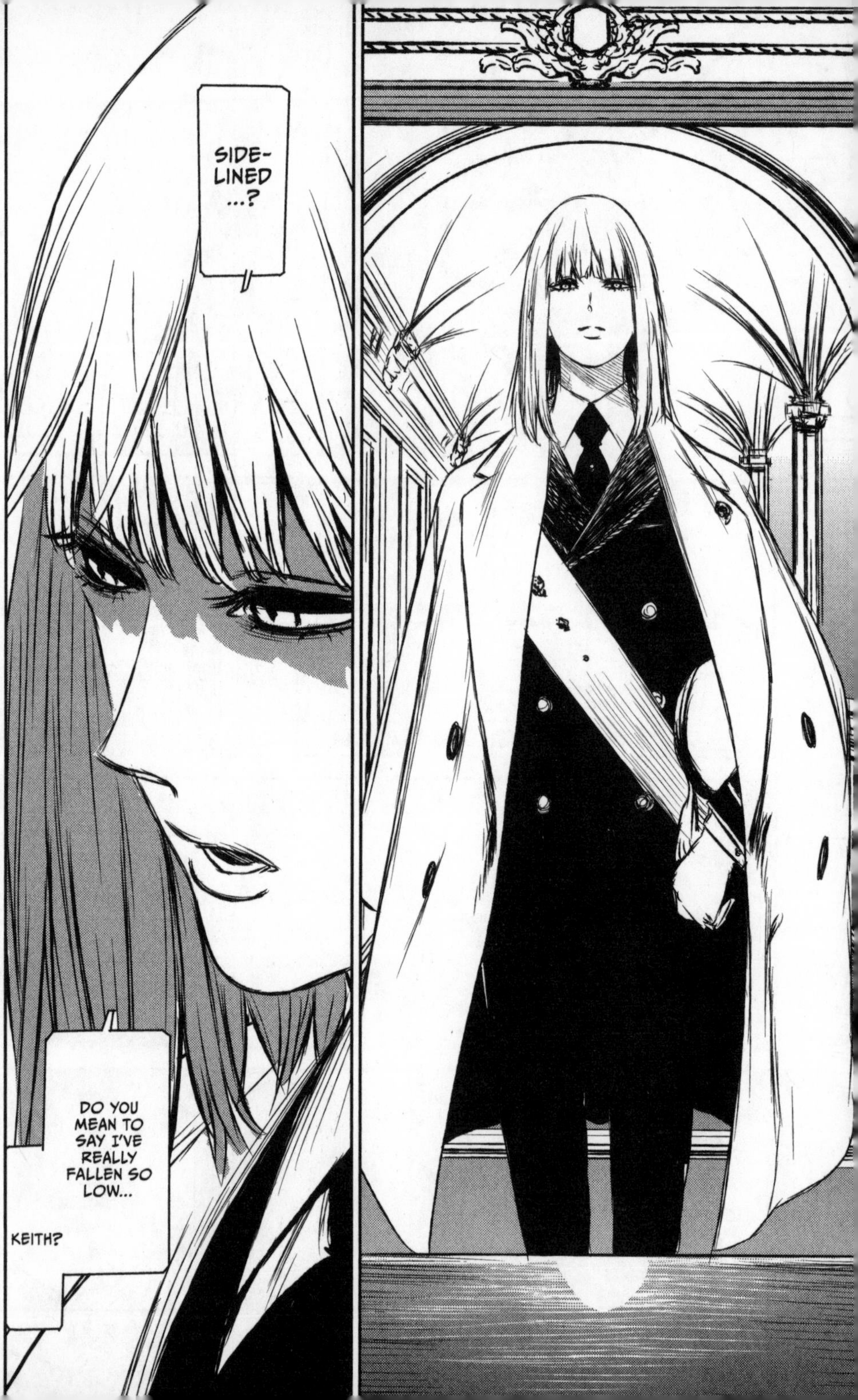
SIDE-LINED ...?
DO YOU MEAN TO SAY I'VE REALLY FALLEN SO LOW...
KEITH?

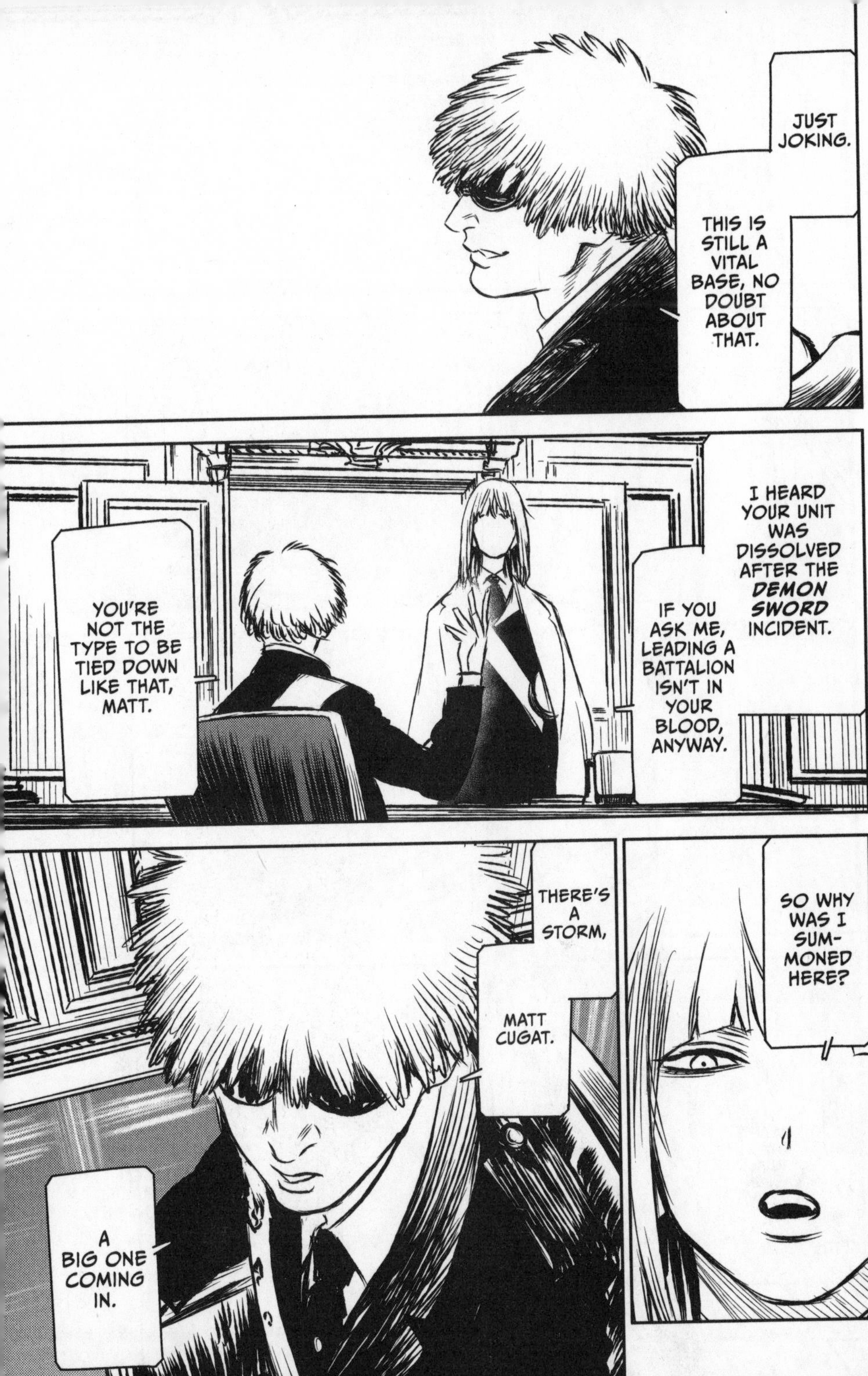
JUST JOKING.
THIS IS STILL A VITAL BASE, NO DOUBT ABOUT THAT.
I HEARD YOUR UNIT WAS DISSOLVED AFTER THE ***DEMON SWORD*** INCIDENT.
IF YOU ASK ME, LEADING A BATTALION ISN'T IN YOUR BLOOD, ANYWAY.
YOU'RE NOT THE TYPE TO BE TIED DOWN LIKE THAT, MATT.
SO WHY WAS I SUMMONED HERE?
THERE'S A STORM,
MATT CUGAT.
A BIG ONE COMING IN.

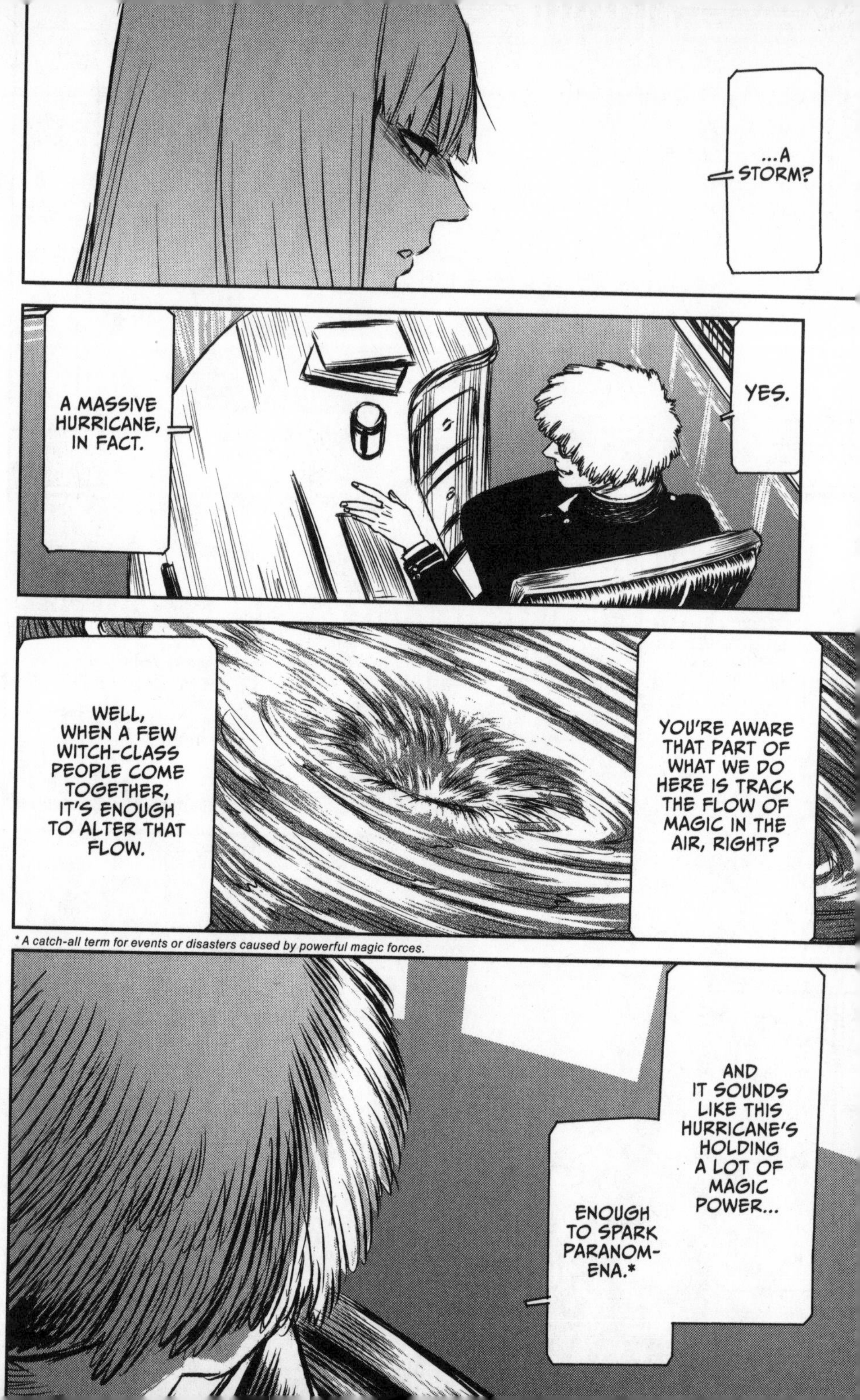
...A STORM?
YES.
A MASSIVE HURRICANE, IN FACT.
YOU'RE AWARE THAT PART OF WHAT WE DO HERE IS TRACK THE FLOW OF MAGIC IN THE AIR, RIGHT?
WELL, WHEN A FEW WITCH-CLASS PEOPLE COME TOGETHER, IT'S ENOUGH TO ALTER THAT FLOW.
AND IT SOUNDS LIKE THIS HURRICANE'S HOLDING A LOT OF MAGIC POWER...
ENOUGH TO SPARK PARANOM-ENA.*

* A catch-all term for events or disasters caused by powerful magic forces.

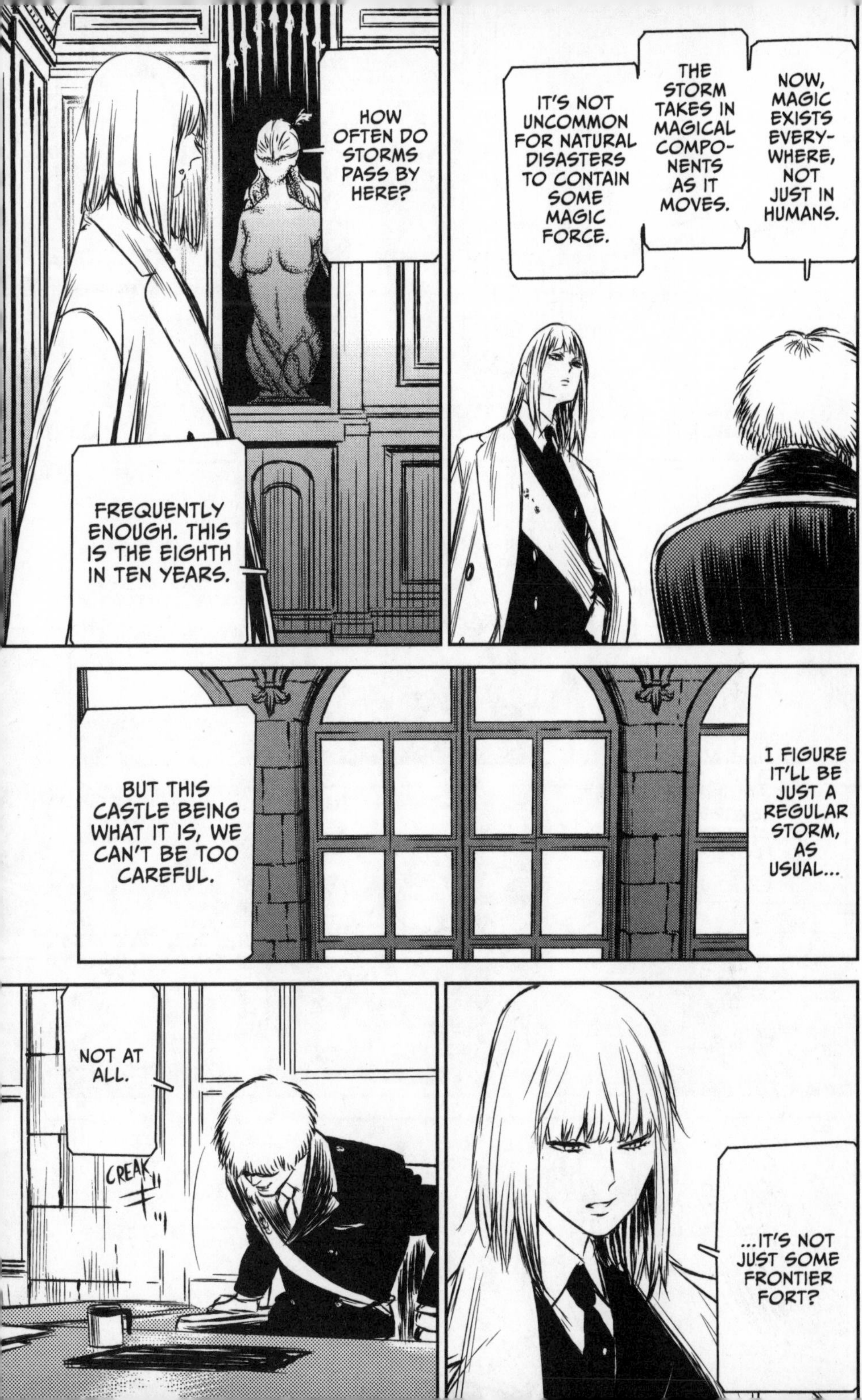
NOW, MAGIC EXISTS EVERYWHERE, NOT JUST IN HUMANS.
THE STORM TAKES IN MAGICAL COMPONENTS AS IT MOVES.
IT'S NOT UNCOMMON FOR NATURAL DISASTERS TO CONTAIN SOME MAGIC FORCE.
HOW OFTEN DO STORMS PASS BY HERE?
FREQUENTLY ENOUGH. THIS IS THE EIGHTH IN TEN YEARS.
I FIGURE IT'LL BE JUST A REGULAR STORM, AS USUAL...
BUT THIS CASTLE BEING WHAT IT IS, WE CAN'T BE TOO CAREFUL.
...IT'S NOT JUST SOME FRONTIER FORT?
NOT AT ALL.
CREAK

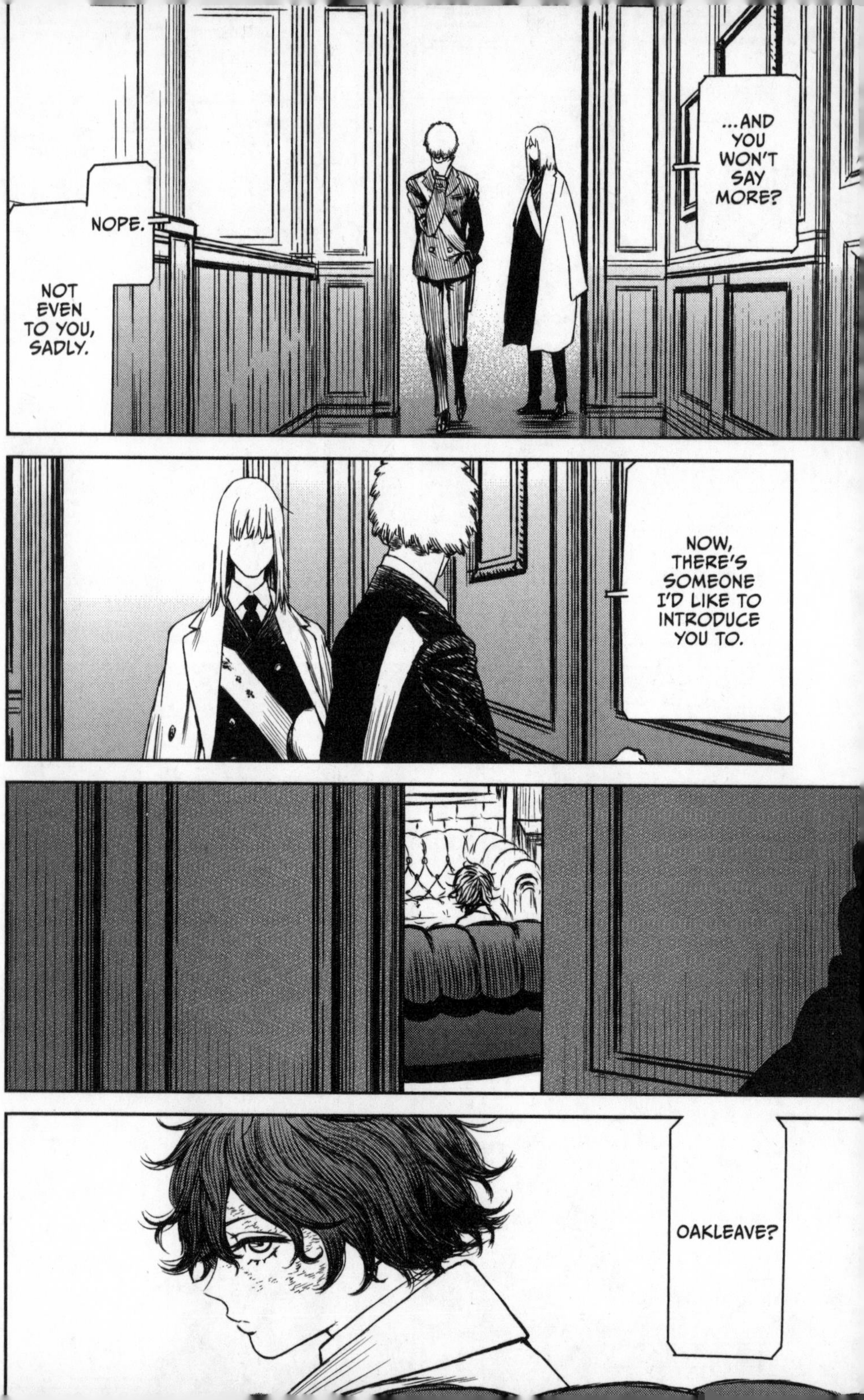
...AND YOU WON'T SAY MORE?
NOPE.
NOT EVEN TO YOU, SADLY.
NOW, THERE'S SOMEONE I'D LIKE TO INTRODUCE YOU TO.
OAKLEAVE?

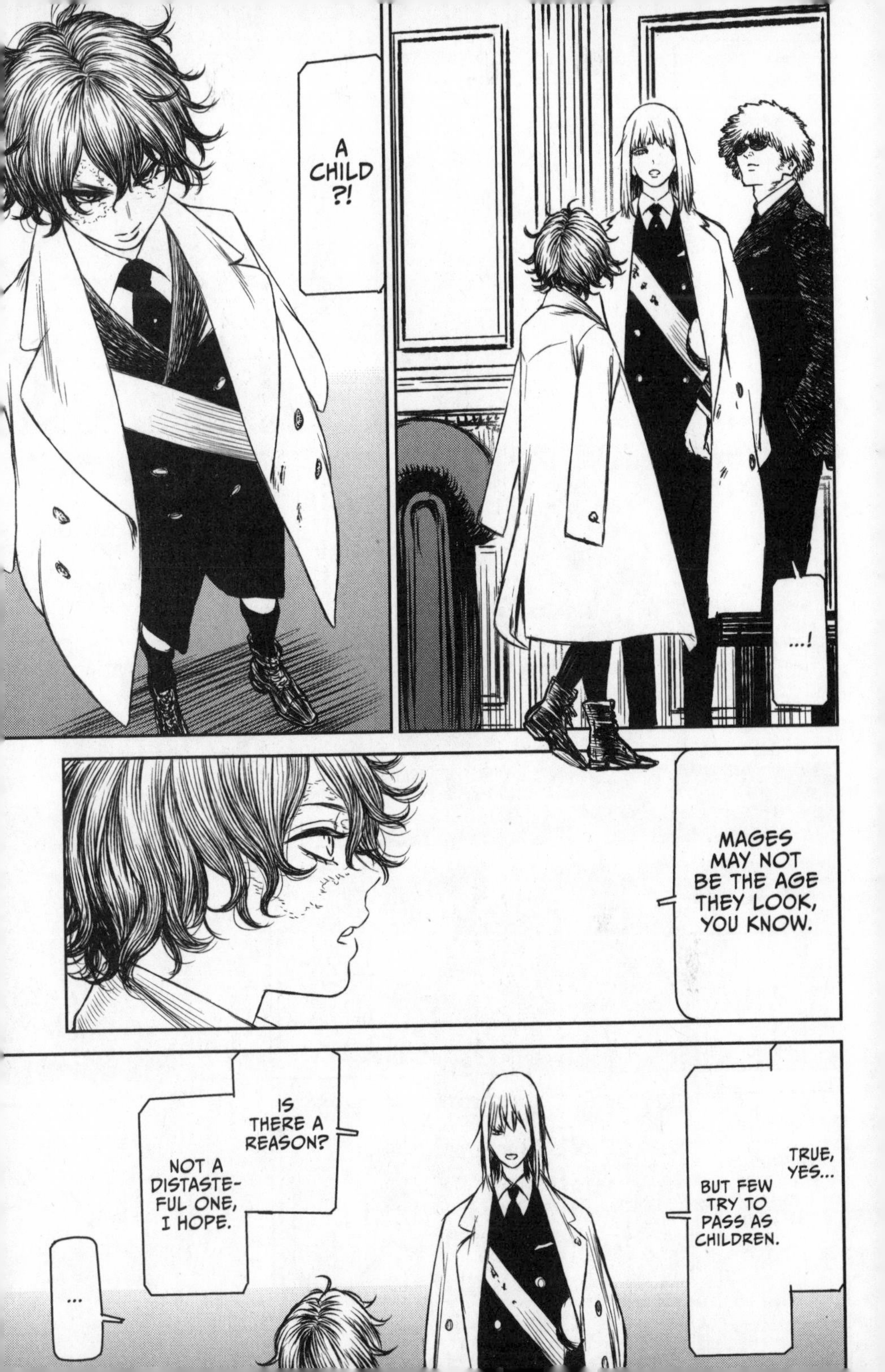
...!
A CHILD ?!
MAGES MAY NOT BE THE AGE THEY LOOK, YOU KNOW.
TRUE, YES...
BUT FEW TRY TO PASS AS CHILDREN.
IS THERE A REASON?
NOT A DISTASTE-FUL ONE, I HOPE.
...

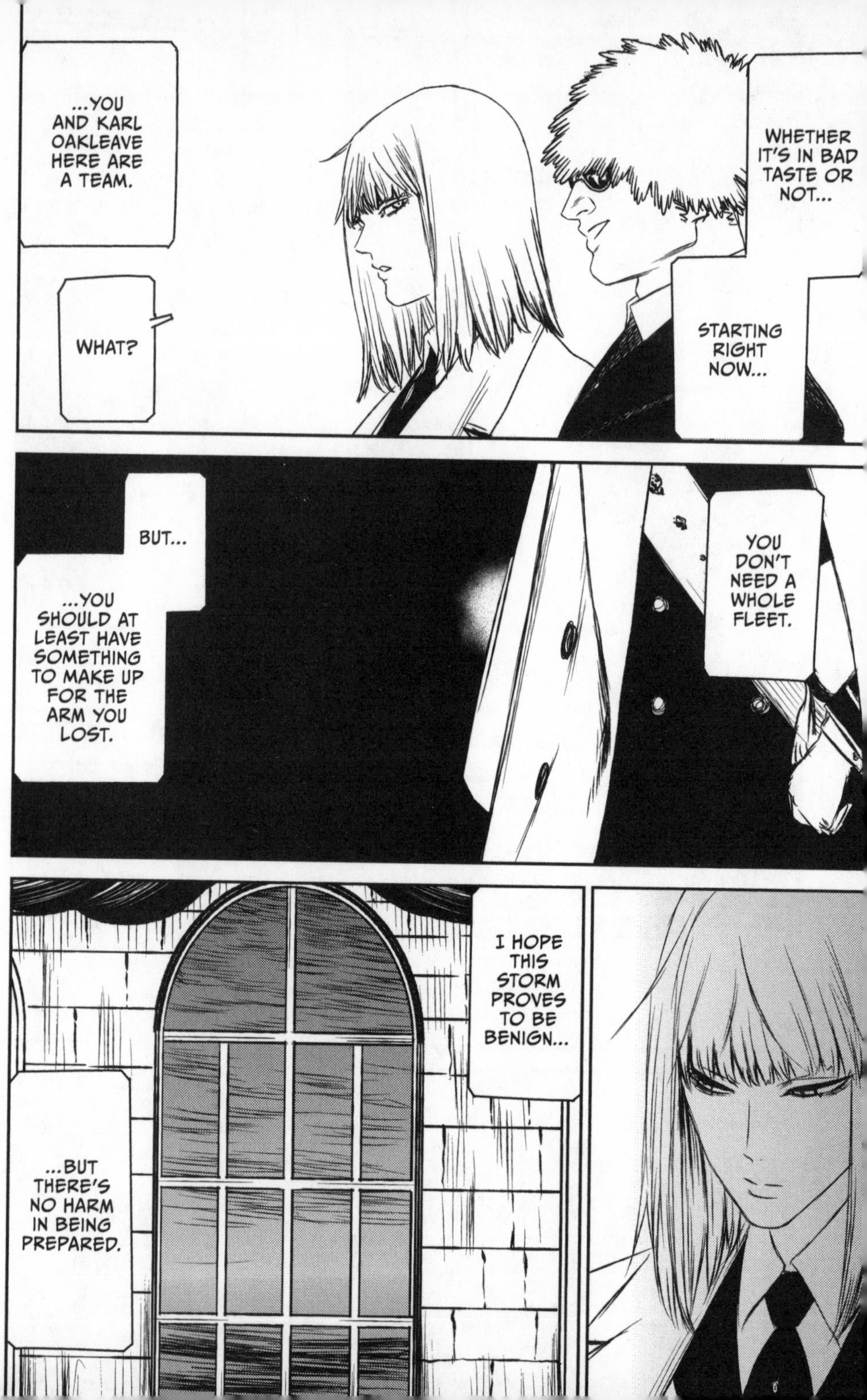
WHETHER IT'S IN BAD TASTE OR NOT...
STARTING RIGHT NOW...
...YOU AND KARL OAKLEAVE HERE ARE A TEAM.
WHAT?
YOU DON'T NEED A WHOLE FLEET.
BUT...
...YOU SHOULD AT LEAST HAVE SOMETHING TO MAKE UP FOR THE ARM YOU LOST.
I HOPE THIS STORM PROVES TO BE BENIGN...
...BUT THERE'S NO HARM IN BEING PREPARED.

IT COULD MAKE LANDFALL AS EARLY AS TOMORROW AFTERNOON.

WE HAVE ENOUGH TROOPS HERE.

AND MATT...

WE AREN'T ALONE.

OTHER FELLOW *KNIGHT COMMANDERS* ARE HERE AS WELL.

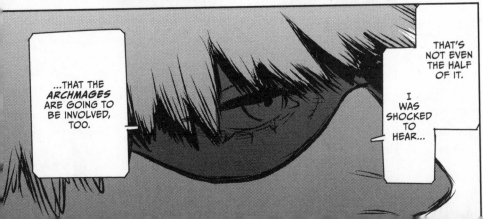

THAT'S NOT EVEN THE HALF OF IT.

I WAS SHOCKED TO HEAR...

...THAT THE *ARCHMAGES* ARE GOING TO BE INVOLVED, TOO.

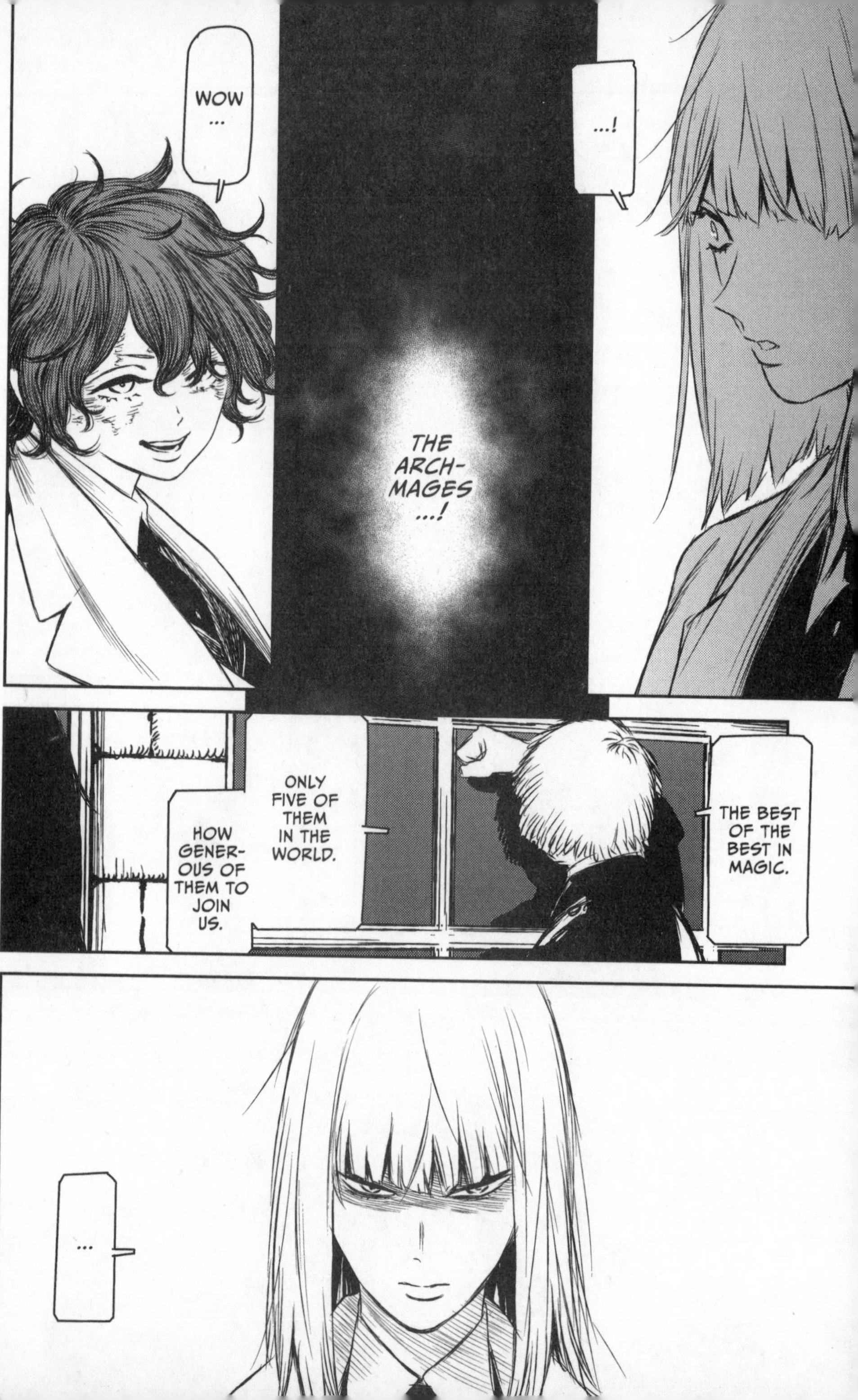
...!
THE ARCH-MAGES ...!
WOW ...
THE BEST OF THE BEST IN MAGIC.
ONLY FIVE OF THEM IN THE WORLD.
HOW GENER-OUS OF THEM TO JOIN US.
...

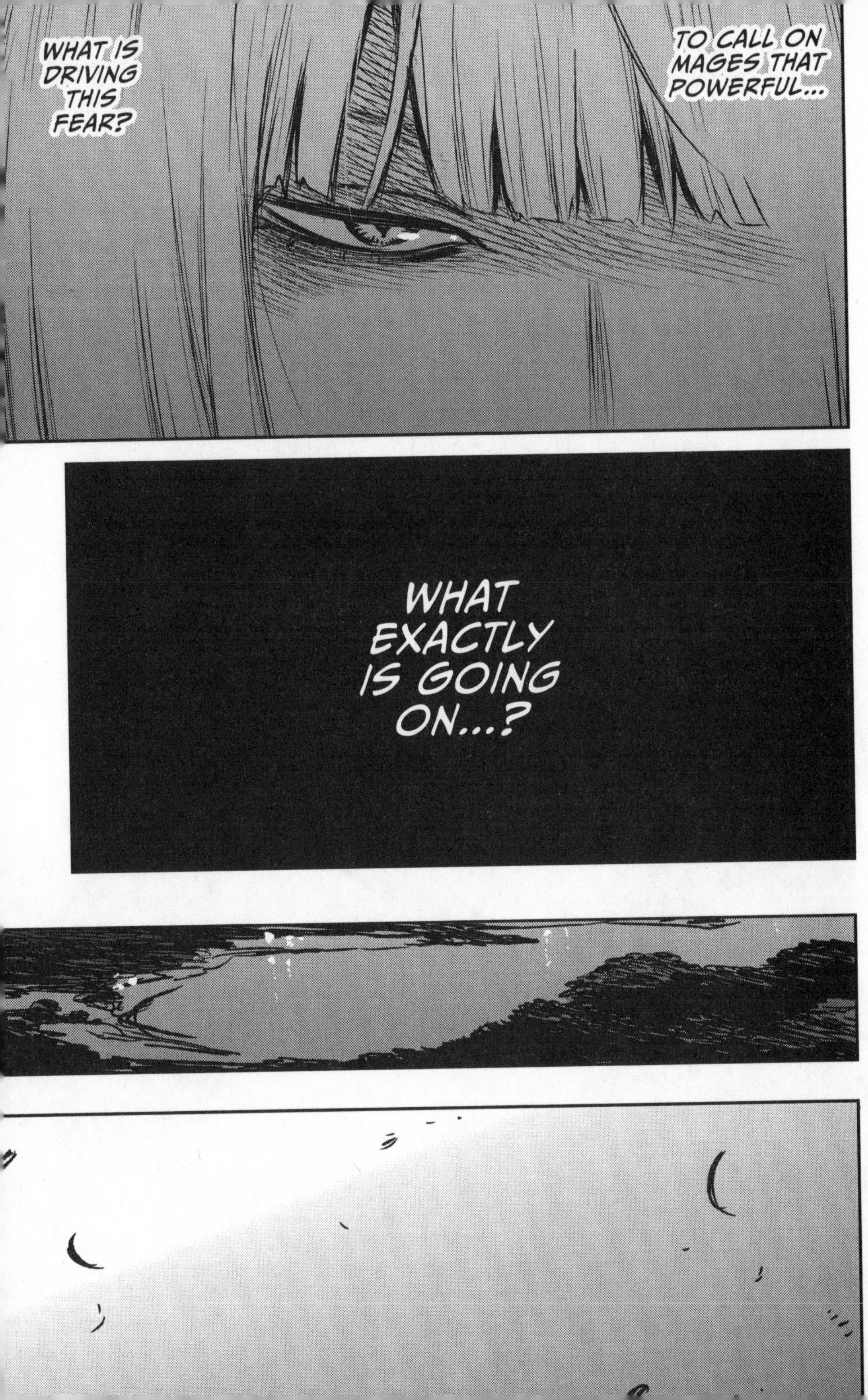
TO CALL ON MAGES THAT POWERFUL...
WHAT IS DRIVING THIS FEAR?
WHAT EXACTLY IS GOING ON...?

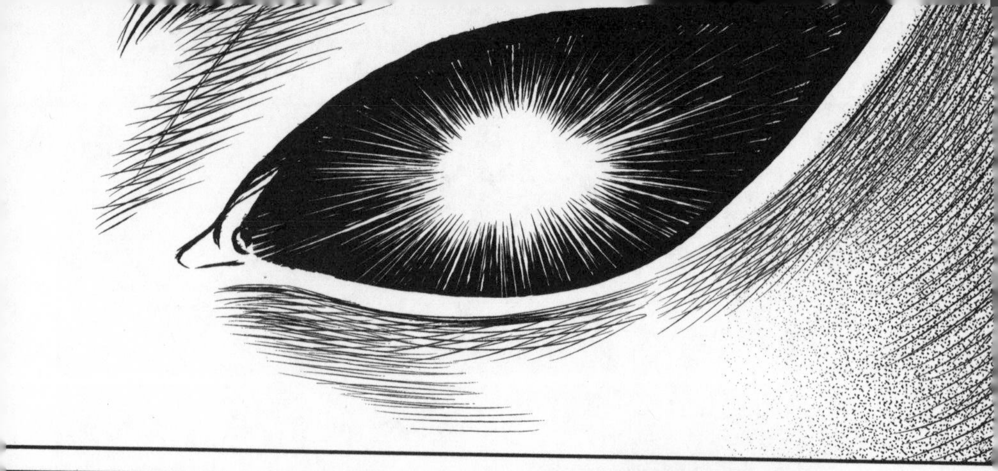
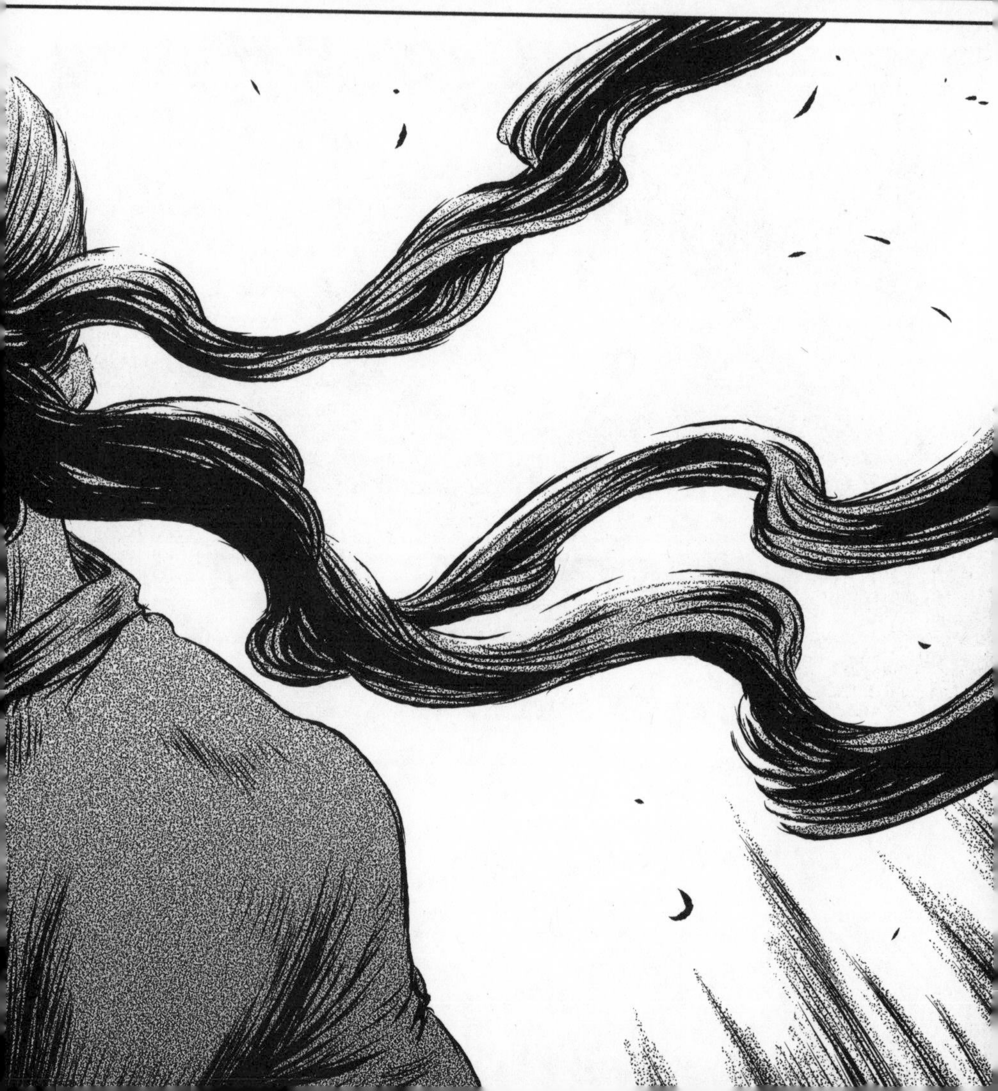

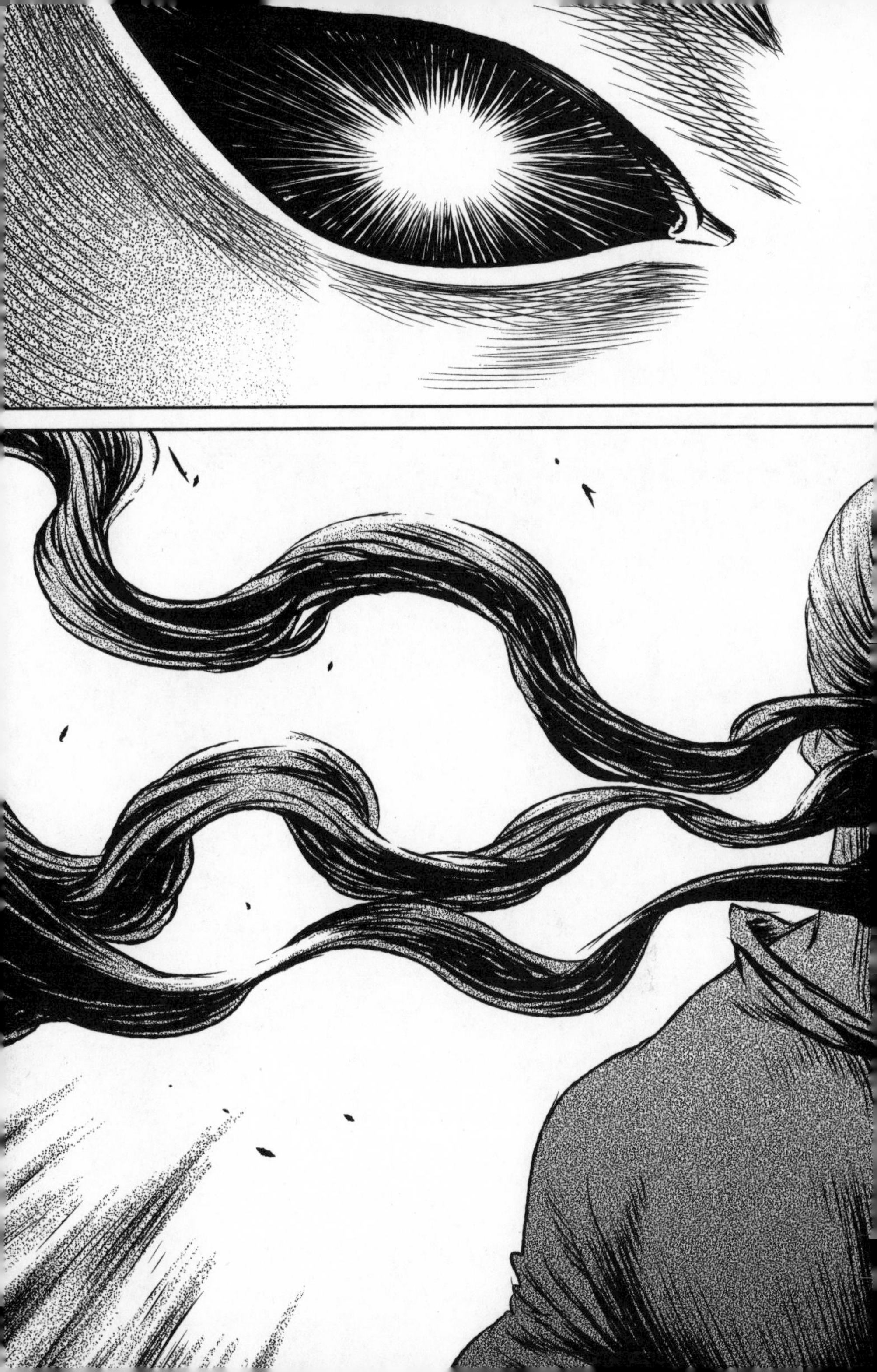

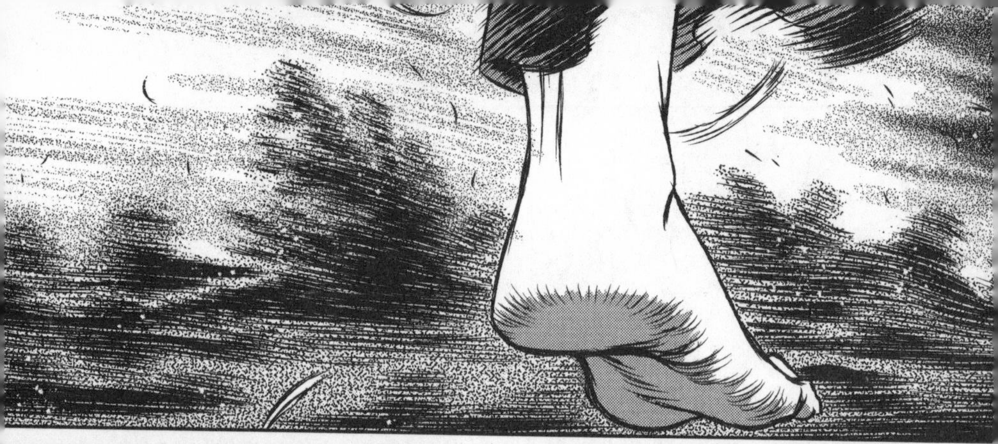
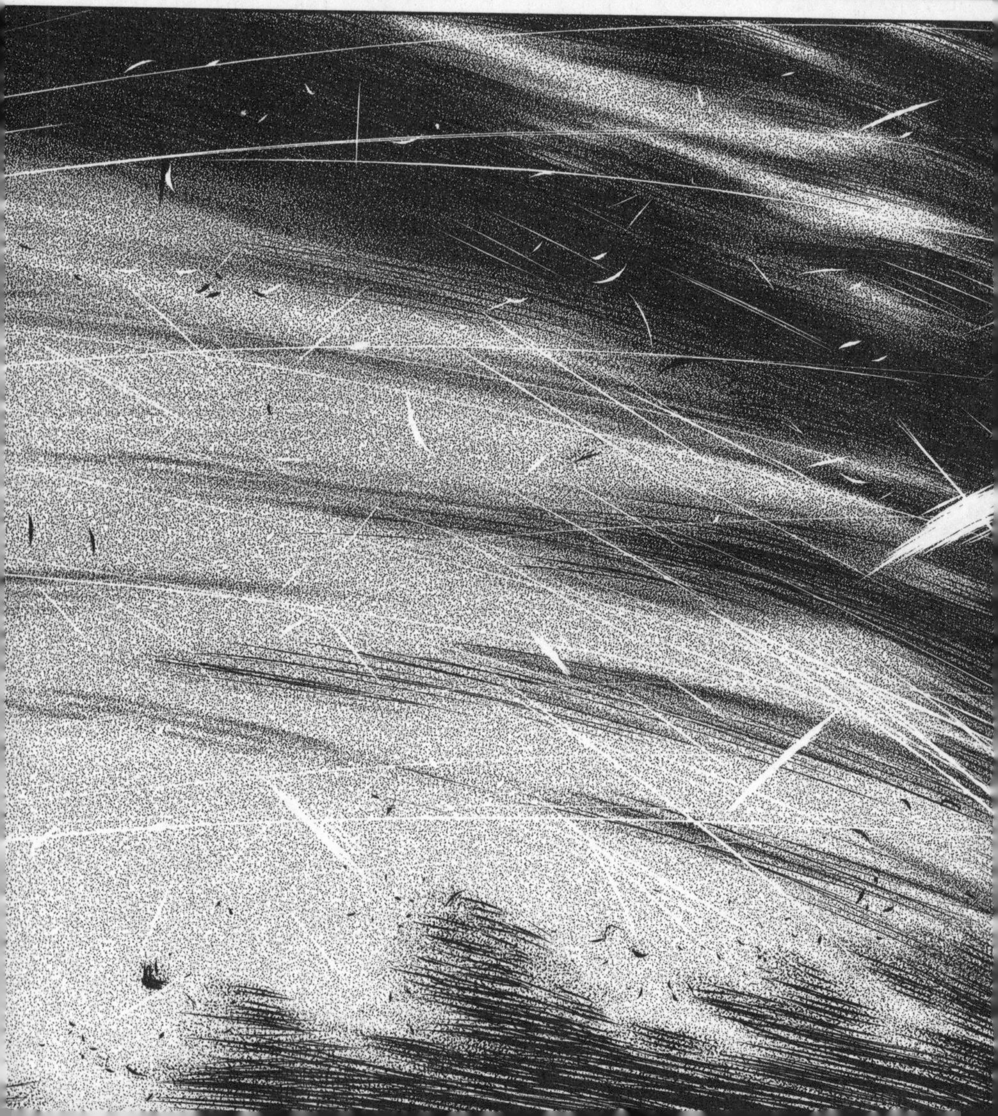

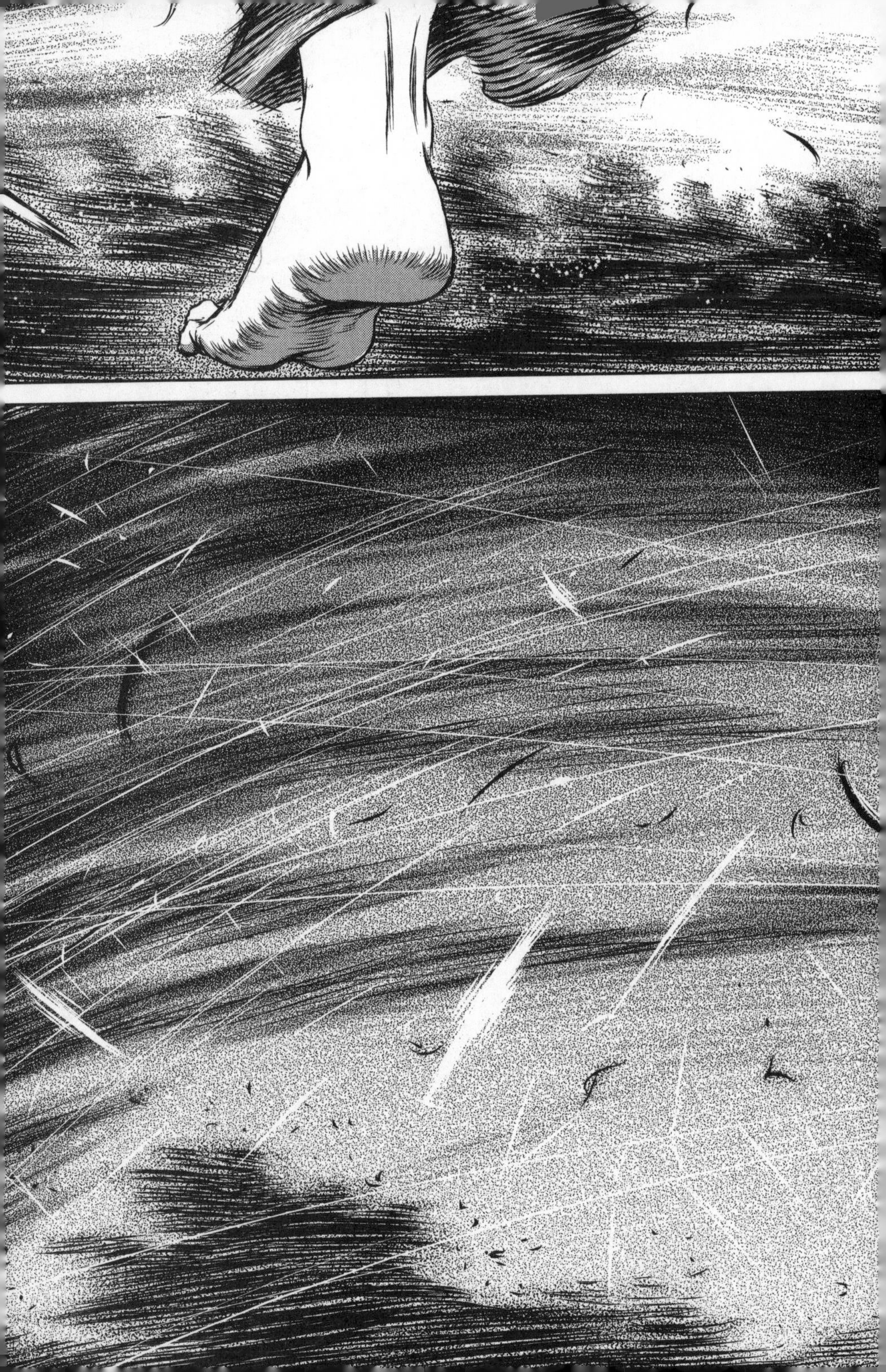

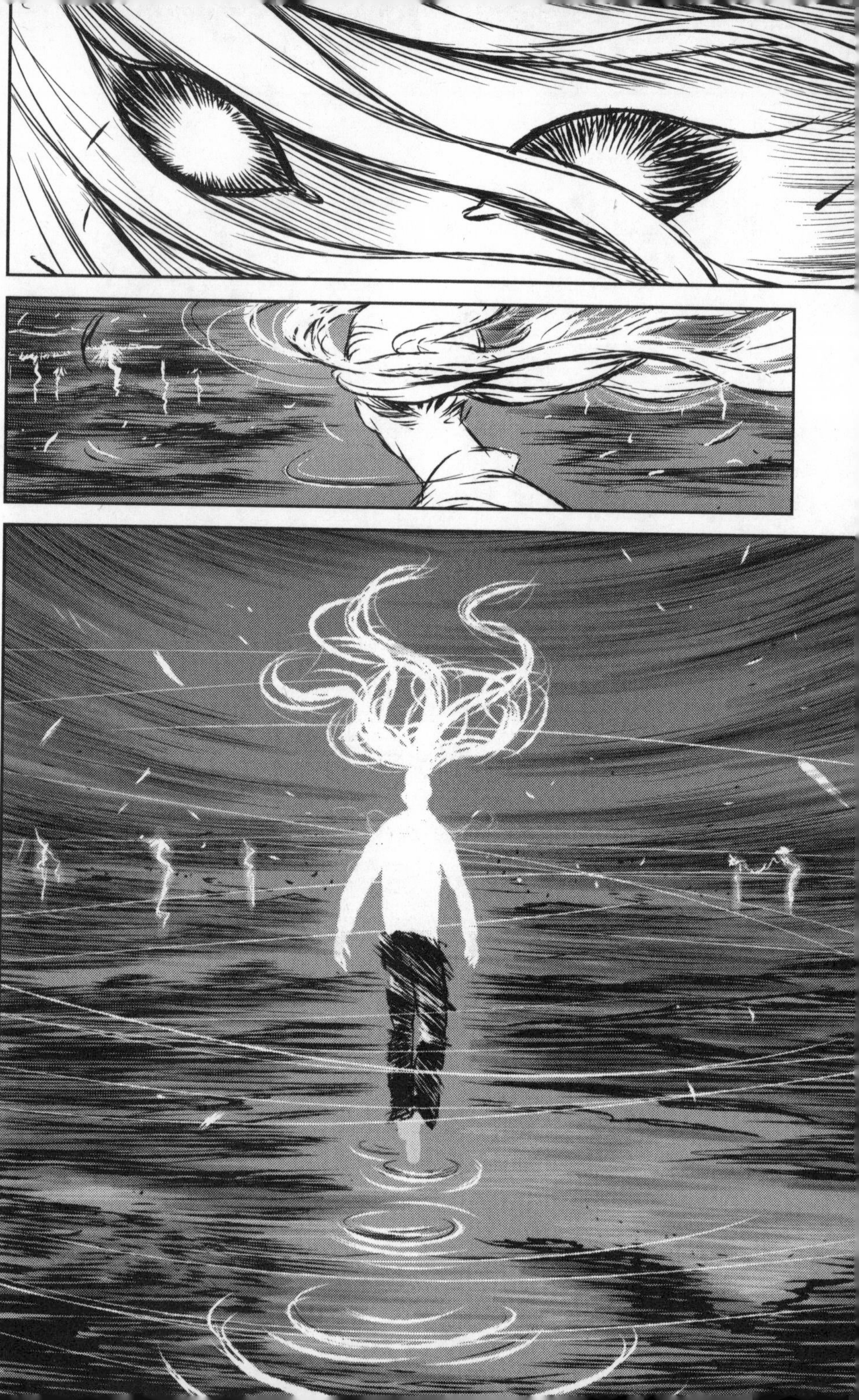

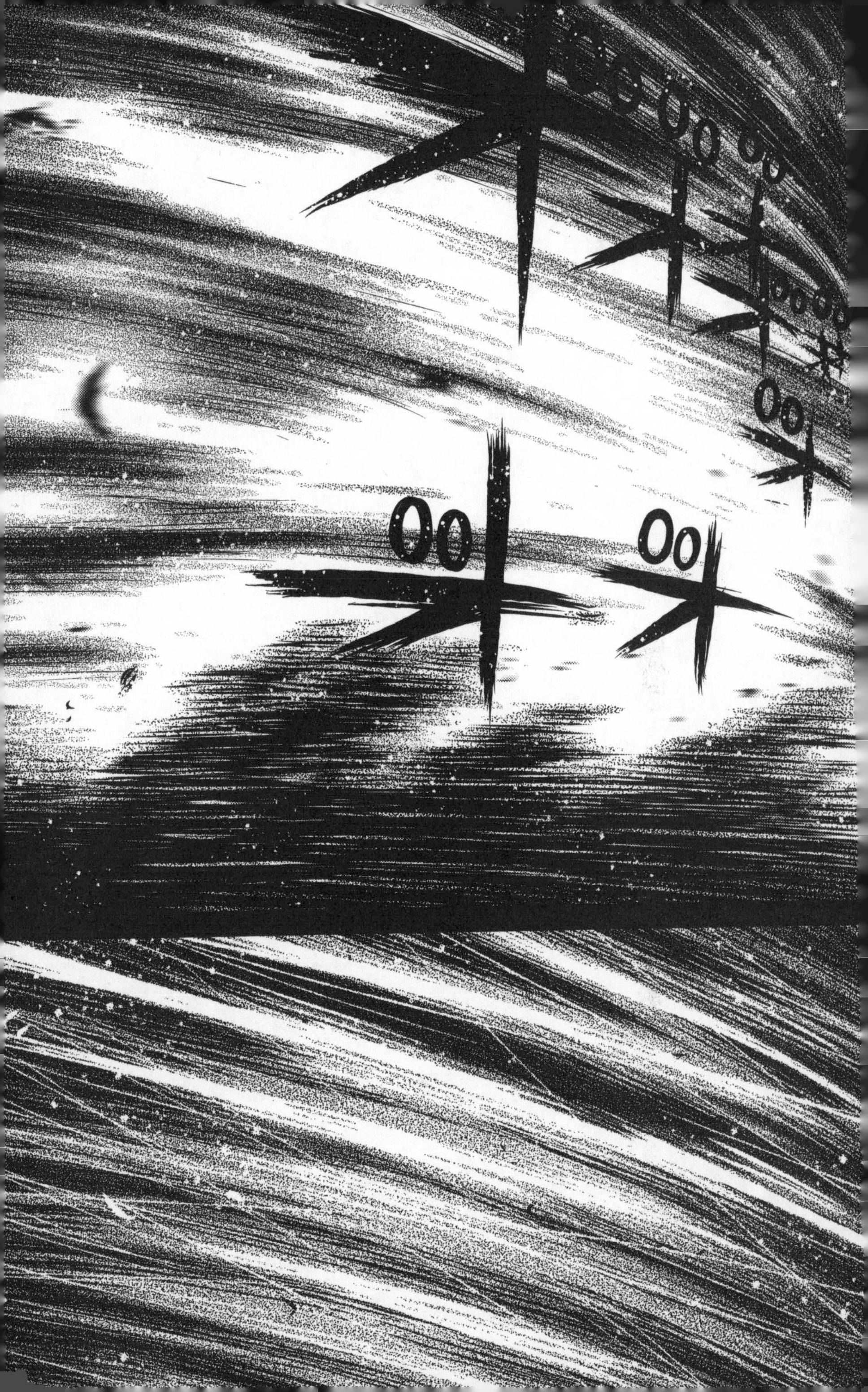

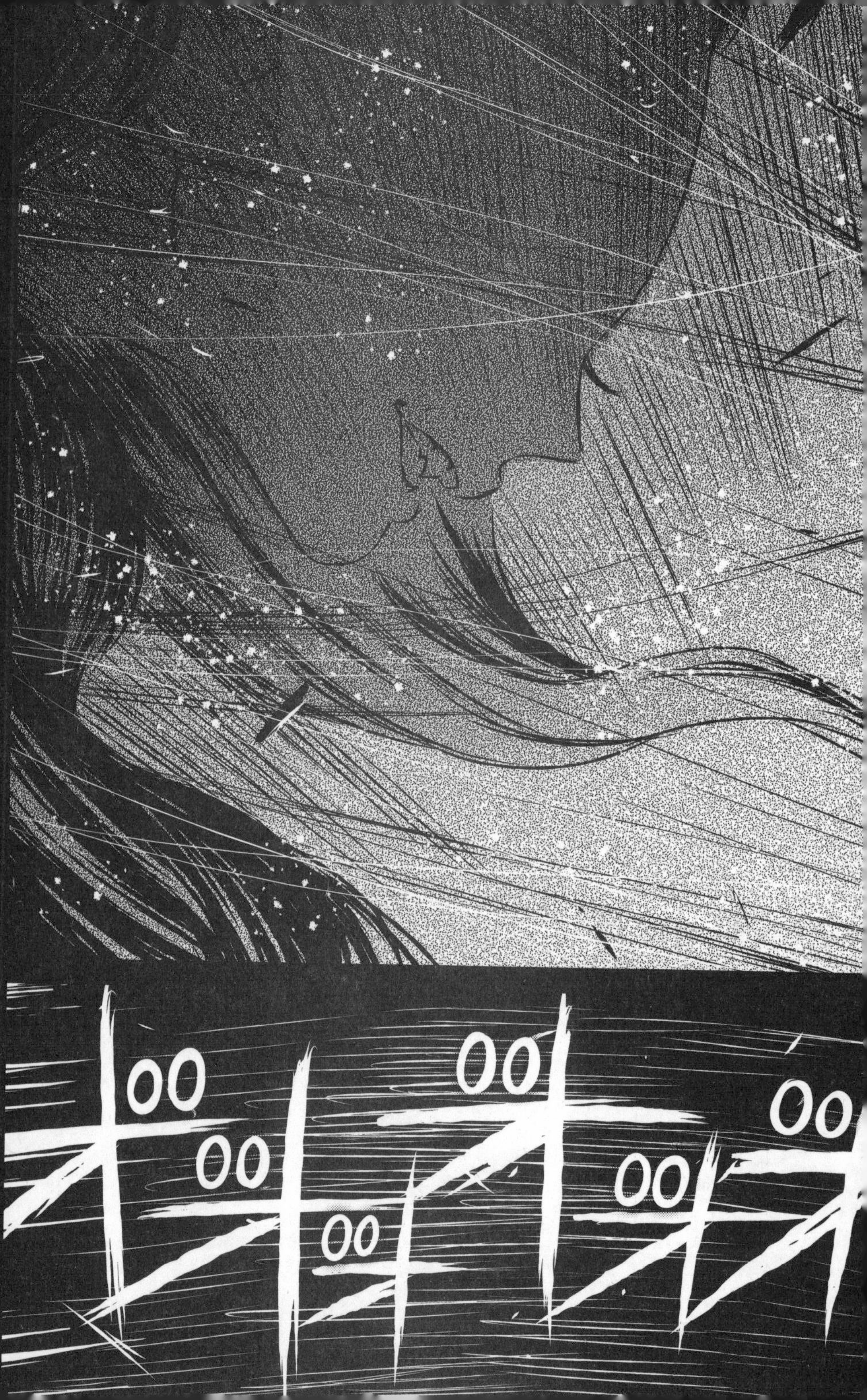
OO
OO
OO
OO
OO
OO

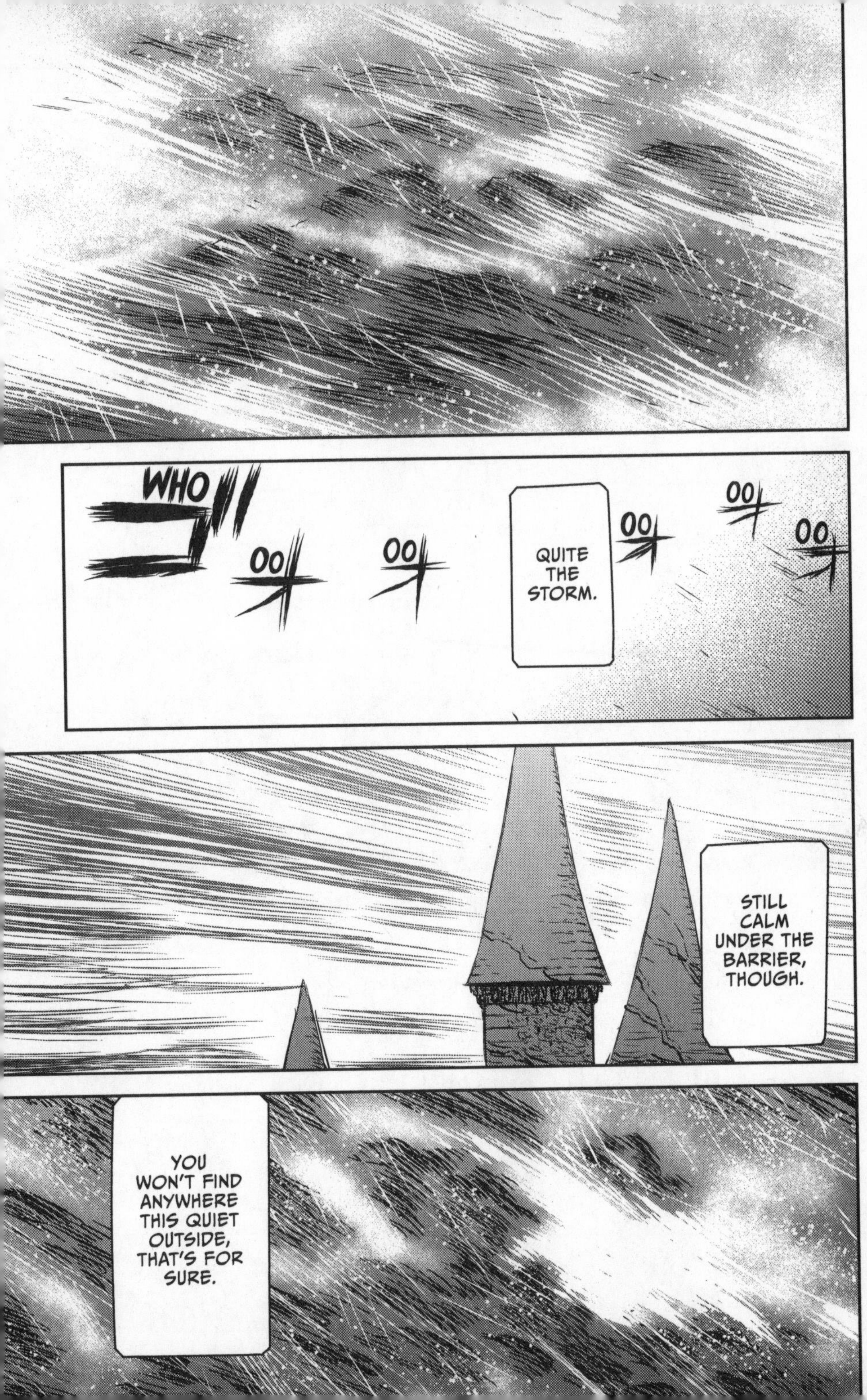
QUITE THE STORM.
WHO OO OO OO OO OO
STILL CALM UNDER THE BARRIER, THOUGH.
YOU WON'T FIND ANYWHERE THIS QUIET OUTSIDE, THAT'S FOR SURE.

CHAPTER 44: CHAOS INSIDE THE STORM—ACT 11

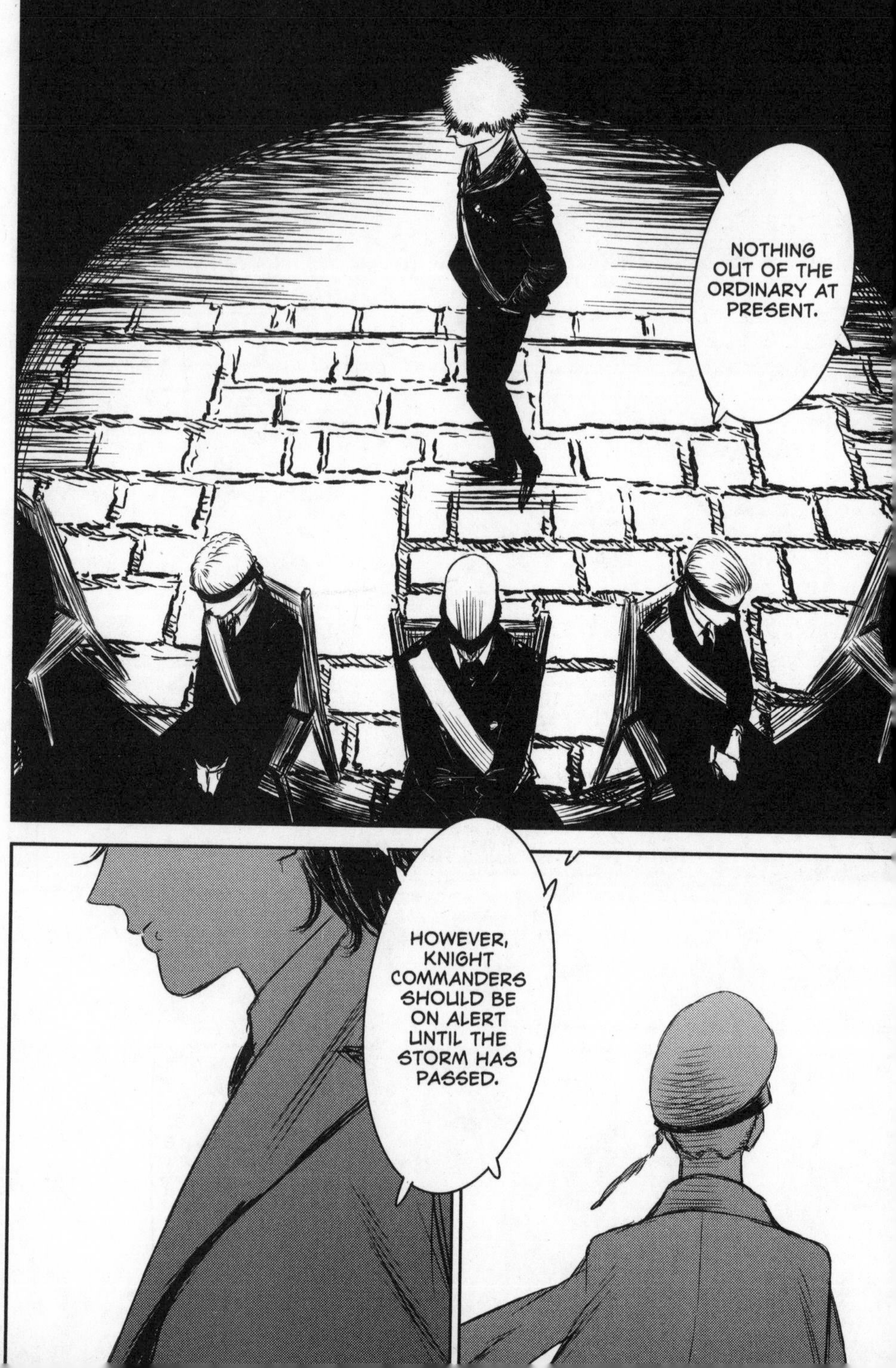
NOTHING OUT OF THE ORDINARY AT PRESENT.
HOWEVER, KNIGHT COMMANDERS SHOULD BE ON ALERT UNTIL THE STORM HAS PASSED.

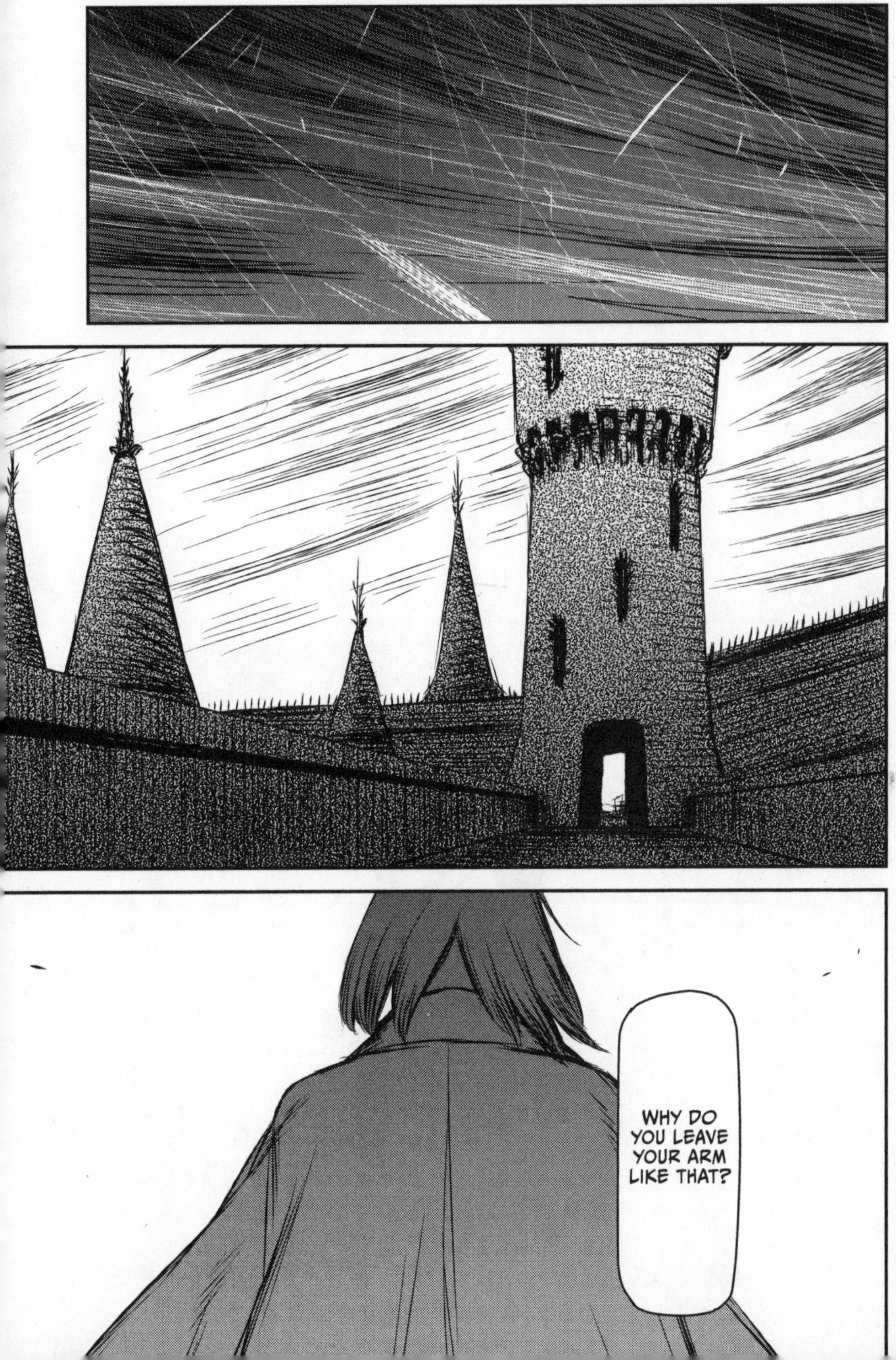
WHY DO YOU LEAVE YOUR ARM LIKE THAT?

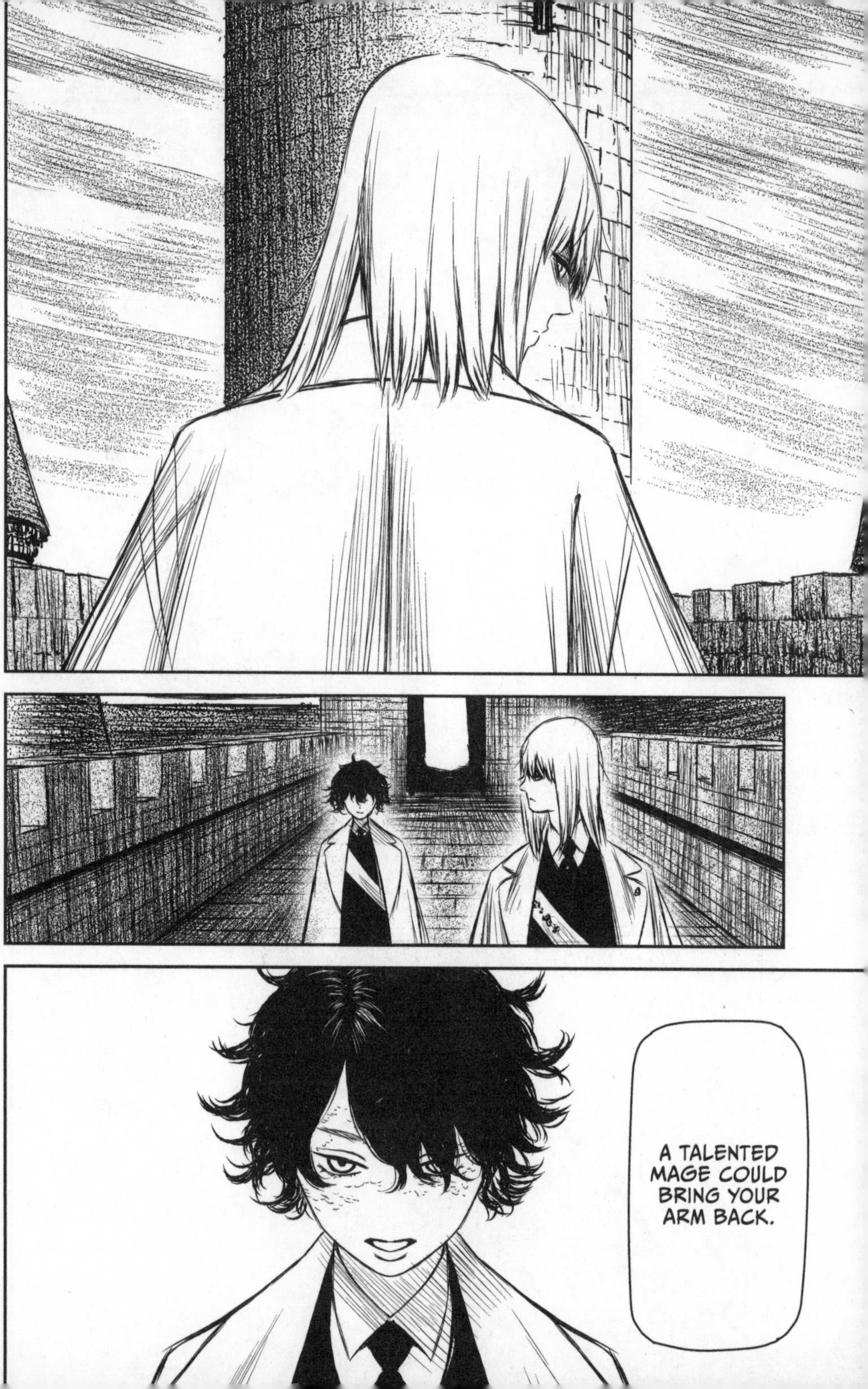
A TALENTED MAGE COULD BRING YOUR ARM BACK.

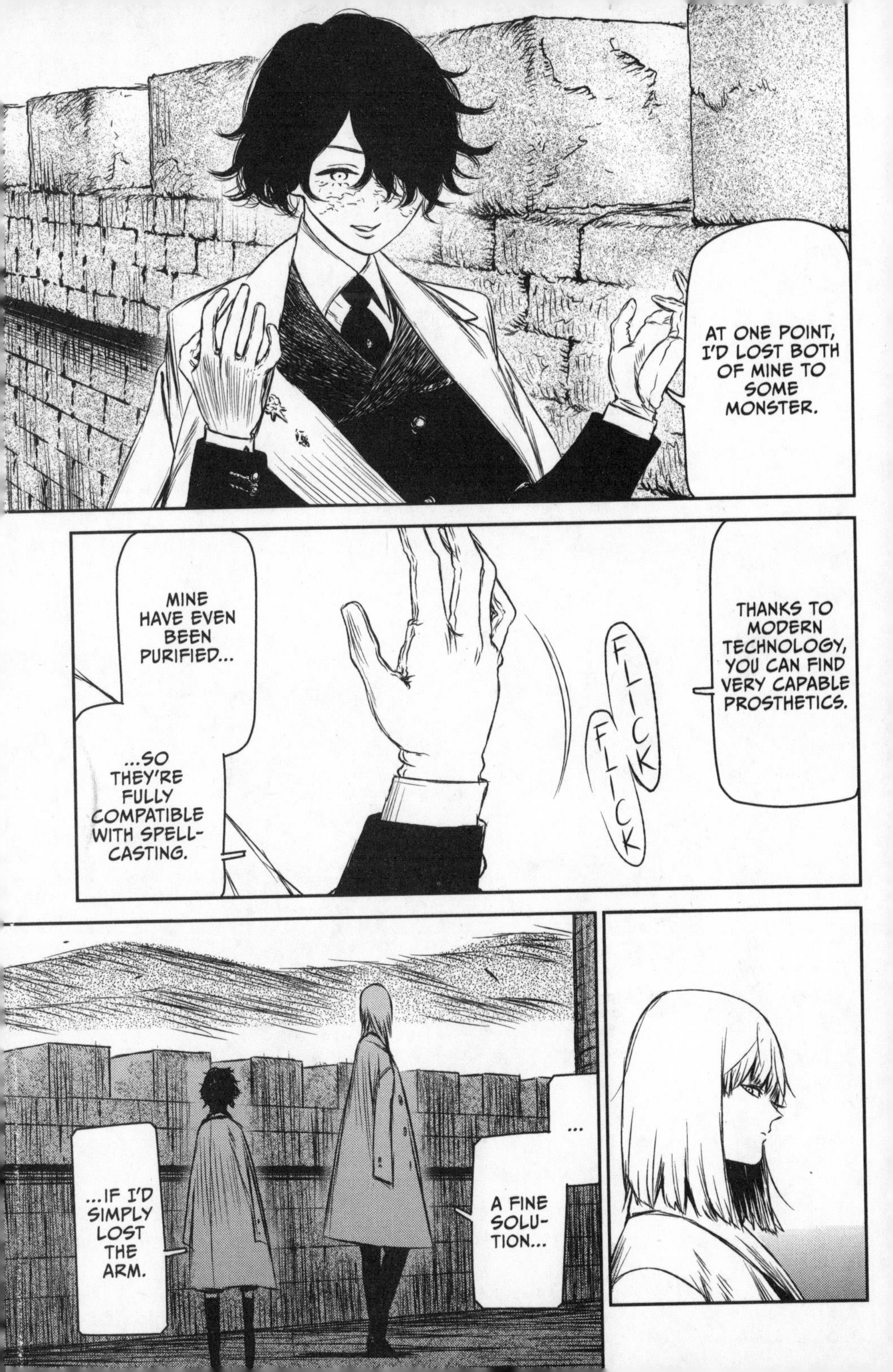
AT ONE POINT, I'D LOST BOTH OF MINE TO SOME MONSTER.
THANKS TO MODERN TECHNOLOGY, YOU CAN FIND VERY CAPABLE PROSTHETICS.
FLICK
FLICK
MINE HAVE EVEN BEEN PURIFIED...
...SO THEY'RE FULLY COMPATIBLE WITH SPELL-CASTING.
...
A FINE SOLUTION...
...IF I'D SIMPLY LOST THE ARM.

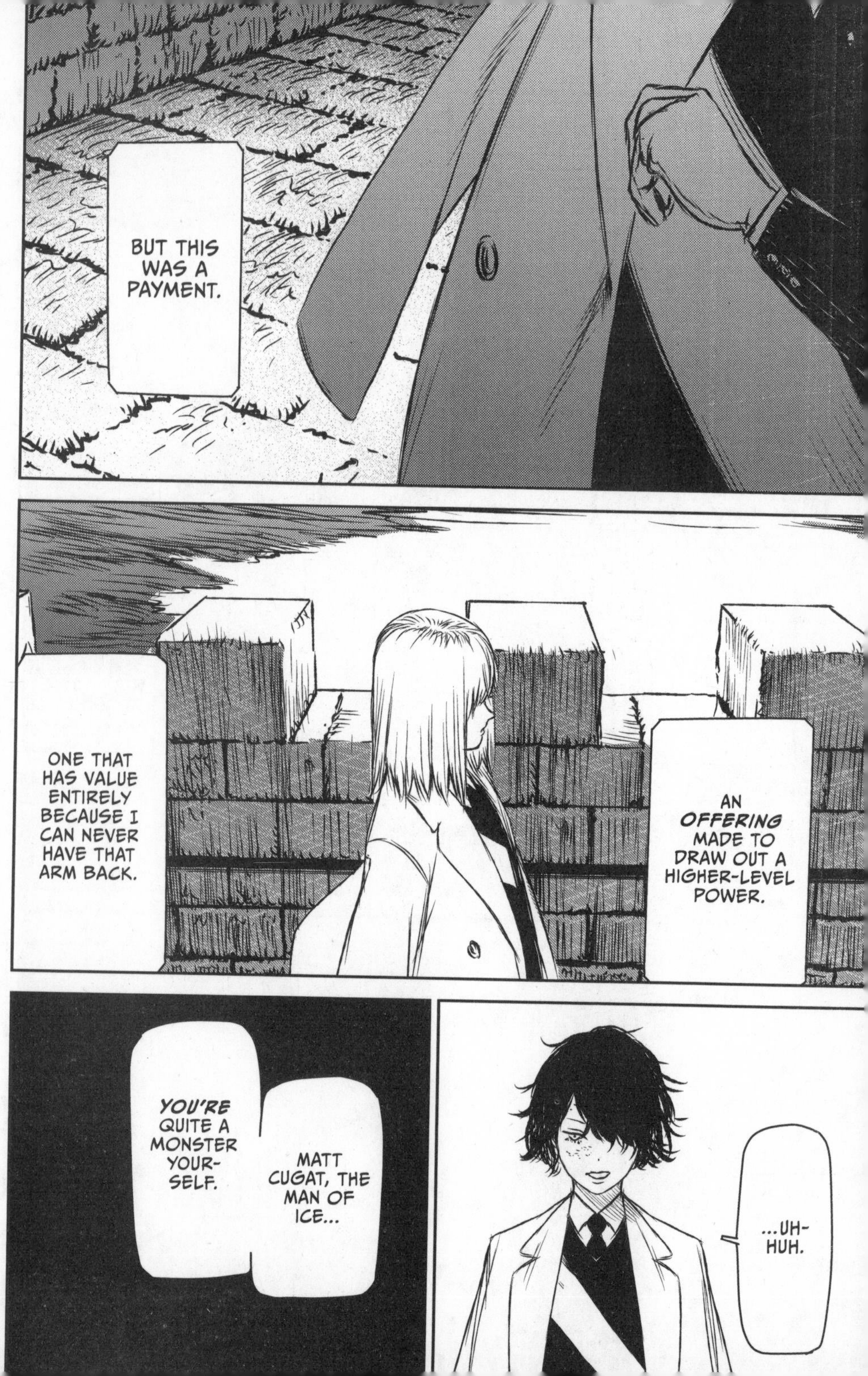

BUT THIS WAS A PAYMENT.
AN *OFFERING* MADE TO DRAW OUT A HIGHER-LEVEL POWER.
ONE THAT HAS VALUE ENTIRELY BECAUSE I CAN NEVER HAVE THAT ARM BACK.
...UH-HUH.
MATT CUGAT, THE MAN OF ICE...
YOU'RE QUITE A MONSTER YOUR-SELF.

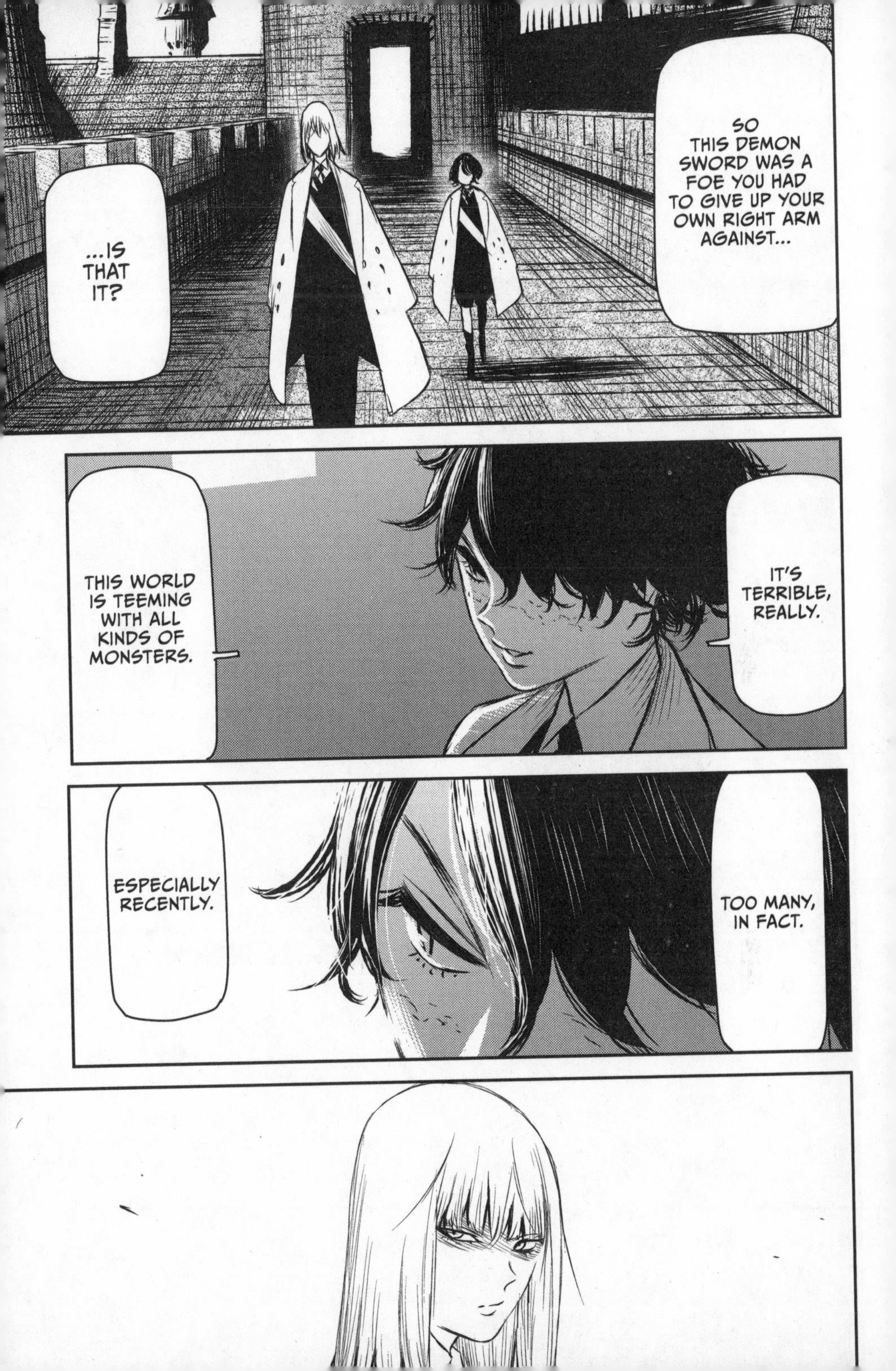
SO THIS DEMON SWORD WAS A FOE YOU HAD TO GIVE UP YOUR OWN RIGHT ARM AGAINST...
...IS THAT IT?
IT'S TERRIBLE, REALLY.
THIS WORLD IS TEEMING WITH ALL KINDS OF MONSTERS.
TOO MANY, IN FACT.
ESPECIALLY RECENTLY.

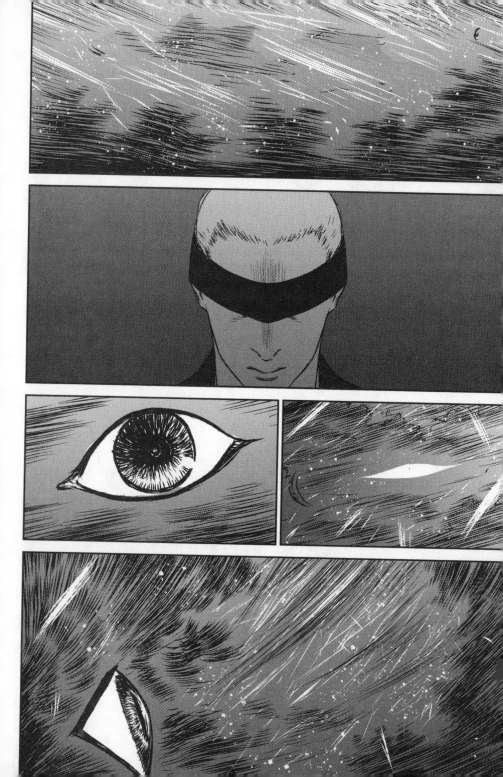

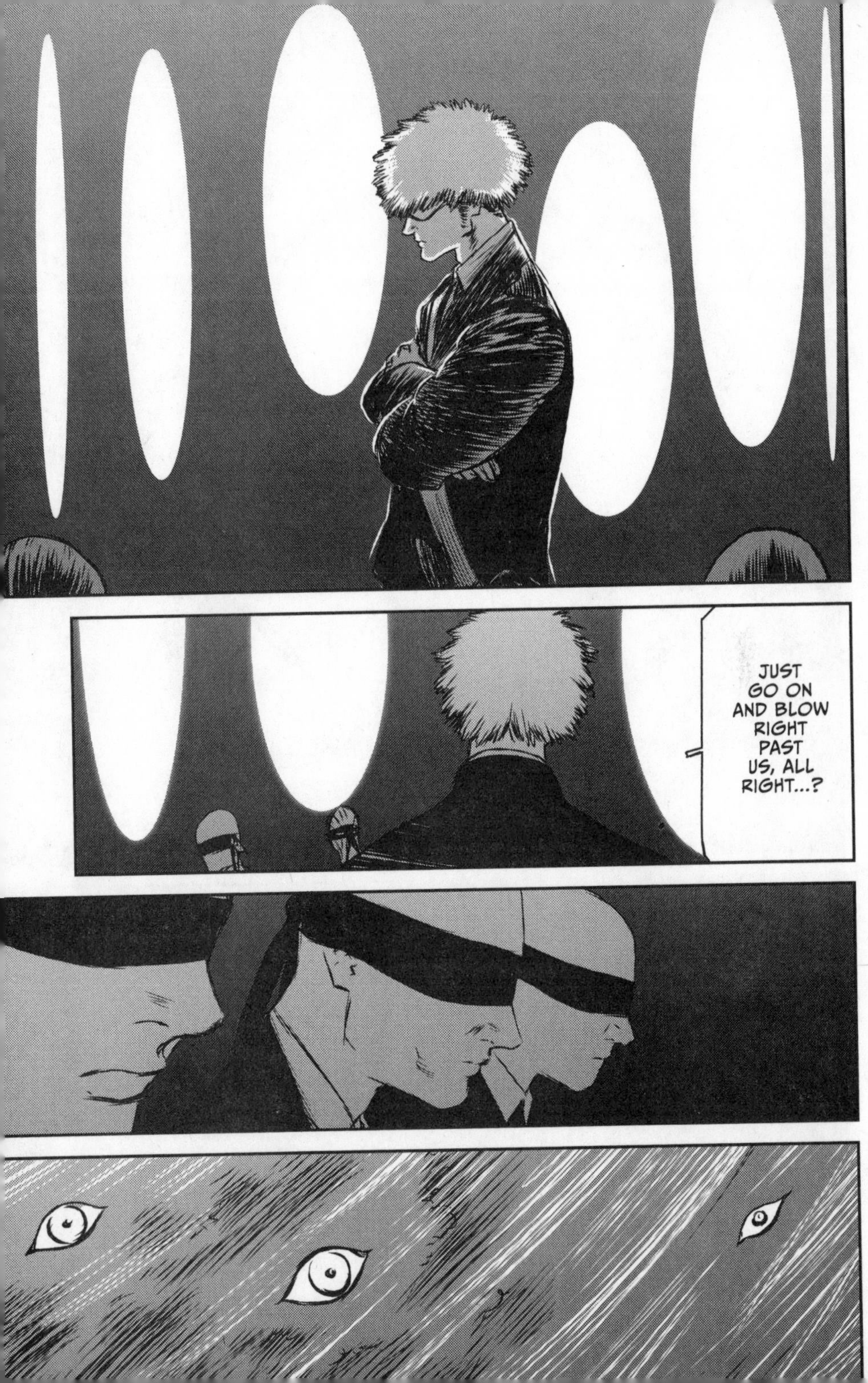
JUST GO ON AND BLOW RIGHT PAST US, ALL RIGHT...?

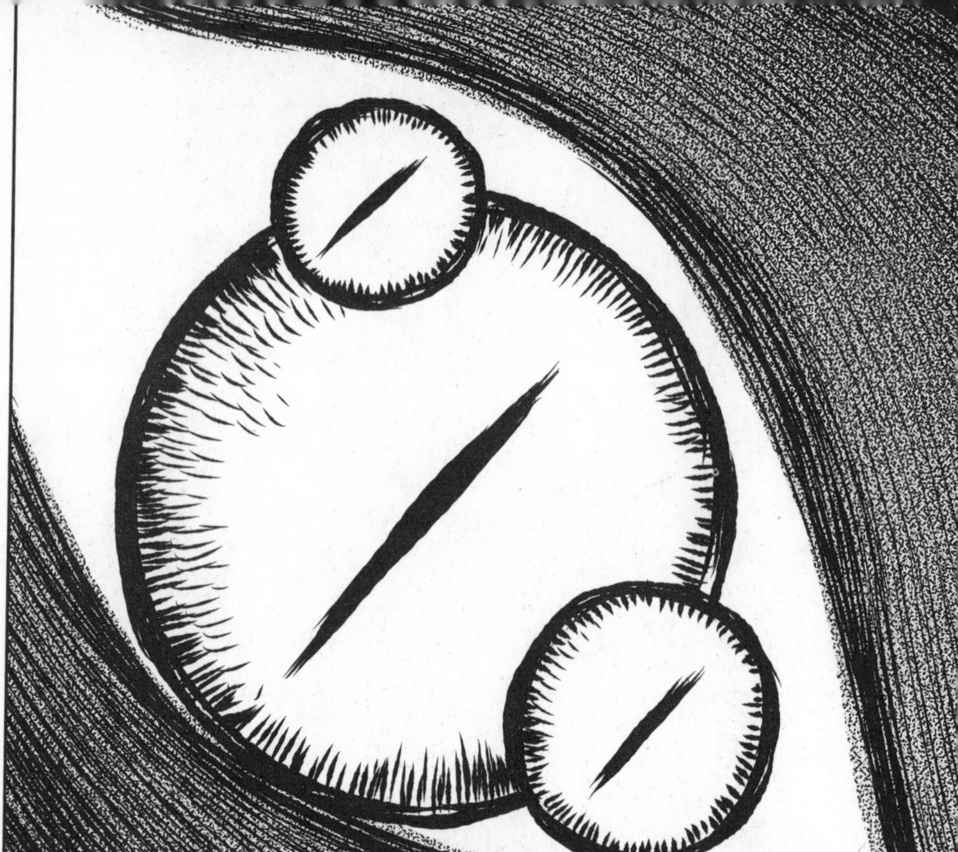

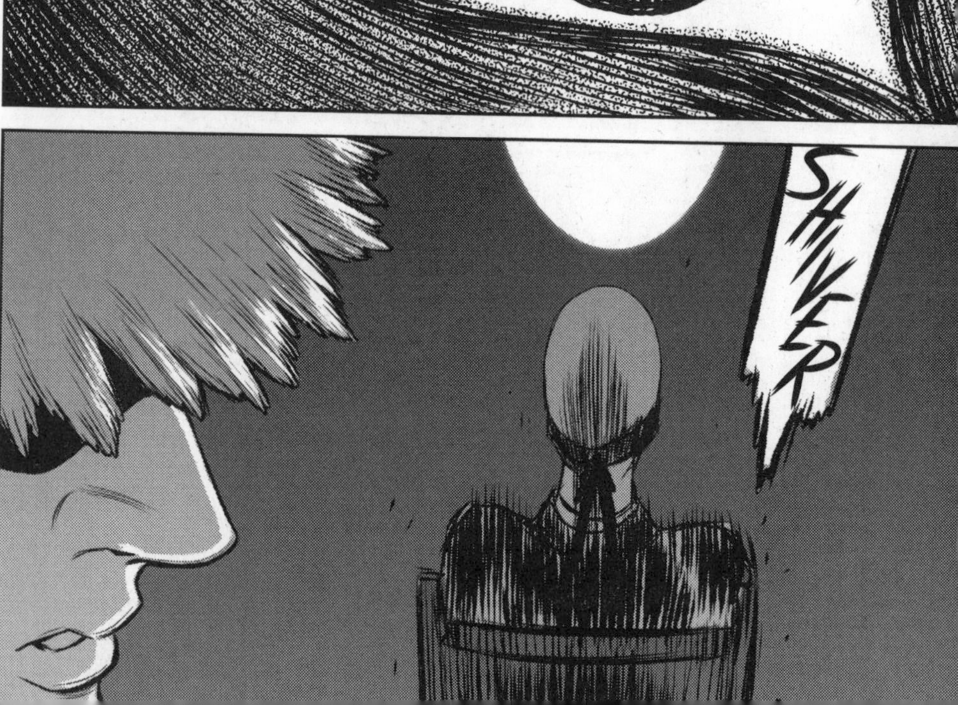
SHIVER

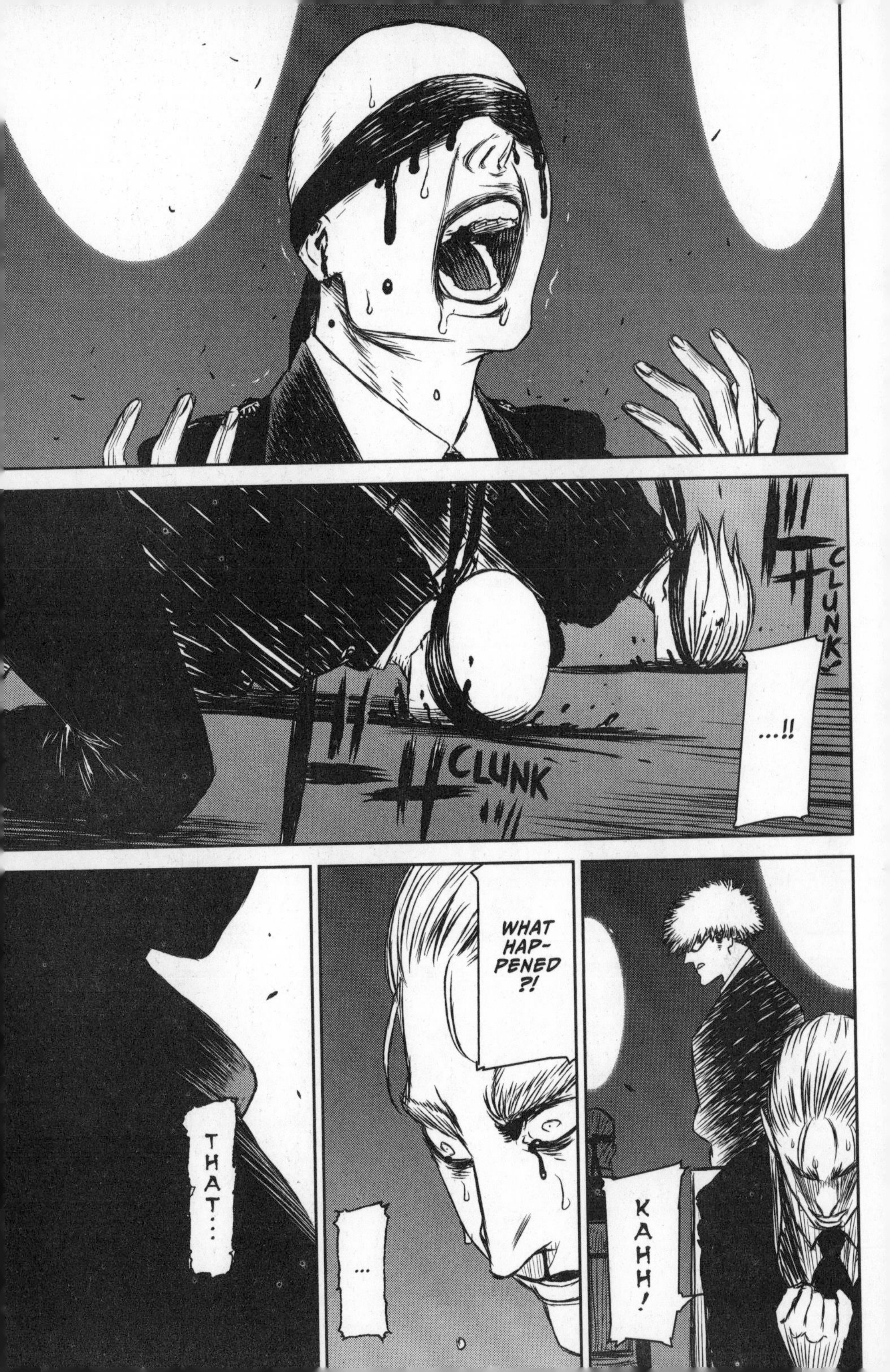
CLUNK
...!!
CLUNK
KAHH!
WHAT HAP-PENED?!
...
THAT...

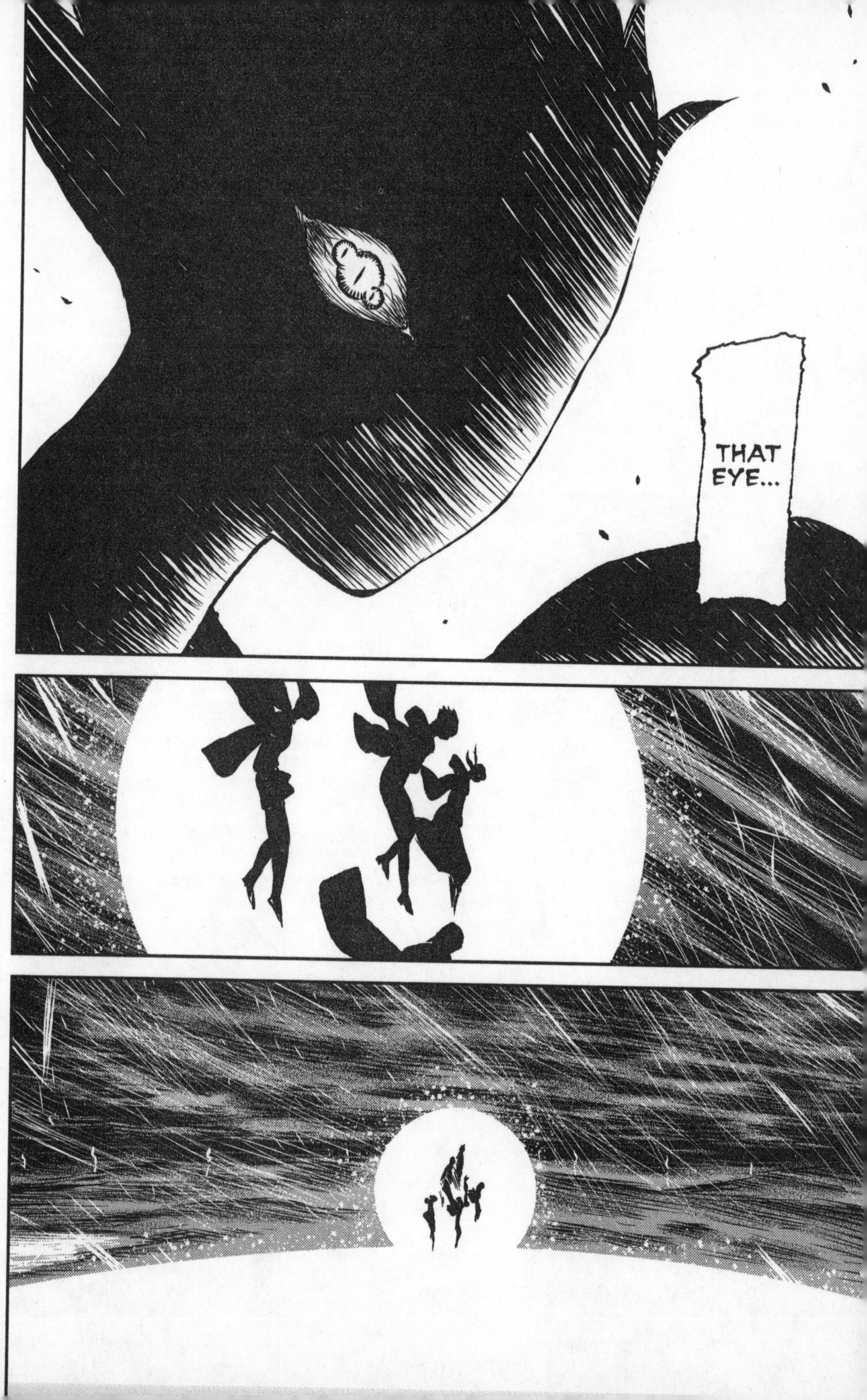
THAT EYE...

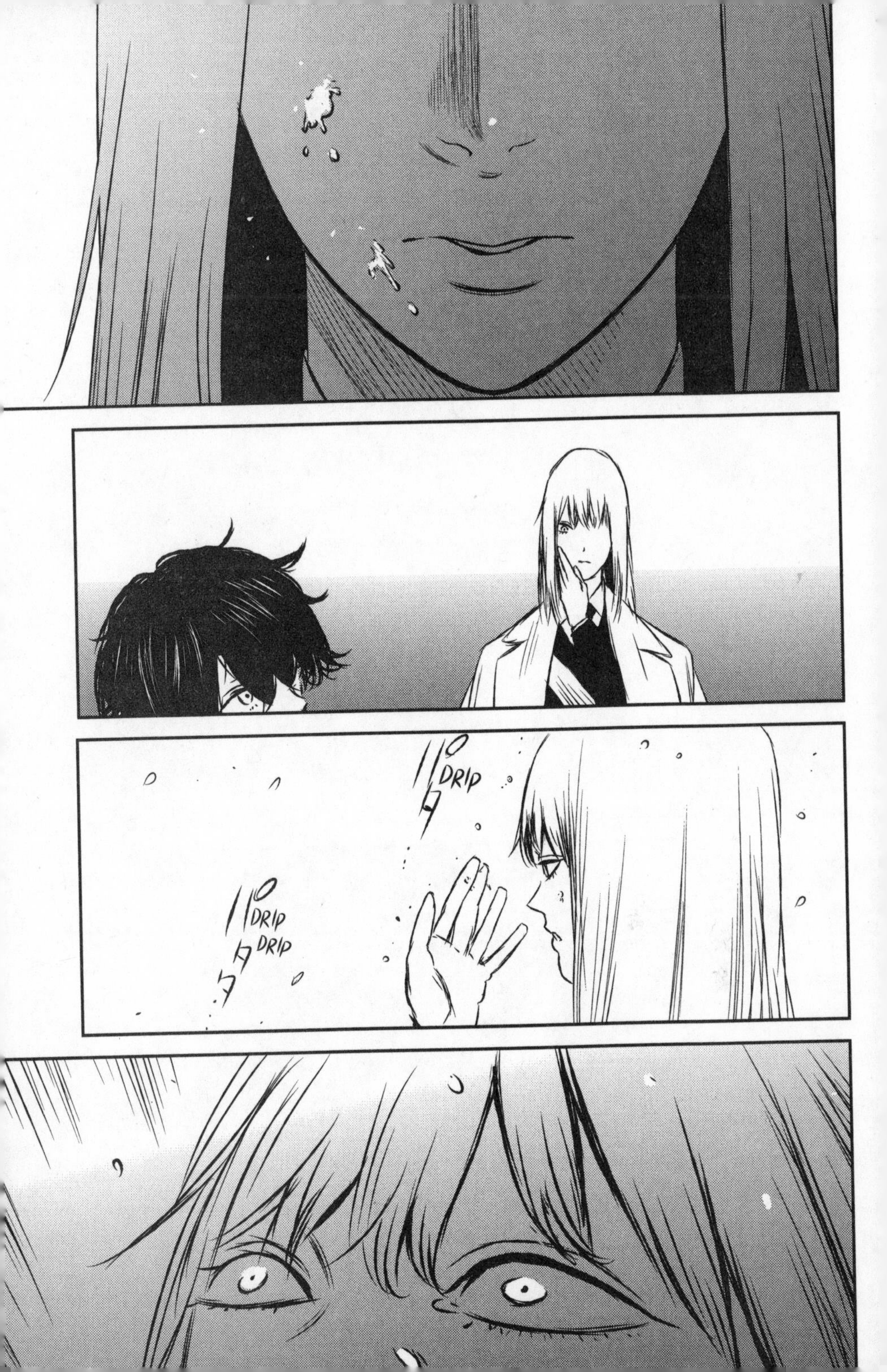
DRIP
DRIP
DRIP

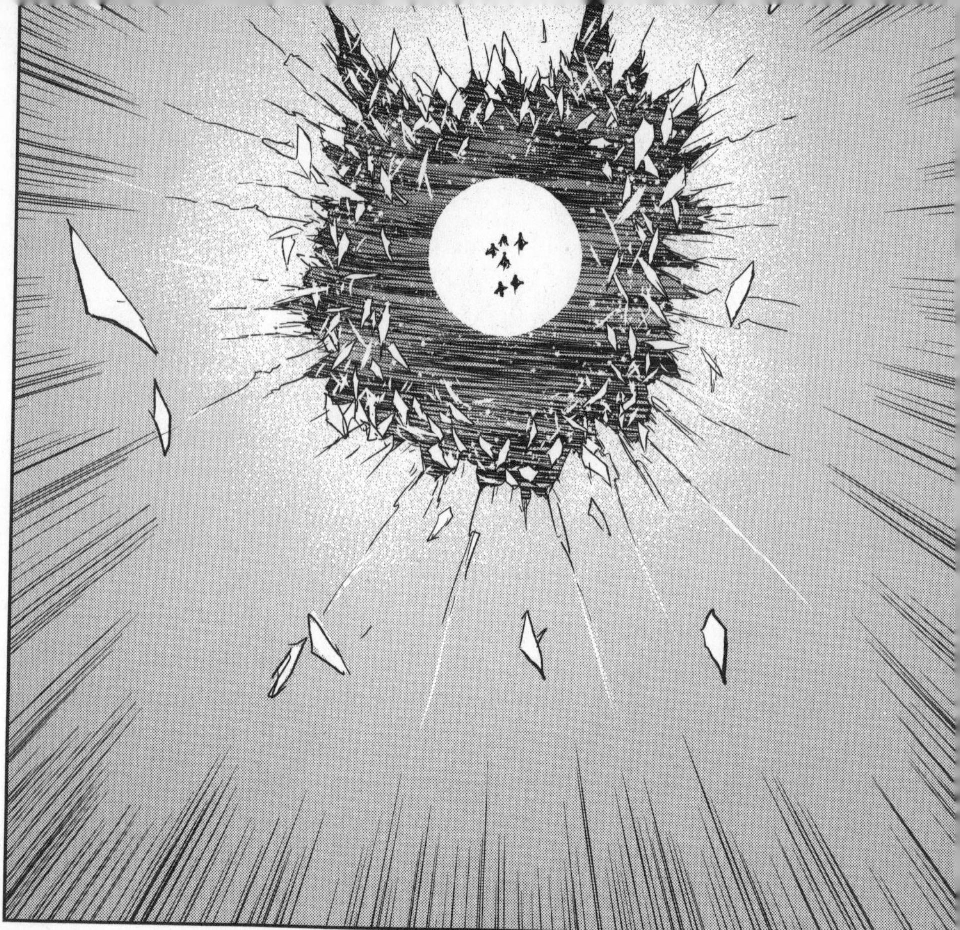

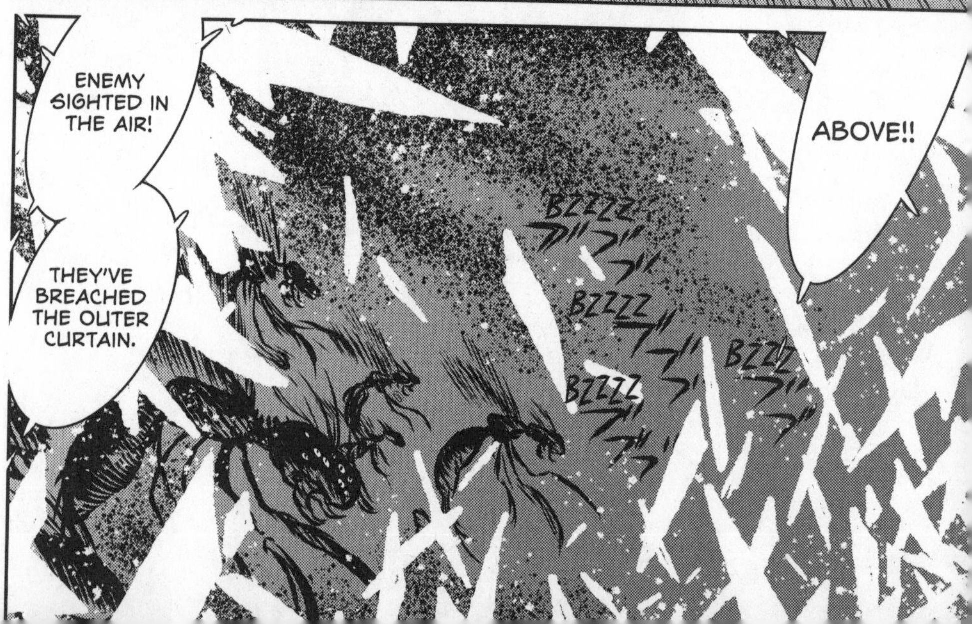
ABOVE!!
ENEMY SIGHTED IN THE AIR!
BZZZZ
BZZZZ
BZZZ
BZZZZ
THEY'VE BREACHED THE OUTER CURTAIN.

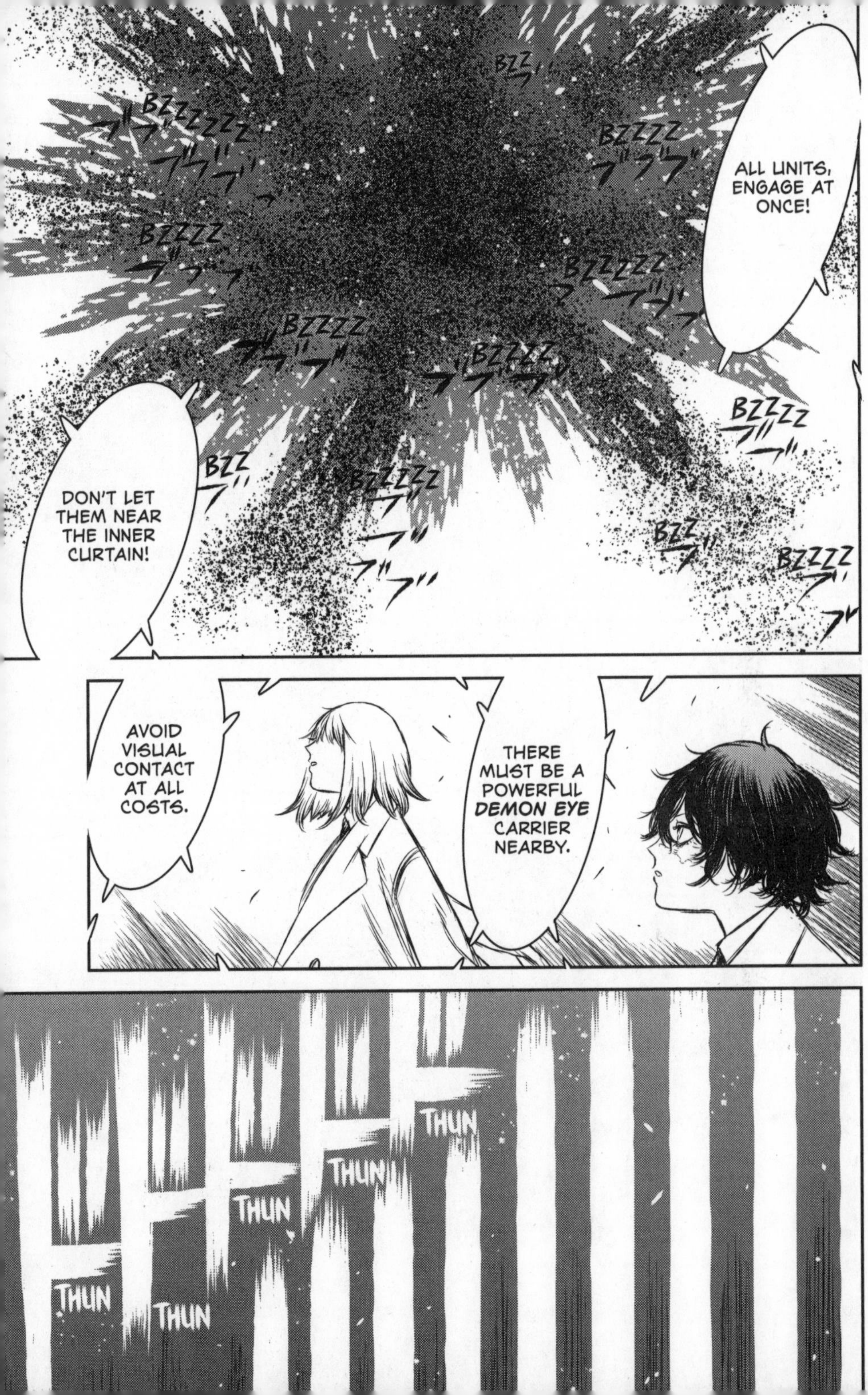
ALL UNITS, ENGAGE AT ONCE!
BZZ
BZZZZ
BZZZZZ
BZZZZZ
BZZZZZZ
BZZZZ
BZZZZZ
BZZZZ
DON'T LET THEM NEAR THE INNER CURTAIN!
BZZ
BZZZZ
BZZZZZ
BZZ
THERE MUST BE A POWERFUL *DEMON EYE* CARRIER NEARBY.
AVOID VISUAL CONTACT AT ALL COSTS.
THUN
THUN
THUN
THUN
THUN

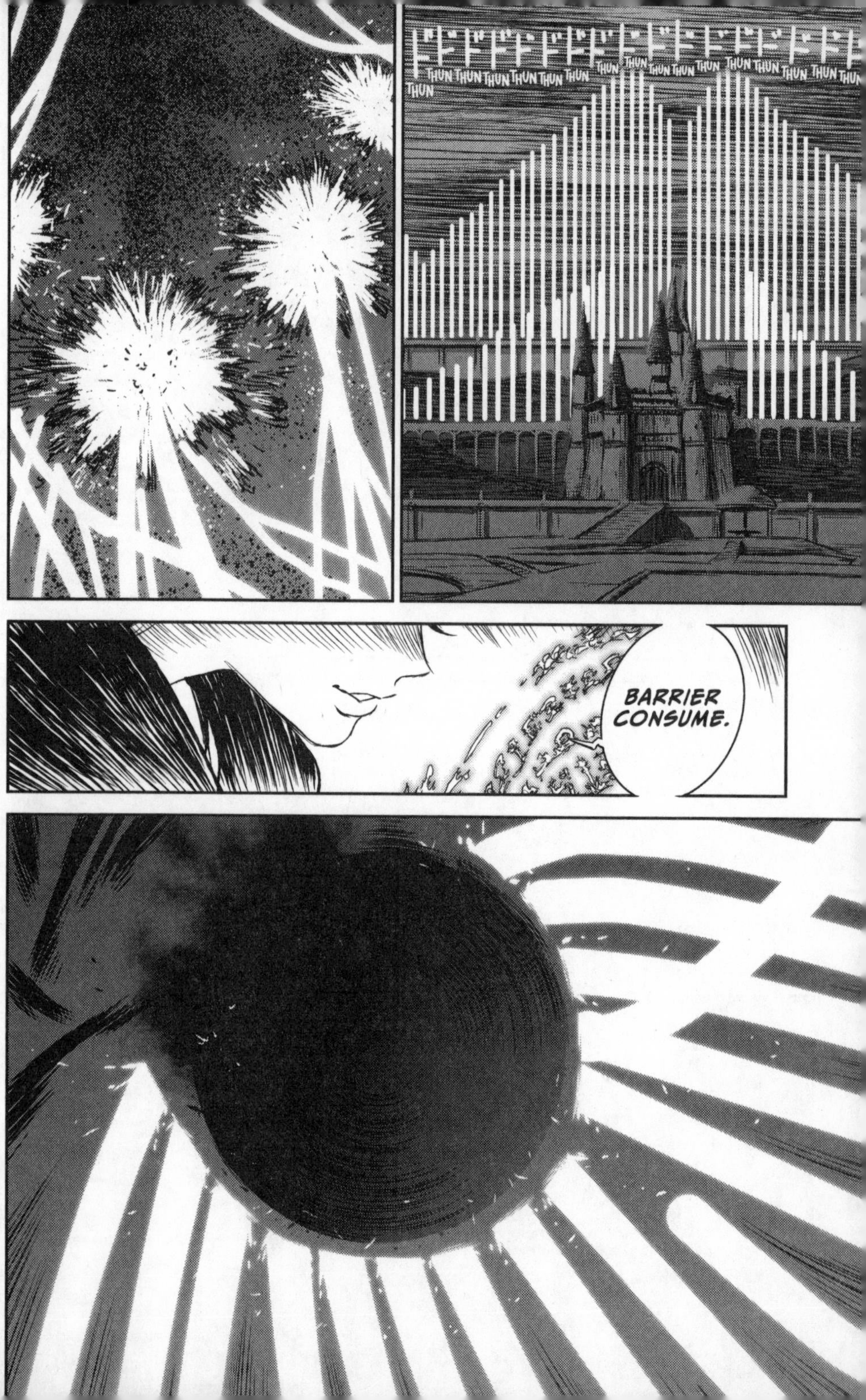
ドドドドドドドドドドドドドドドドド
THUN THUN THUN THUN THUN THUN THUN THUN THUN THUN THUN THUN THUN THUN THUN THUN THUN THUN
BARRIER CONSUME.

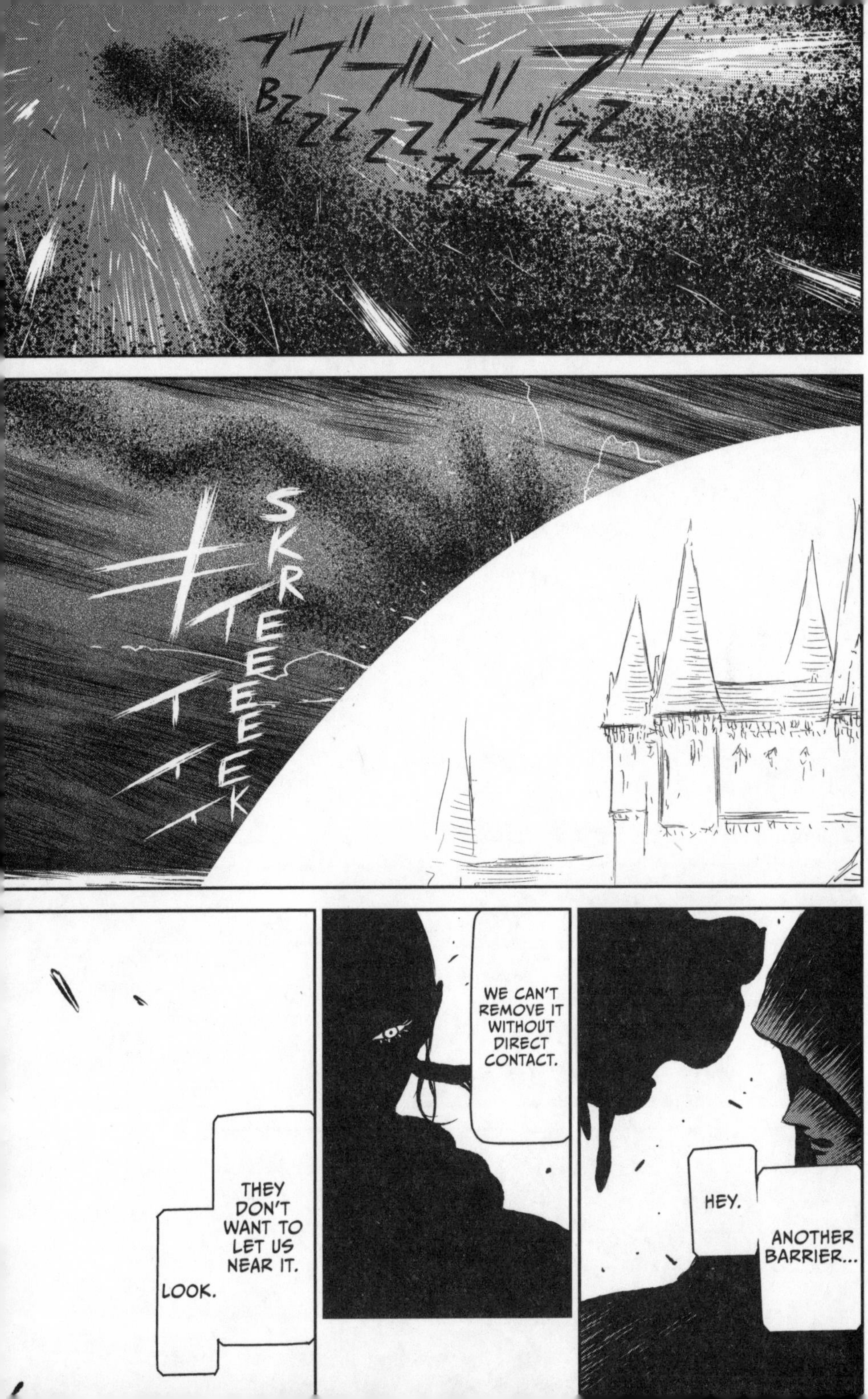
BZZZZZZZZZZZ
SKREEEEEEK
ANOTHER BARRIER...
HEY.
WE CAN'T REMOVE IT WITHOUT DIRECT CONTACT.
THEY DON'T WANT TO LET US NEAR IT.
LOOK.

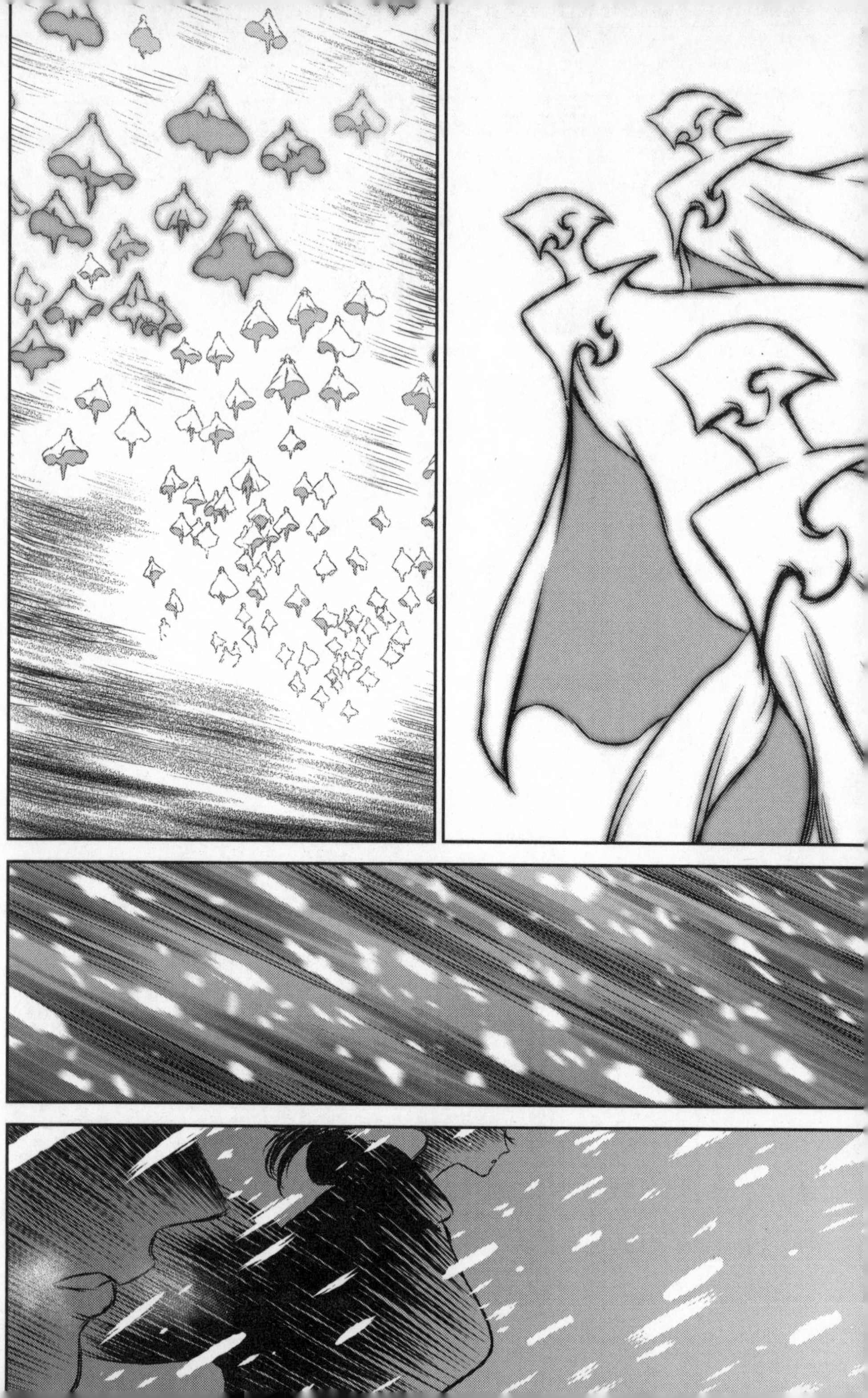

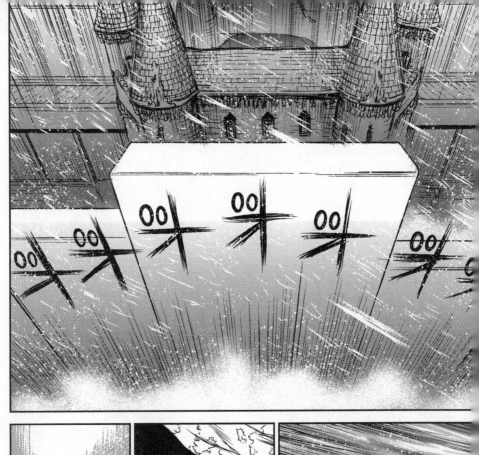

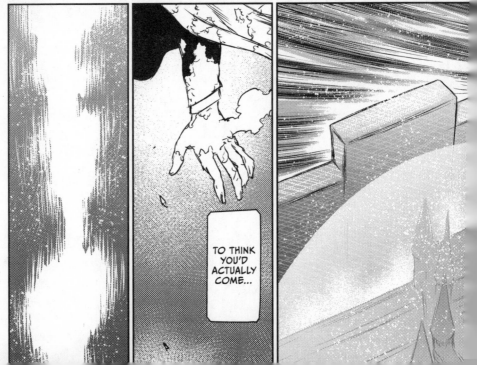

TO THINK
YOU'D
ACTUALLY
COME...

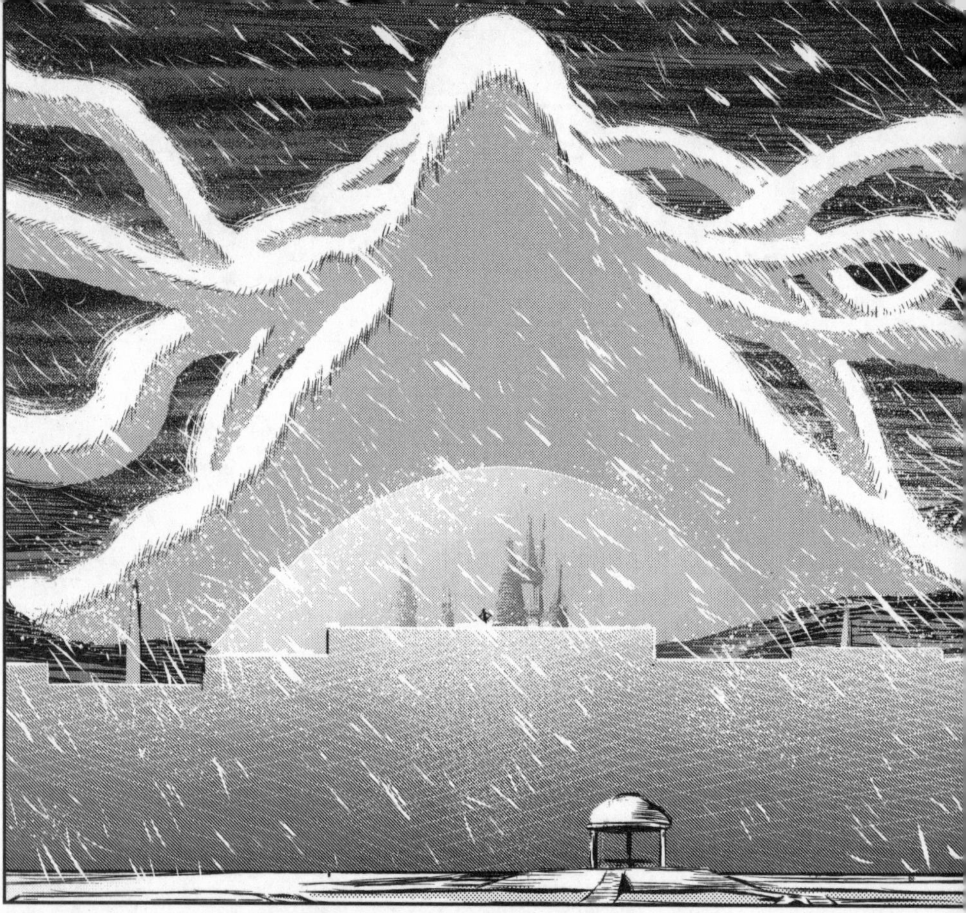

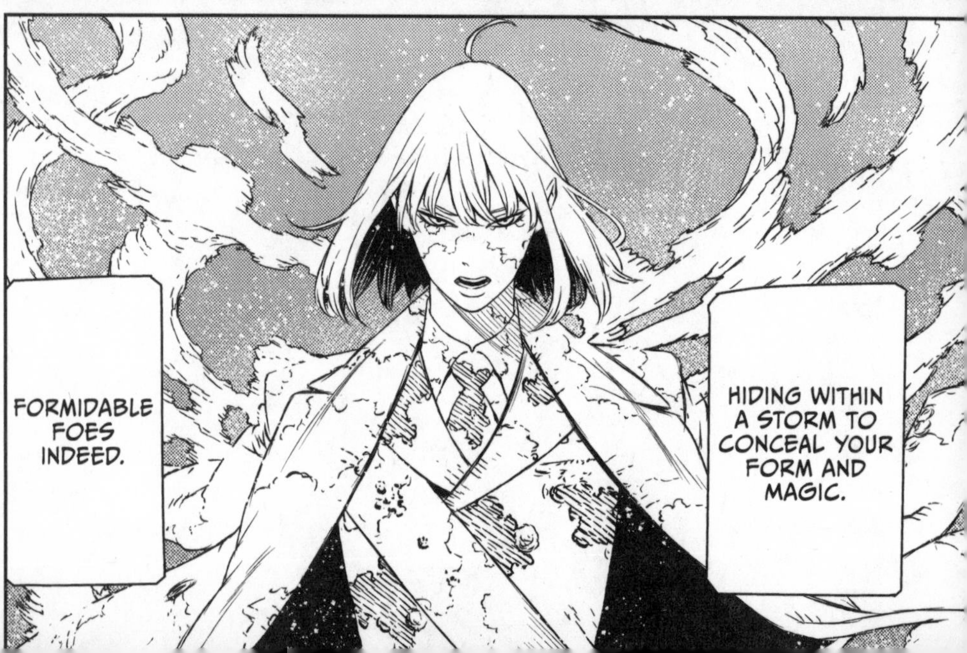
HIDING WITHIN A STORM TO CONCEAL YOUR FORM AND MAGIC.
FORMIDABLE FOES INDEED.

SO HE'S THE ONE THEY SAY CAN ACTUALLY POSE A THREAT TO WITCHES.
THE SO-CALLED *MAN OF ICE.*
WE DIDN'T *ASK* YOU TO TURN THIS HURRICANE INTO A SNOWSTORM.

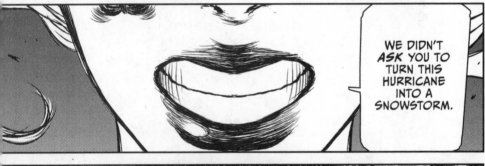

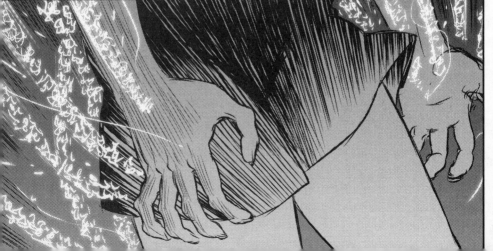

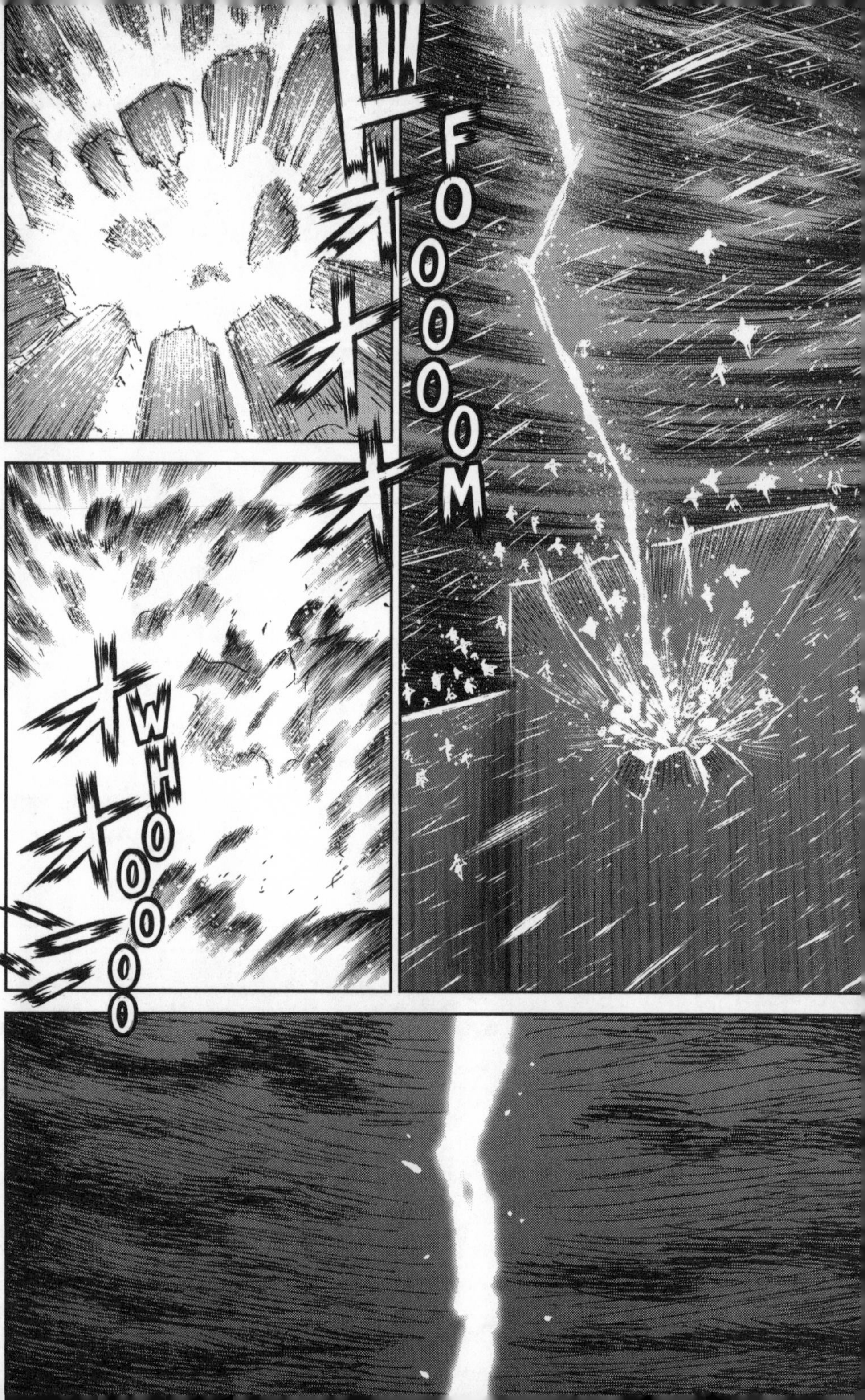
FOOOOOM
WHOOOOO

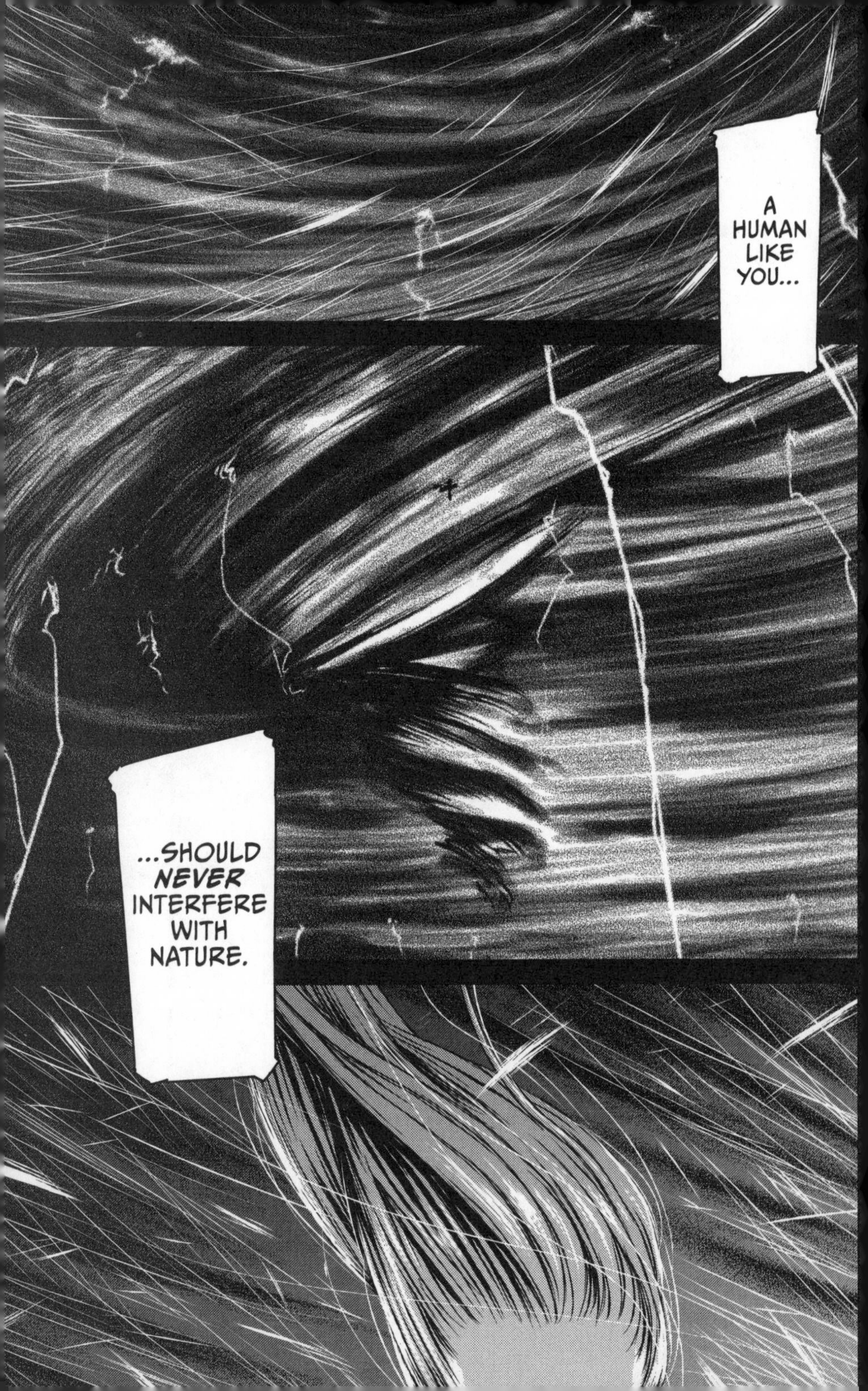
A HUMAN LIKE YOU...
...SHOULD *NEVER* INTERFERE WITH NATURE.

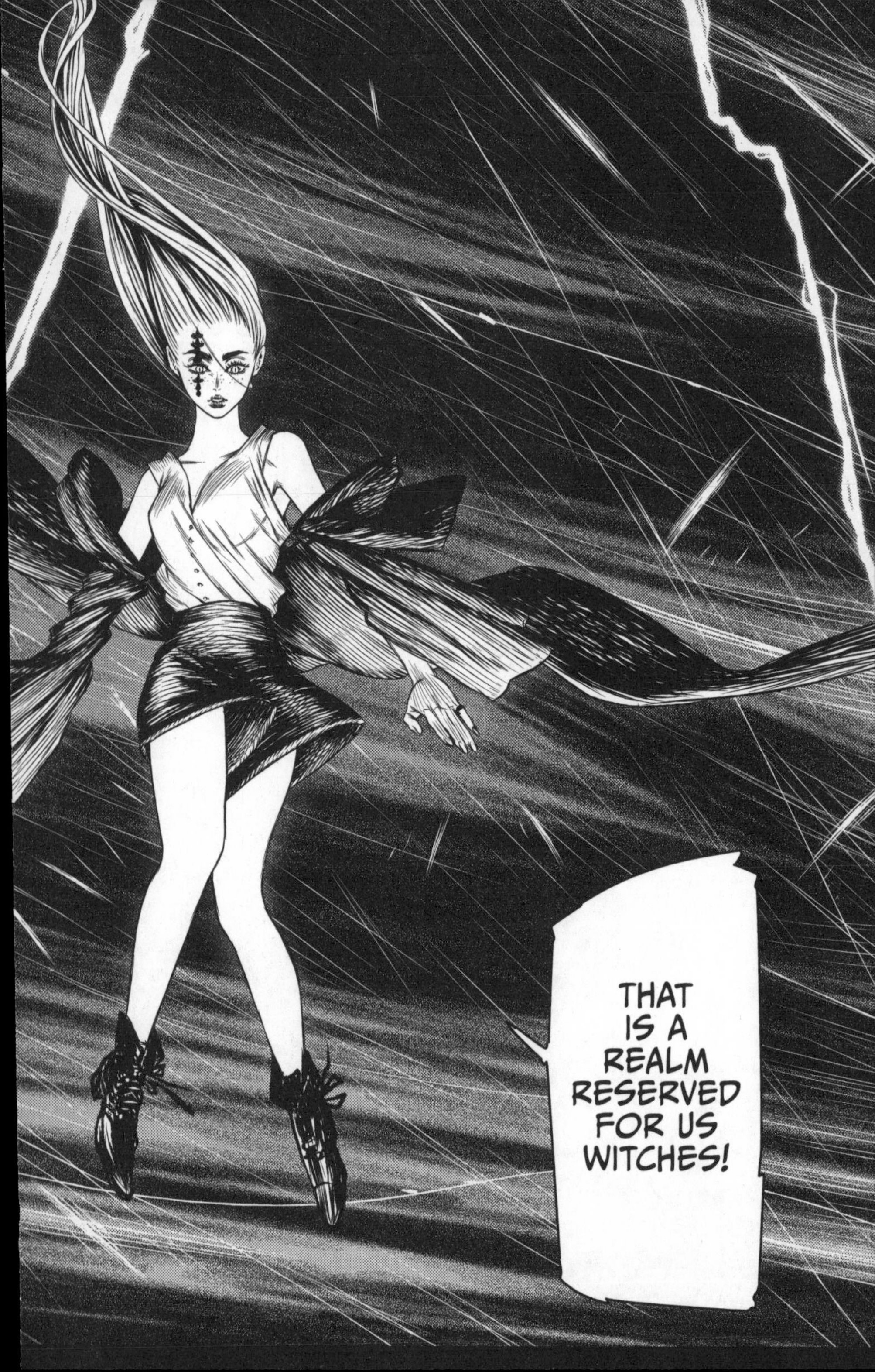
THAT IS A REALM RESERVED FOR US WITCHES!

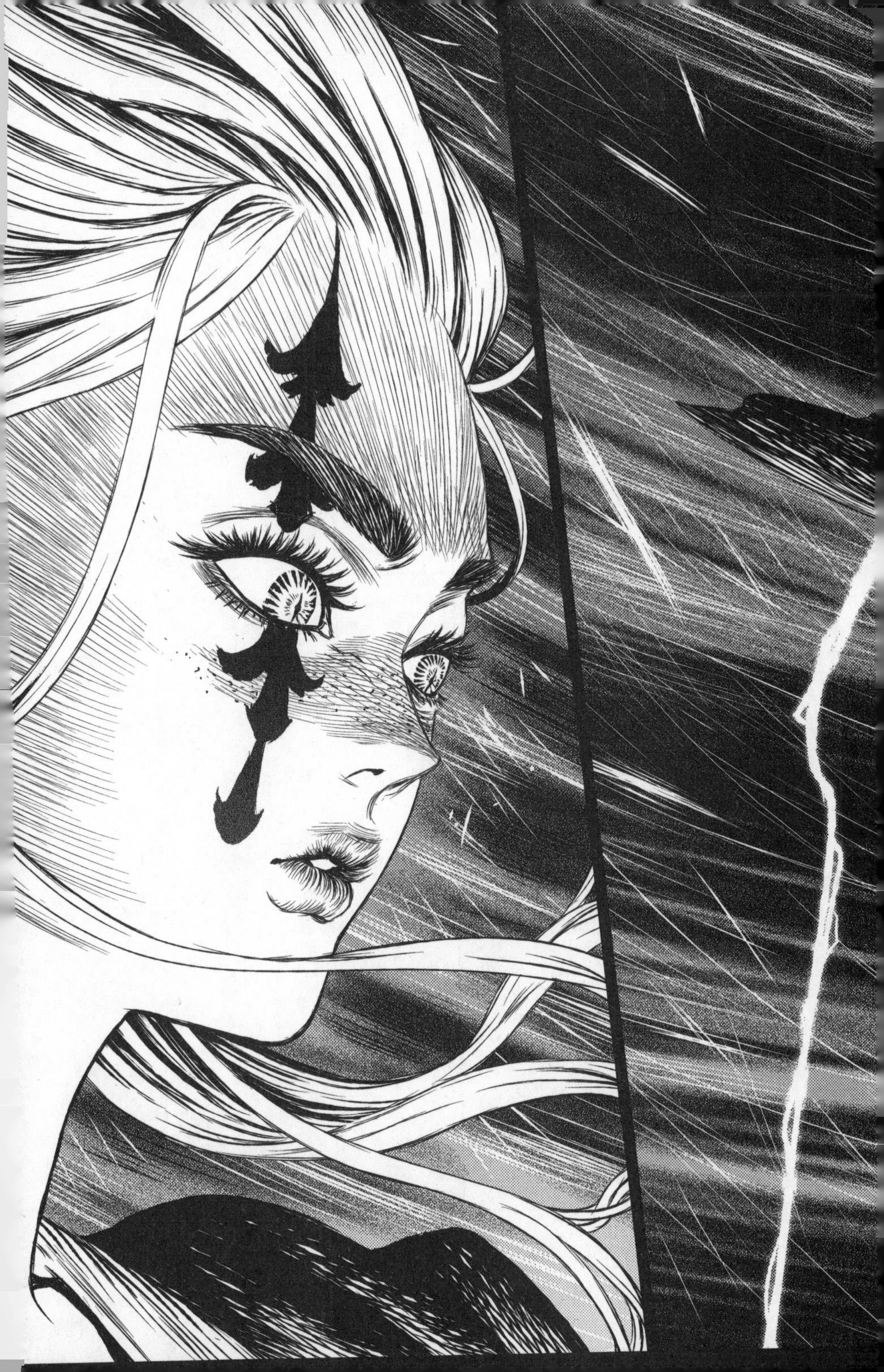

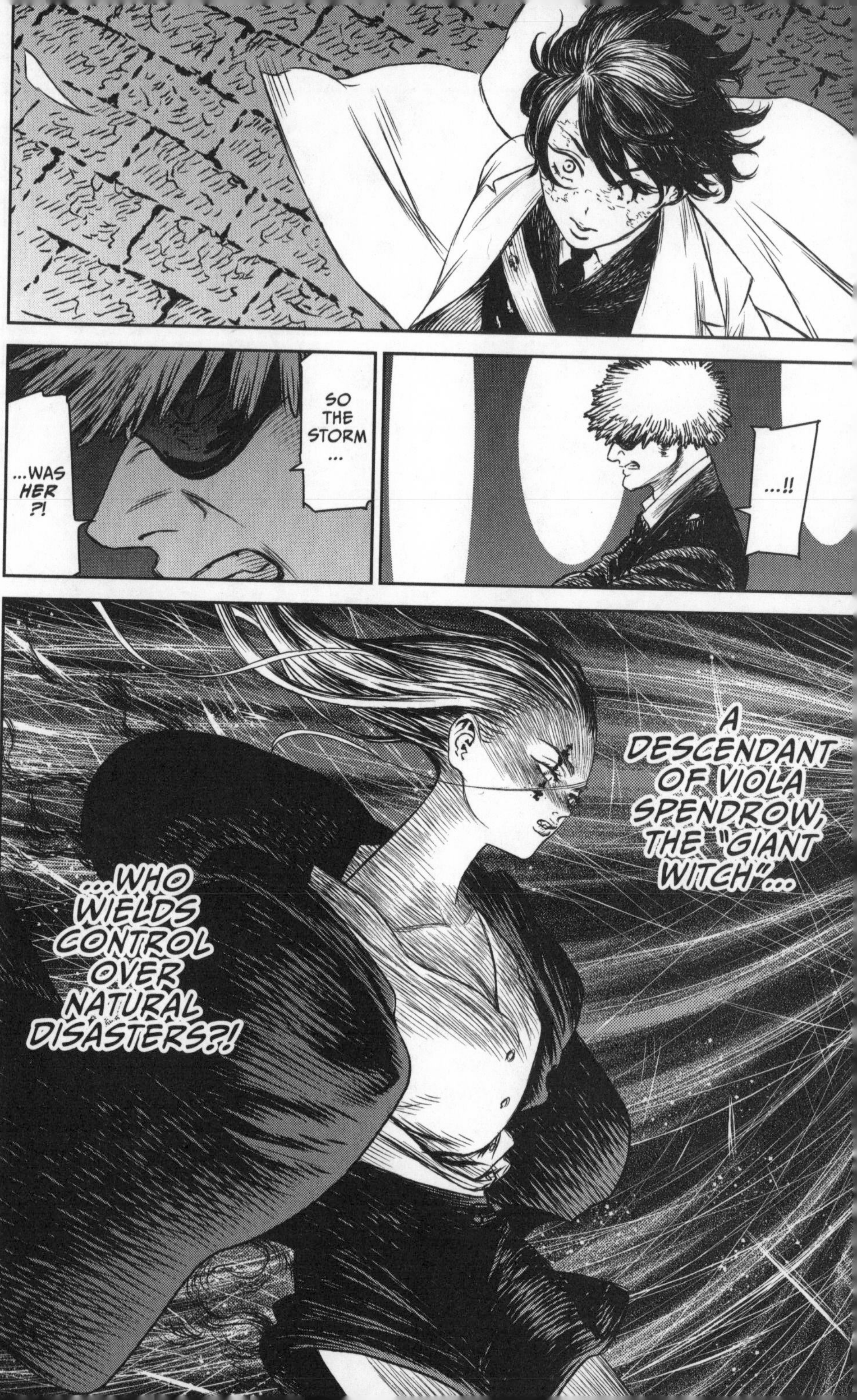
...!!
SO THE STORM...
...WAS HER?!
A DESCENDANT OF VIOLA SPENDROW, THE "GIANT WITCH"...
...WHO WIELDS CONTROL OVER NATURAL DISASTERS?!

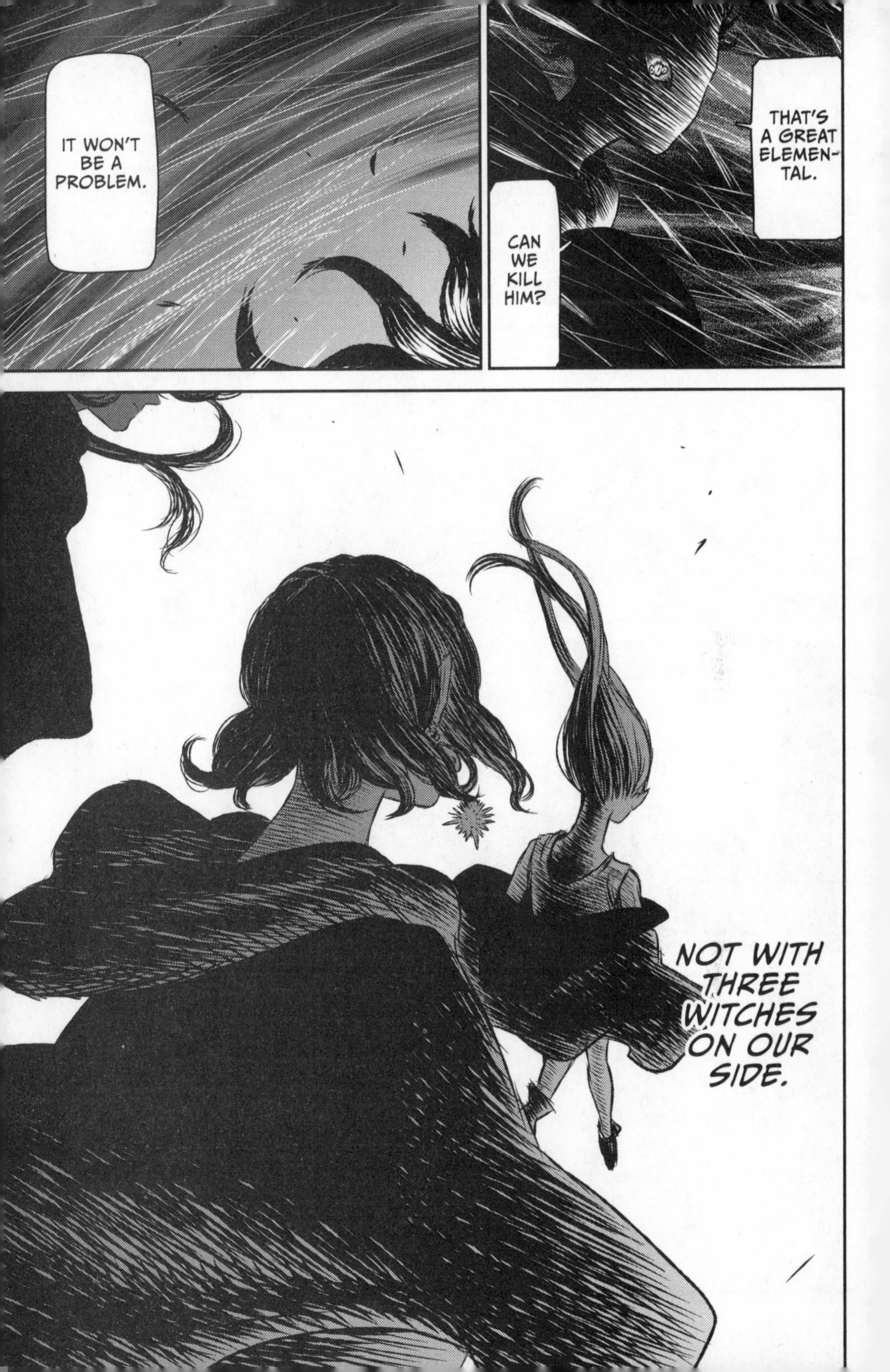
THAT'S A GREAT ELEMENTAL.
CAN WE KILL HIM?
IT WON'T BE A PROBLEM.
NOT WITH THREE WITCHES ON OUR SIDE.

SIIIP

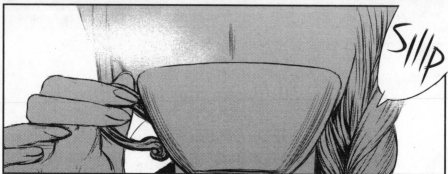

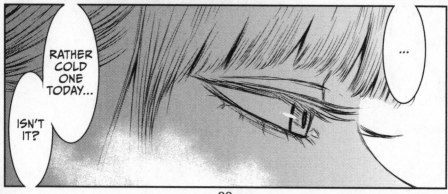

RATHER COLD ONE TODAY...

ISN'T IT?

...

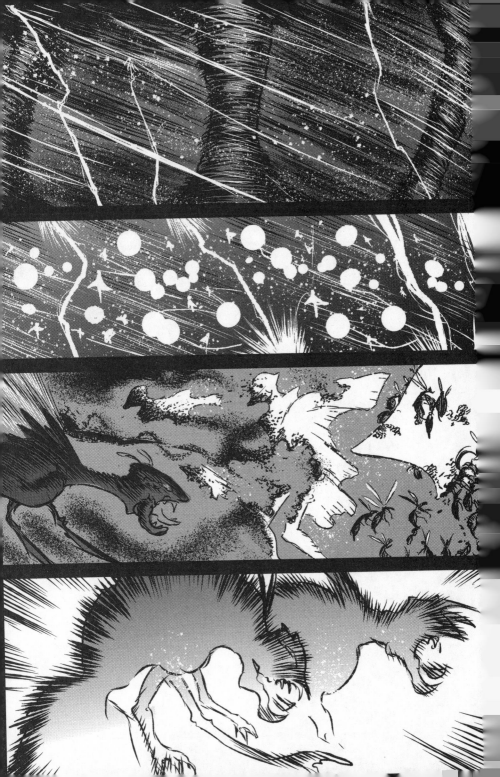

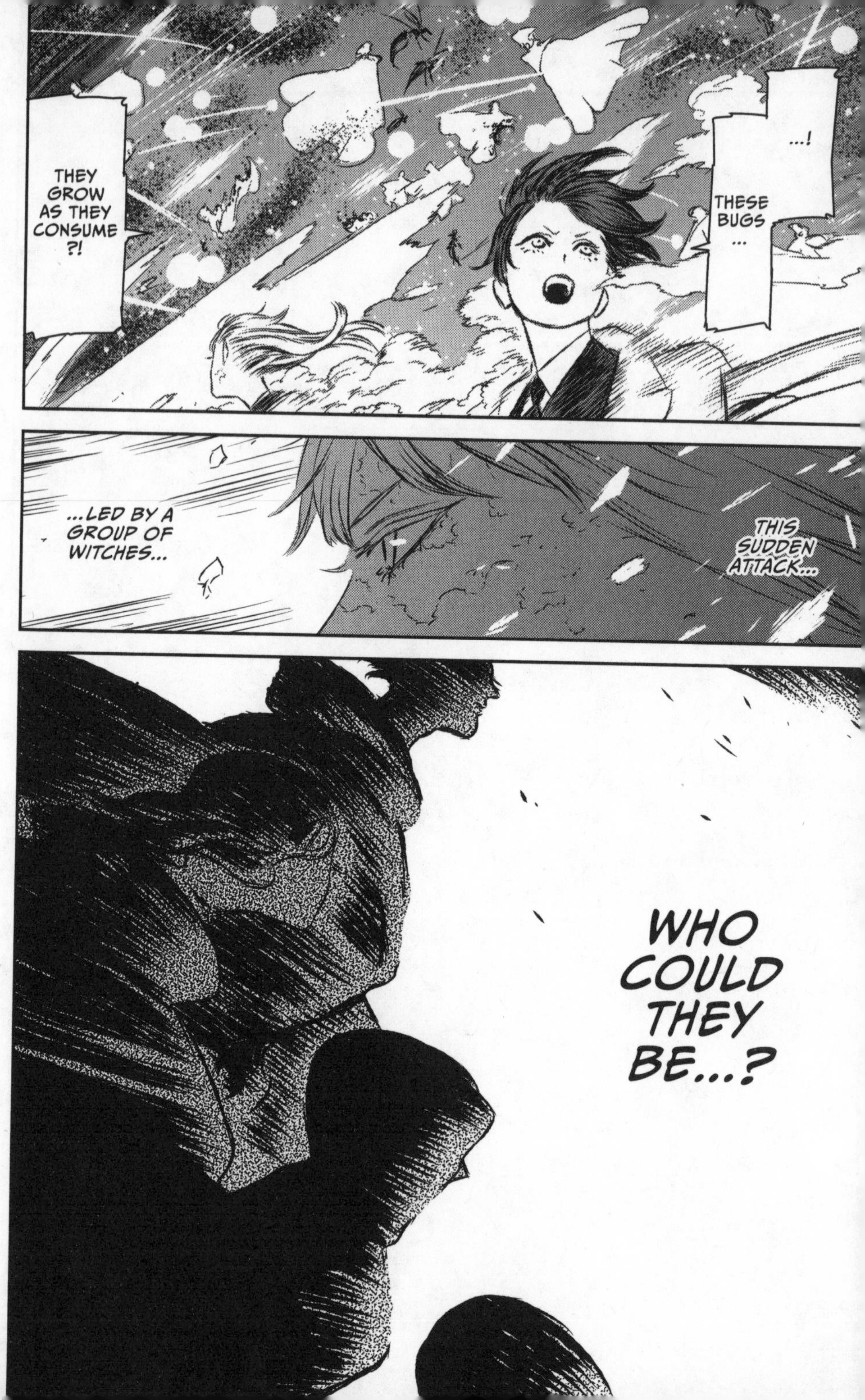
...! THESE BUGS ...
THEY GROW AS THEY CONSUME ?!
THIS SUDDEN ATTACK...
...LED BY A GROUP OF WITCHES...
WHO COULD THEY BE...?

CHAPTER 45: CHAOS INSIDE THE STORM—ACT III

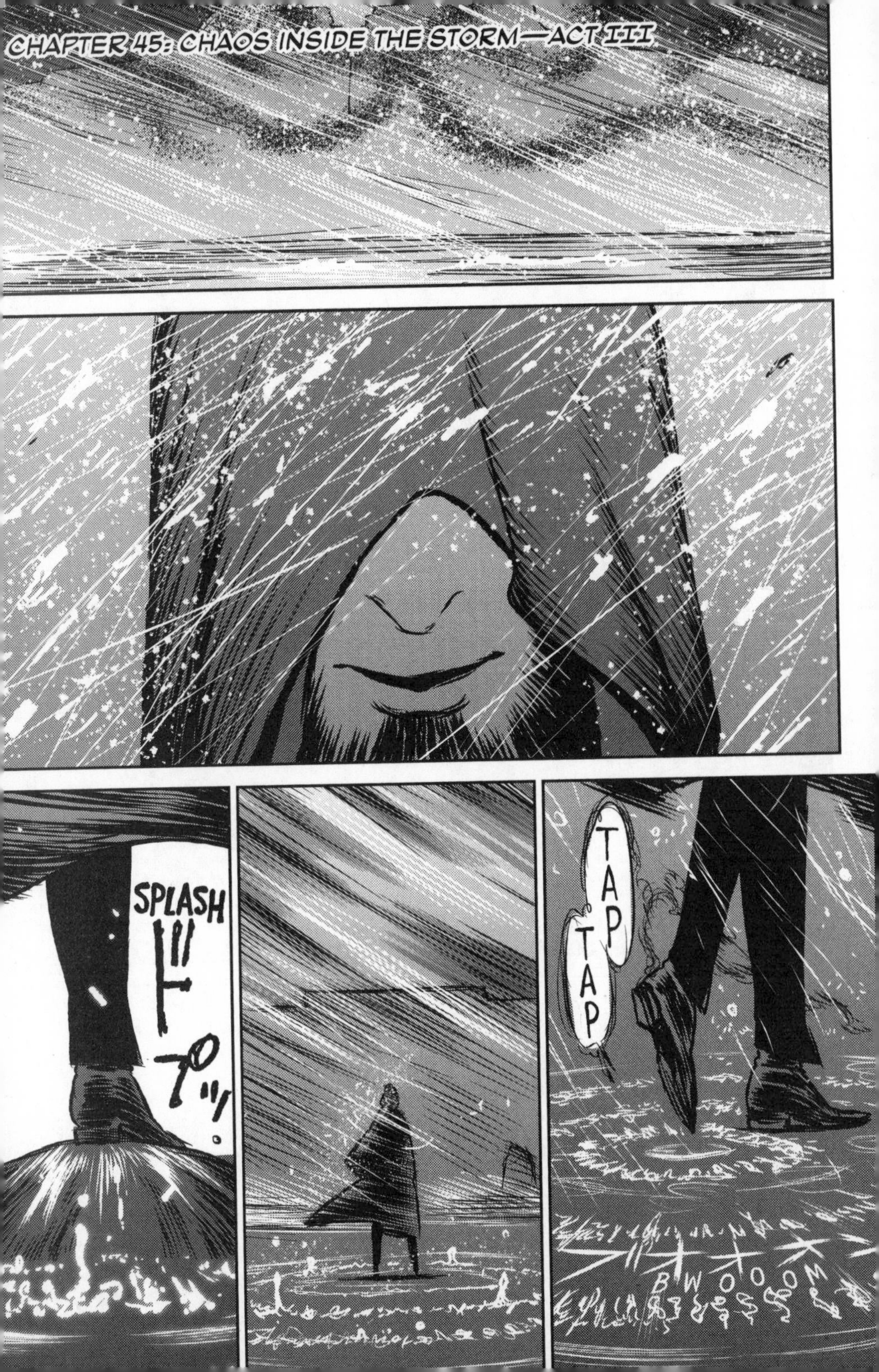
TAP
TAP
BWOOOM
SPLASH

HHHOSPLRRRRR RRRSH

A SUMMONING SPELL...!

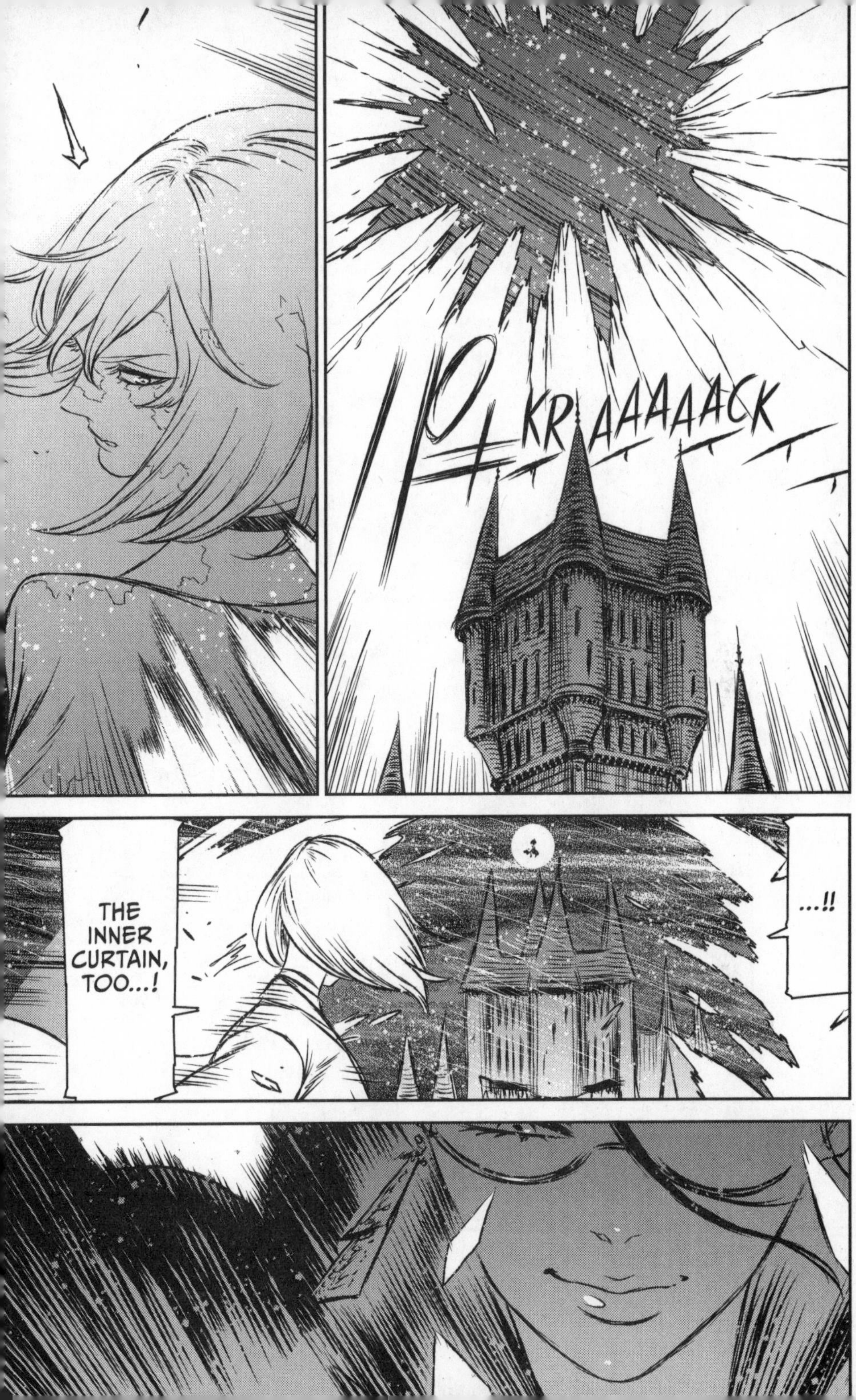
KRAAAAACK
...!!
THE INNER CURTAIN, TOO...!

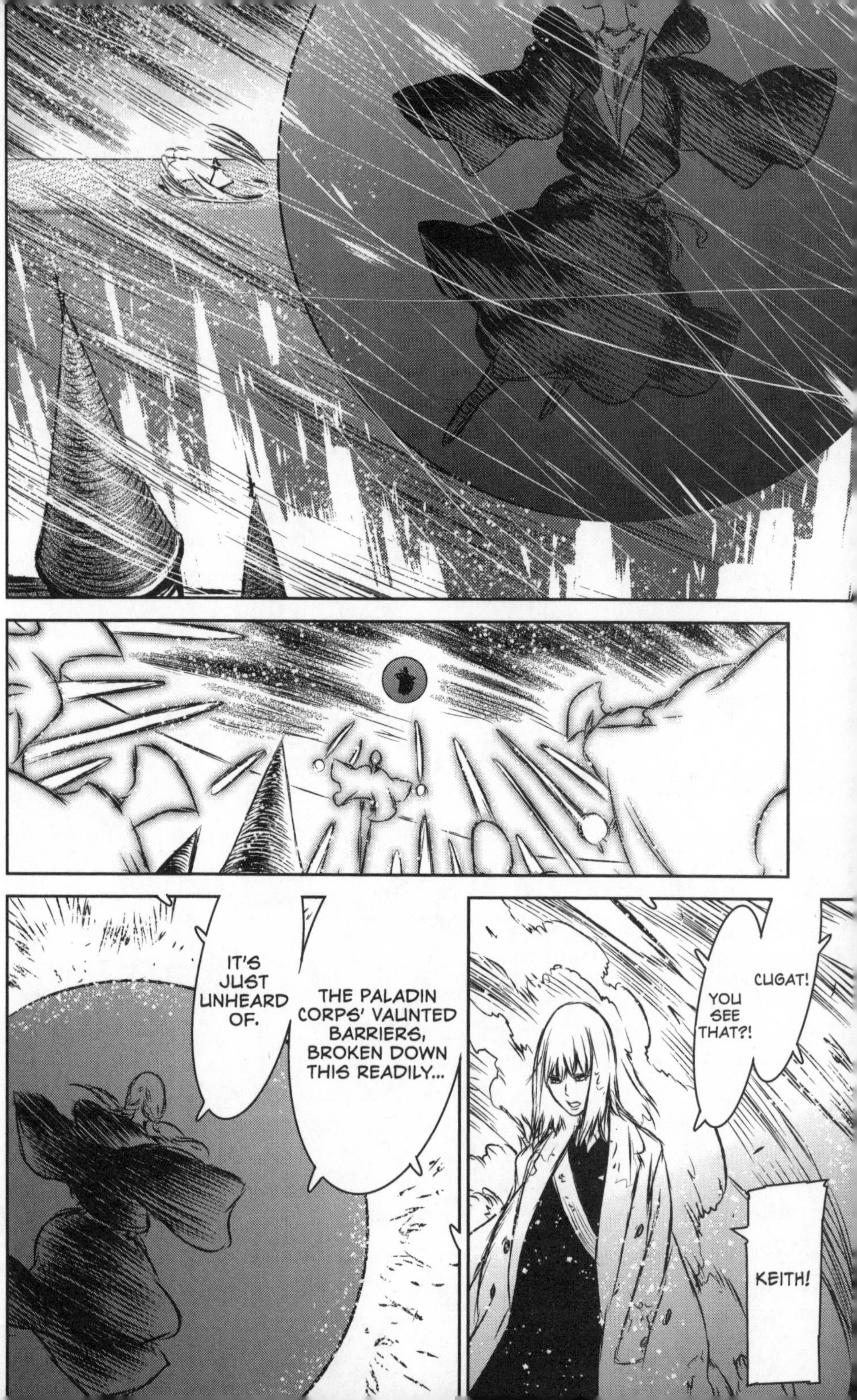
CUGAT!
YOU SEE THAT?!
KEITH!
THE PALADIN CORPS' VAUNTED BARRIERS, BROKEN DOWN THIS READILY...
IT'S JUST UNHEARD OF.

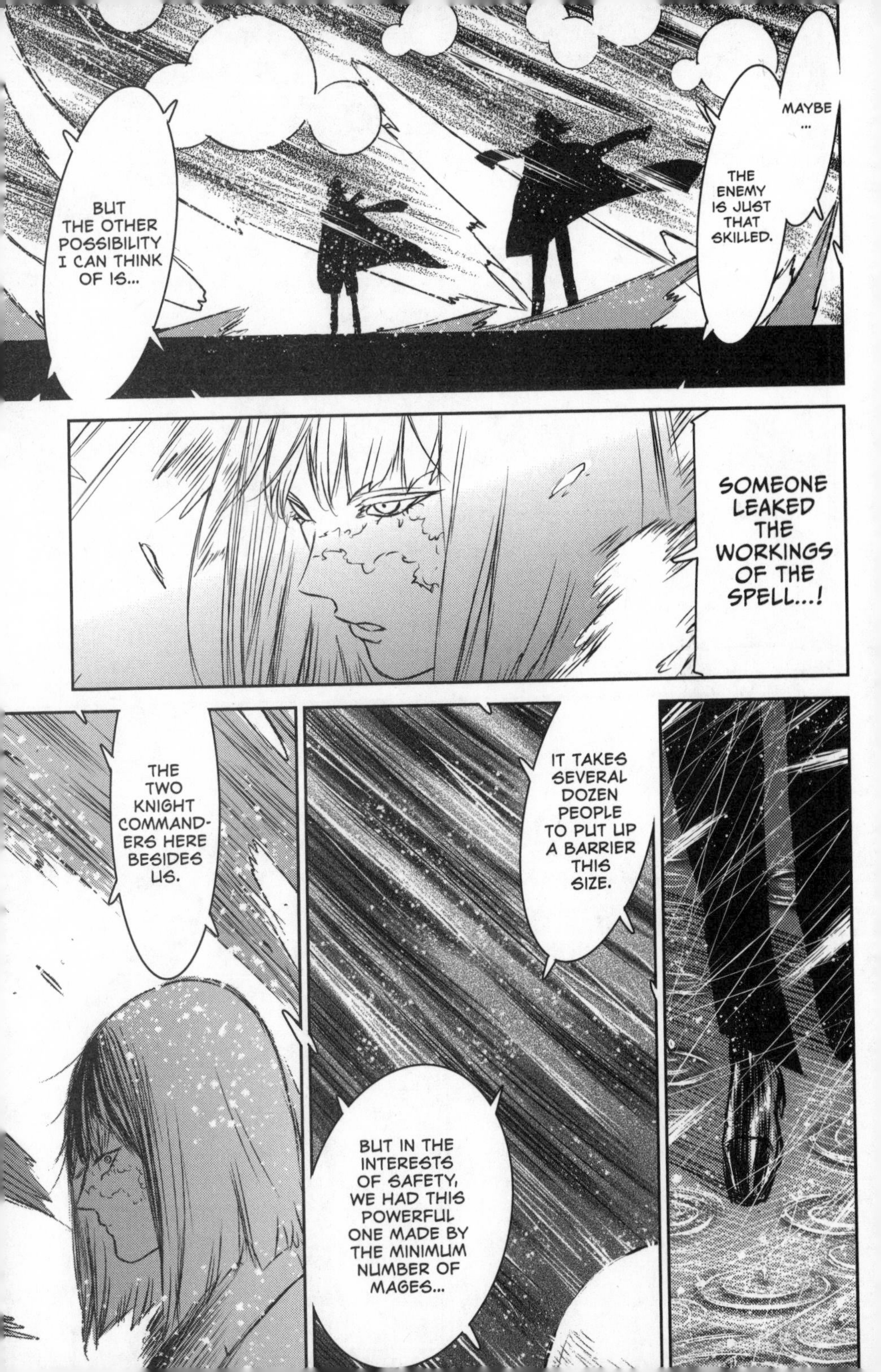
MAYBE...
THE ENEMY IS JUST THAT SKILLED.
BUT THE OTHER POSSIBILITY I CAN THINK OF IS...
SOMEONE LEAKED THE WORKINGS OF THE SPELL...!
IT TAKES SEVERAL DOZEN PEOPLE TO PUT UP A BARRIER THIS SIZE.
BUT IN THE INTERESTS OF SAFETY, WE HAD THIS POWERFUL ONE MADE BY THE MINIMUM NUMBER OF MAGES...
THE TWO KNIGHT COMMAND-ERS HERE BESIDES US.

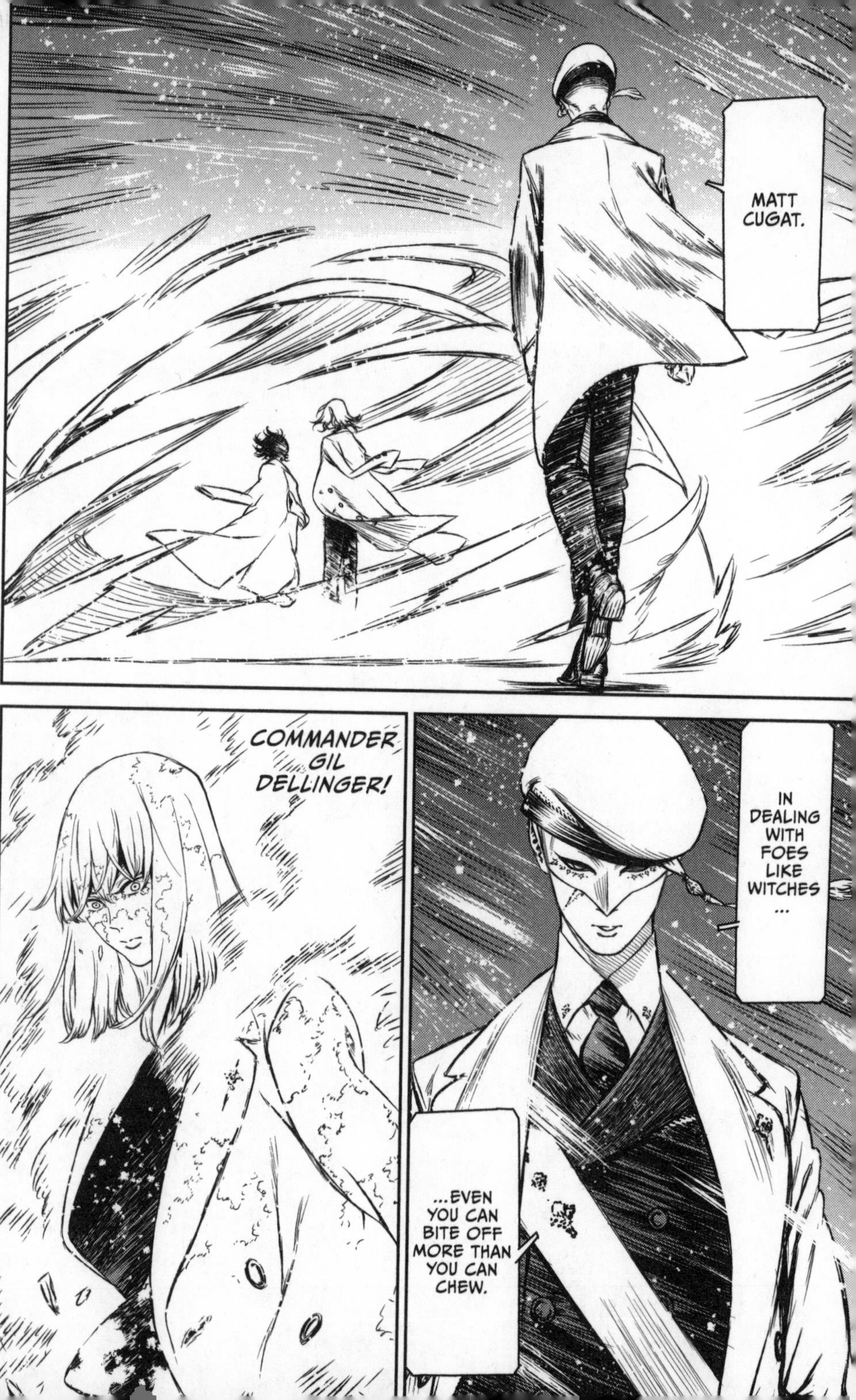
MATT CUGAT.
IN DEALING WITH FOES LIKE WITCHES ...
...EVEN YOU CAN BITE OFF MORE THAN YOU CAN CHEW.
COMMANDER GIL DELLINGER!

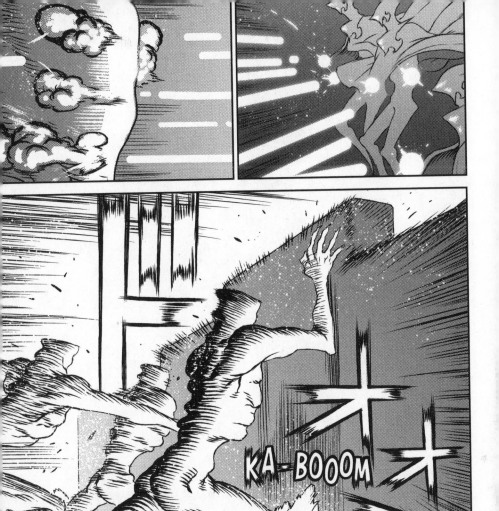

KA-BOOOM

KRAK

KRAK

KRAK

NGH.....!

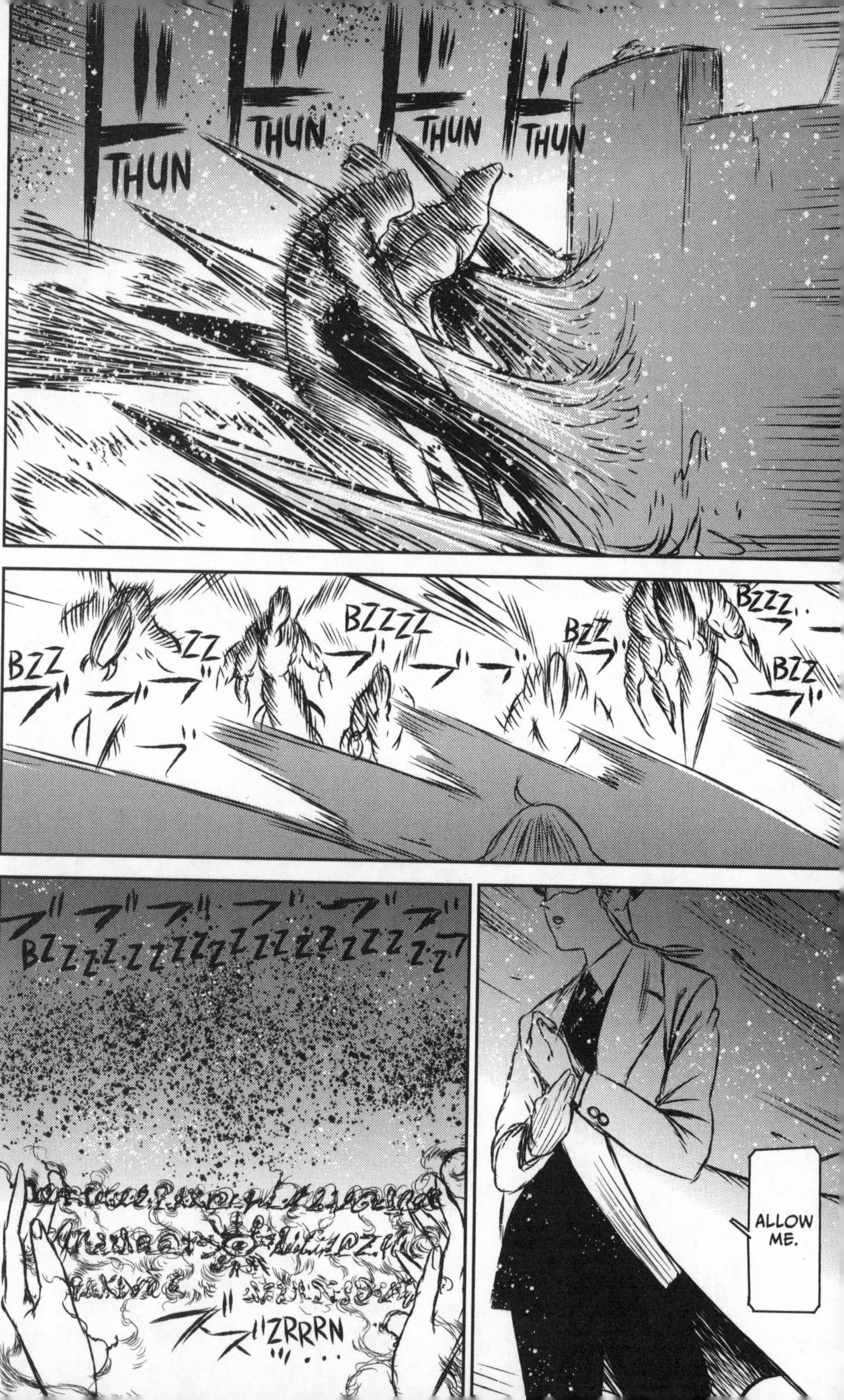
THUN
THUN
THUN
THUN
BZZZ..
BZZ
BZZ
BZZZZZ
ZZ
BZZ
ALLOW ME.
BZZZZZZZZZZZZZZZZZZZZ
ZRRRN...

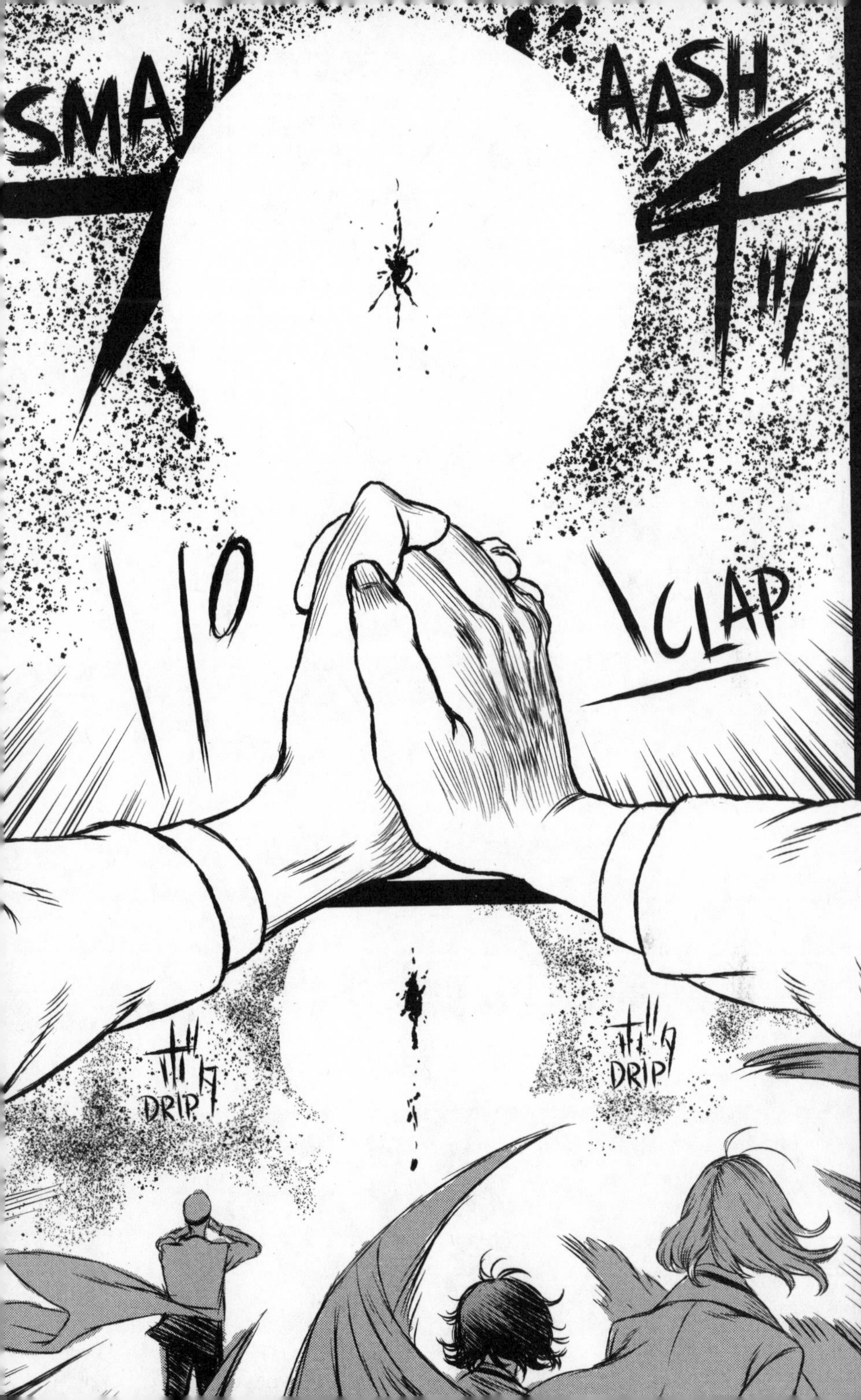
SMAAASH
CLAP
DRIP
DRIP

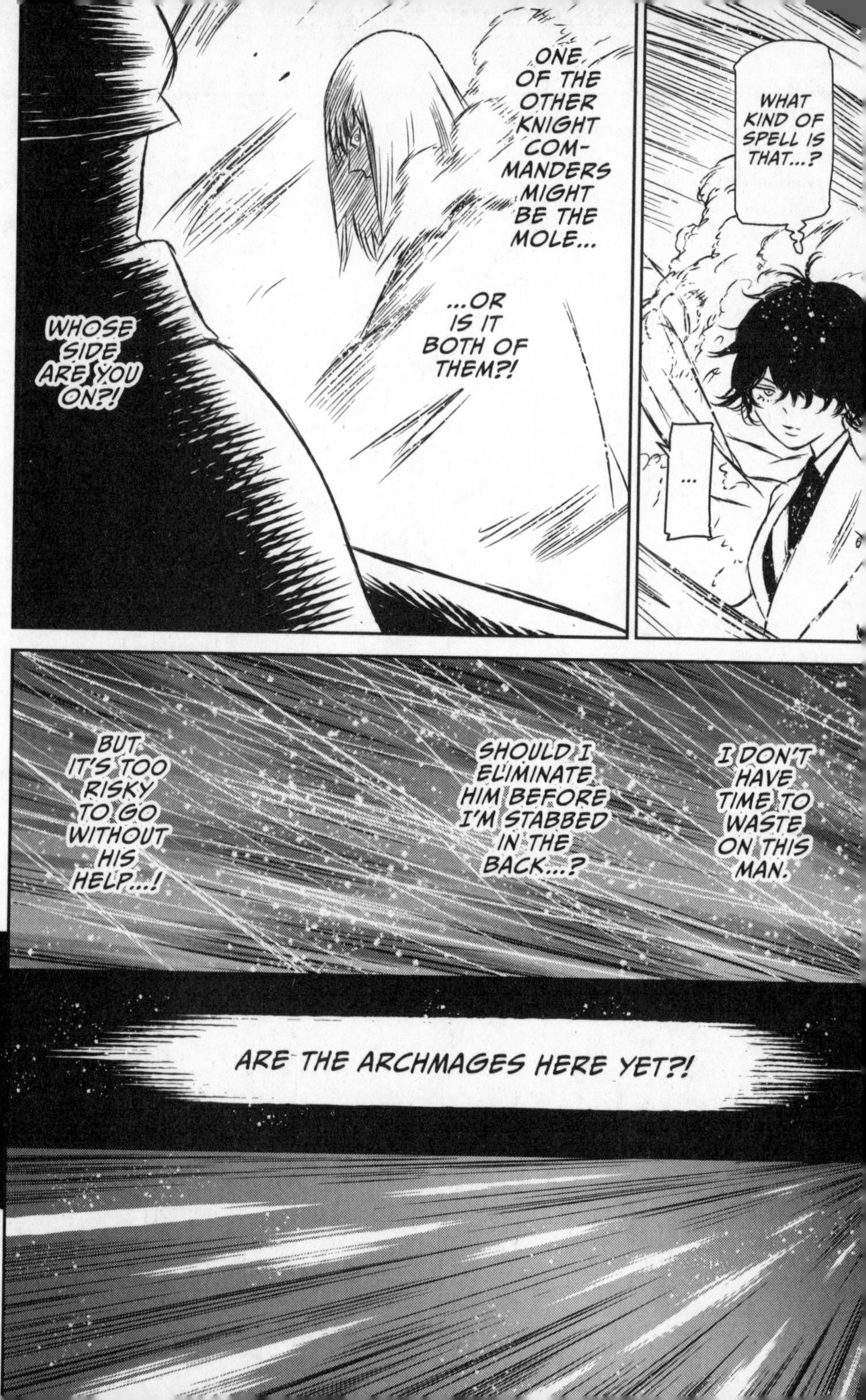
WHAT KIND OF SPELL IS THAT...?
...
ONE OF THE OTHER KNIGHT COM-MANDERS MIGHT BE THE MOLE...
...OR IS IT BOTH OF THEM?!
WHOSE SIDE ARE YOU ON?!
I DON'T HAVE TIME TO WASTE ON THIS MAN.
SHOULD I ELIMINATE HIM BEFORE I'M STABBED IN THE BACK...?
BUT IT'S TOO RISKY TO GO WITHOUT HIS HELP...!
ARE THE ARCHMAGES HERE YET?!

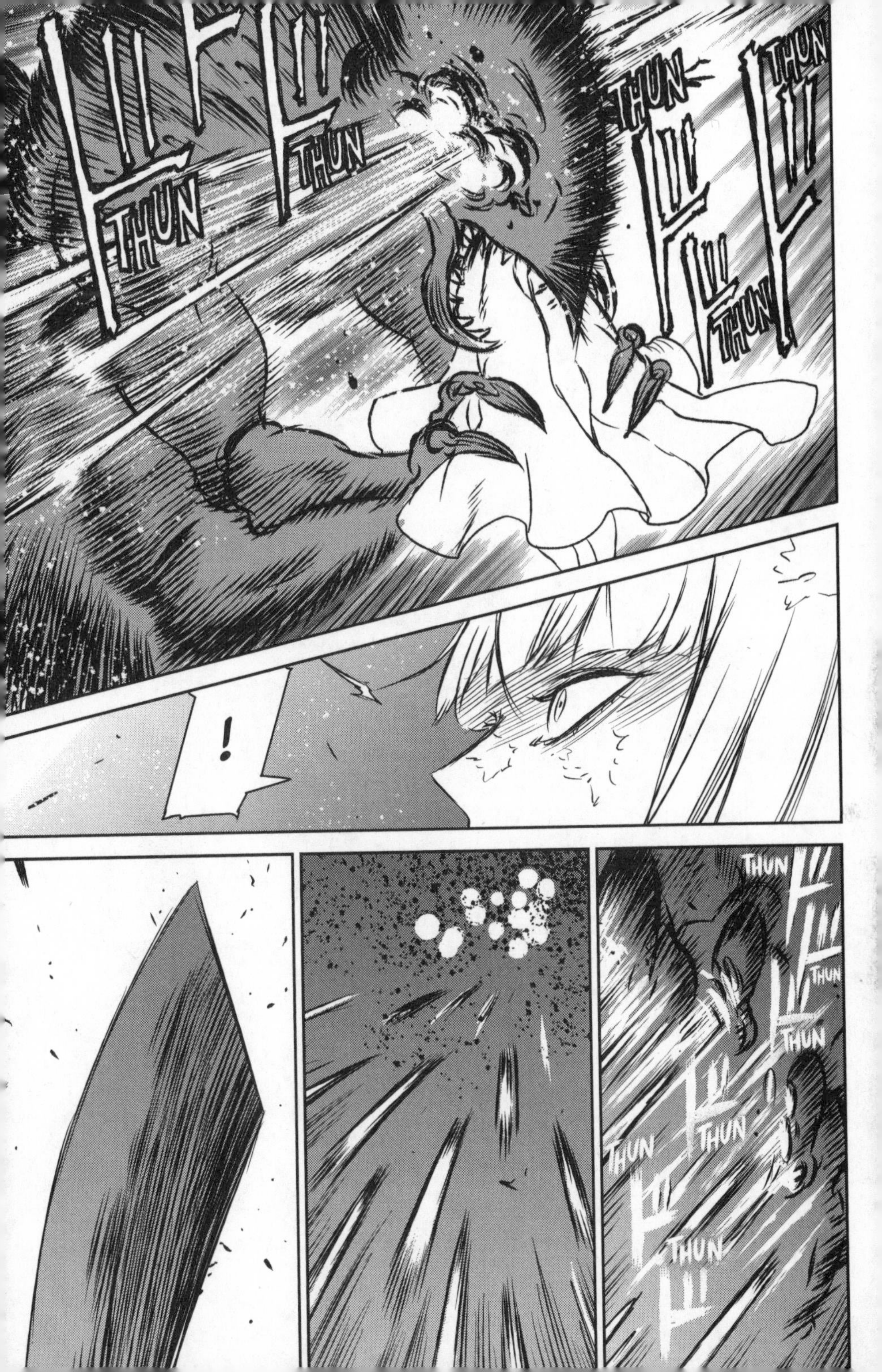
THUN
THUN
THUN
THUN
THUN
THUN
!
THUN
THUN
THUN
THUN
THUN
THUN

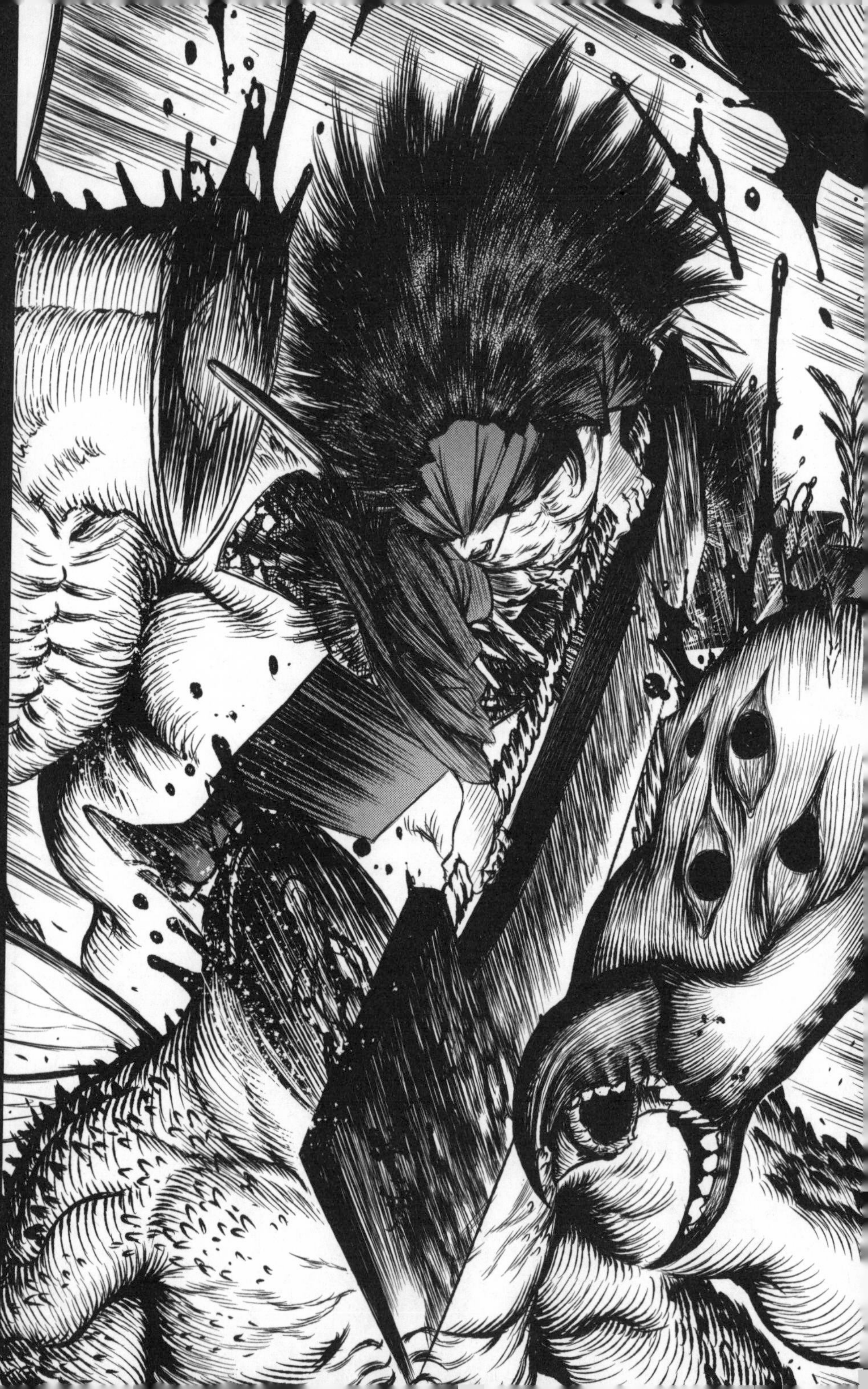

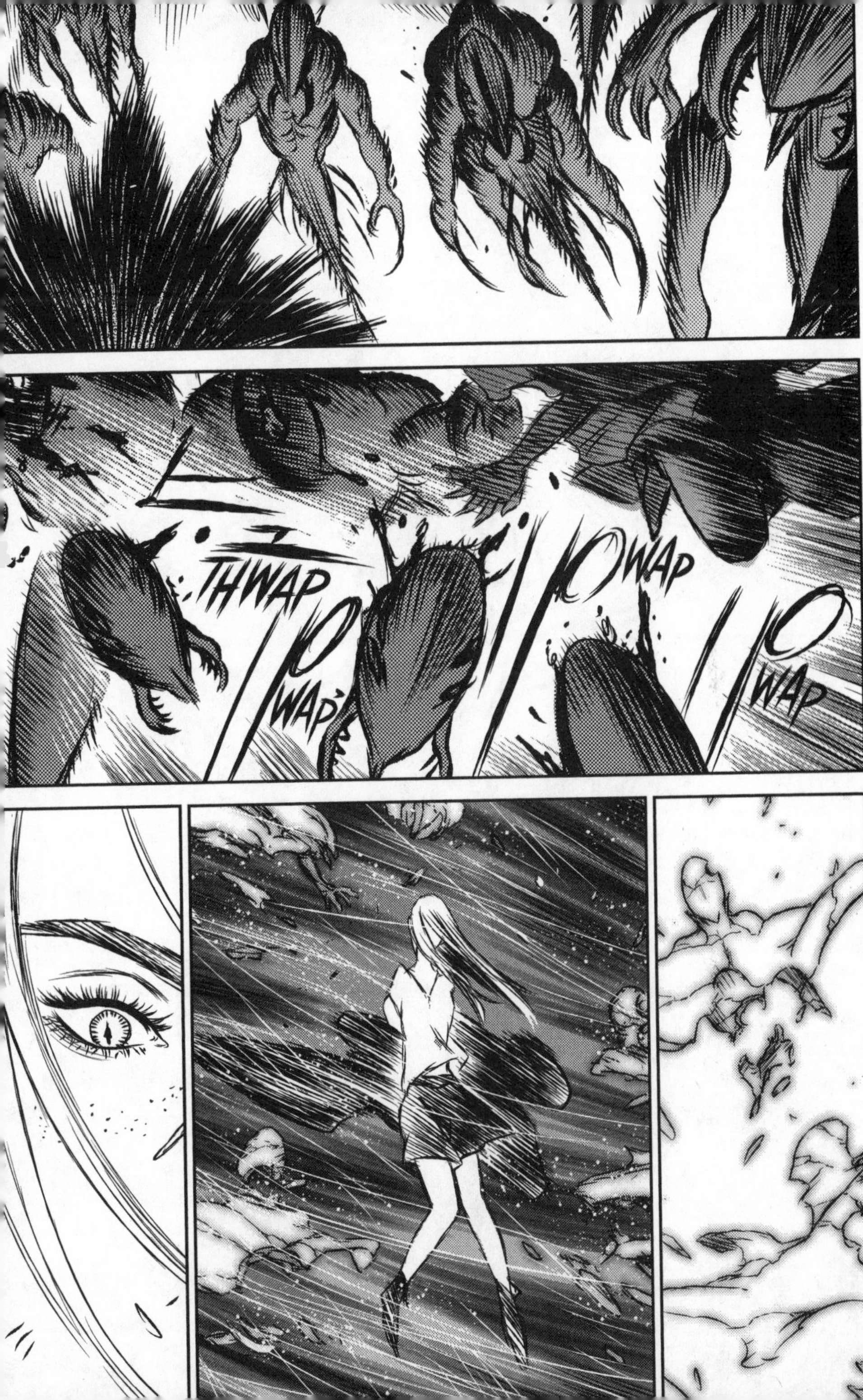
WAP
WAP
THWAP
WAP

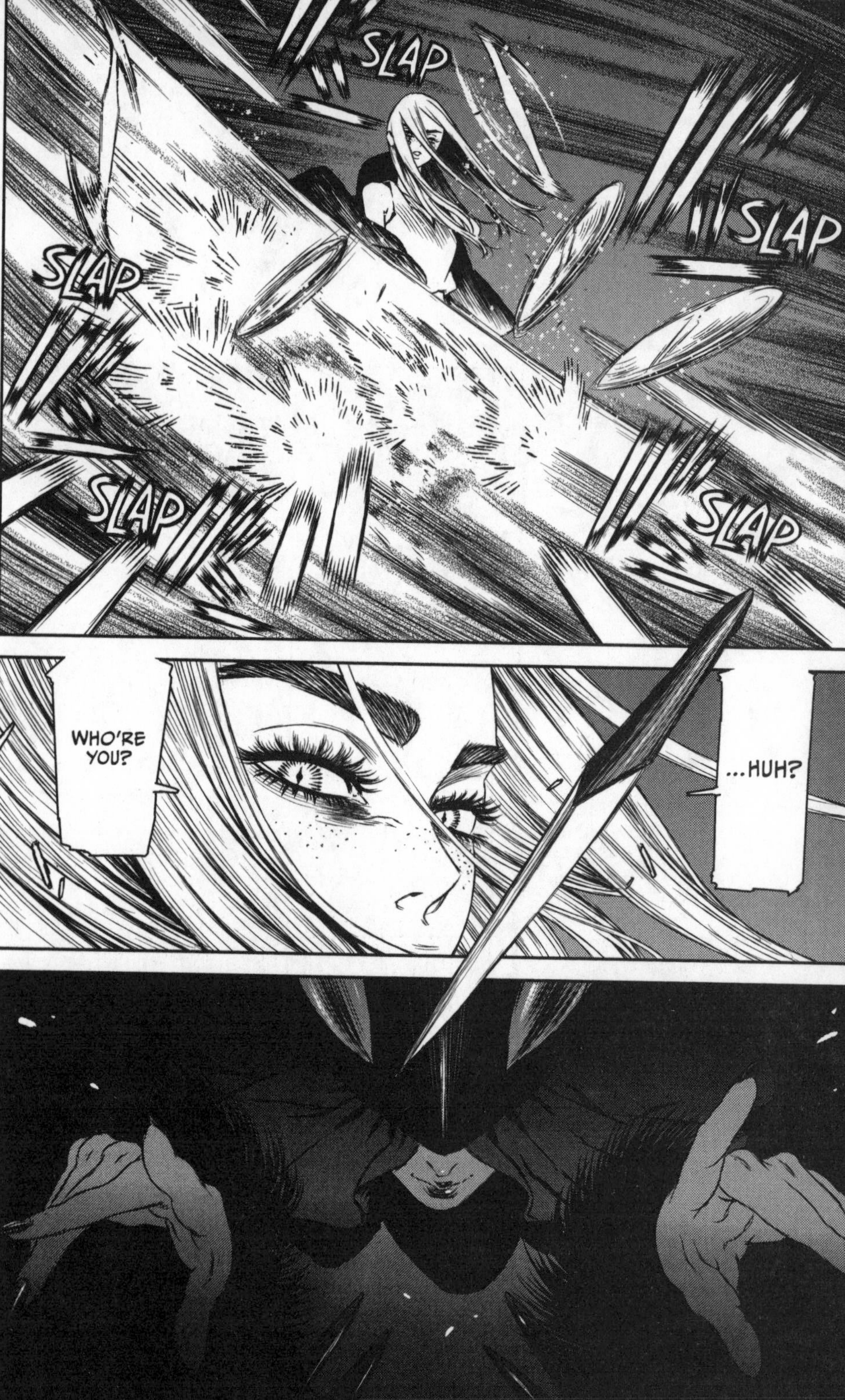
SLAP
SLAP
SLAP
SLAP
SLAP
...HUH?
WHO'RE YOU?

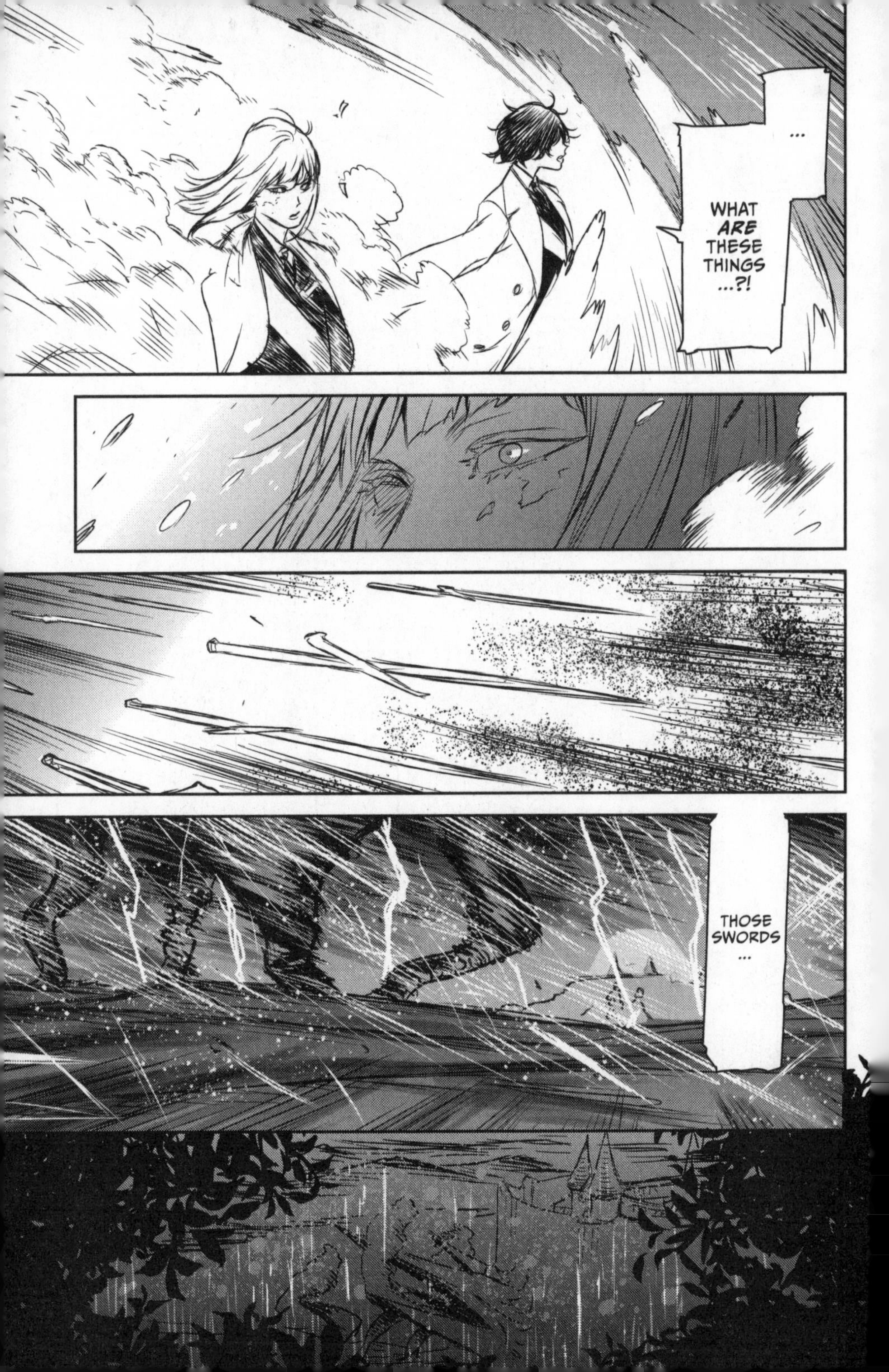
...
WHAT *ARE* THESE THINGS ...?!
THOSE SWORDS ...

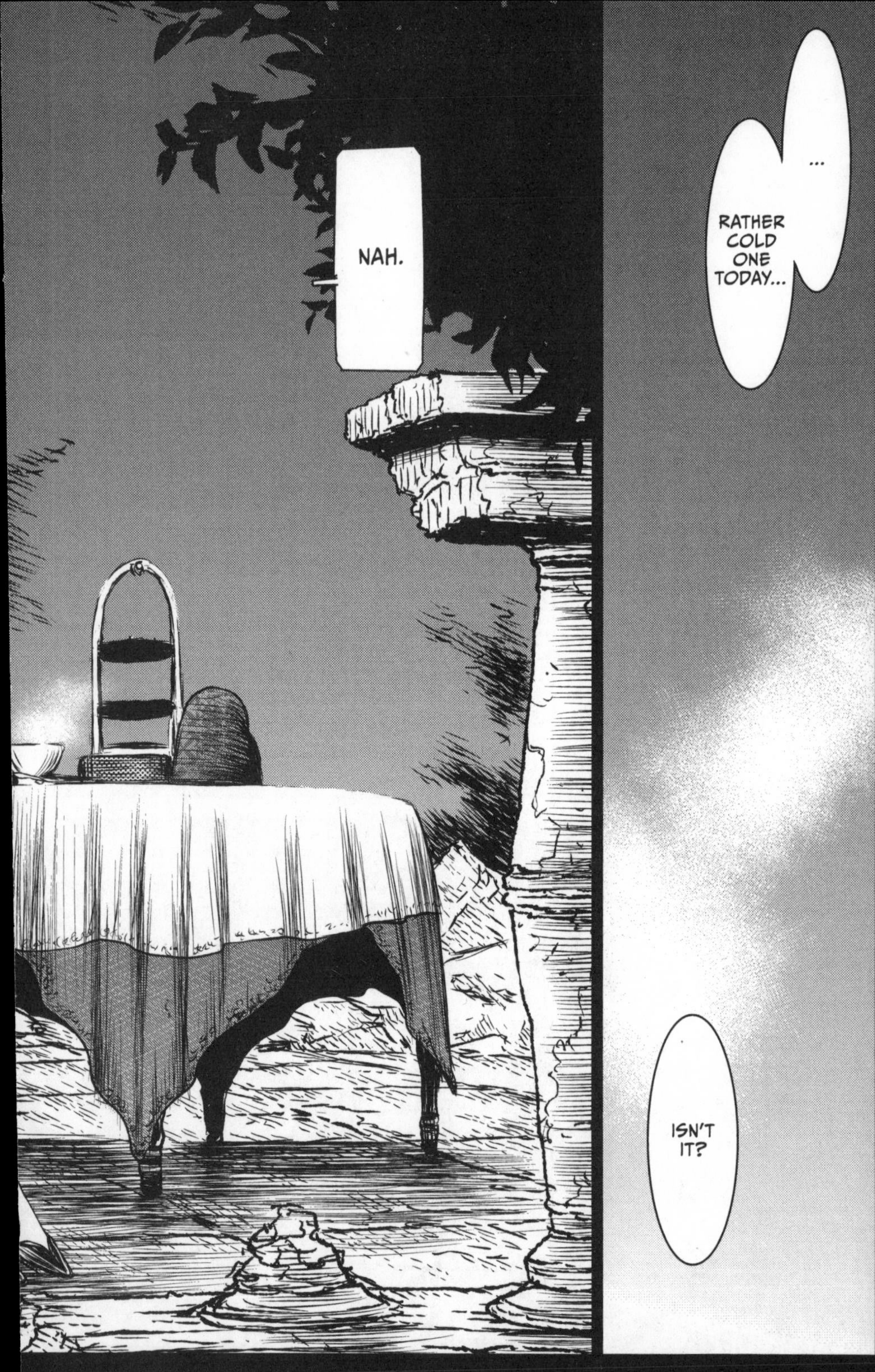
...
RATHER COLD ONE TODAY...
ISN'T IT?
NAH.

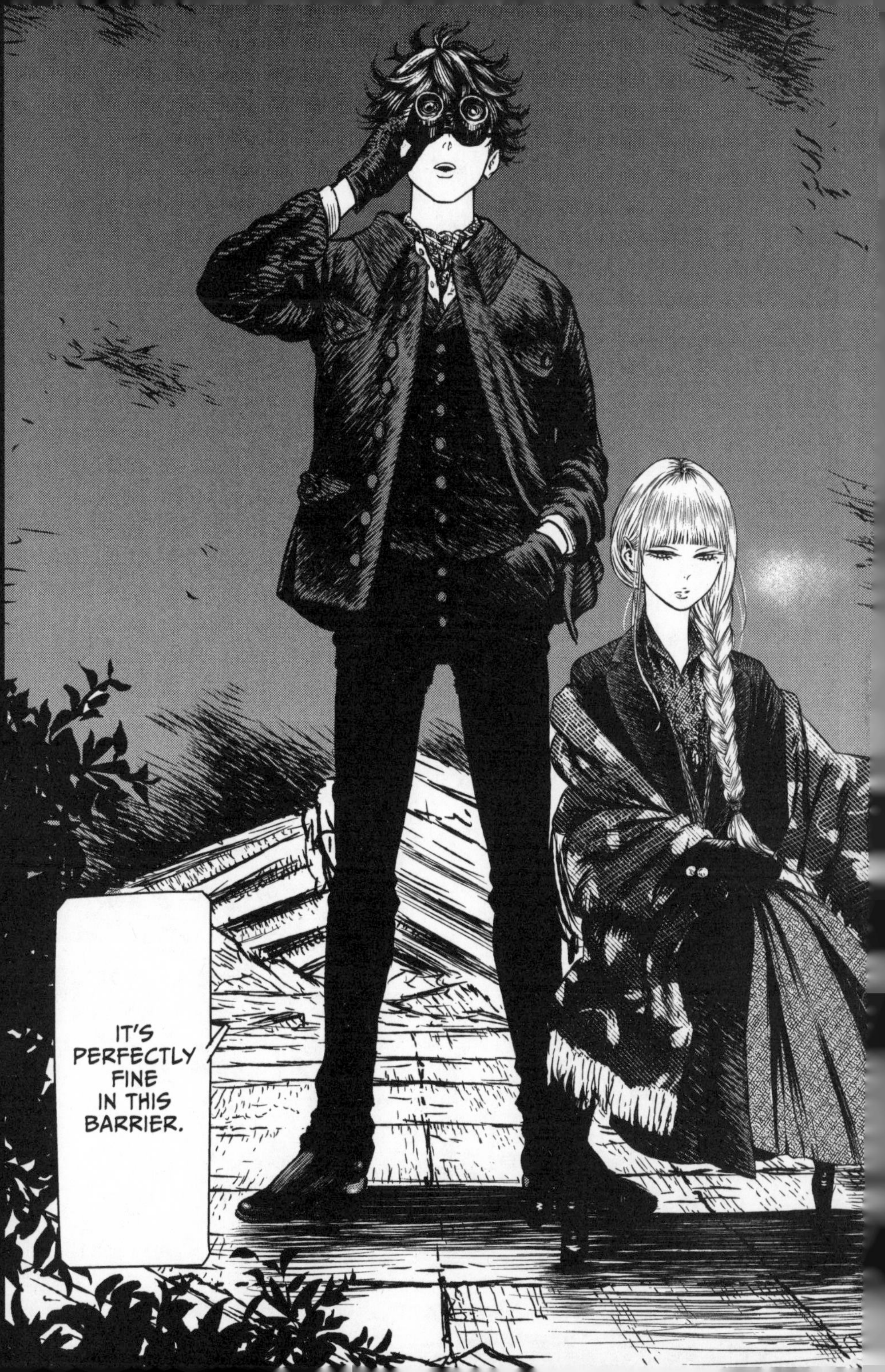
IT'S PERFECTLY FINE IN THIS BARRIER.

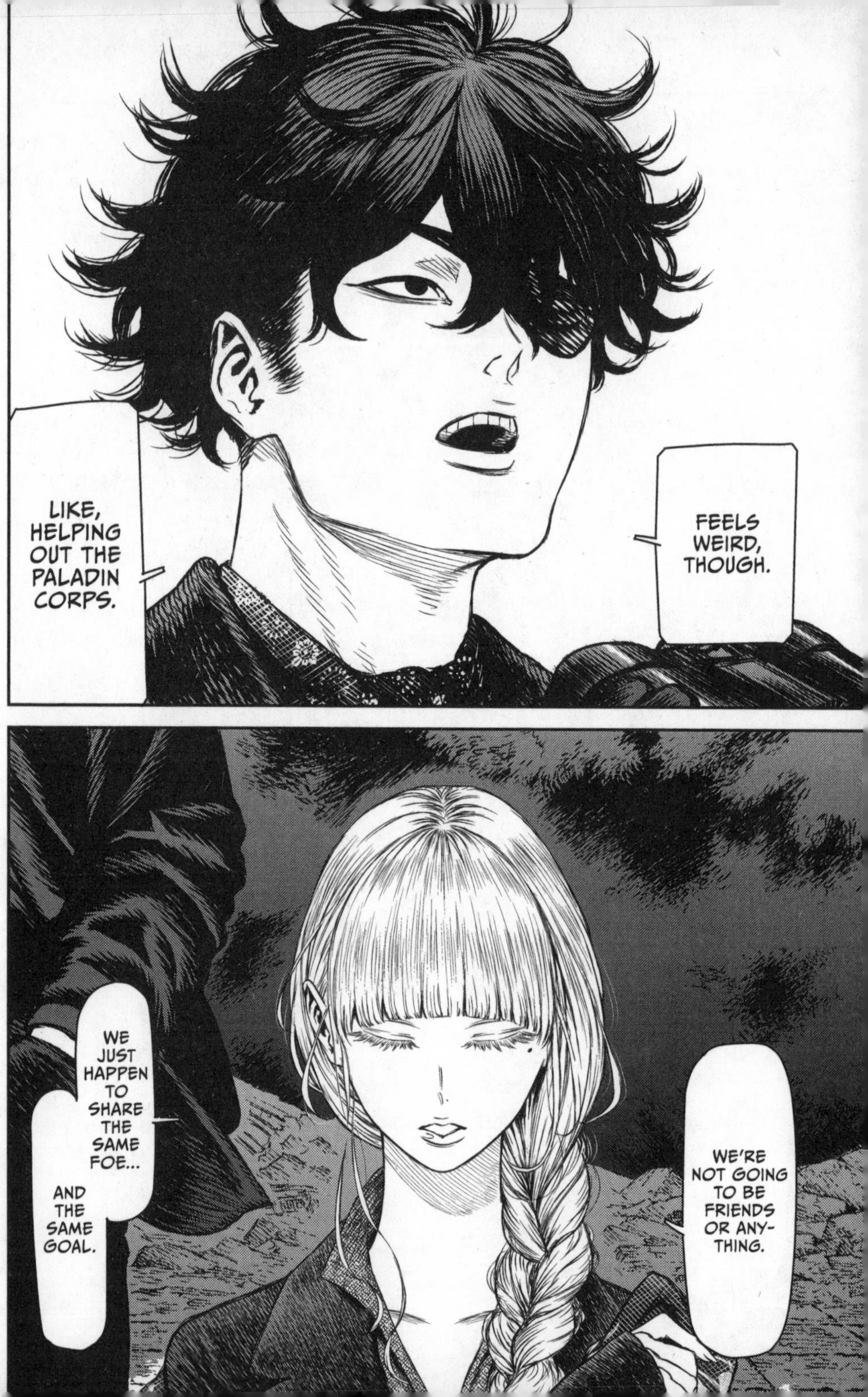
FEELS WEIRD, THOUGH.
LIKE, HELPING OUT THE PALADIN CORPS.
WE'RE NOT GOING TO BE FRIENDS OR ANY-THING.
WE JUST HAPPEN TO SHARE THE SAME FOE...
AND THE SAME GOAL.

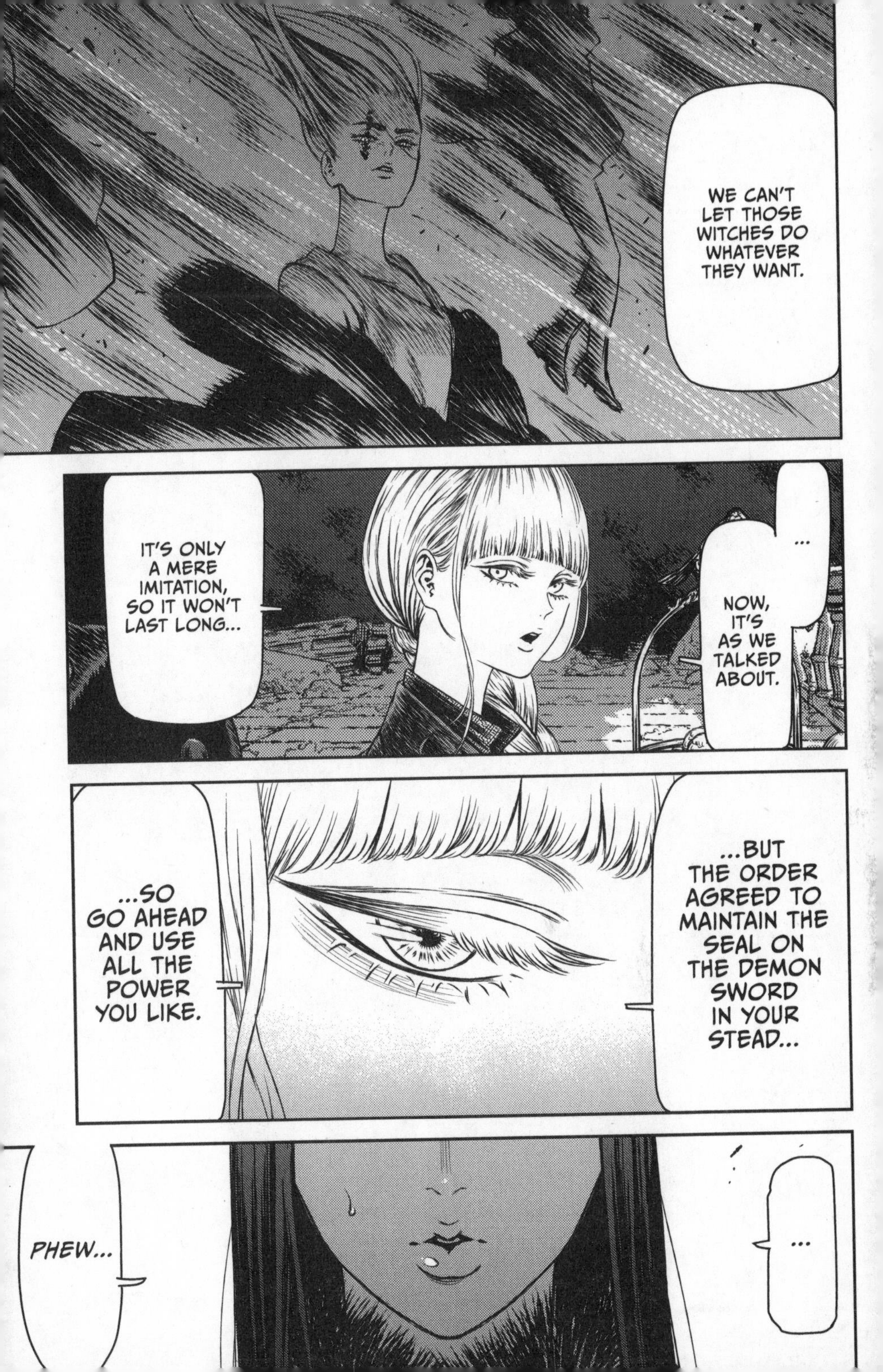
WE CAN'T LET THOSE WITCHES DO WHATEVER THEY WANT.
...
NOW, IT'S AS WE TALKED ABOUT.
IT'S ONLY A MERE IMITATION, SO IT WON'T LAST LONG...
...BUT THE ORDER AGREED TO MAINTAIN THE SEAL ON THE DEMON SWORD IN YOUR STEAD...
...SO GO AHEAD AND USE ALL THE POWER YOU LIKE.
...
PHEW...

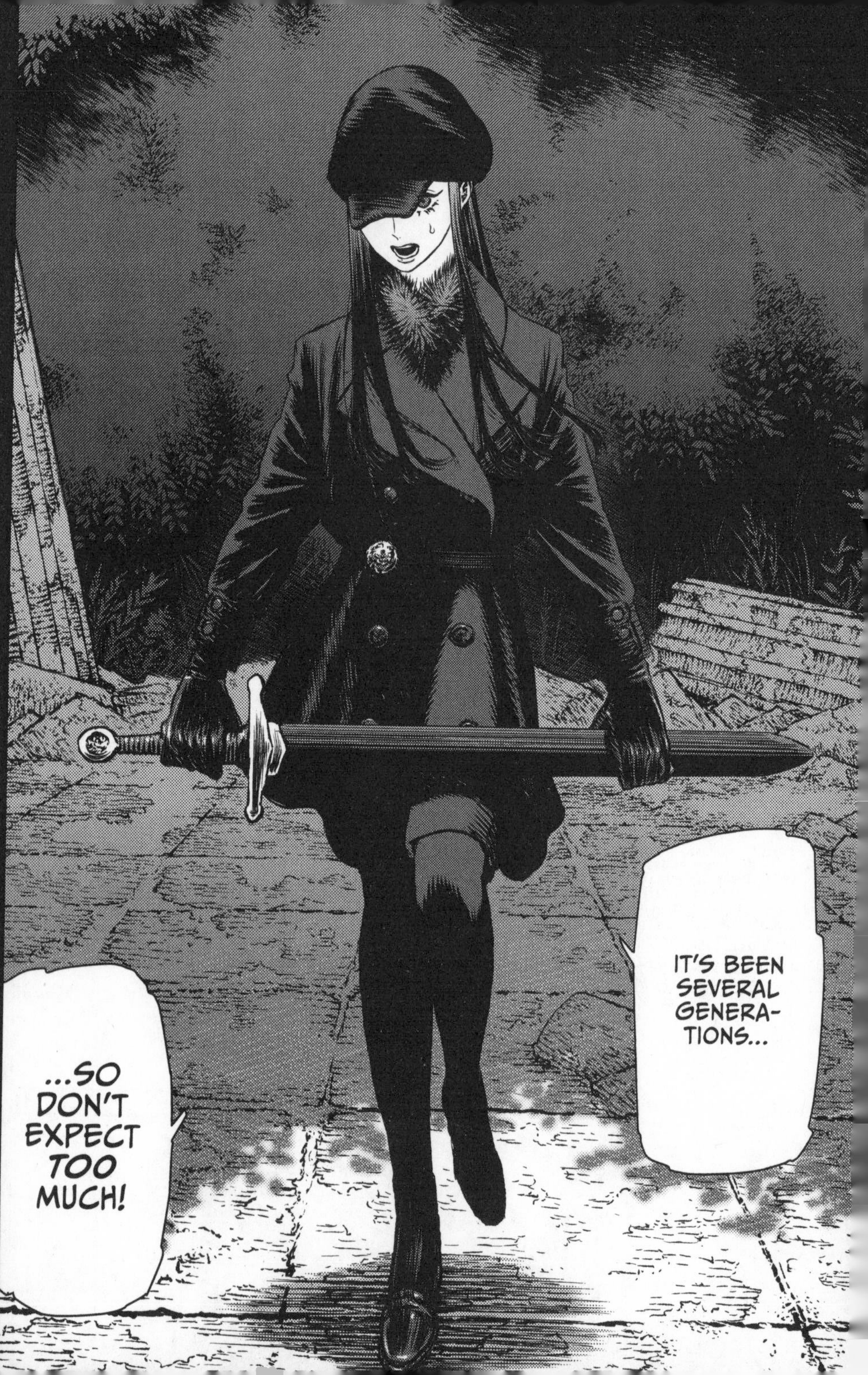
IT'S BEEN SEVERAL GENERATIONS...
...SO DON'T EXPECT TOO MUCH!

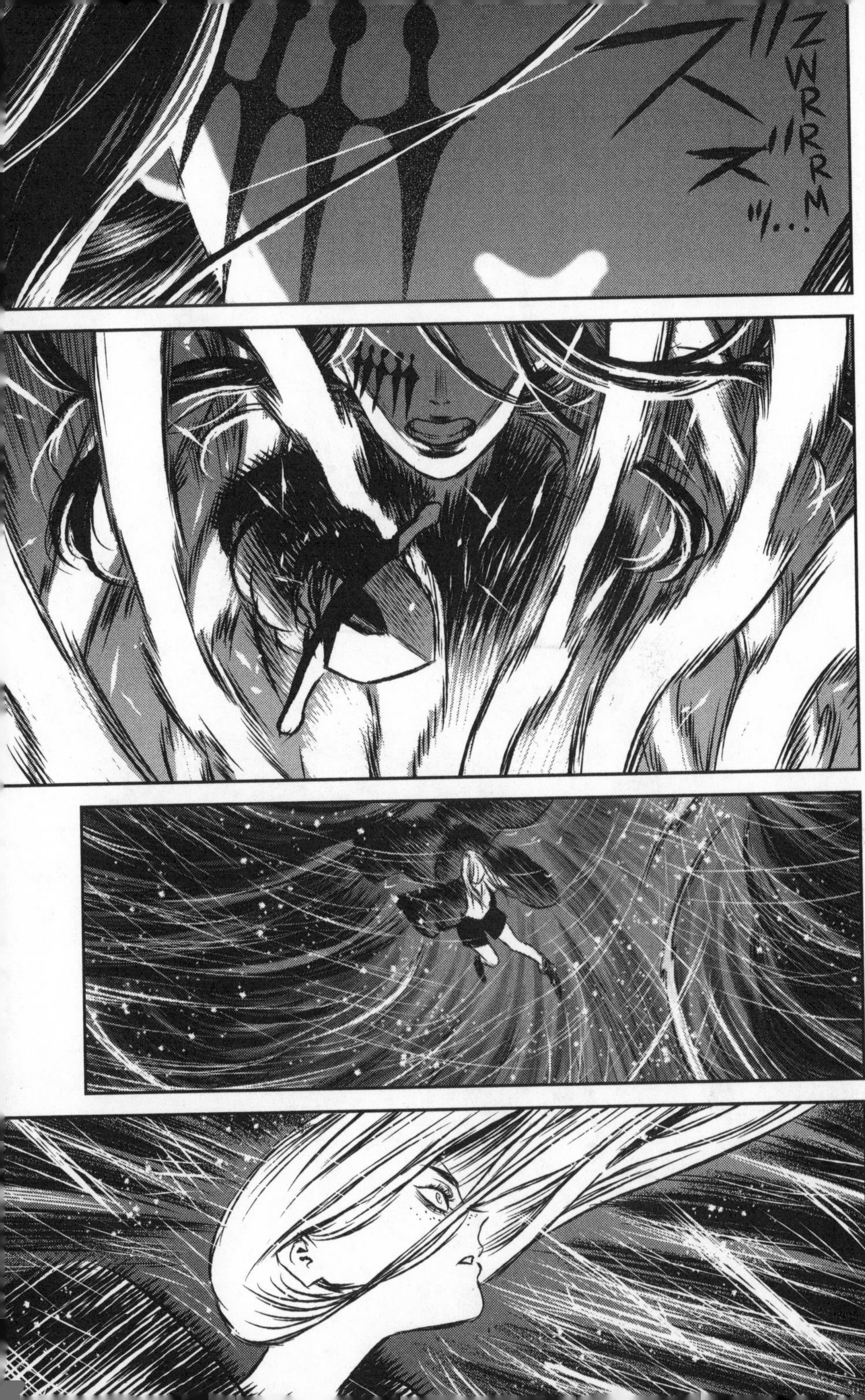
ZWRRRM...!

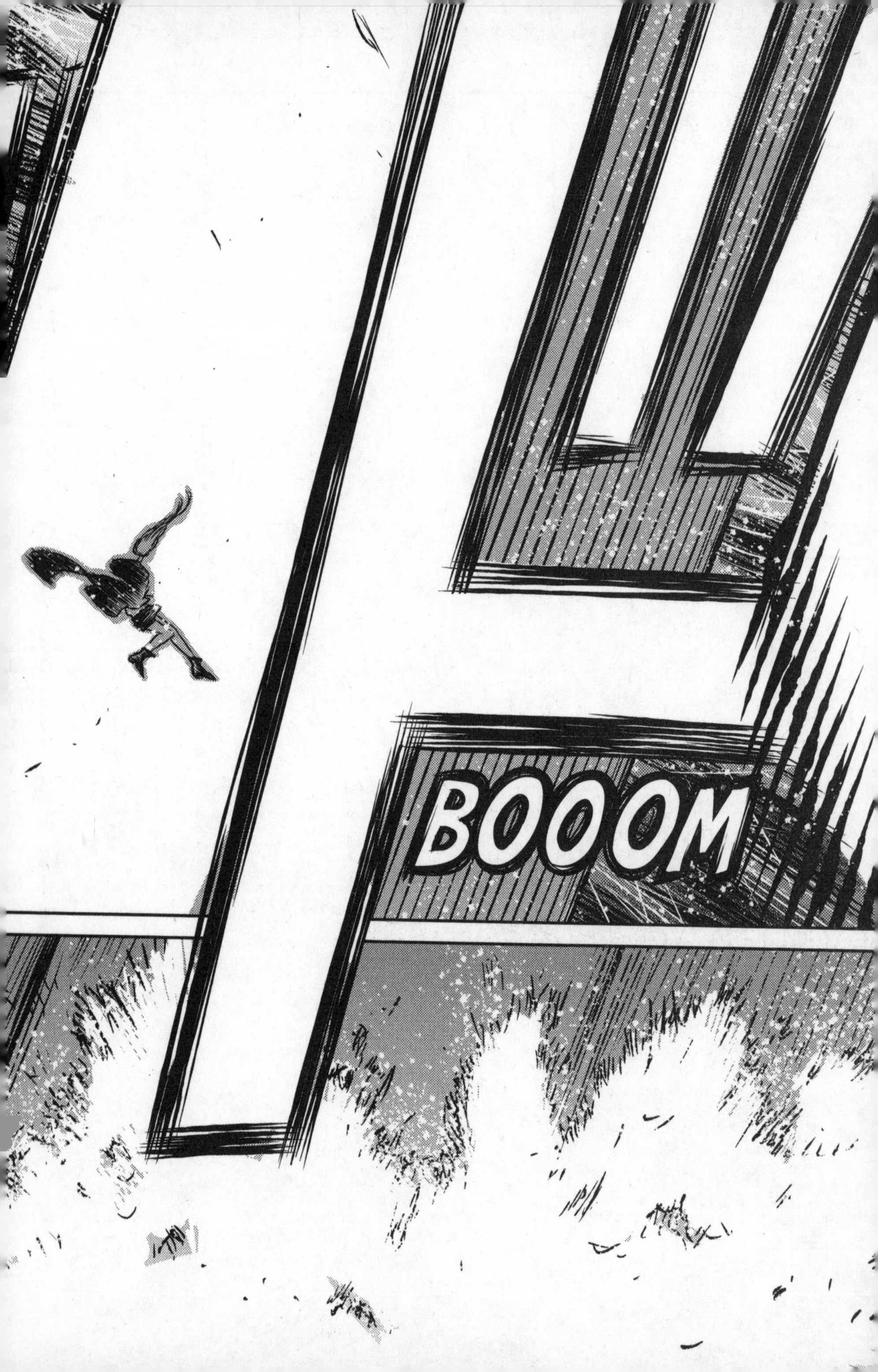
BOOOM

Chapter 46: Chaos Inside the Storm—Act IV

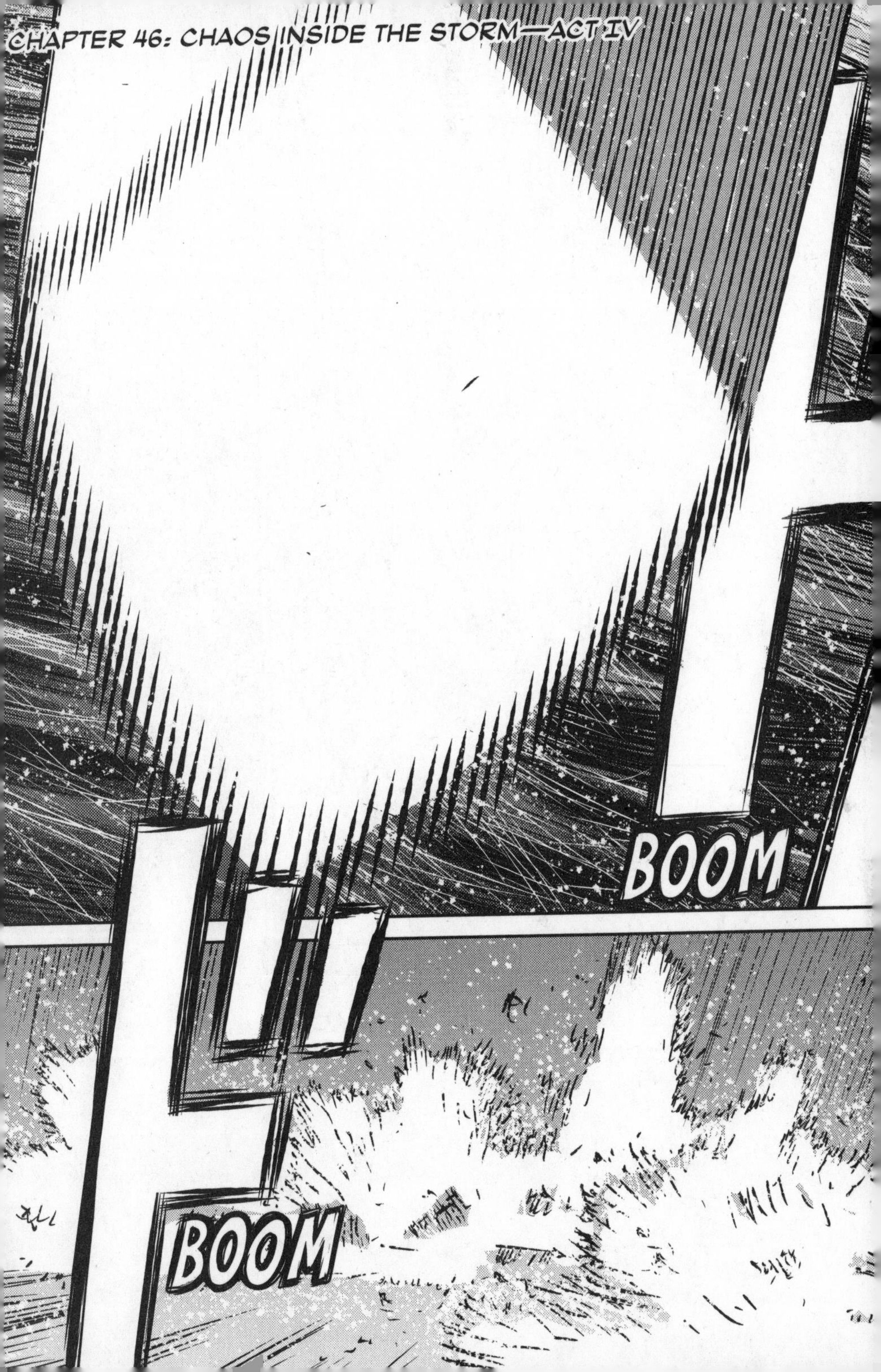
BOOM
BOOM

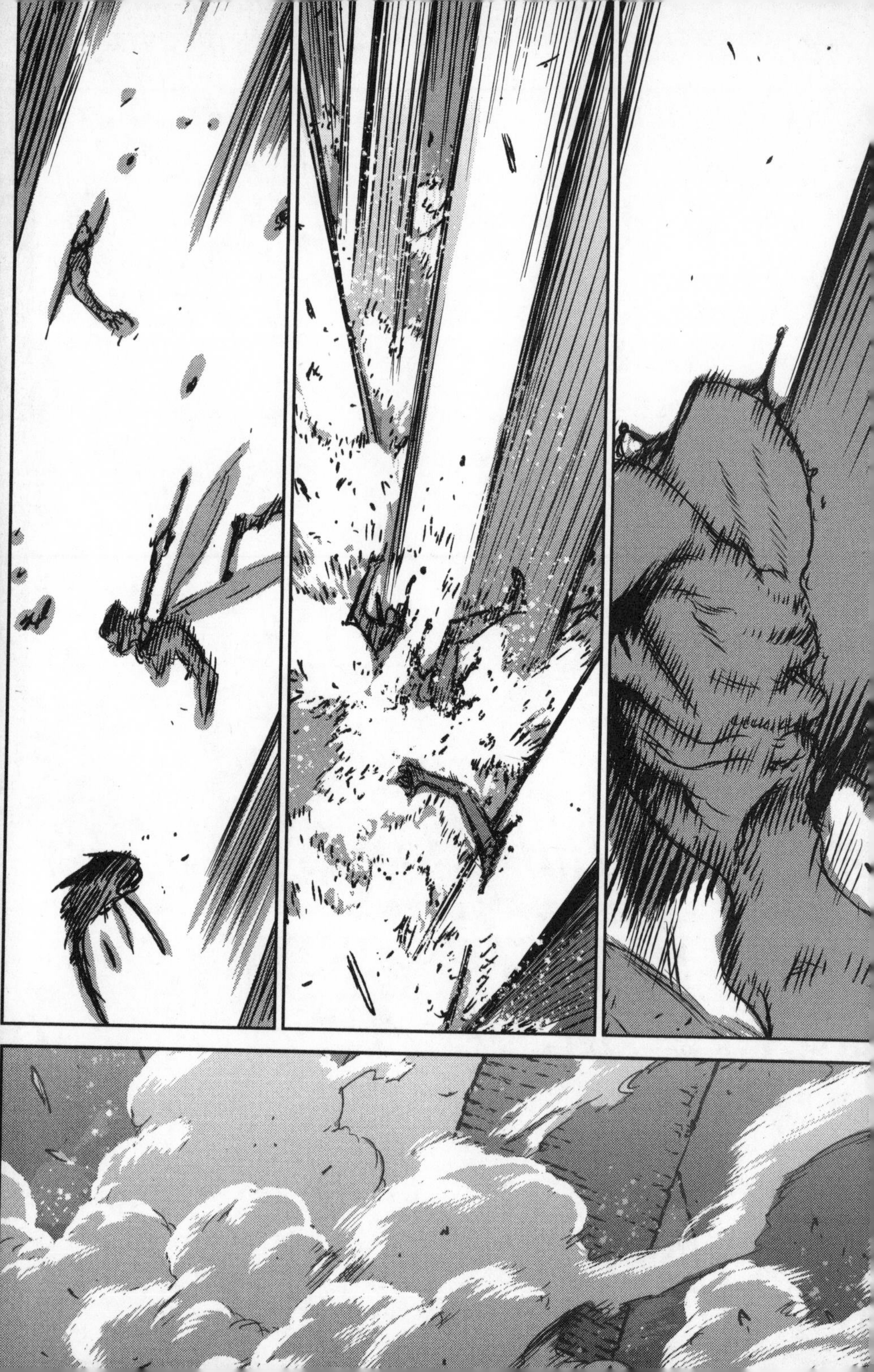

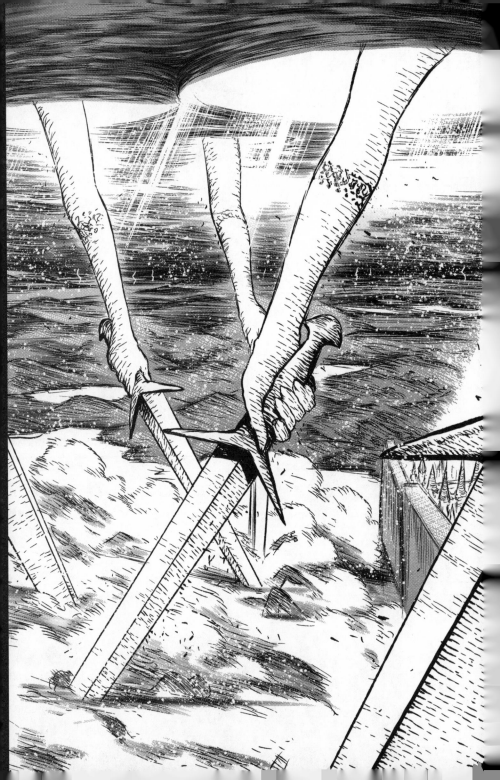

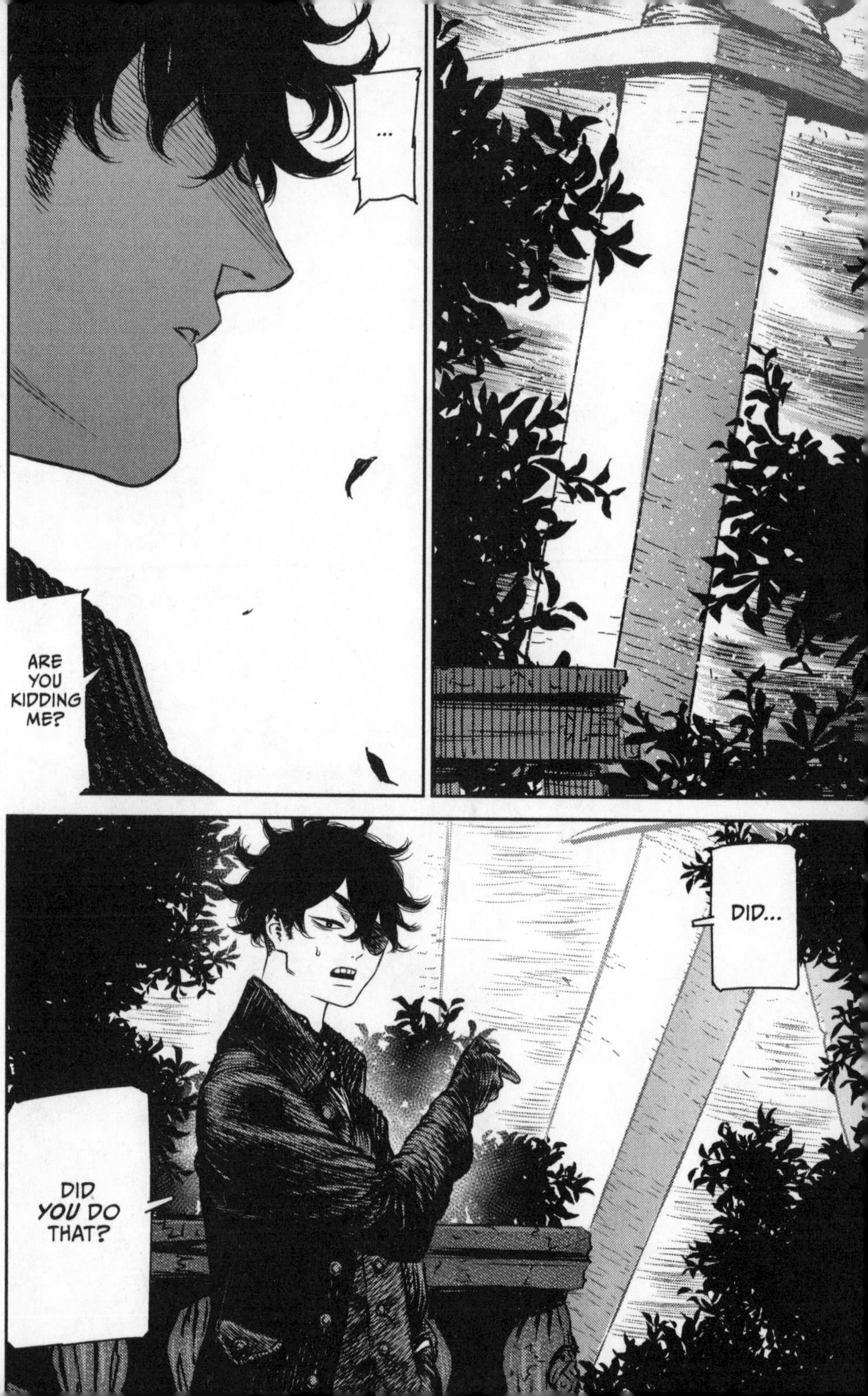
...
ARE YOU KIDDING ME?
DID...
DID *YOU* DO THAT?

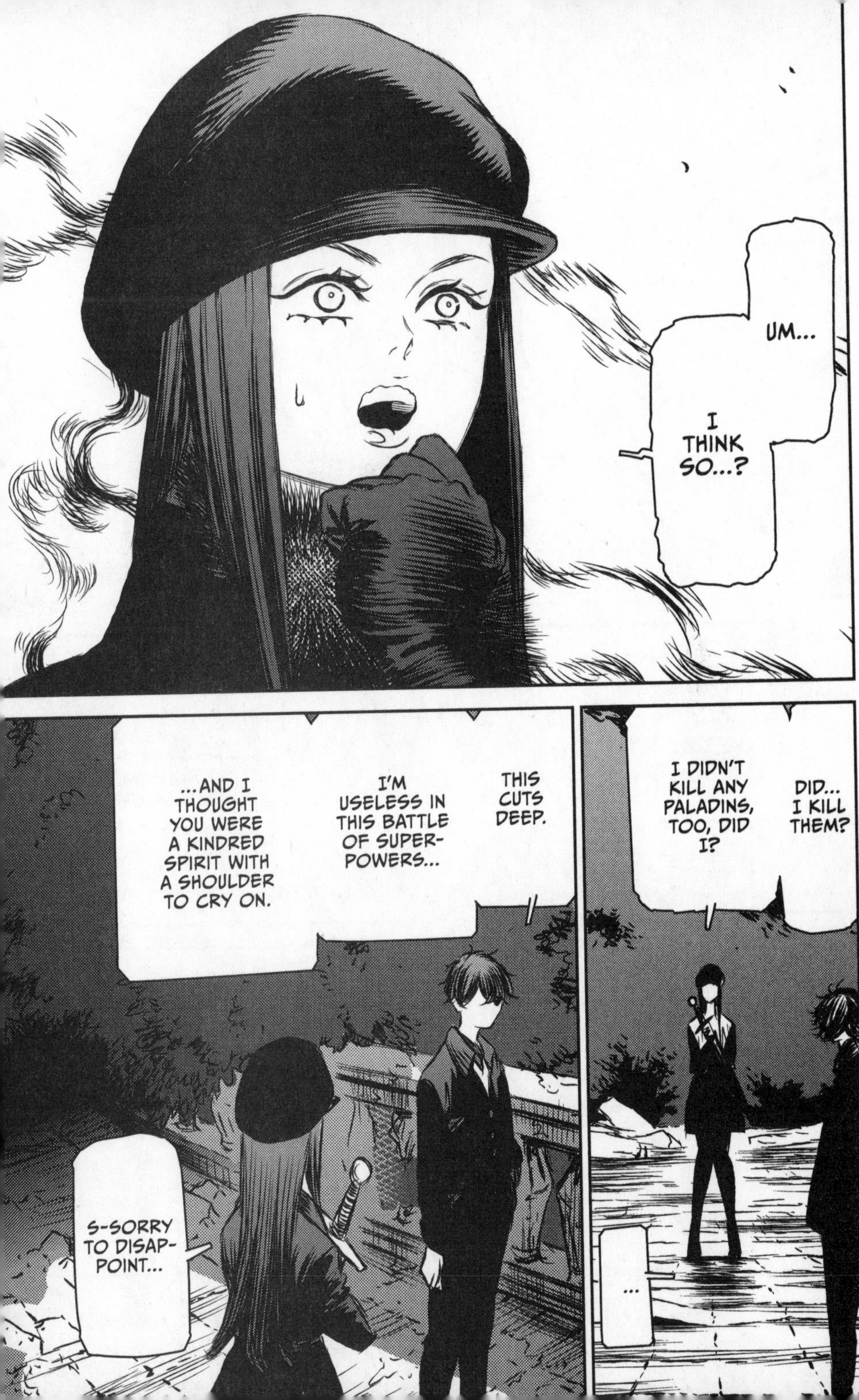
UM...
I THINK SO...?
DID... I KILL THEM?
I DIDN'T KILL ANY PALADINS, TOO, DID I?
...
THIS CUTS DEEP.
I'M USELESS IN THIS BATTLE OF SUPER-POWERS...
...AND I THOUGHT YOU WERE A KINDRED SPIRIT WITH A SHOULDER TO CRY ON.
S-SORRY TO DISAP-POINT...

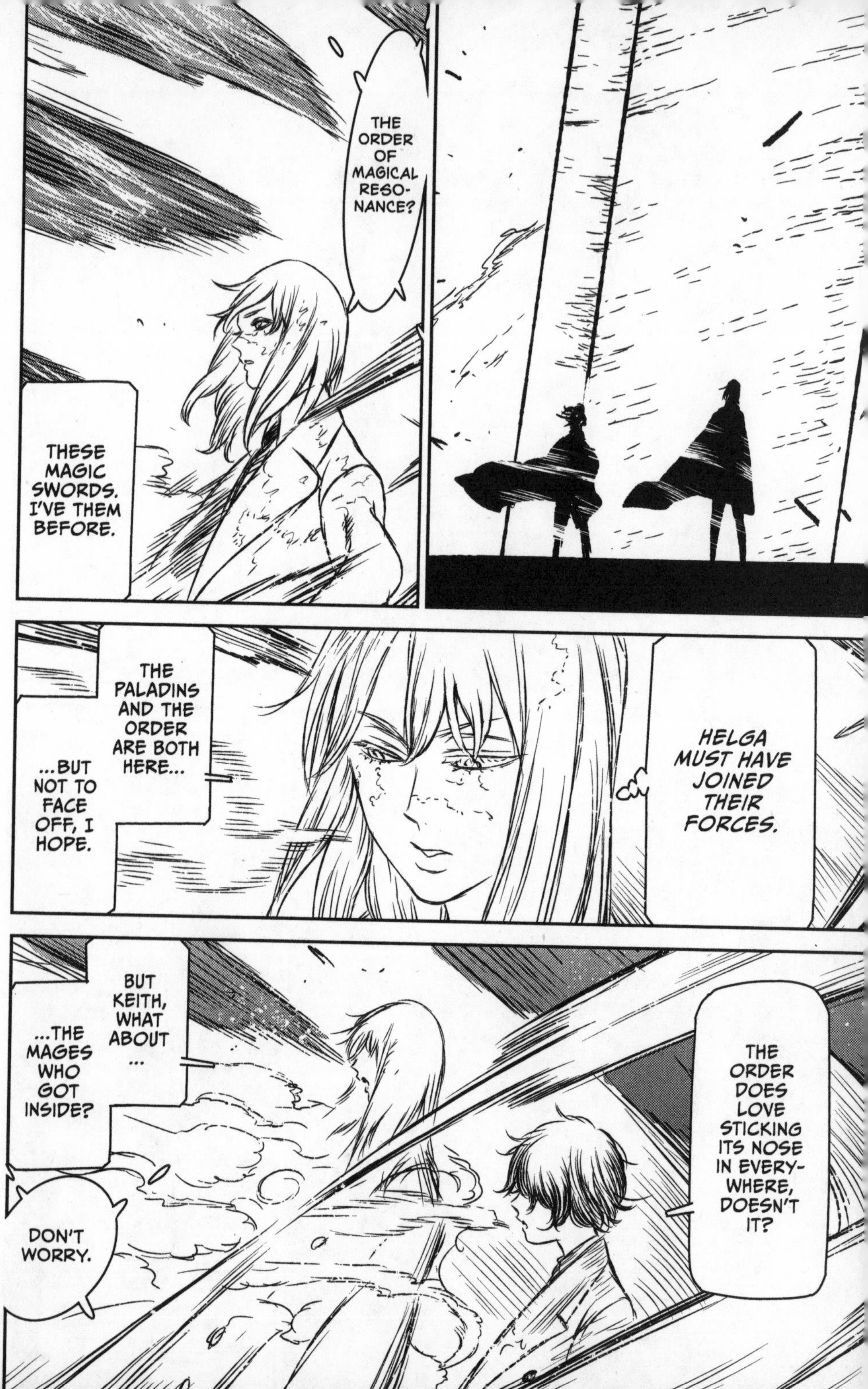
THE ORDER OF MAGICAL RESONANCE?
THESE MAGIC SWORDS. I'VE THEM BEFORE.
HELGA MUST HAVE JOINED THEIR FORCES.
THE PALADINS AND THE ORDER ARE BOTH HERE...
...BUT NOT TO FACE OFF, I HOPE.
THE ORDER DOES LOVE STICKING ITS NOSE IN EVERY-WHERE, DOESN'T IT?
BUT KEITH, WHAT ABOUT ...
...THE MAGES WHO GOT INSIDE?
DON'T WORRY.

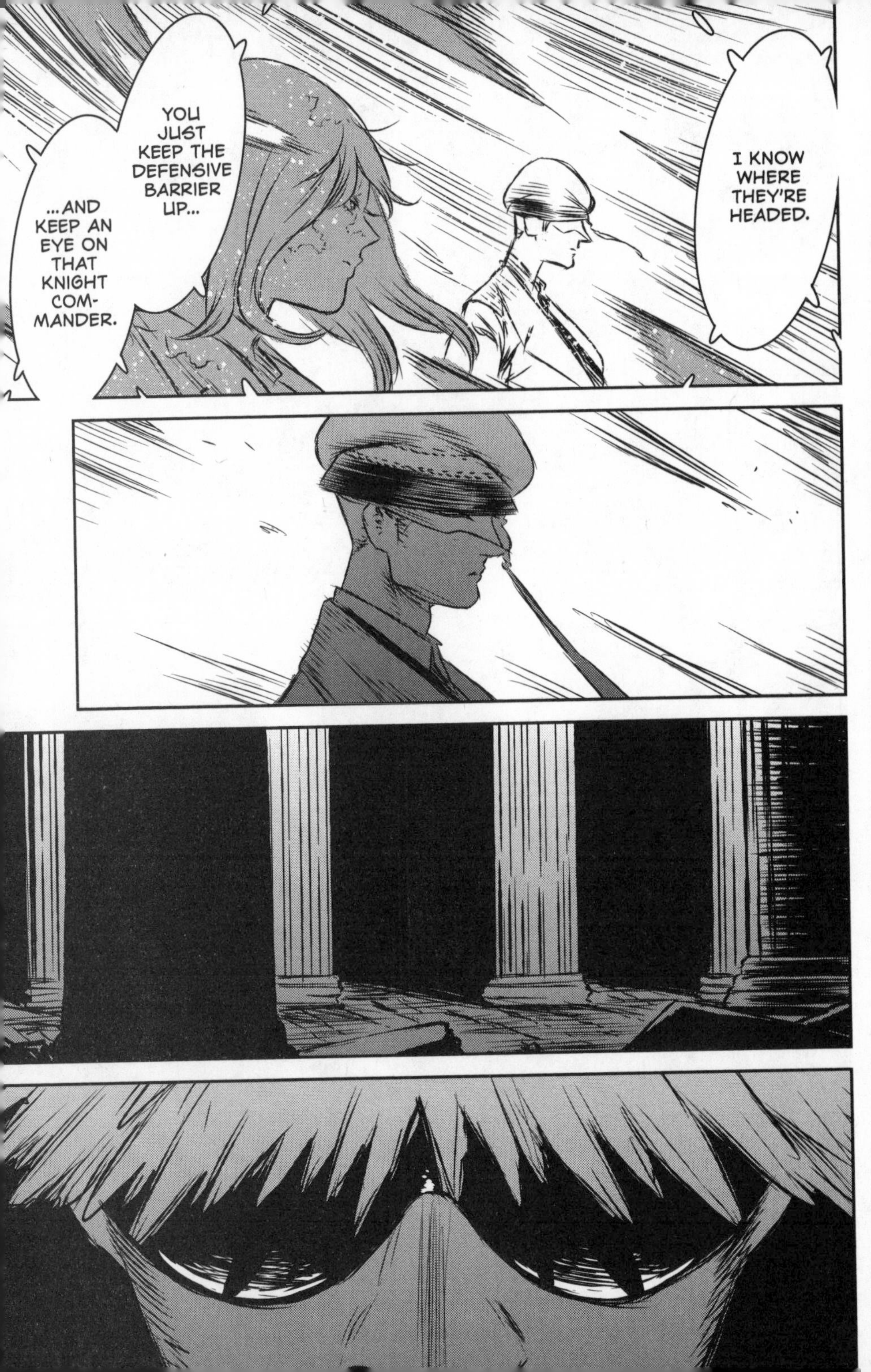
I KNOW WHERE THEY'RE HEADED.
YOU JUST KEEP THE DEFENSIVE BARRIER UP...
...AND KEEP AN EYE ON THAT KNIGHT COM-MANDER.

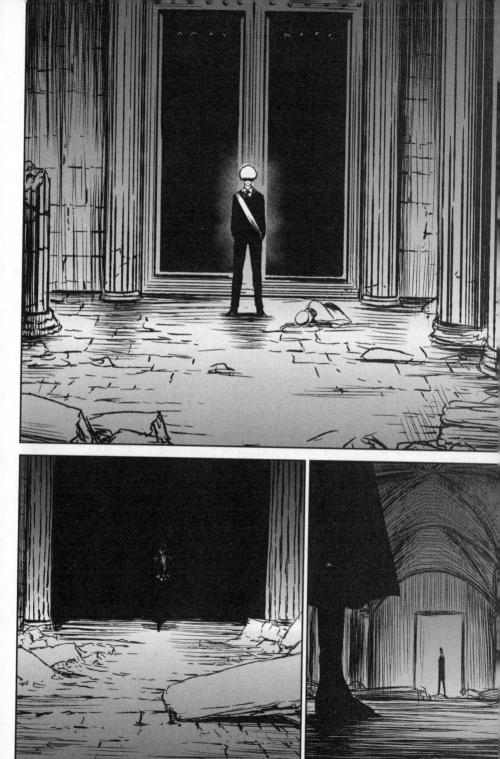

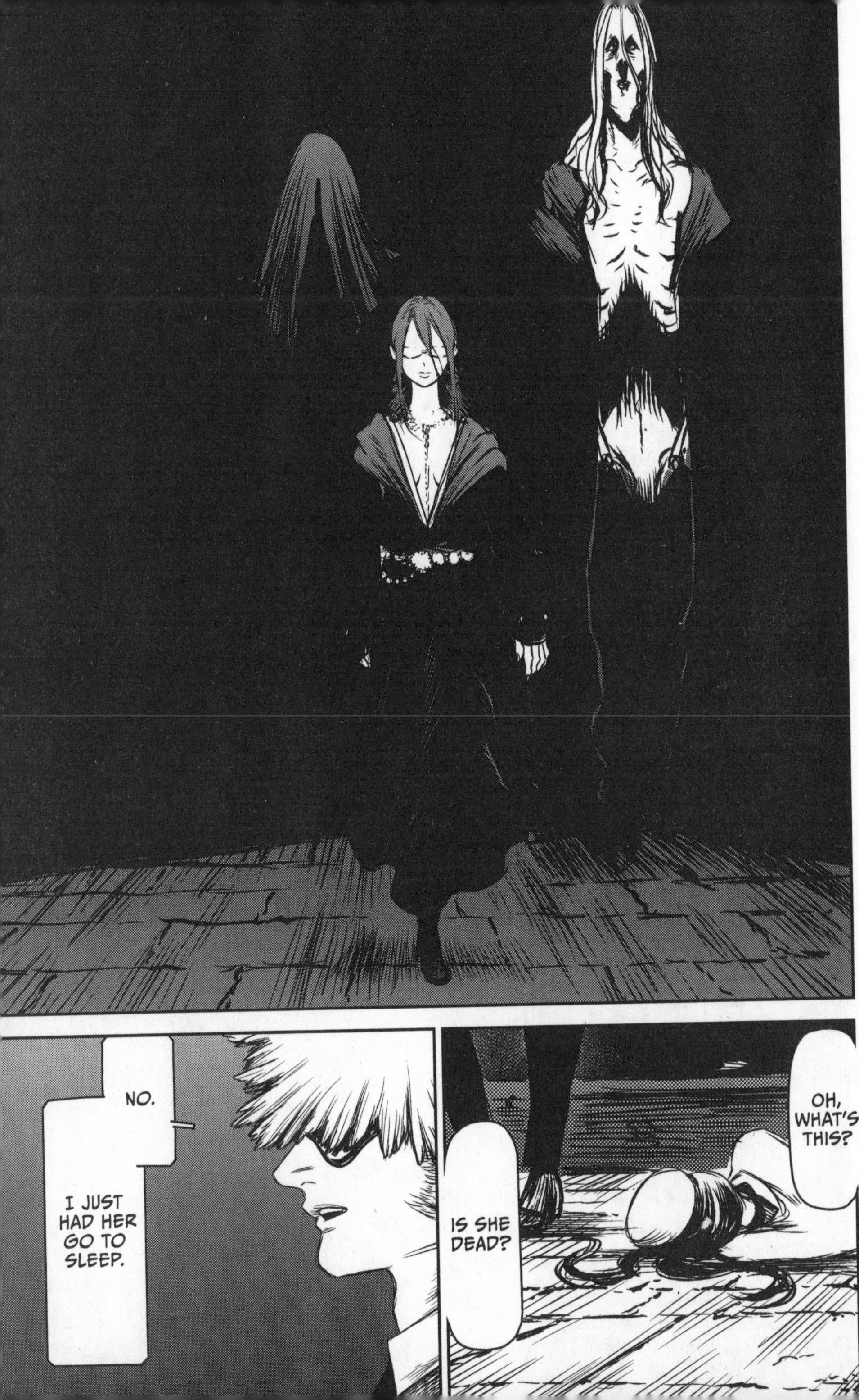
OH, WHAT'S THIS?
IS SHE DEAD?
NO.
I JUST HAD HER GO TO SLEEP.

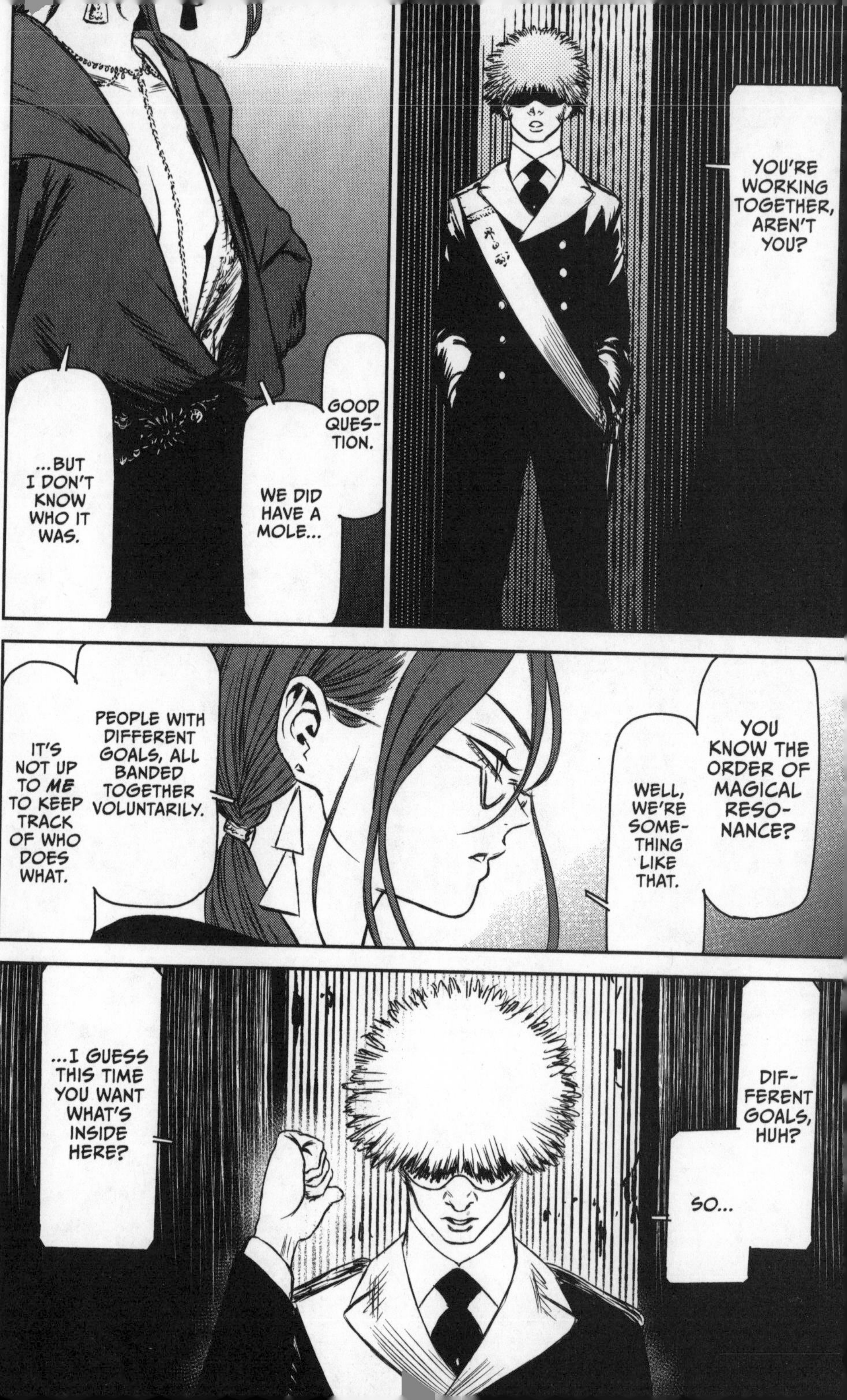
YOU'RE WORKING TOGETHER, AREN'T YOU?
GOOD QUESTION.
WE DID HAVE A MOLE...
...BUT I DON'T KNOW WHO IT WAS.
YOU KNOW THE ORDER OF MAGICAL RESONANCE?
WELL, WE'RE SOMETHING LIKE THAT.
PEOPLE WITH DIFFERENT GOALS, ALL BANDED TOGETHER VOLUNTARILY.
IT'S NOT UP TO *ME* TO KEEP TRACK OF WHO DOES WHAT.
DIFFERENT GOALS, HUH?
SO...
...I GUESS THIS TIME YOU WANT WHAT'S INSIDE HERE?

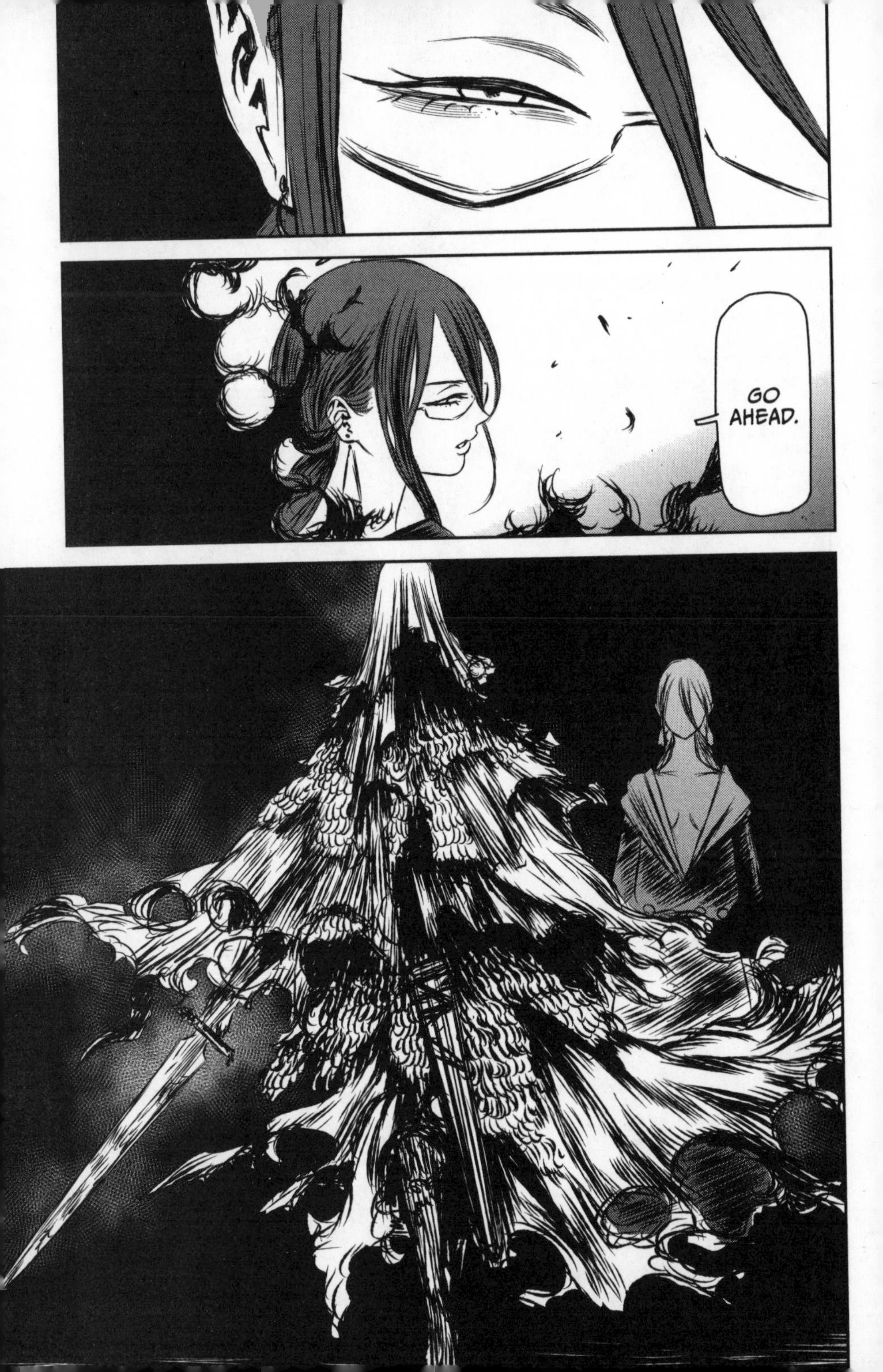
GO AHEAD.

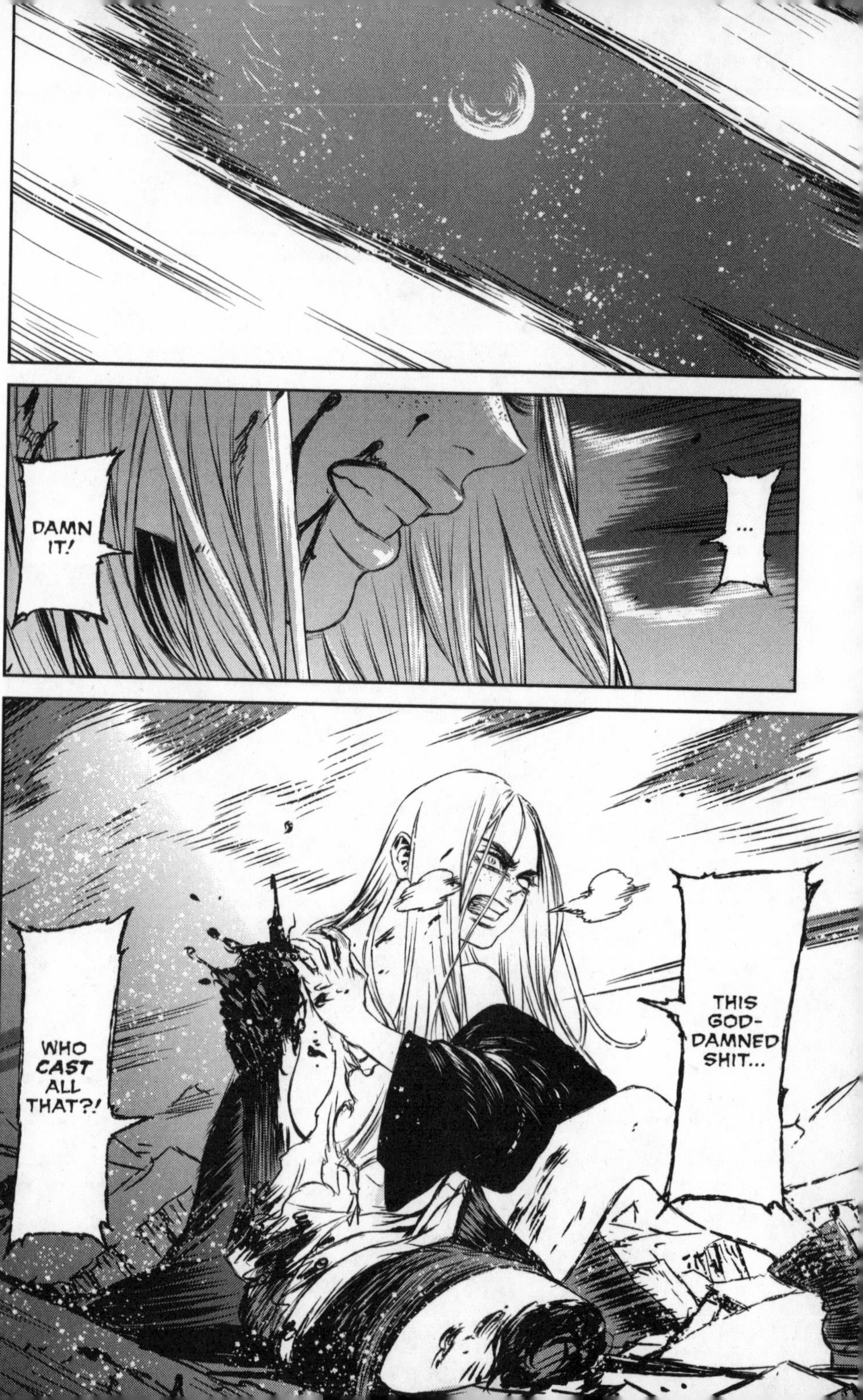
...
DAMN IT!
THIS GOD-DAMNED SHIT...
WHO CAST ALL THAT?!

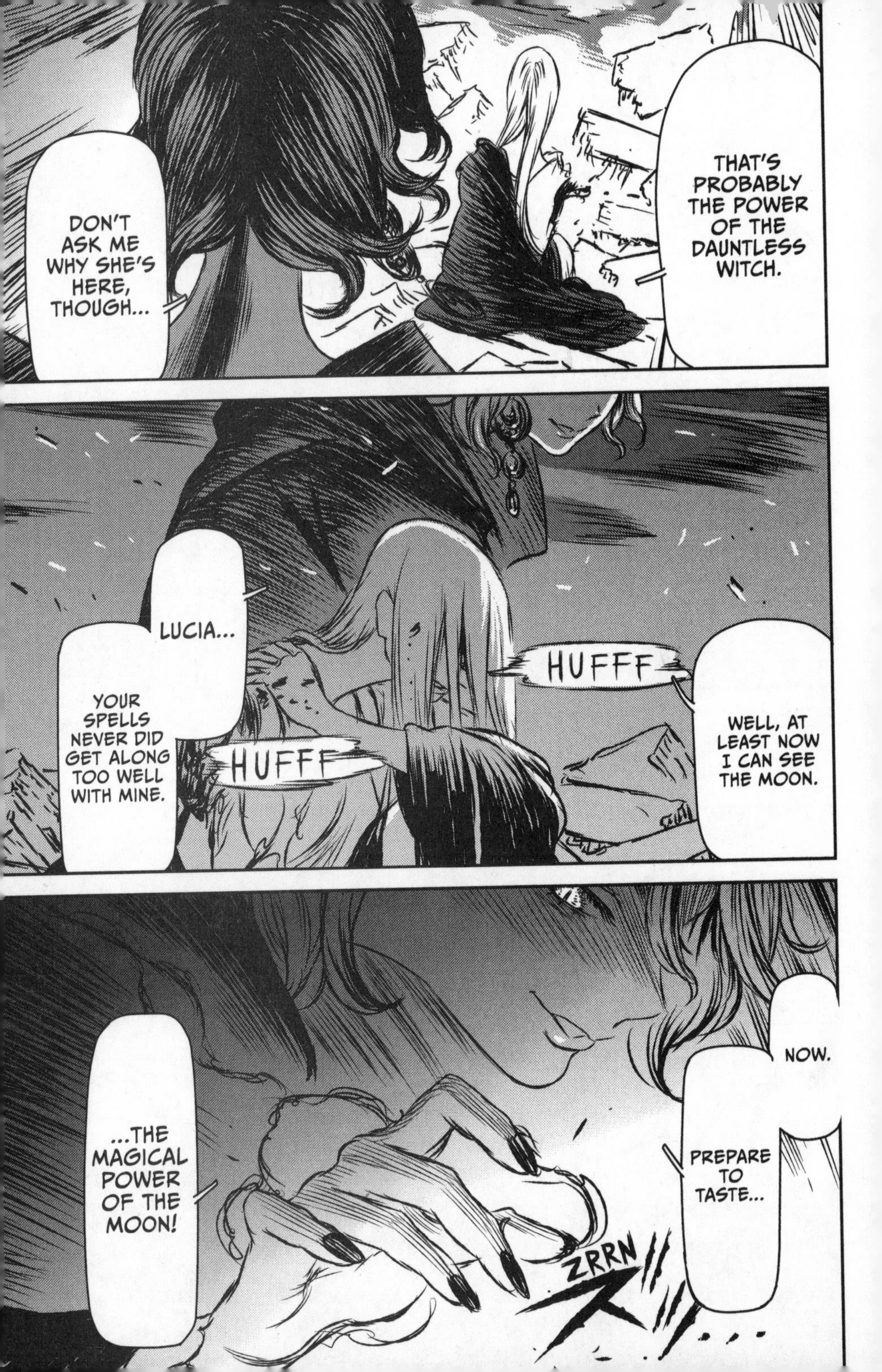
THAT'S PROBABLY THE POWER OF THE DAUNTLESS WITCH.
DON'T ASK ME WHY SHE'S HERE, THOUGH...
WELL, AT LEAST NOW I CAN SEE THE MOON.
HUFFF
LUCIA...
HUFFF
YOUR SPELLS NEVER DID GET ALONG TOO WELL WITH MINE.
NOW.
PREPARE TO TASTE...
...THE MAGICAL POWER OF THE MOON!
ZRRN

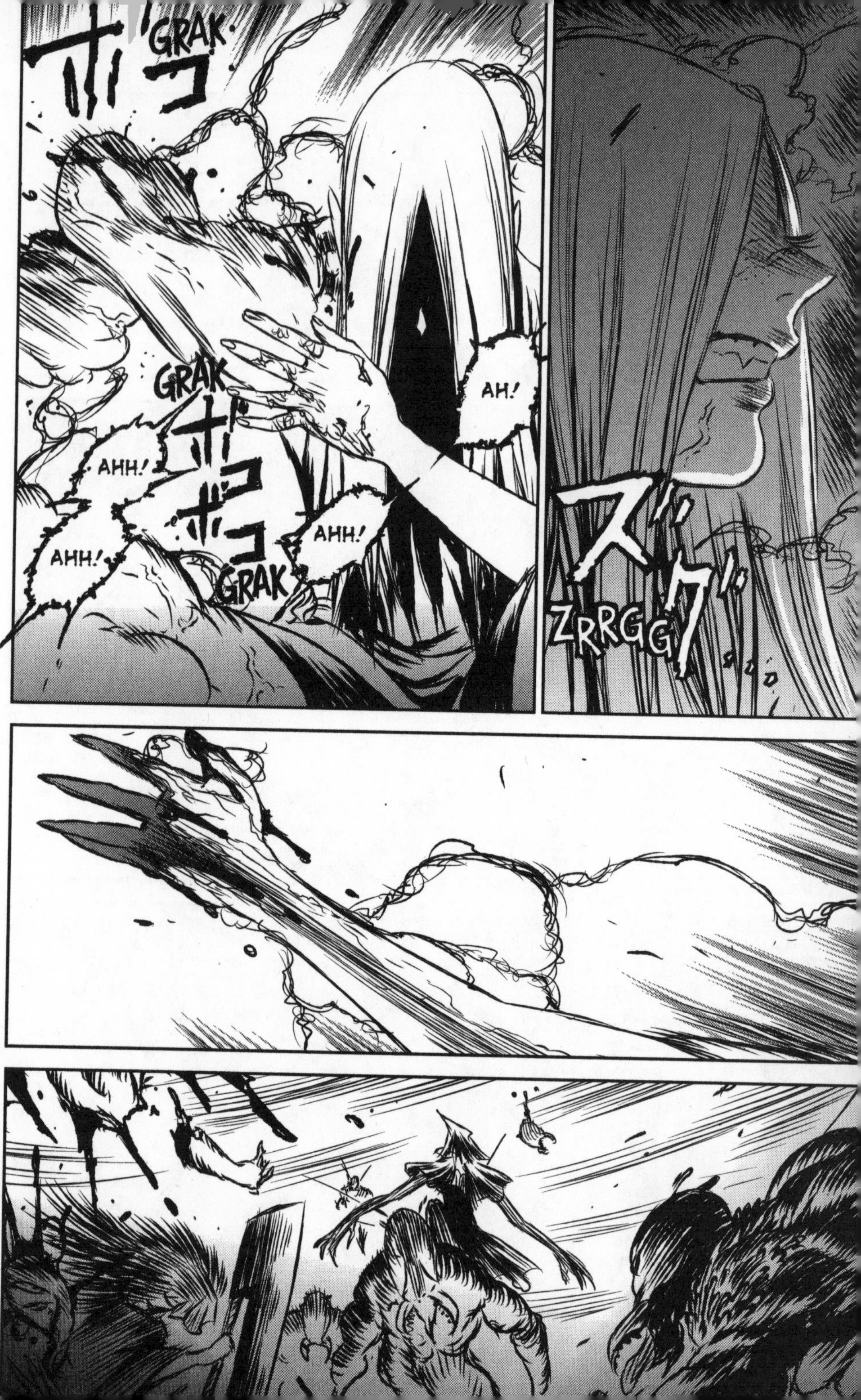
ZRRGG
GRAK
AH!
GRAK
AHH!
AHH!
AHH!
GRAK

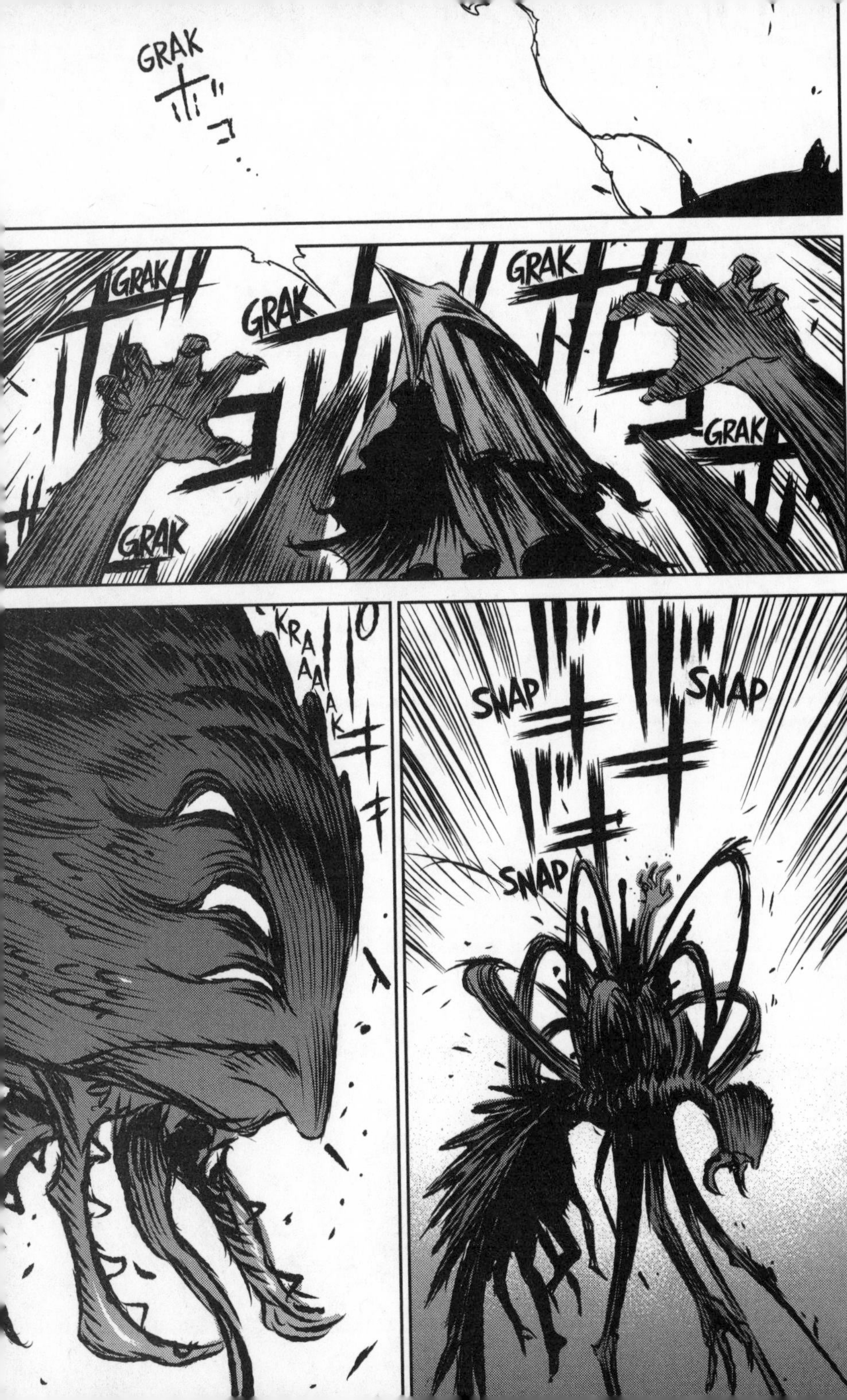
GRAK
GRAK
GRAK
GRAK
GRAK
GRAK
SNAP
SNAP
SNAP
KRAAAAAK

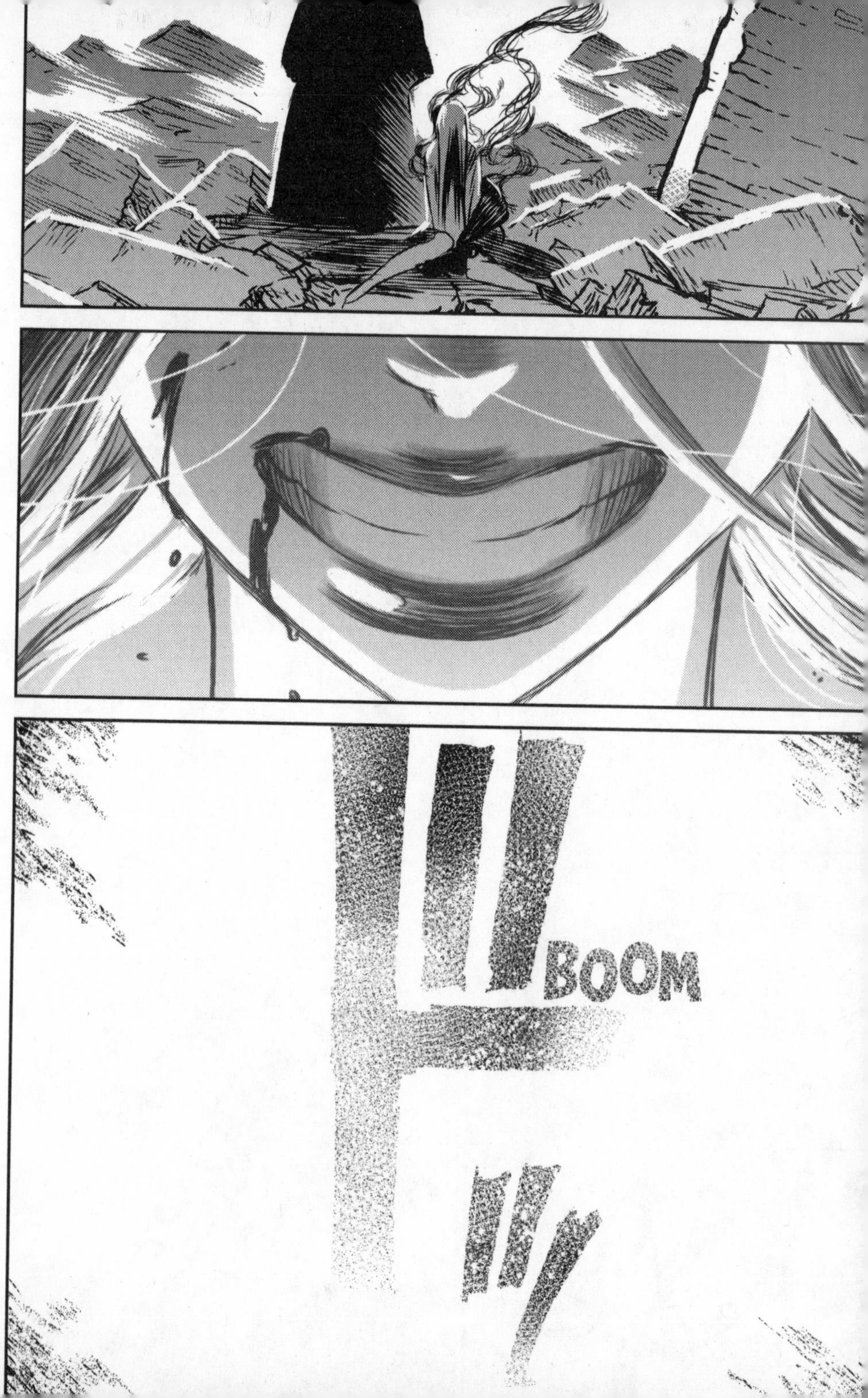
BOOM

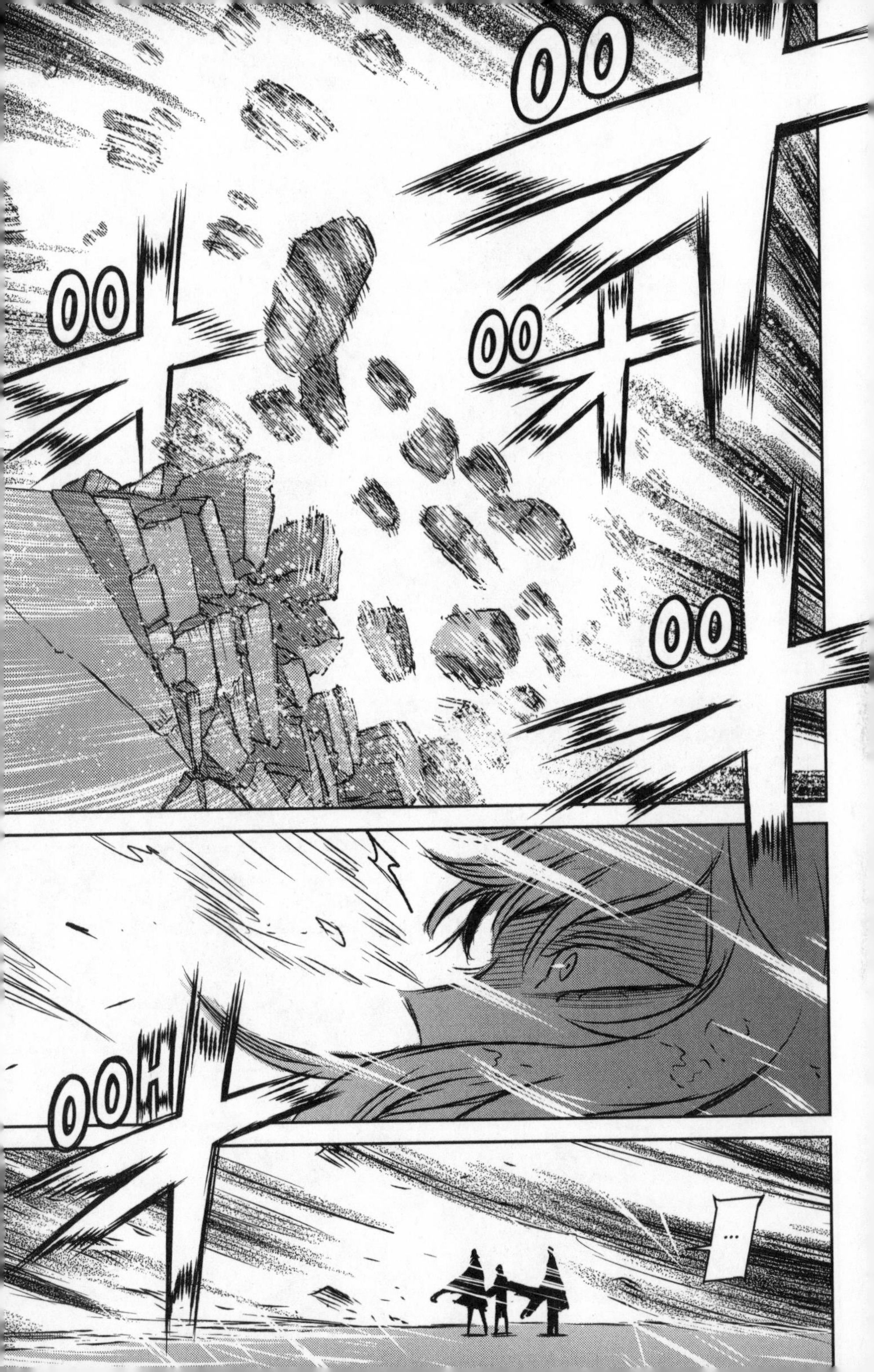
OO
OO
OO
OO
OOH
...

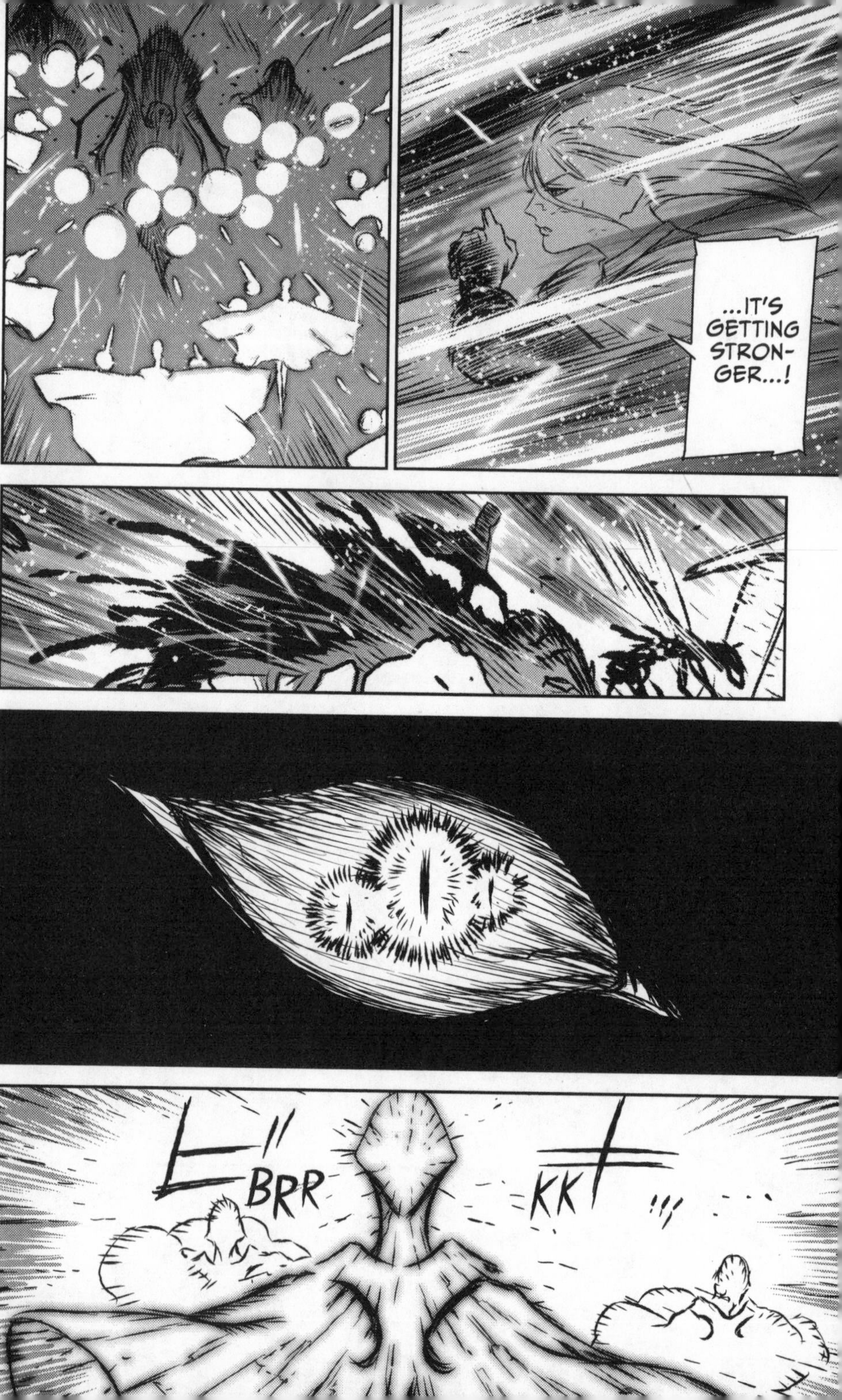
...IT'S GETTING STRON-GER...!
BRR
KK
!!!

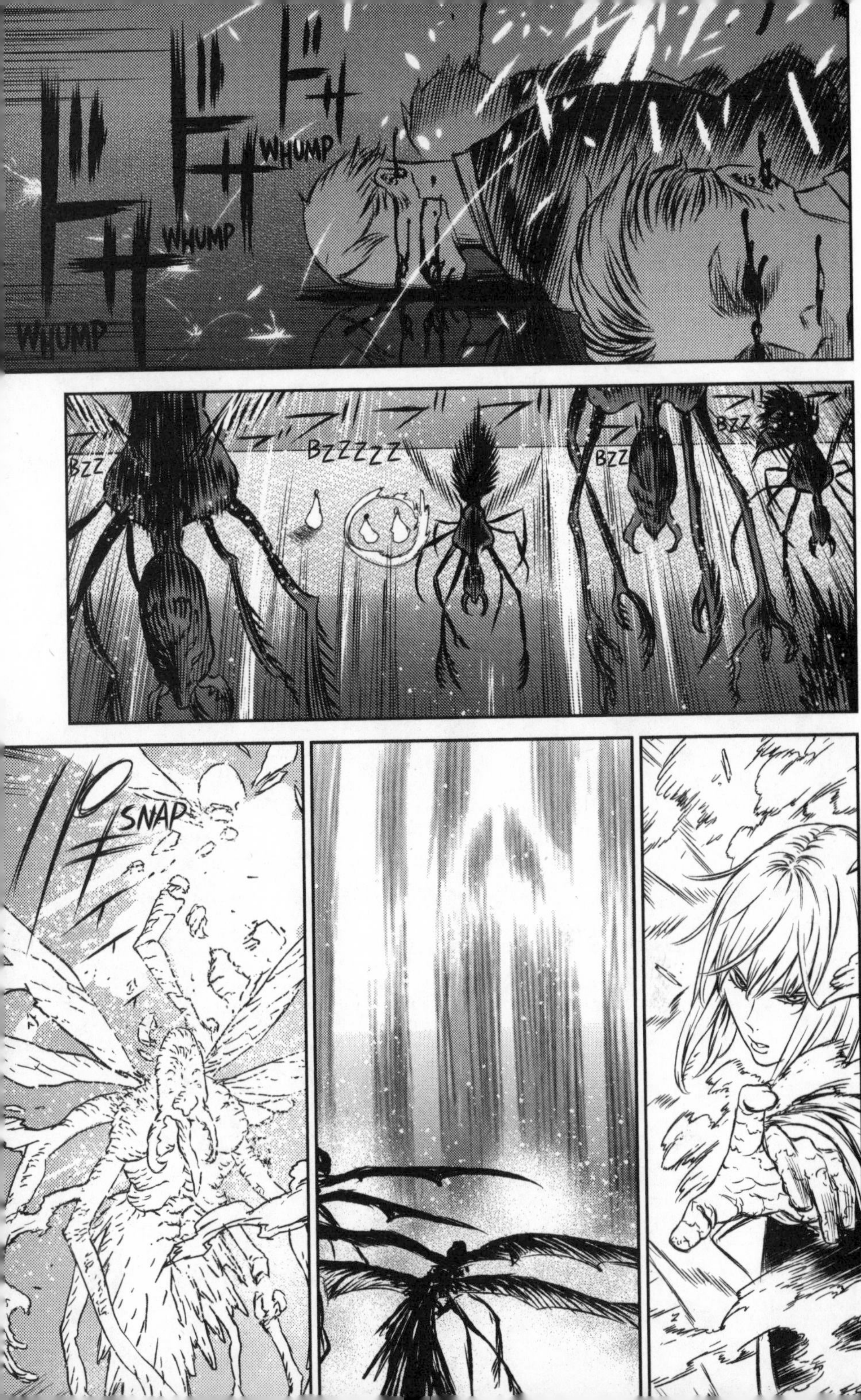
WHUMP
WHUMP
WHUMP
BZZ
BZZ
BZZZZZ
BZZ
SNAP

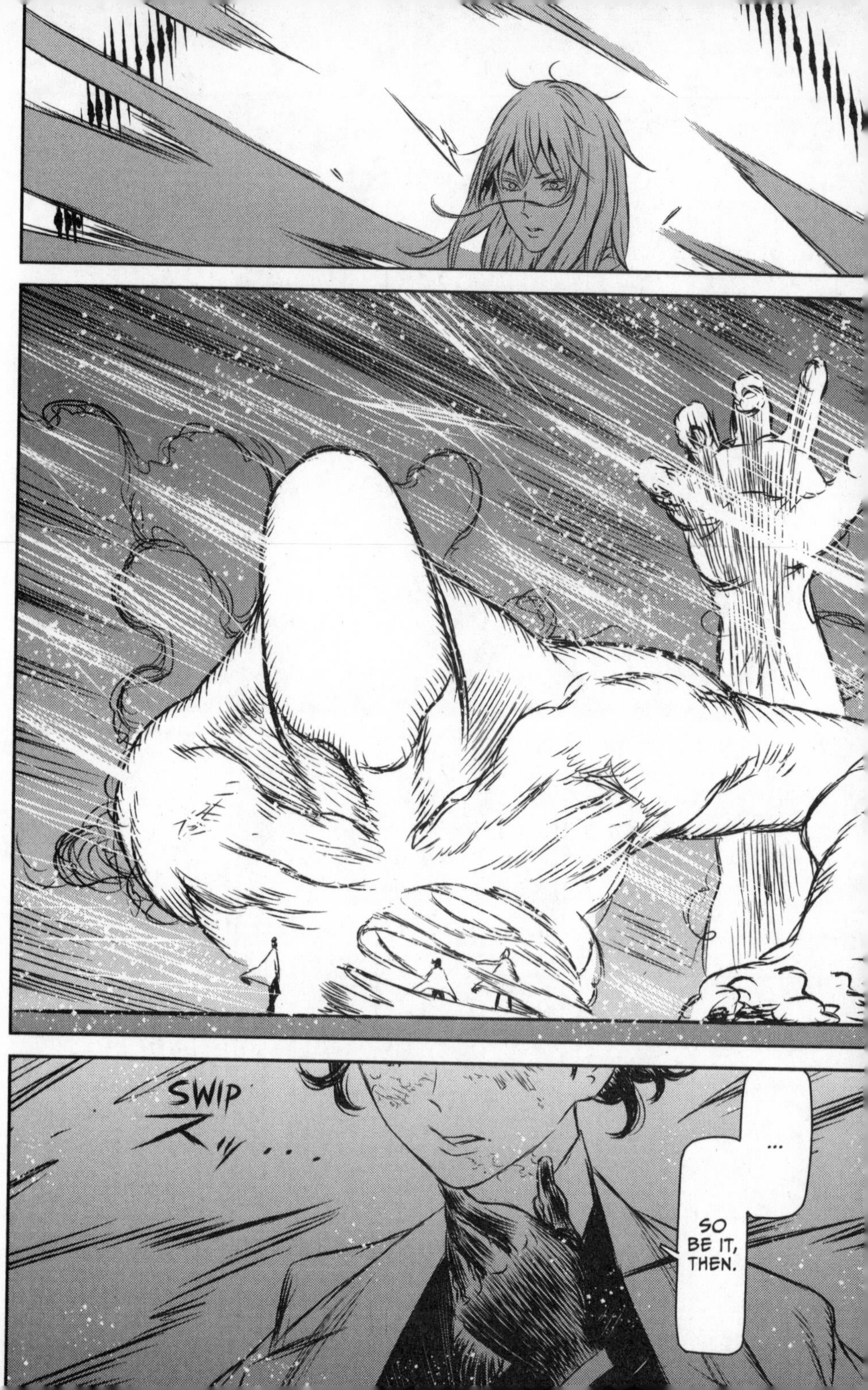
...
SO BE IT, THEN.
SWIP
スッ...

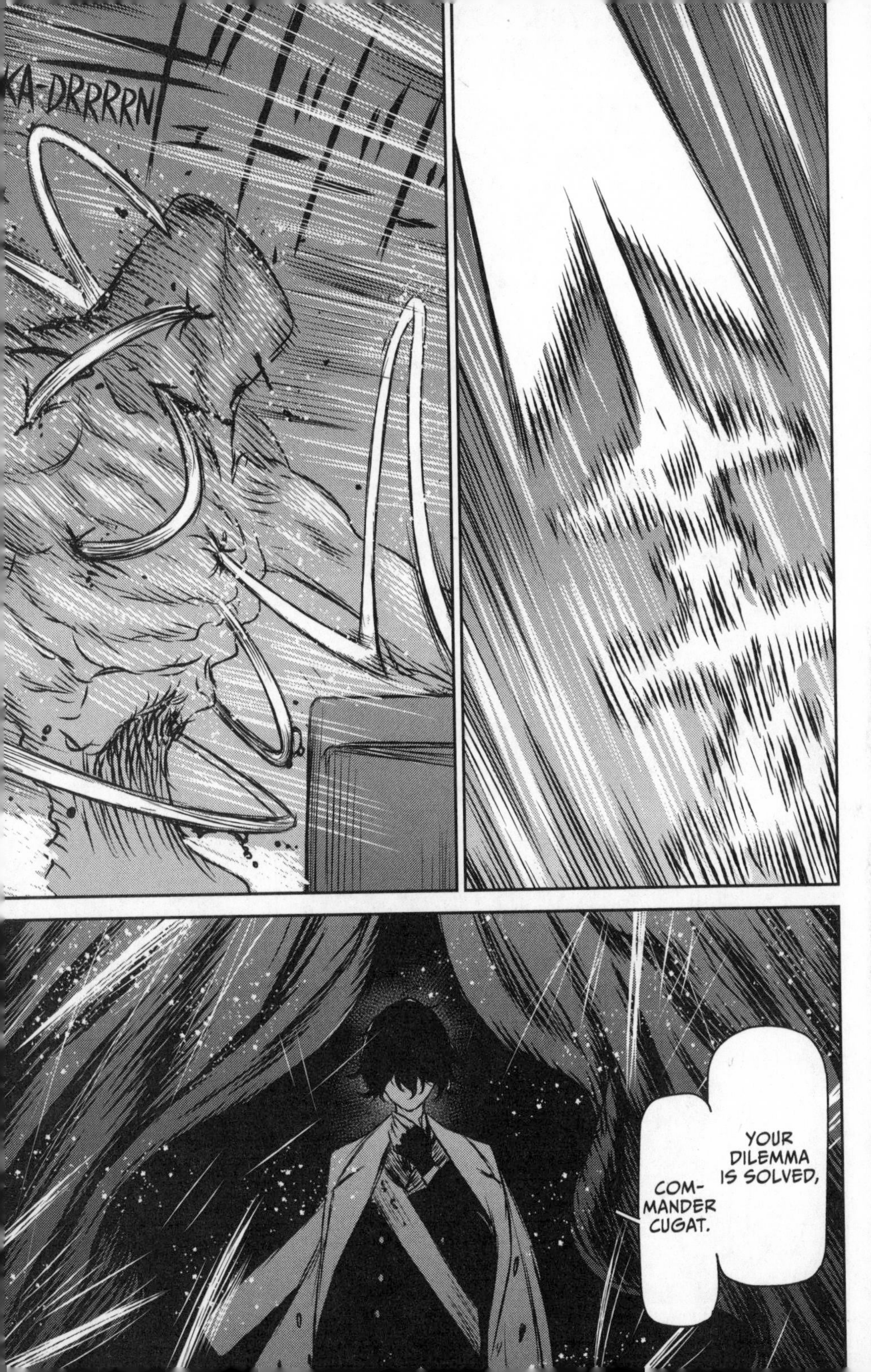
KA-DRRRRN
YOUR DILEMMA IS SOLVED,
COM-MANDER CUGAT.

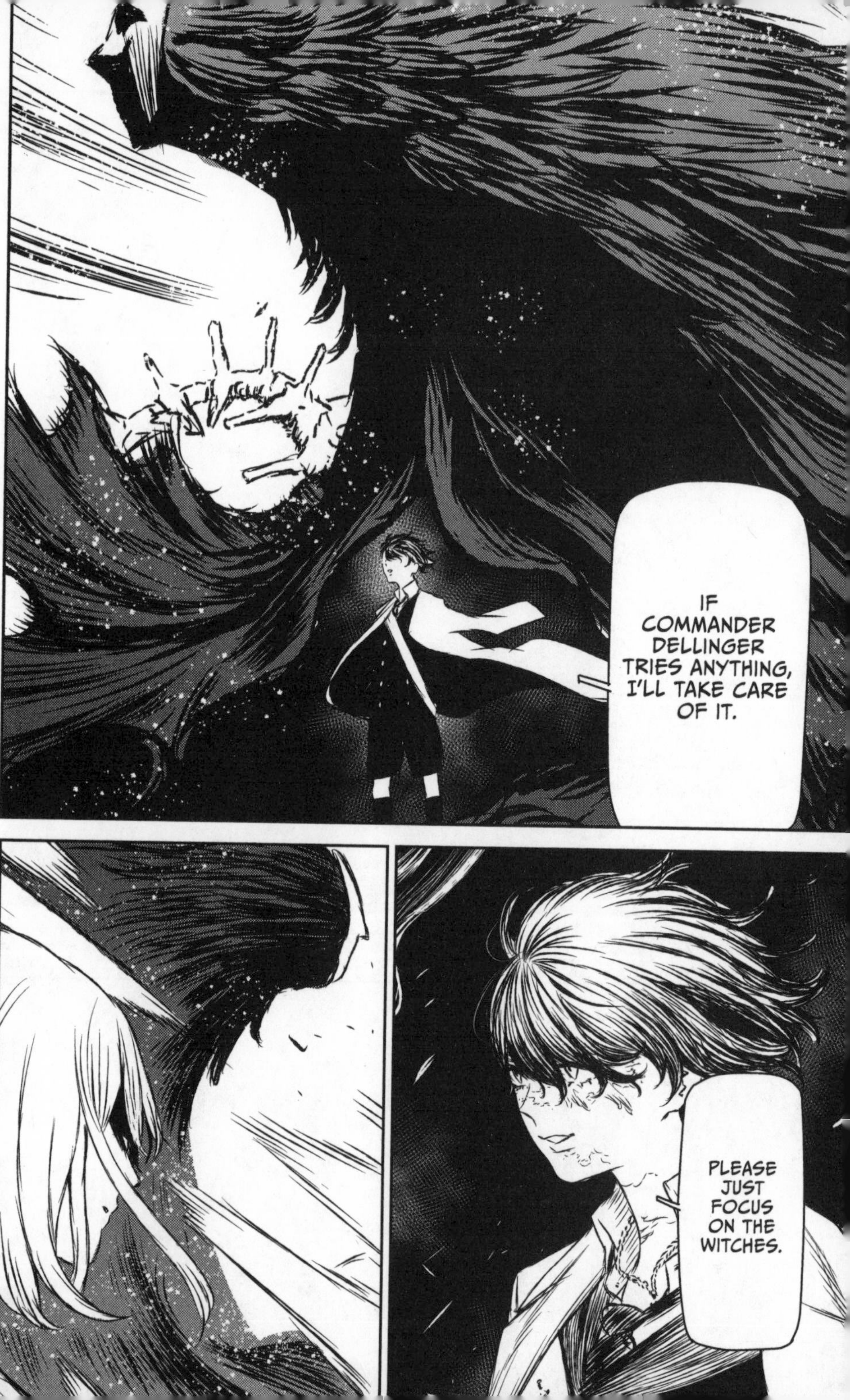
IF COMMANDER DELLINGER TRIES ANYTHING, I'LL TAKE CARE OF IT.
PLEASE JUST FOCUS ON THE WITCHES.

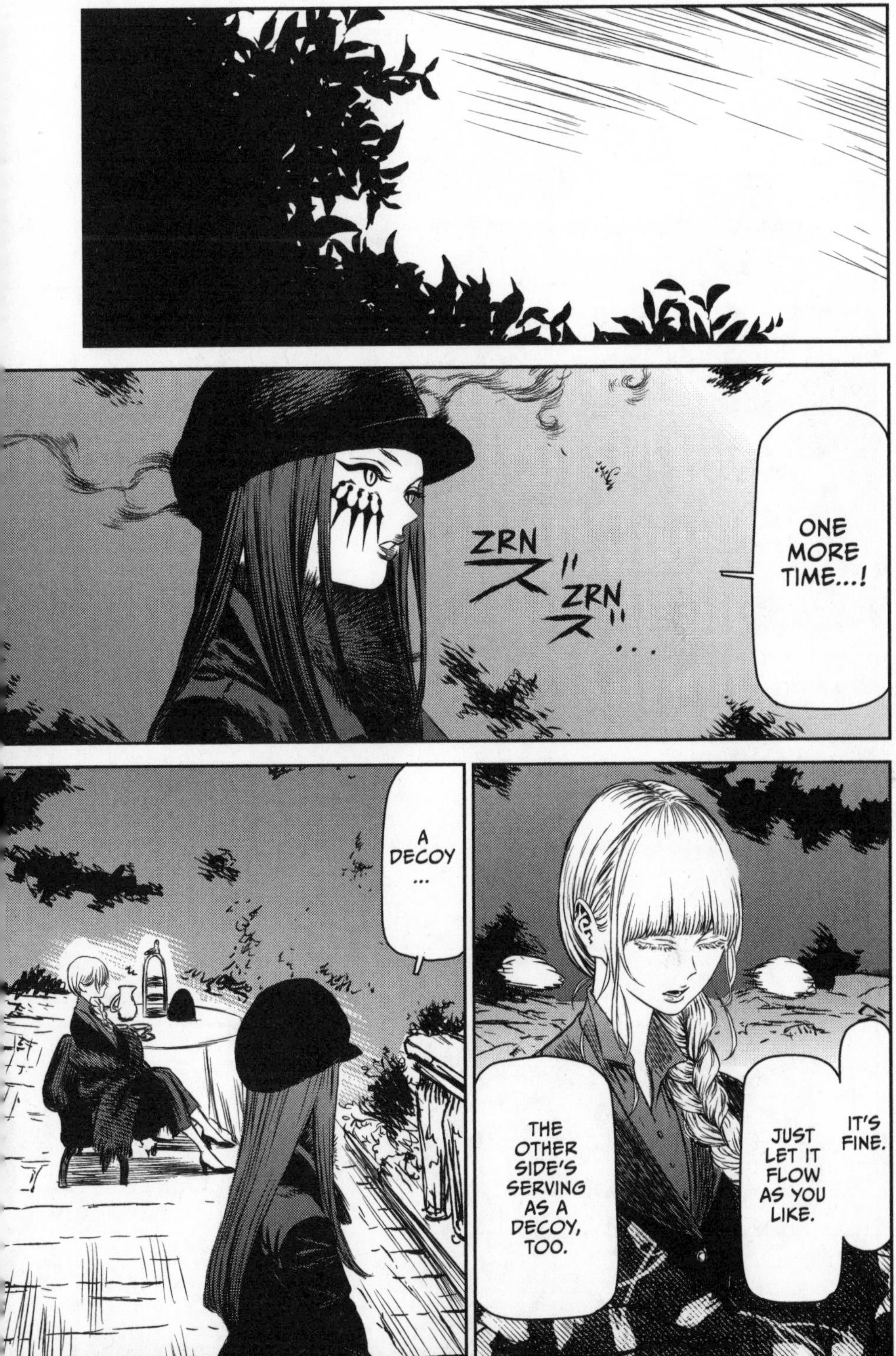
ONE MORE TIME...!
ZRN
ZRN...
IT'S FINE.
JUST LET IT FLOW AS YOU LIKE.
THE OTHER SIDE'S SERVING AS A DECOY, TOO.
A DECOY ...

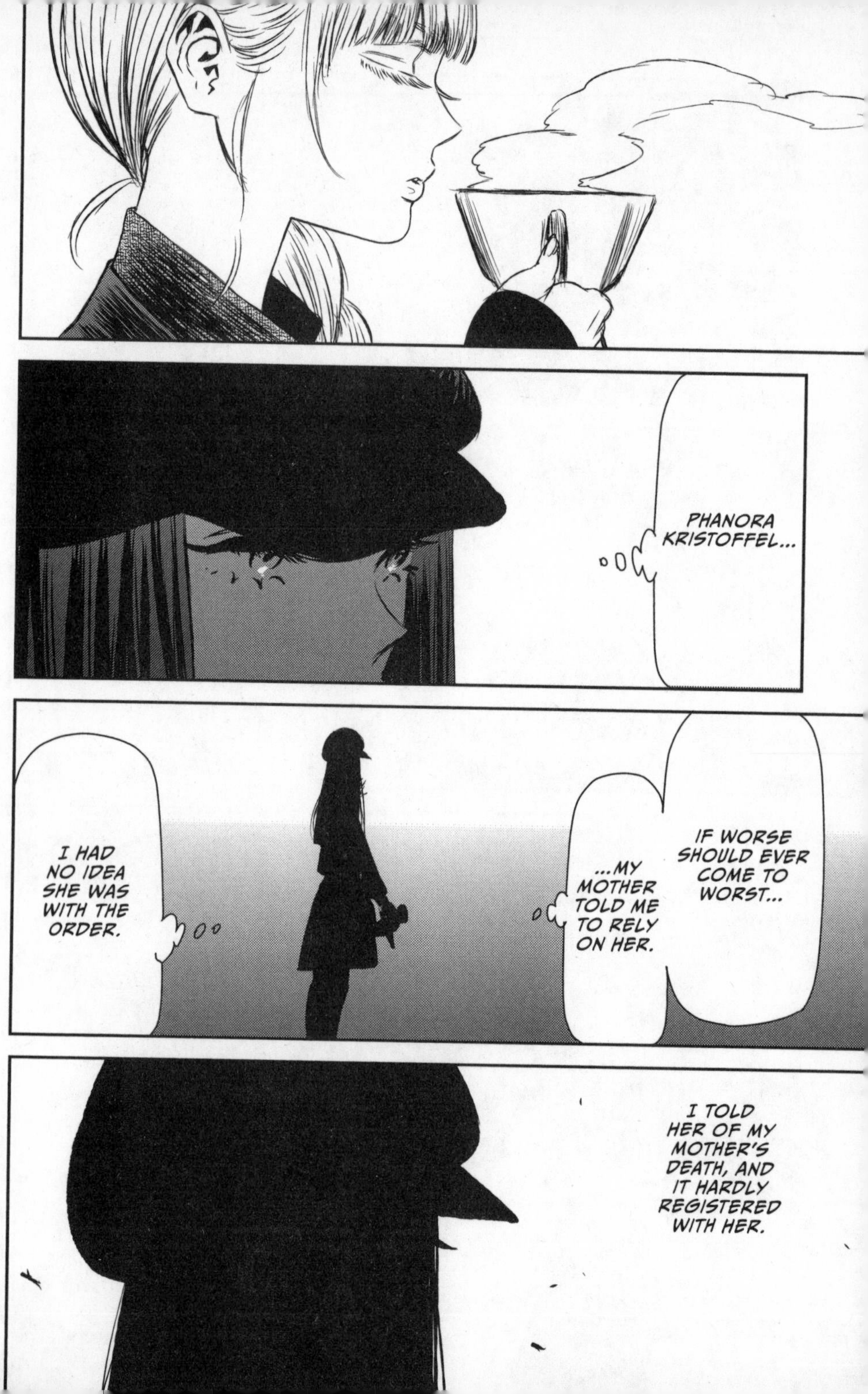
PHANORA KRISTOFFEL...
IF WORSE SHOULD EVER COME TO WORST...
...MY MOTHER TOLD ME TO RELY ON HER.
I HAD NO IDEA SHE WAS WITH THE ORDER.
I TOLD HER OF MY MOTHER'S DEATH, AND IT HARDLY REGISTERED WITH HER.

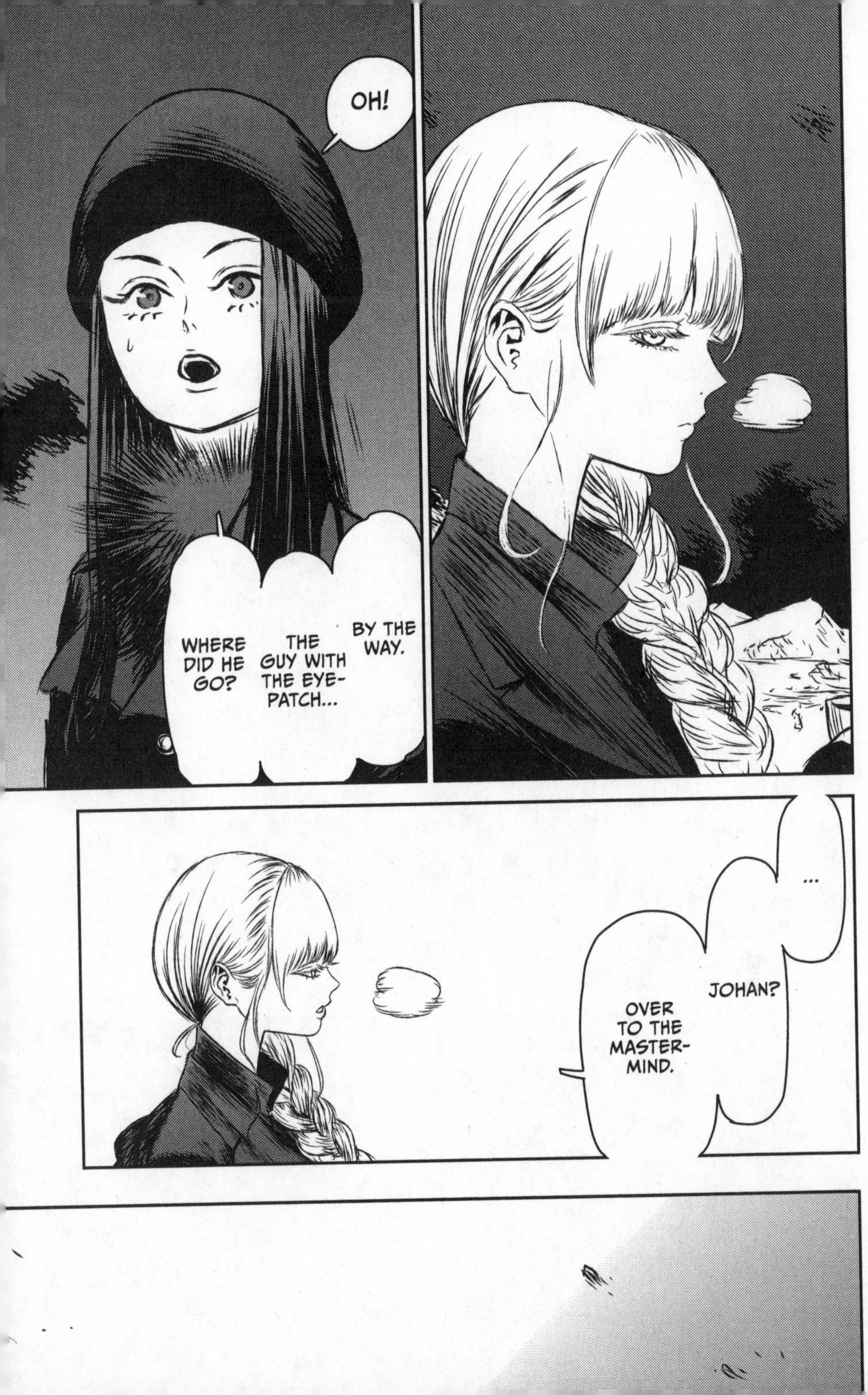
OH!
BY THE WAY.
THE GUY WITH THE EYE-PATCH...
WHERE DID HE GO?
...
JOHAN?
OVER TO THE MASTER-MIND.

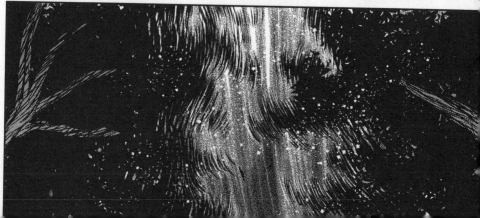

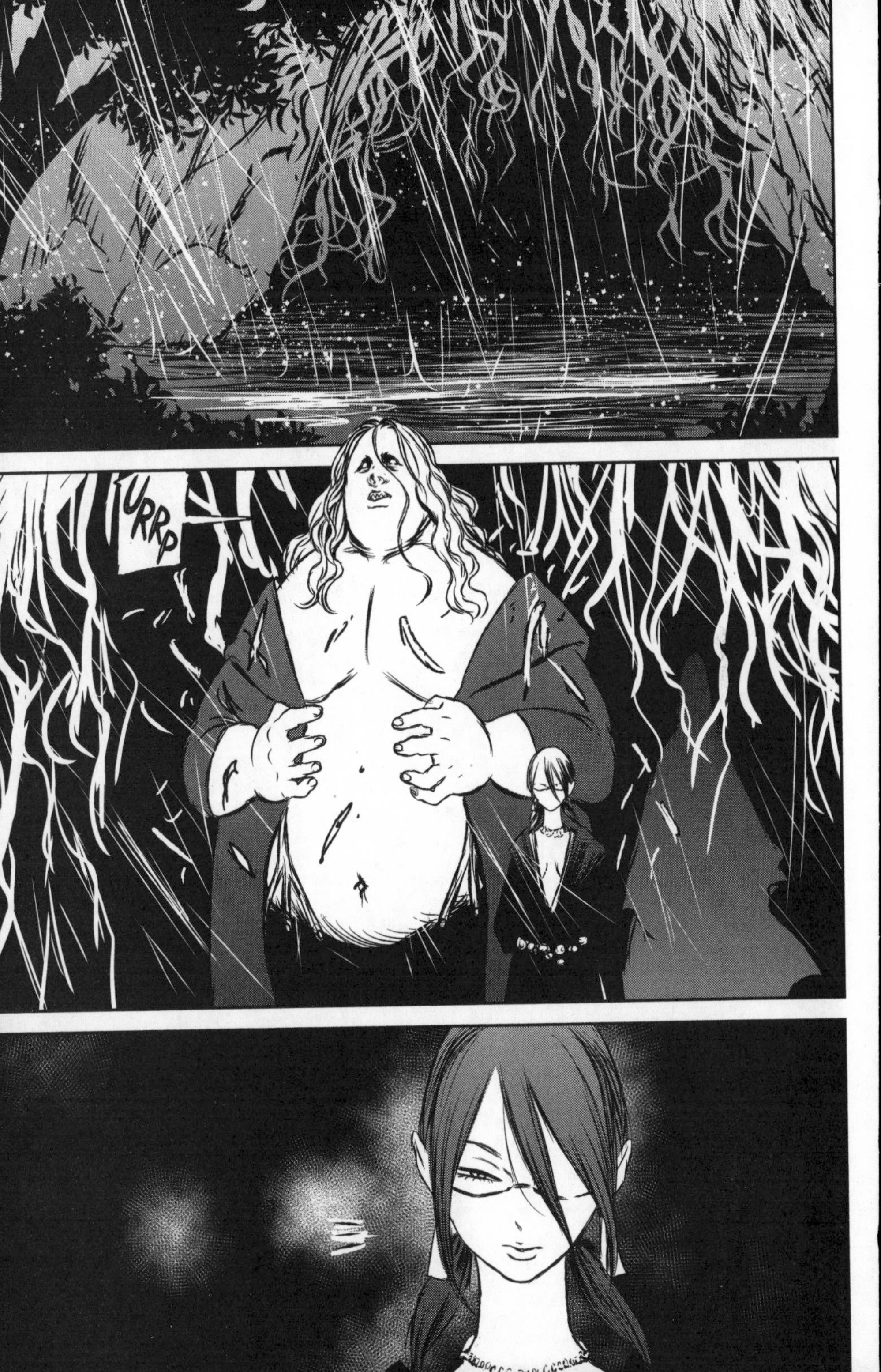
URRRP

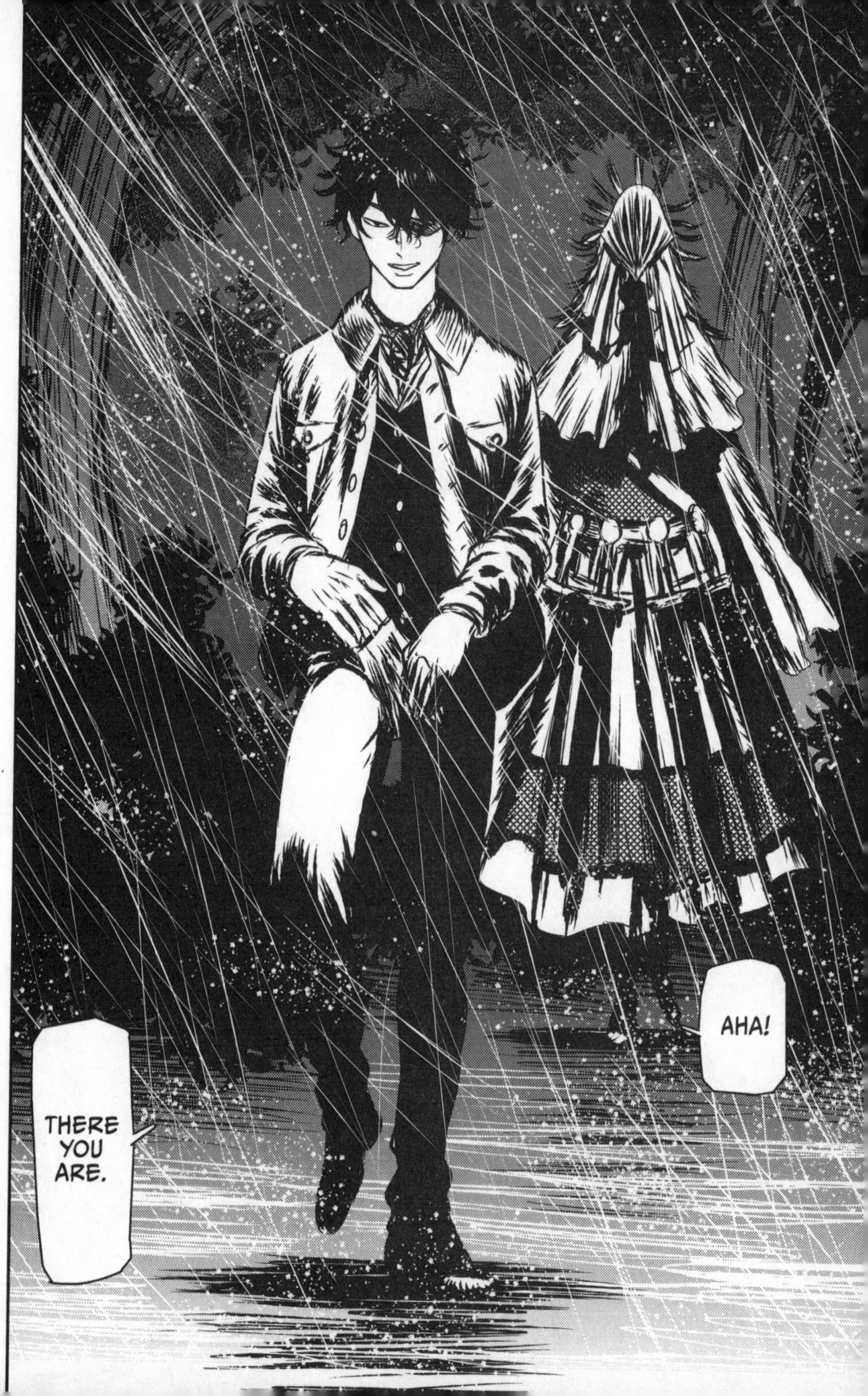
AHA!
THERE YOU ARE.

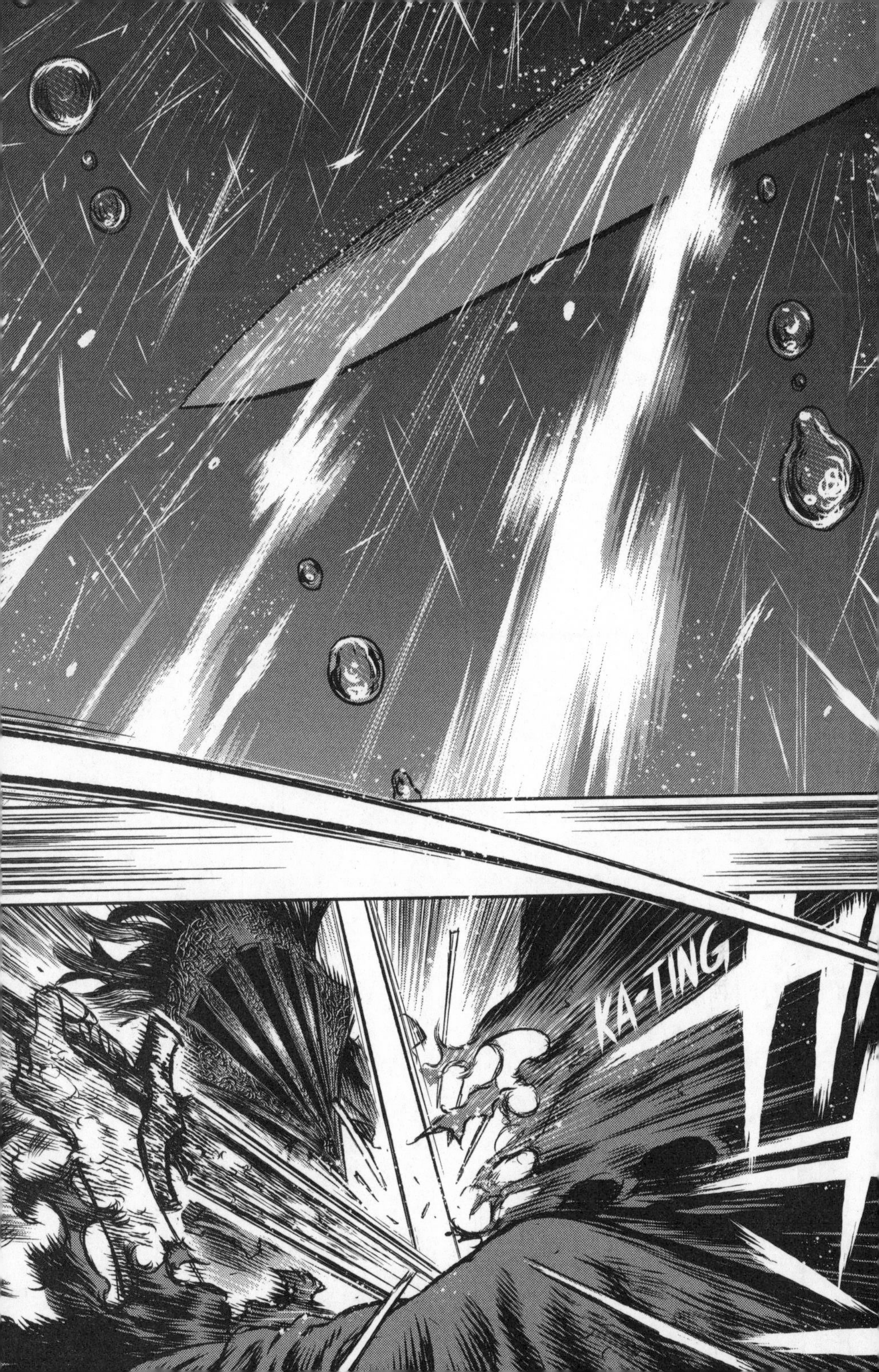
KA-TING

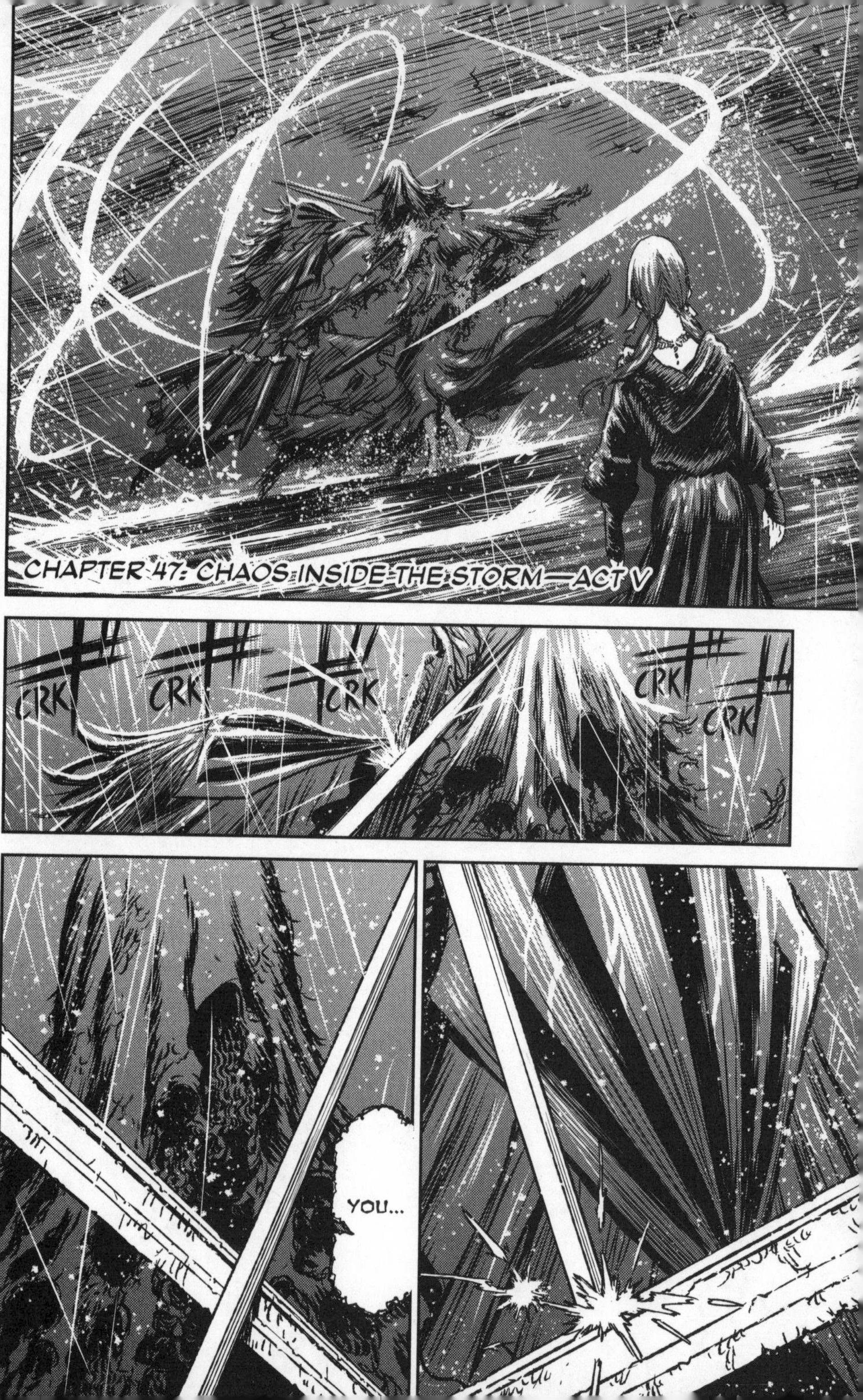
CHAPTER 47: CHAOS INSIDE THE STORM—ACT V
CRK
CRK
CRK
CRK
CRK
YOU...

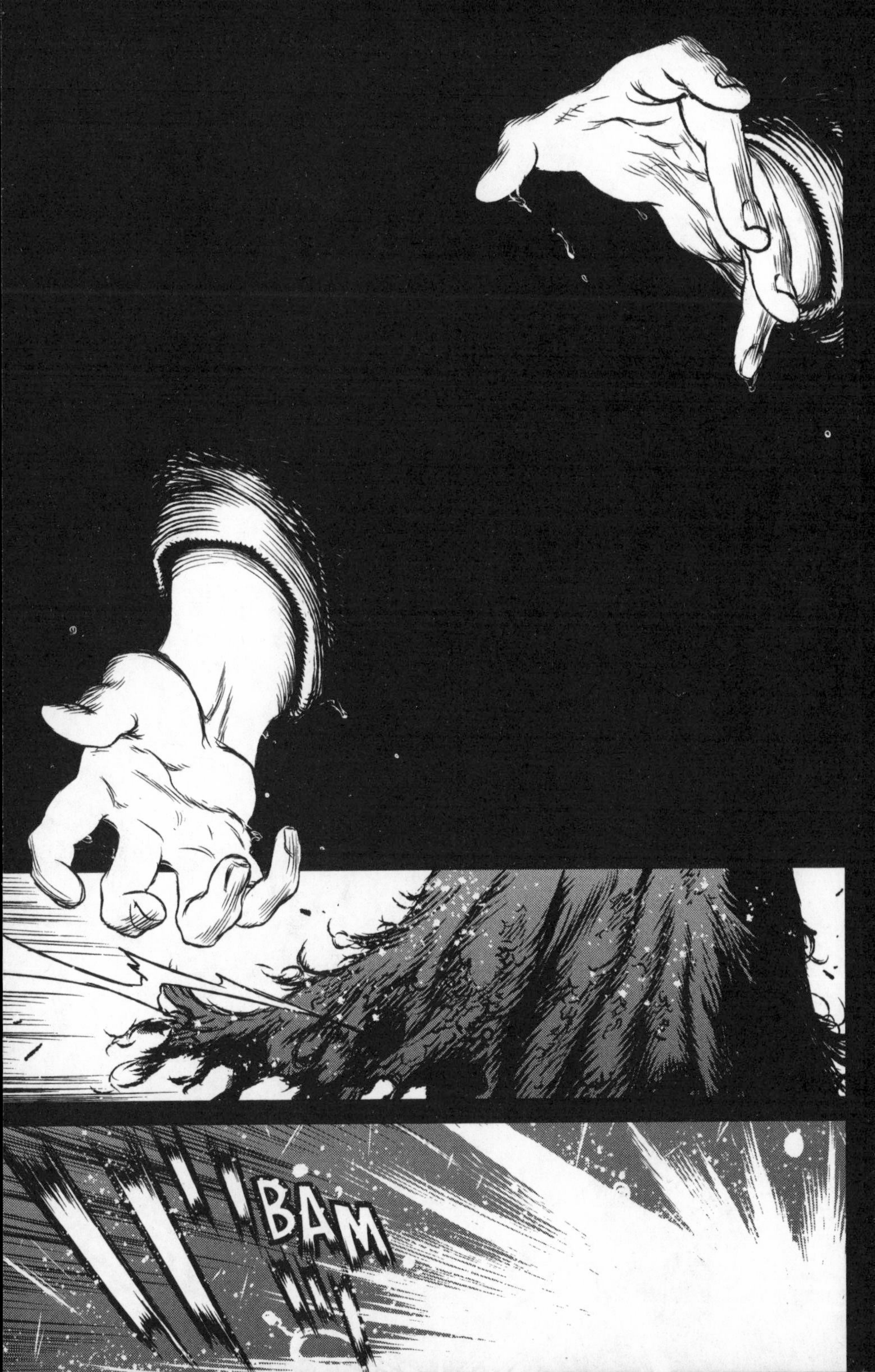
BAM

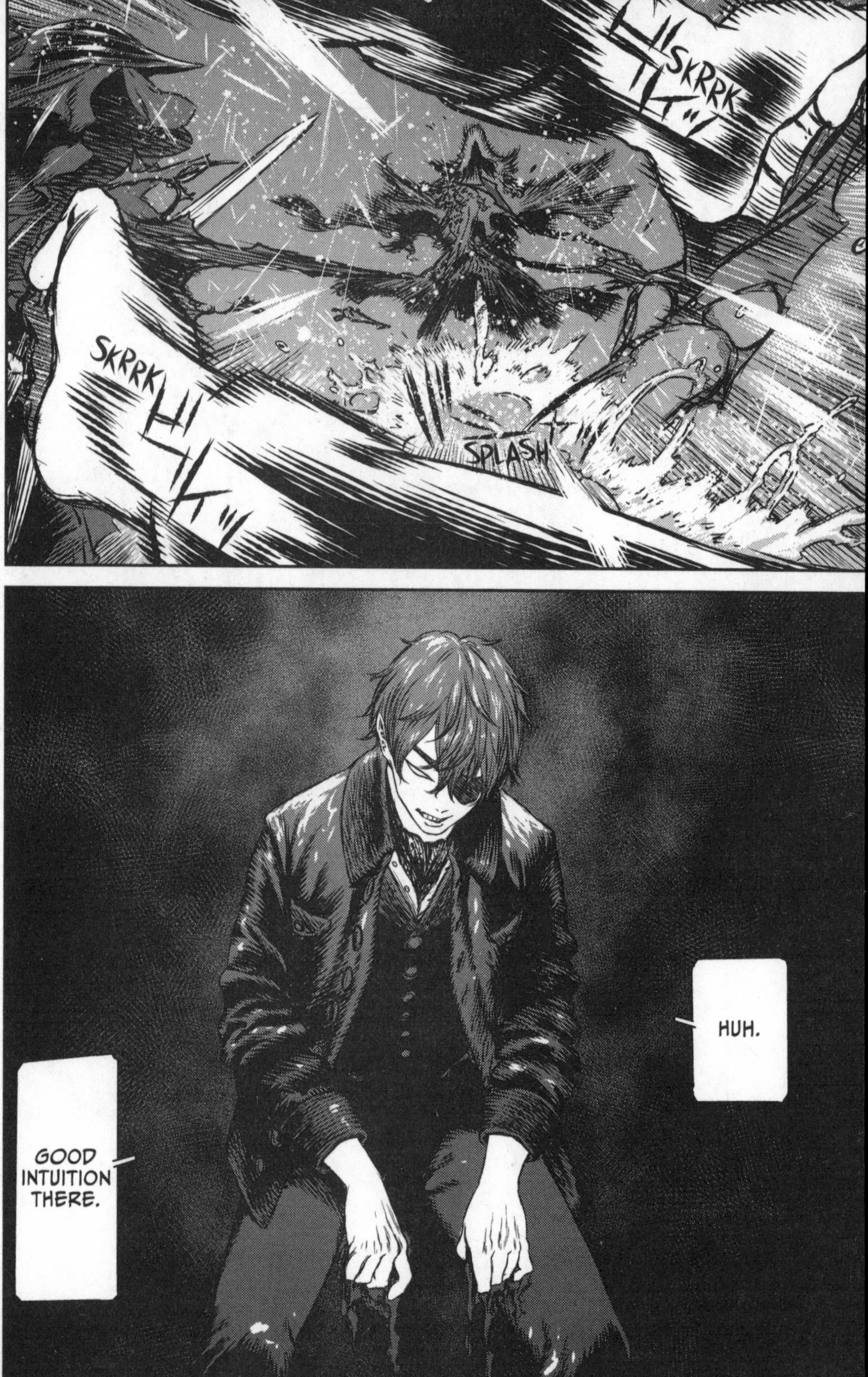
SKRRK
SKRRK
SPLASH
HUH.
GOOD INTUITION THERE.

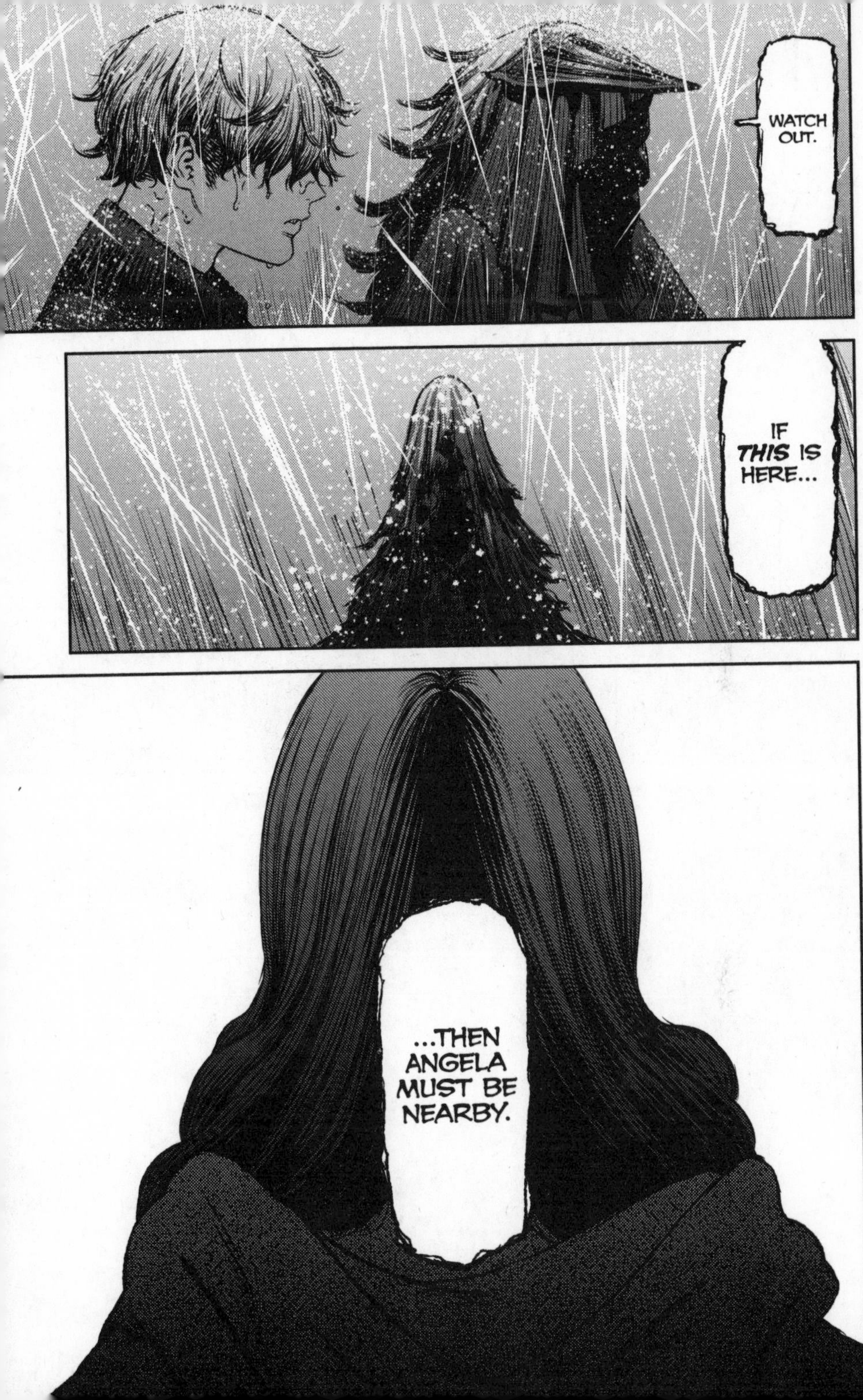
WATCH OUT.
IF *THIS* IS HERE...
...THEN ANGELA MUST BE NEARBY.

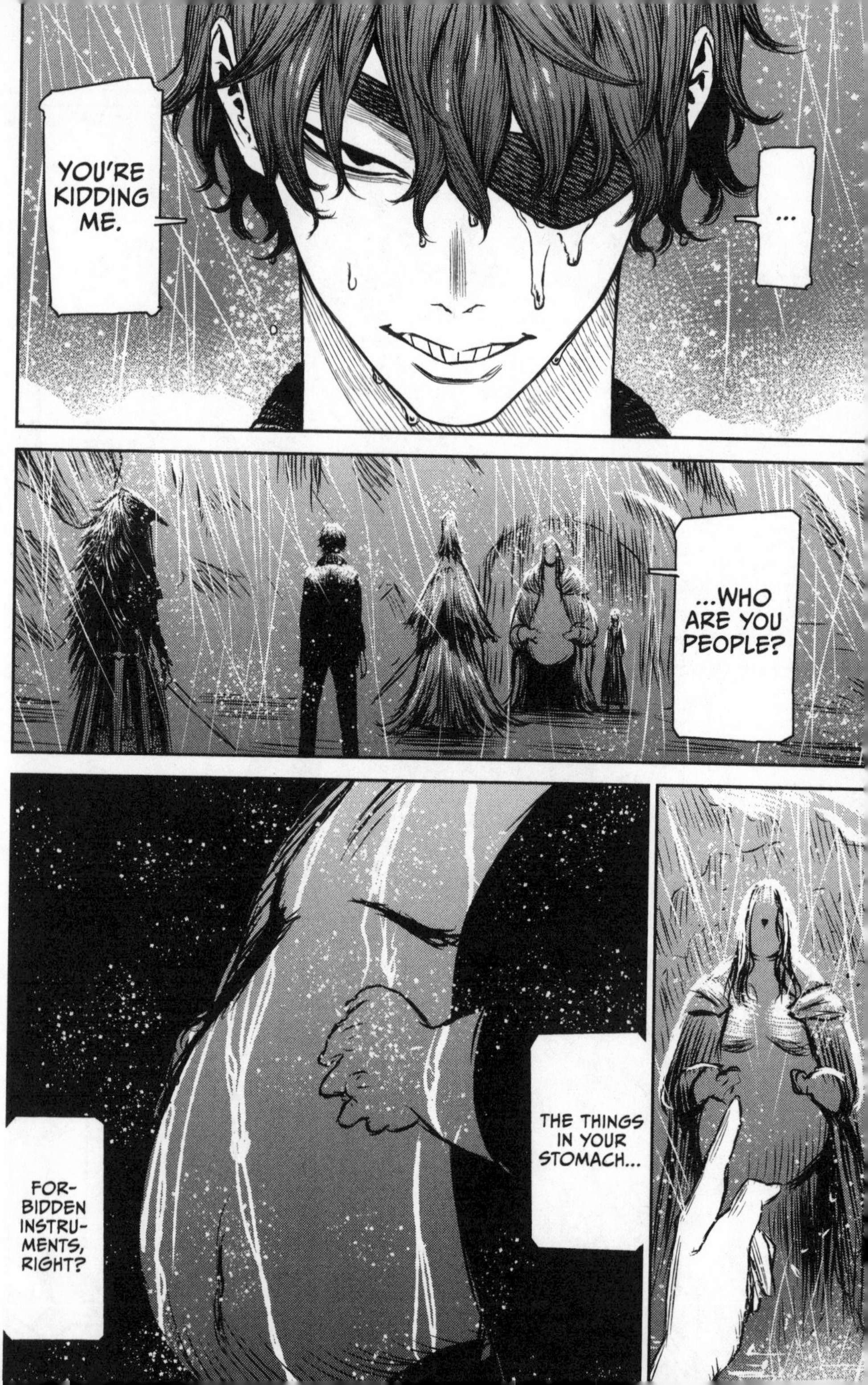
...
YOU'RE KIDDING ME.
...WHO ARE YOU PEOPLE?
THE THINGS IN YOUR STOMACH...
FOR-BIDDEN INSTRU-MENTS, RIGHT?

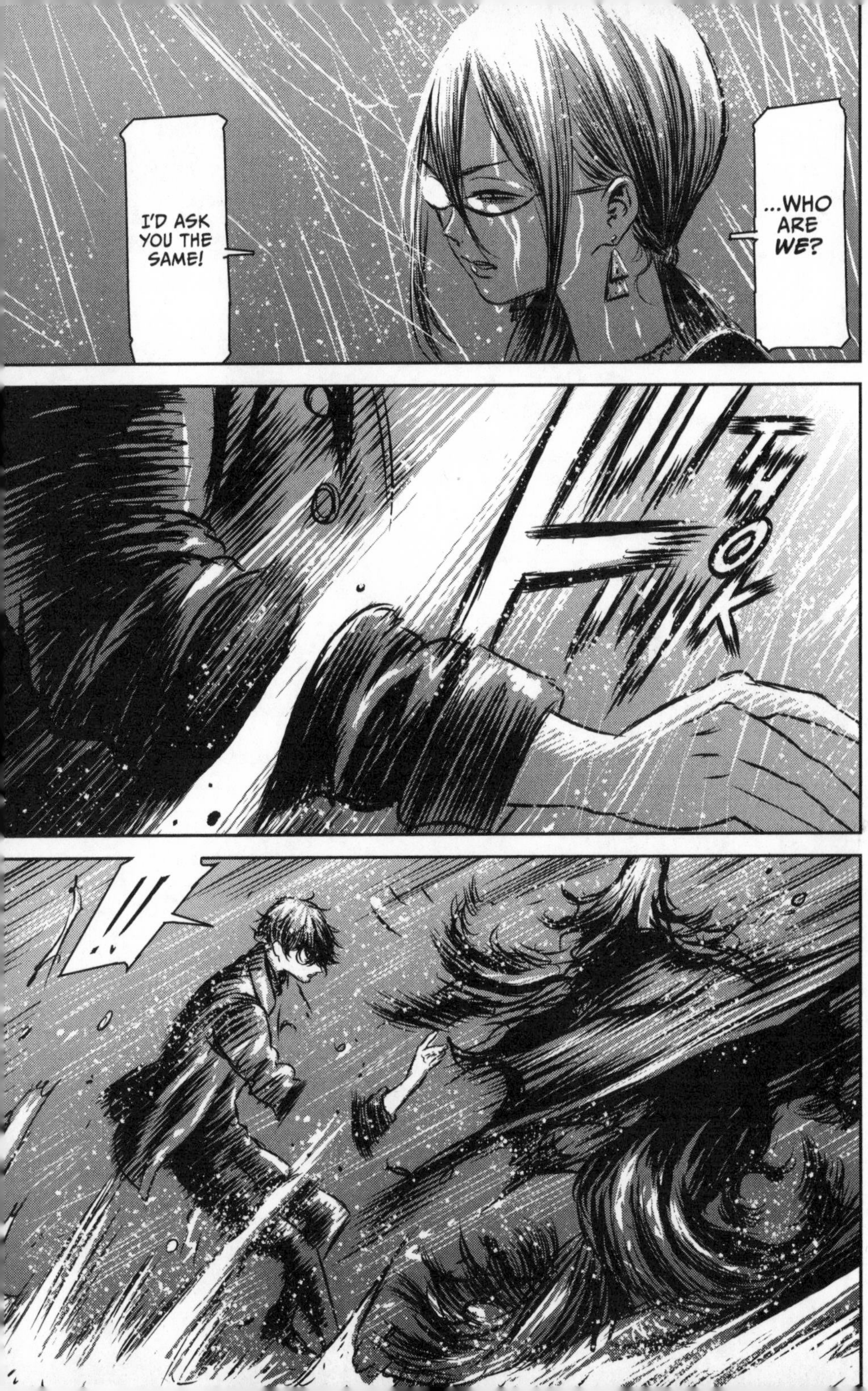
...WHO ARE WE?
I'D ASK YOU THE SAME!
THOK
!!

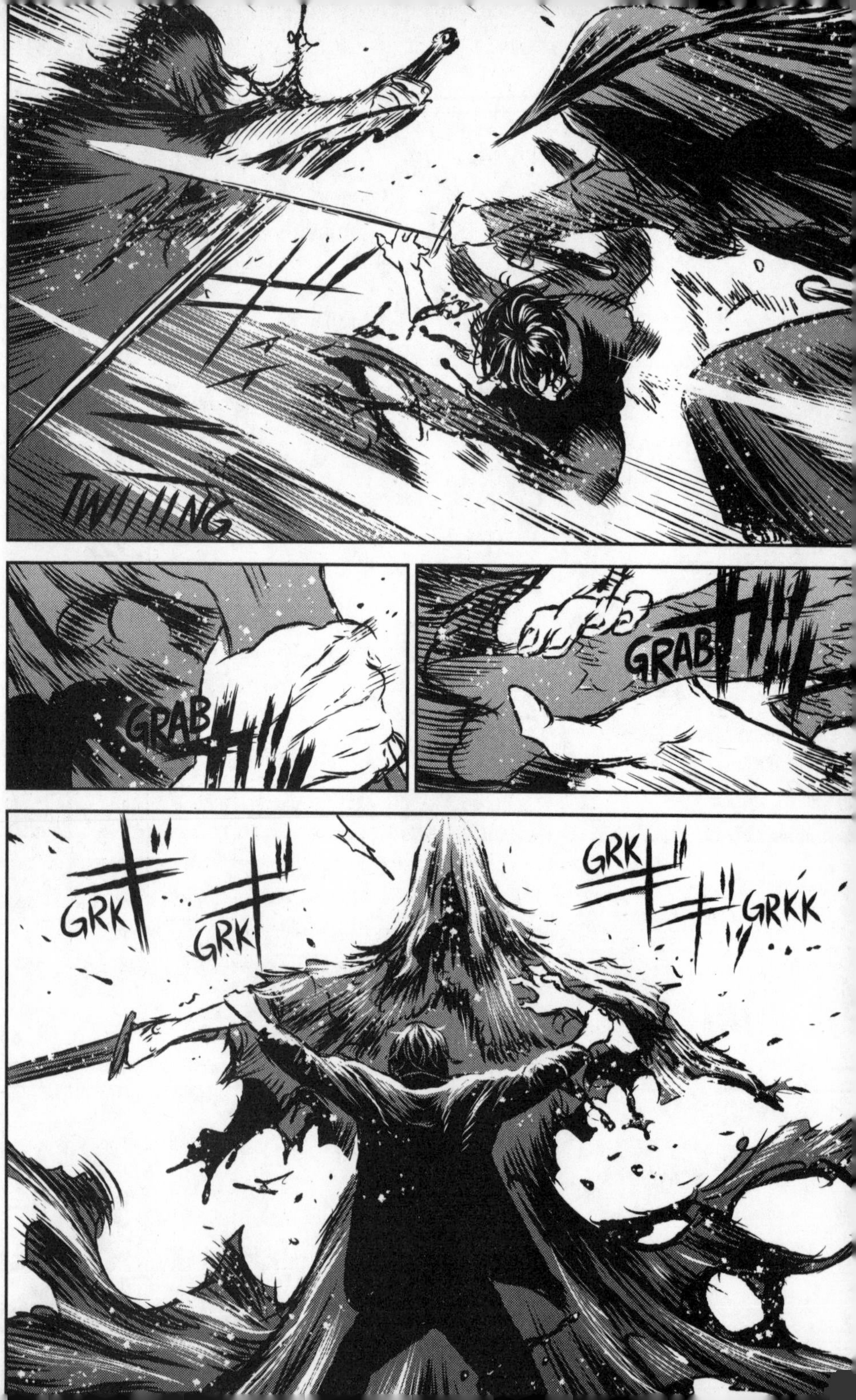
TWIIIING
GRAB
GRAB
GRK
GRKK
GRK
GRK

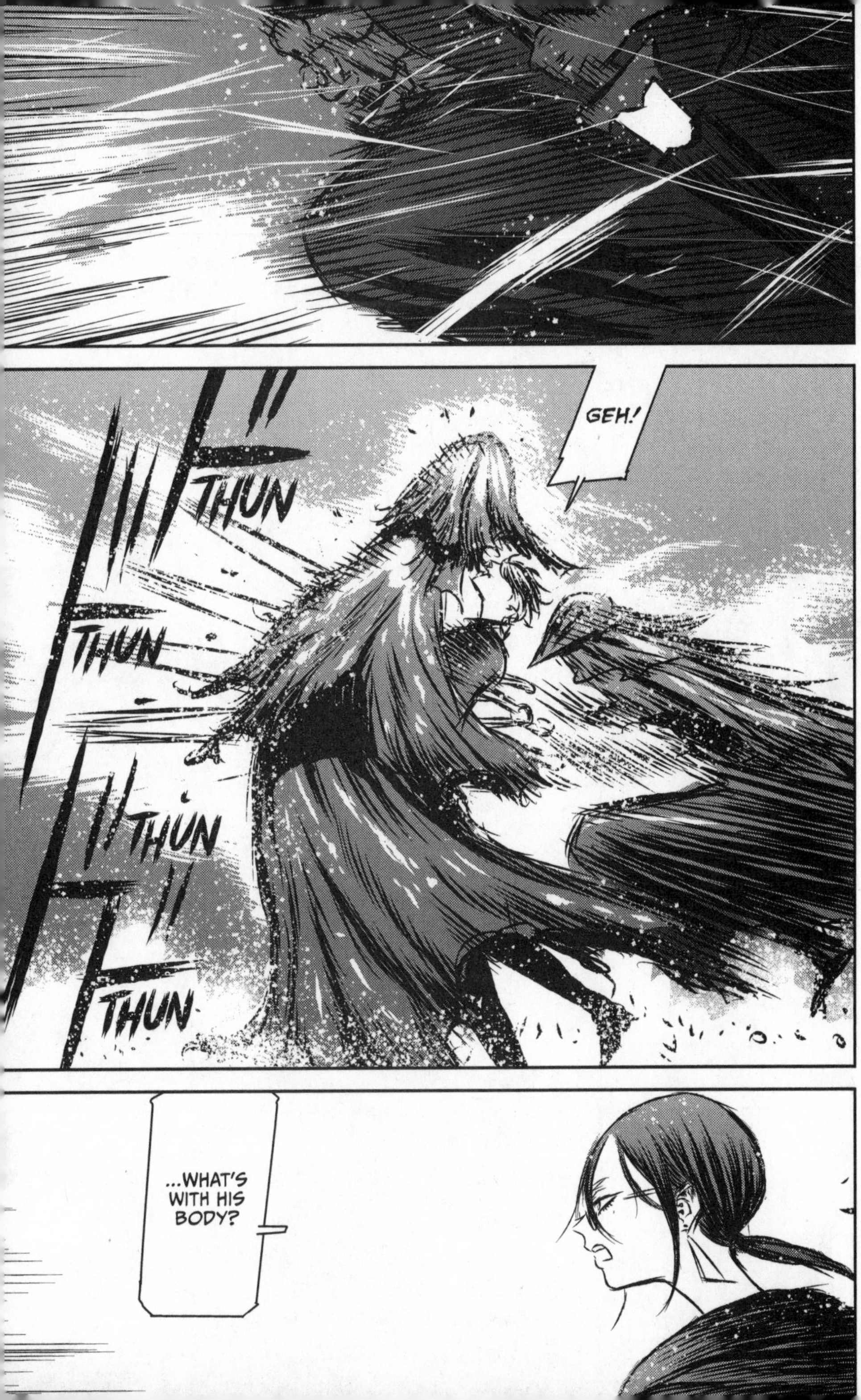
GEH!
THUN
THUN
THUN
THUN
...WHAT'S WITH HIS BODY?

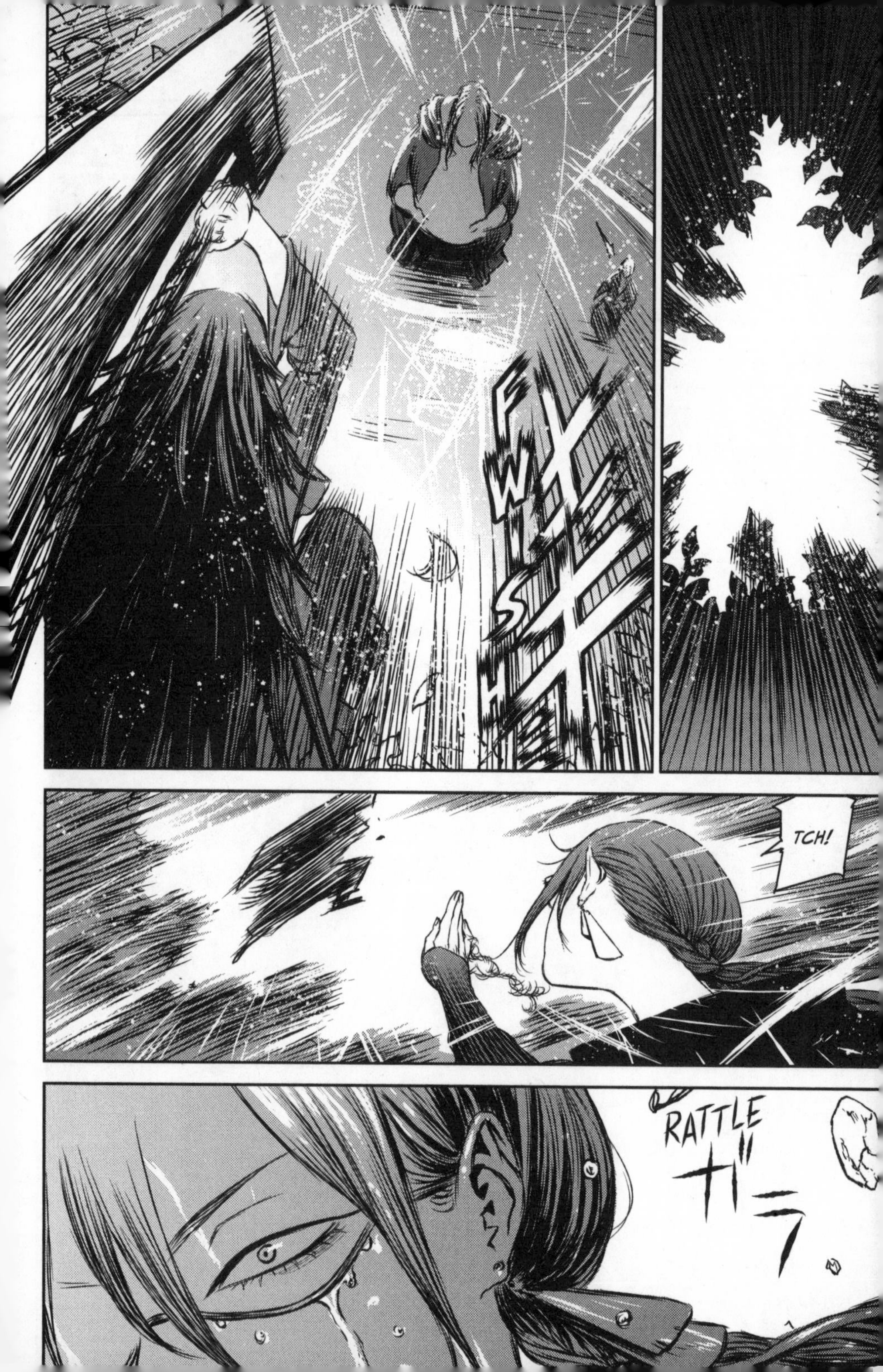
FWISH
TCH!
RATTLE

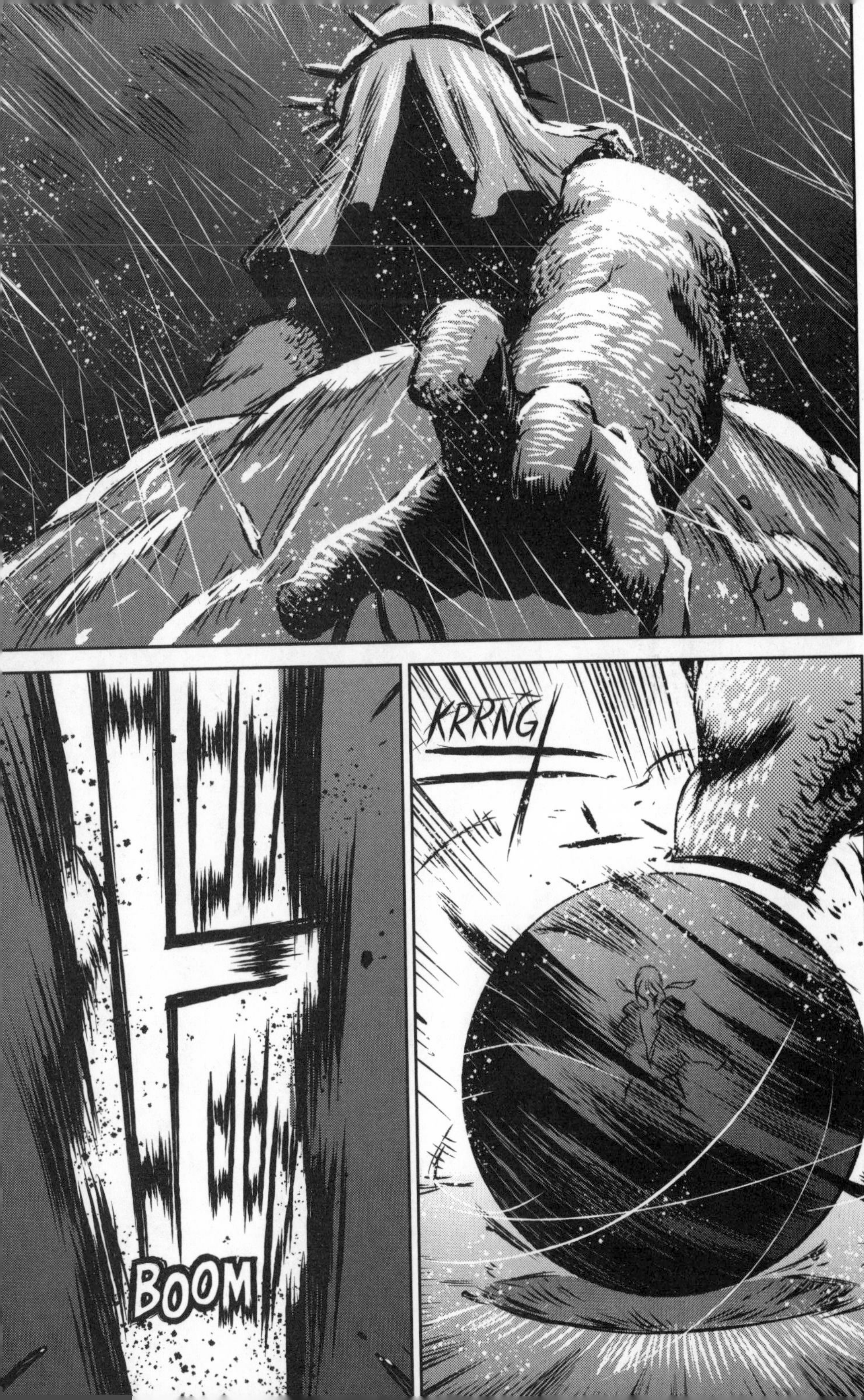
KRRNG!
BOOM

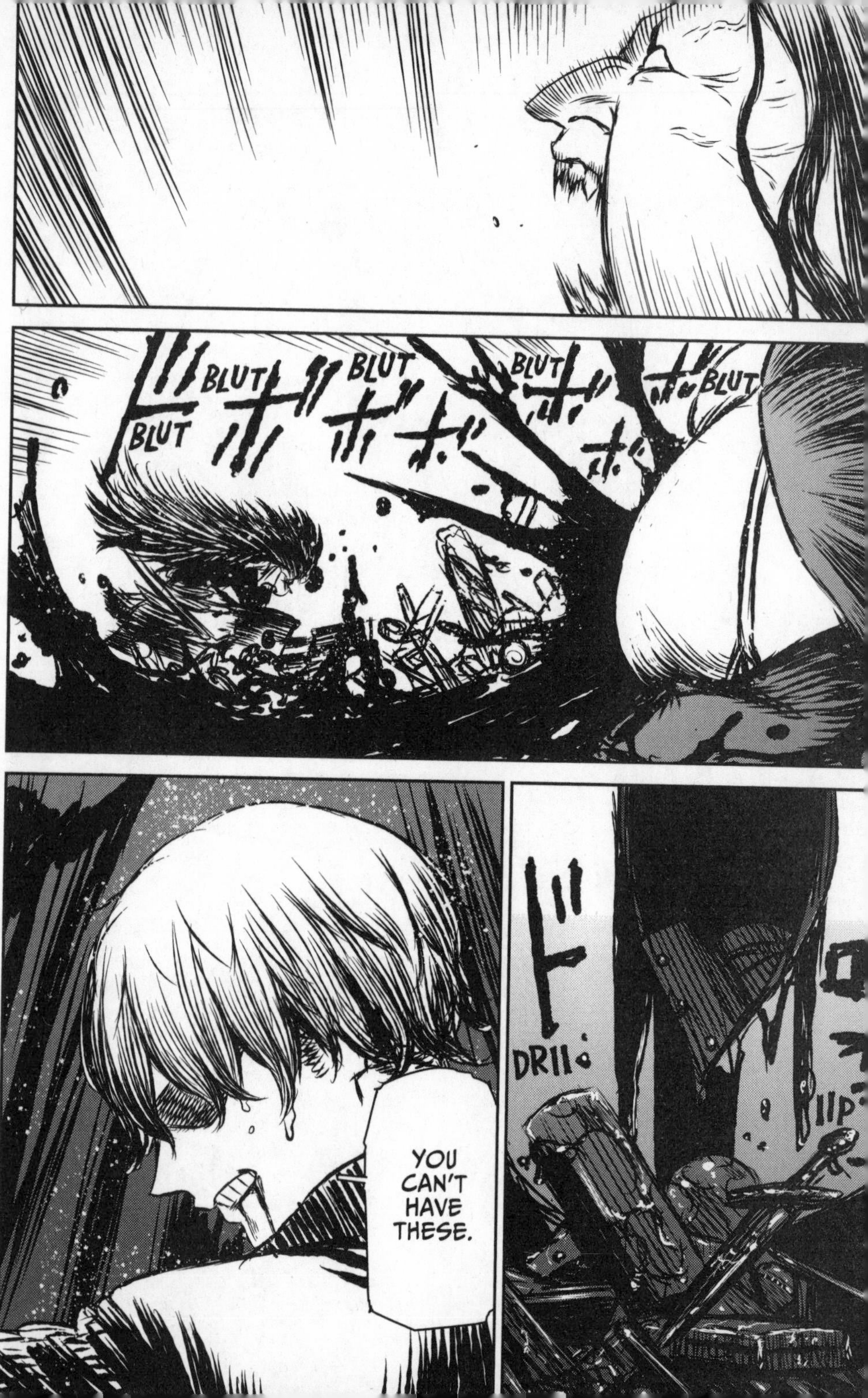
BLUT
BLUT
BLUT
BLUT
BLUT
DRII
IIP
YOU CAN'T HAVE THESE.

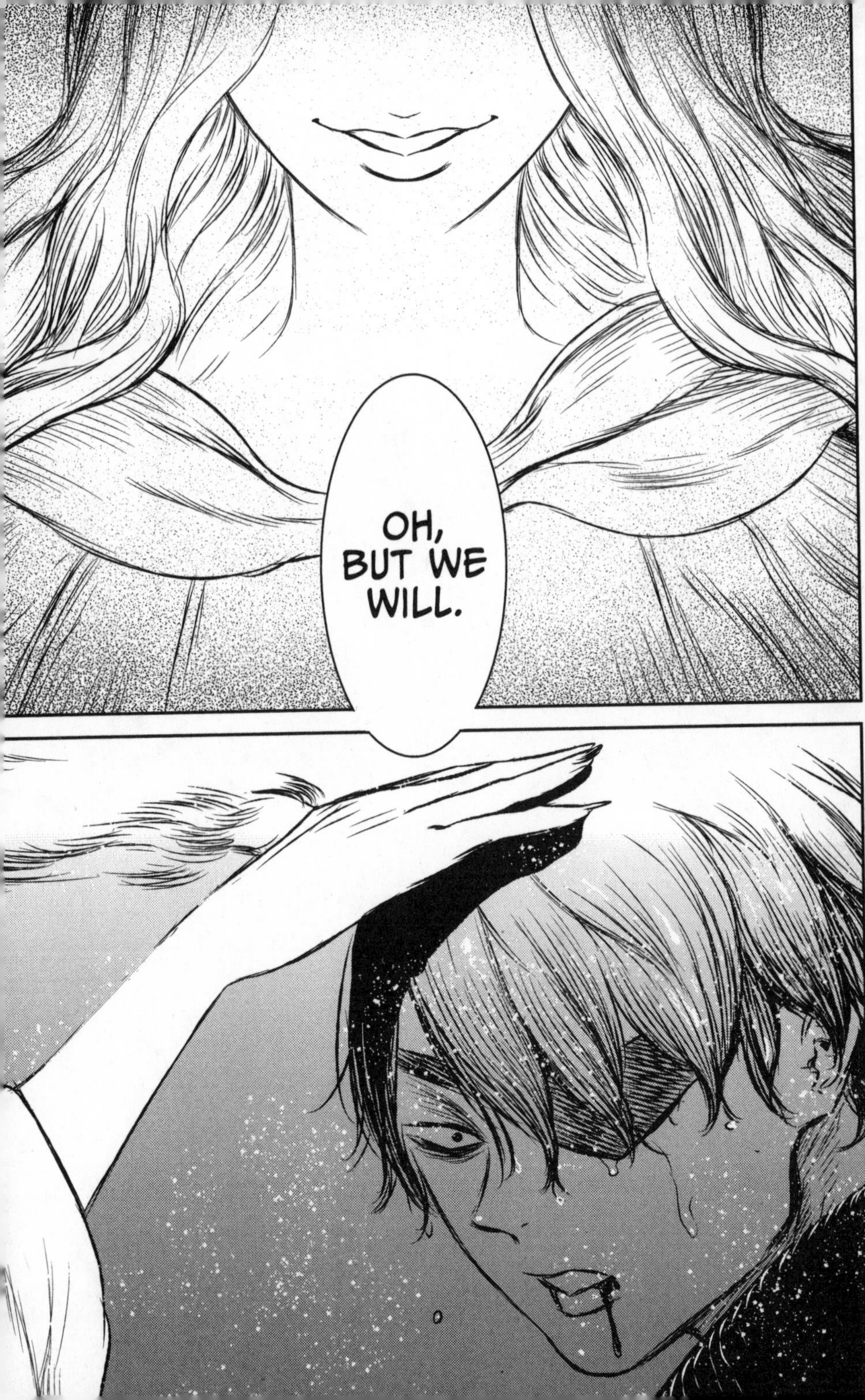
OH, BUT WE WILL.

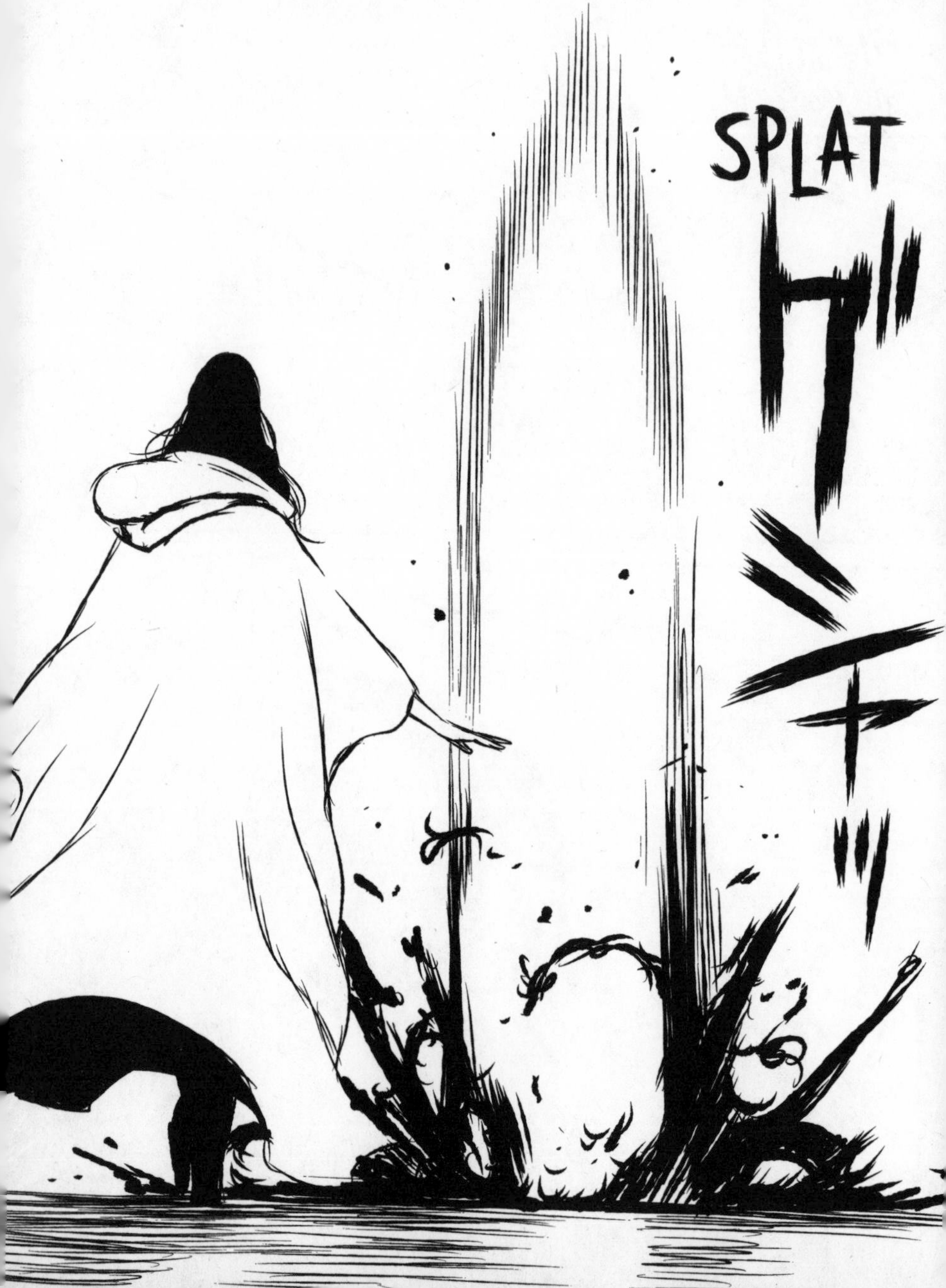
SPLAT

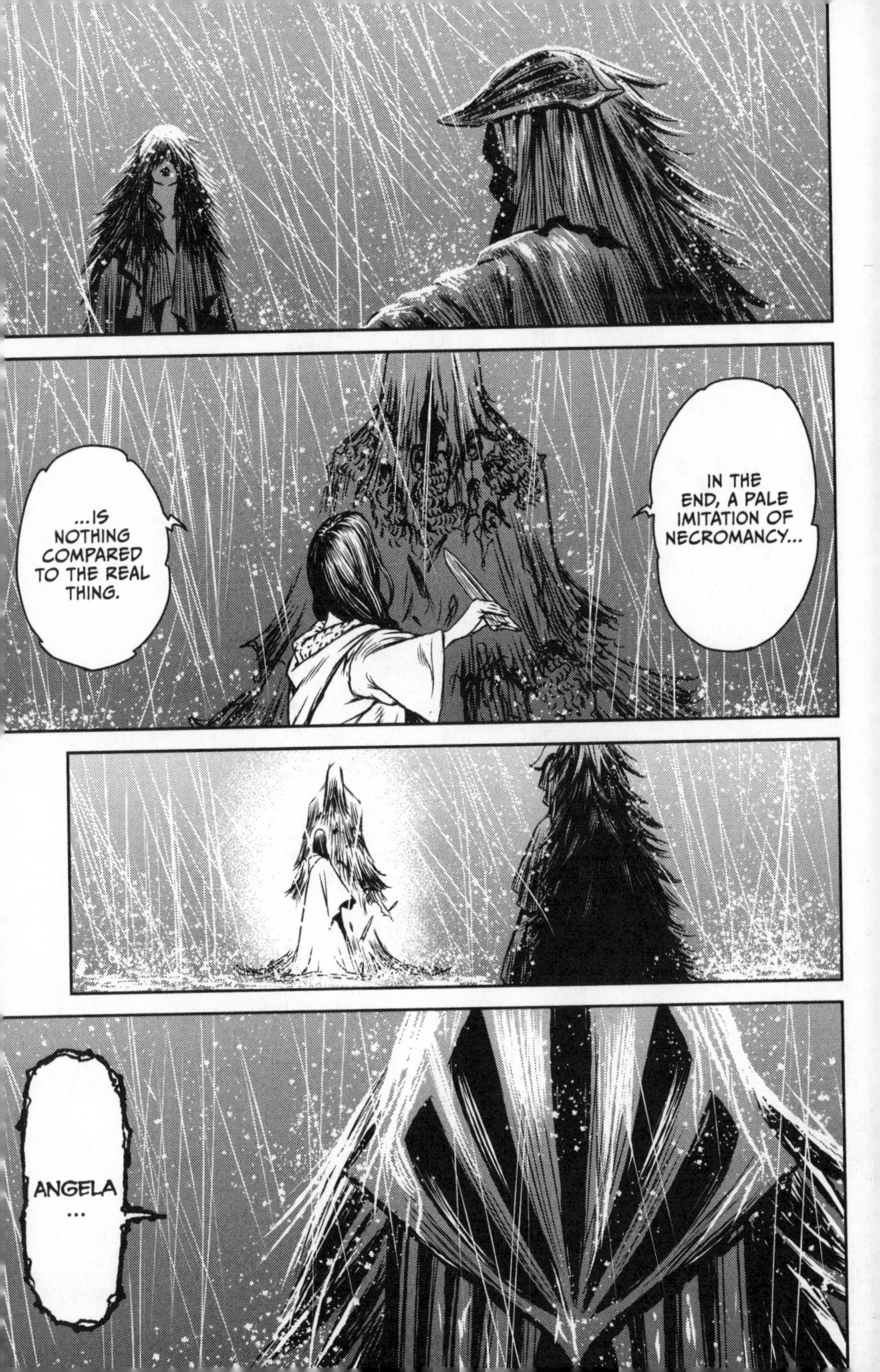
IN THE END, A PALE IMITATION OF NECROMANCY...
...IS NOTHING COMPARED TO THE REAL THING.
ANGELA ...

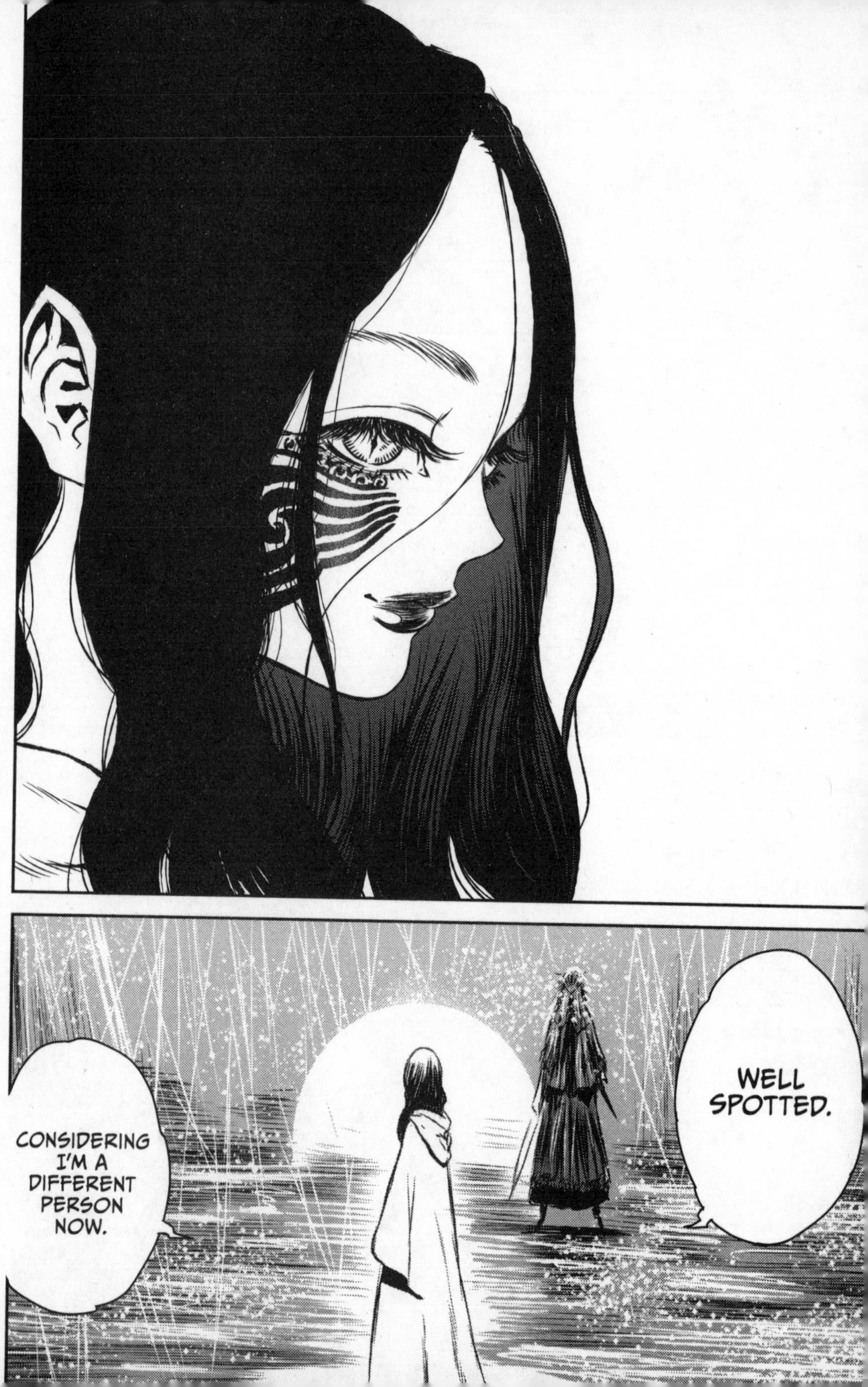
WELL SPOTTED.
CONSIDERING I'M A DIFFERENT PERSON NOW.

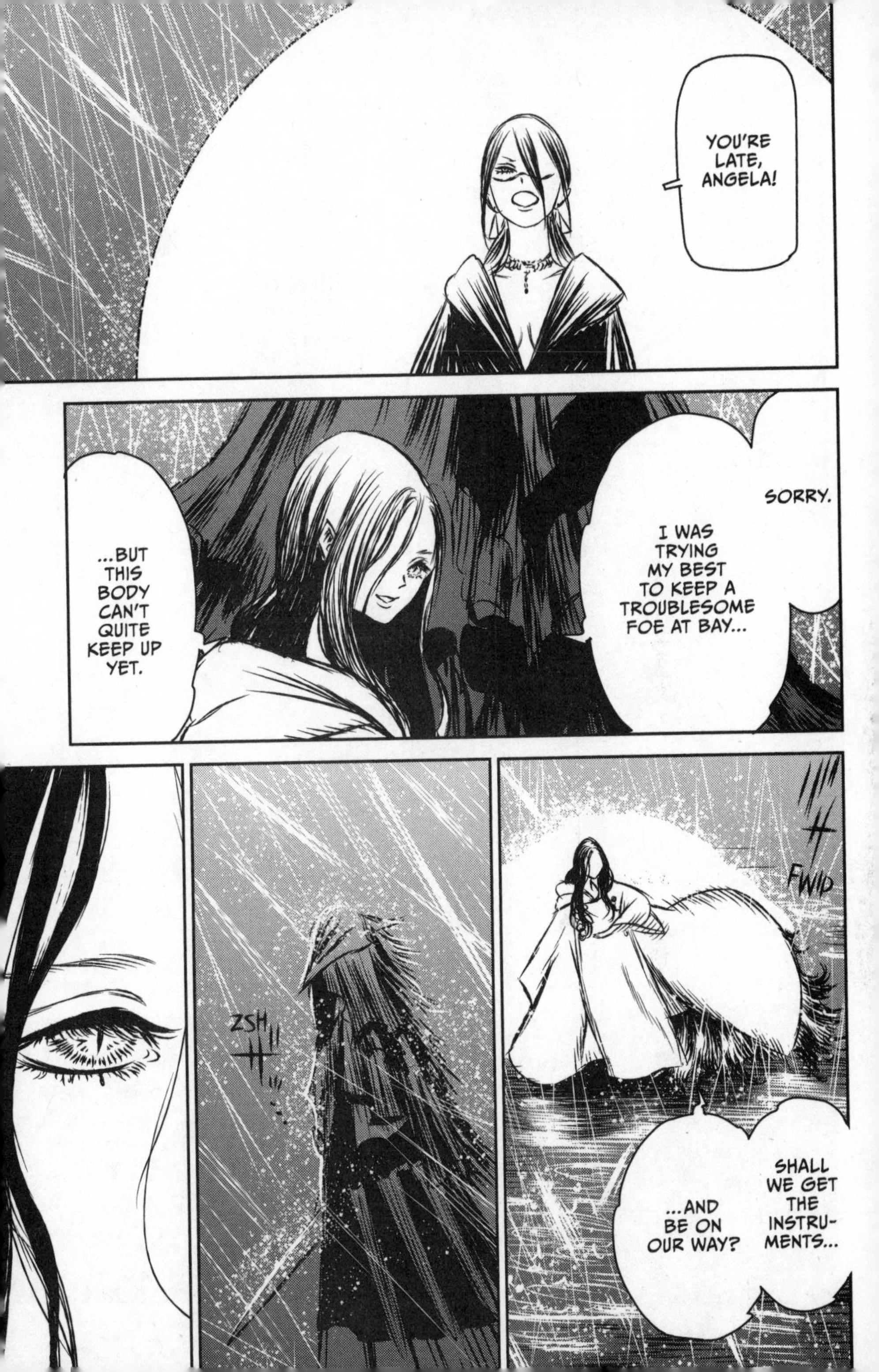
YOU'RE LATE, ANGELA!
SORRY.
I WAS TRYING MY BEST TO KEEP A TROUBLESOME FOE AT BAY...
...BUT THIS BODY CAN'T QUITE KEEP UP YET.
FWIP
SHALL WE GET THE INSTRU-MENTS...
...AND BE ON OUR WAY?
ZSH

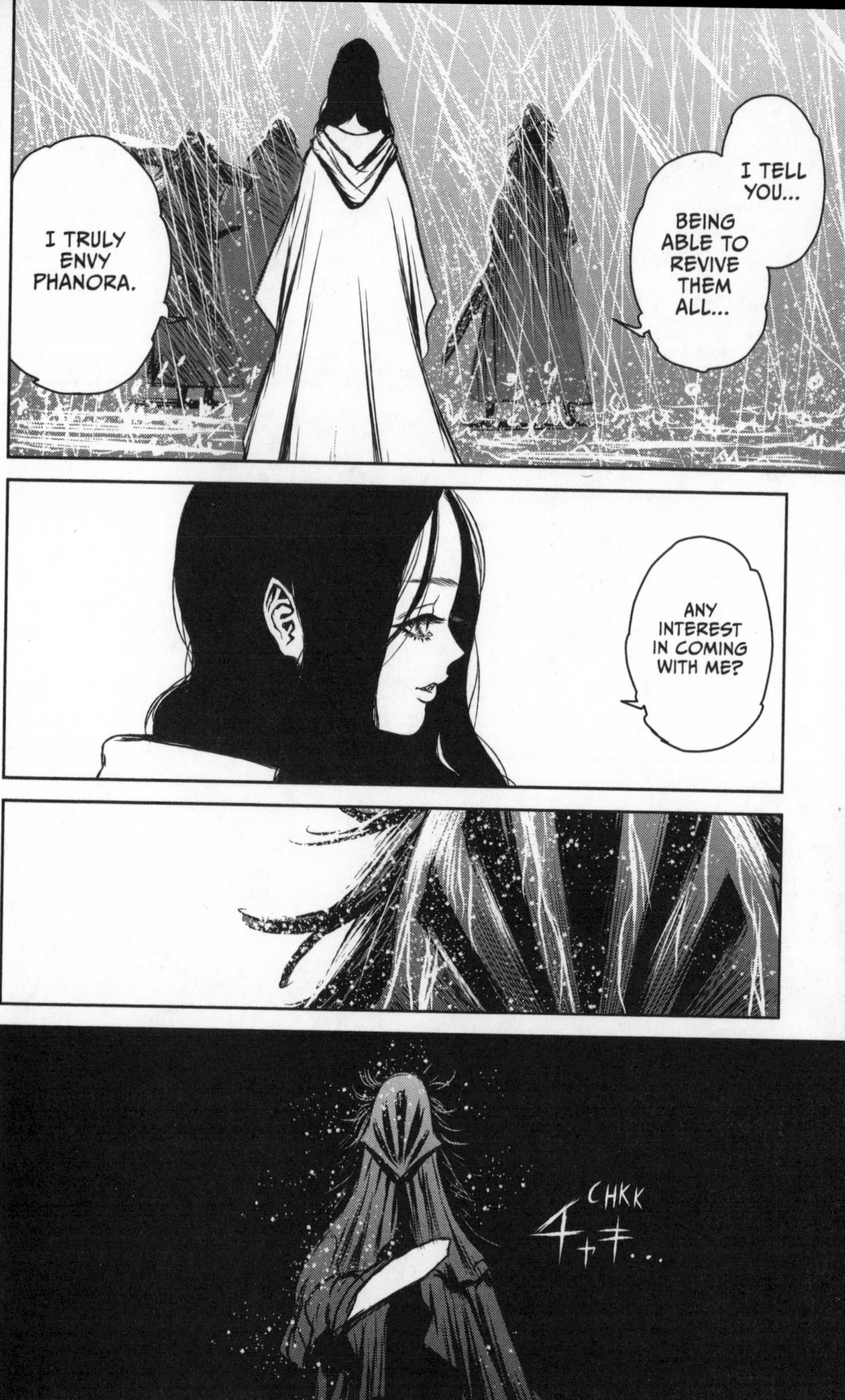
I TELL YOU... BEING ABLE TO REVIVE THEM ALL...
I TRULY ENVY PHANORA.
ANY INTEREST IN COMING WITH ME?
CHKK

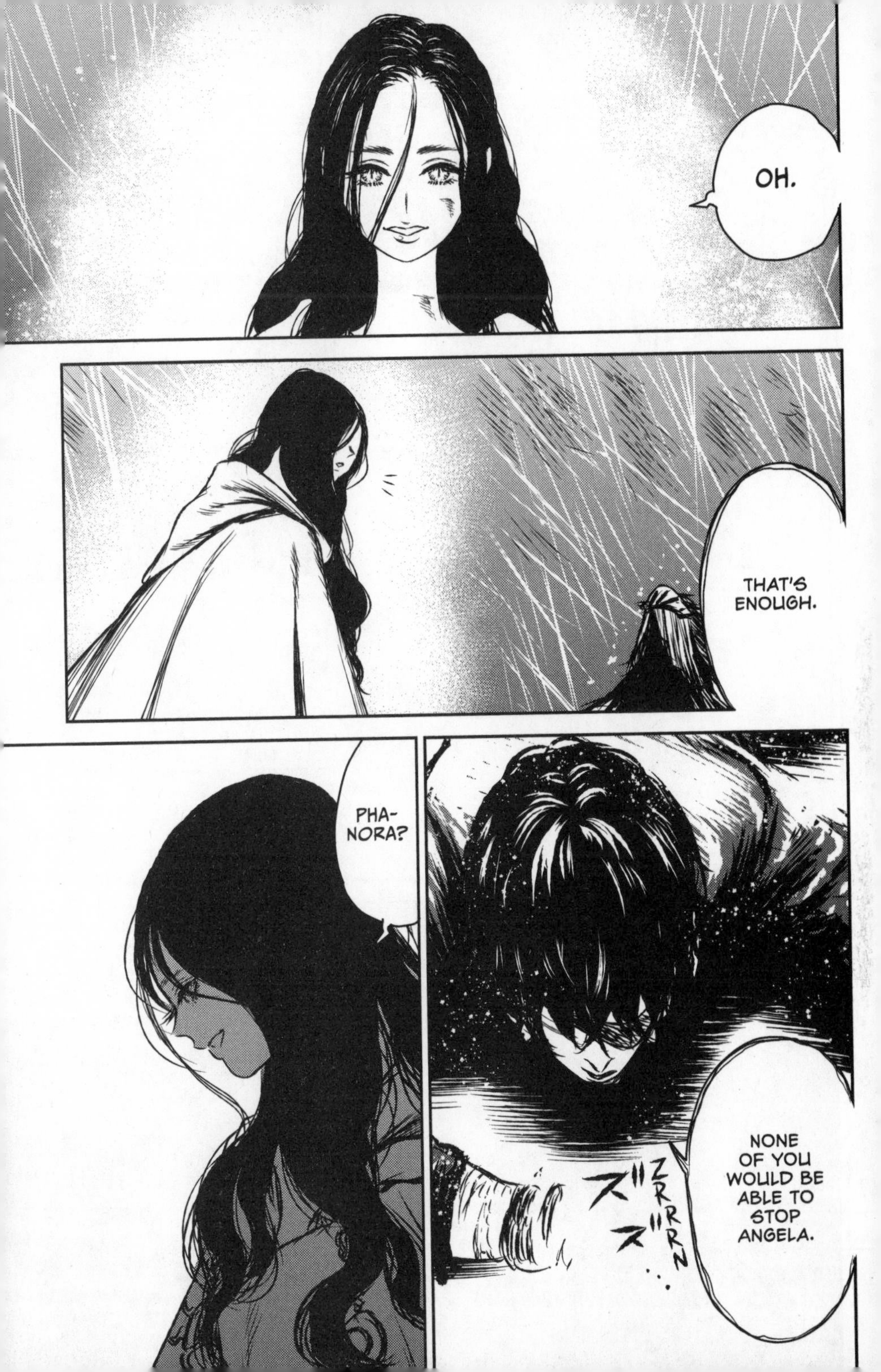
OH.
THAT'S ENOUGH.
NONE OF YOU WOULD BE ABLE TO STOP ANGELA.
ZRRRN...
PHA-NORA?

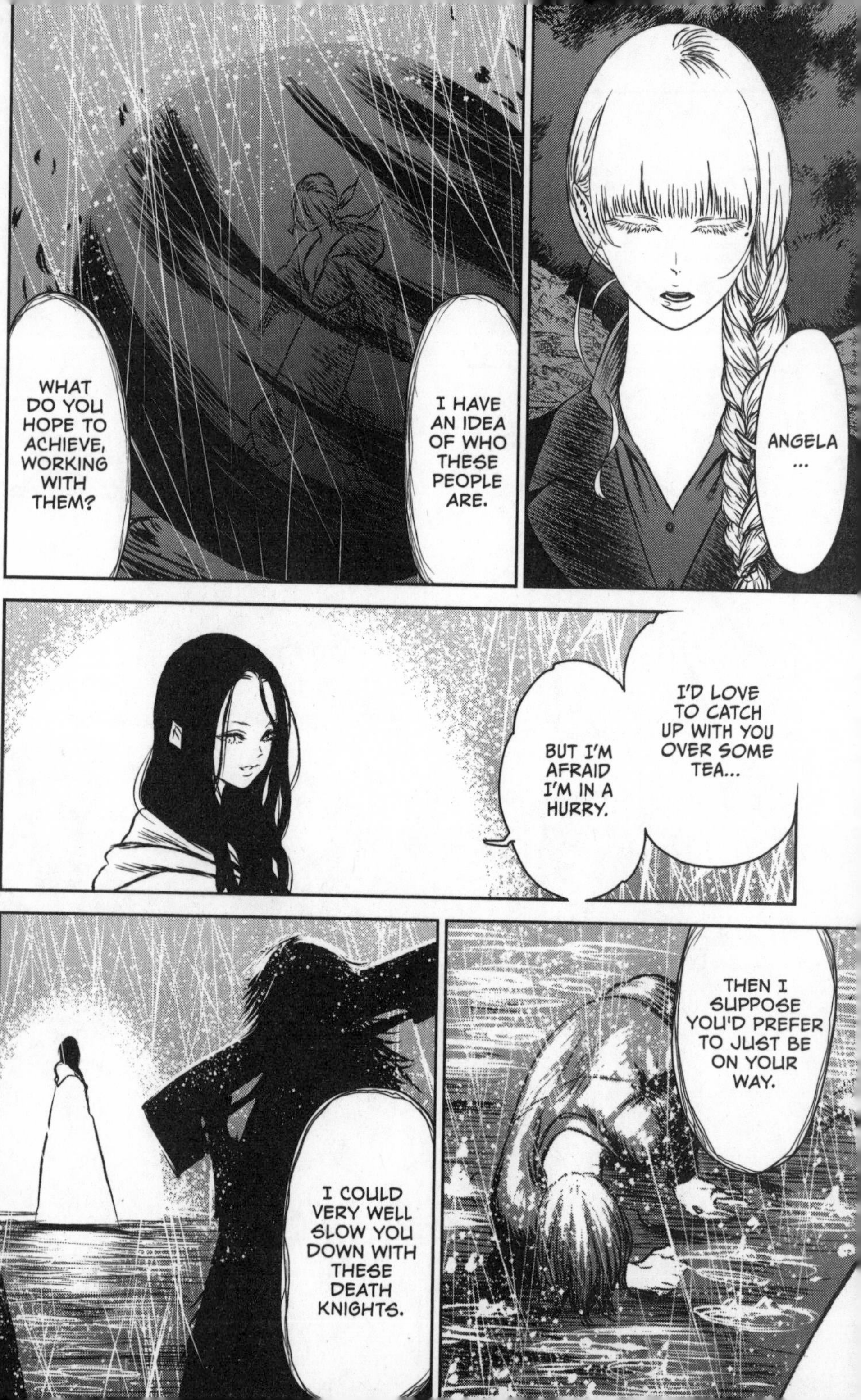
ANGELA ...
I HAVE AN IDEA OF WHO THESE PEOPLE ARE.
WHAT DO YOU HOPE TO ACHIEVE, WORKING WITH THEM?
I'D LOVE TO CATCH UP WITH YOU OVER SOME TEA...
BUT I'M AFRAID I'M IN A HURRY.
THEN I SUPPOSE YOU'D PREFER TO JUST BE ON YOUR WAY.
I COULD VERY WELL SLOW YOU DOWN WITH THESE DEATH KNIGHTS.

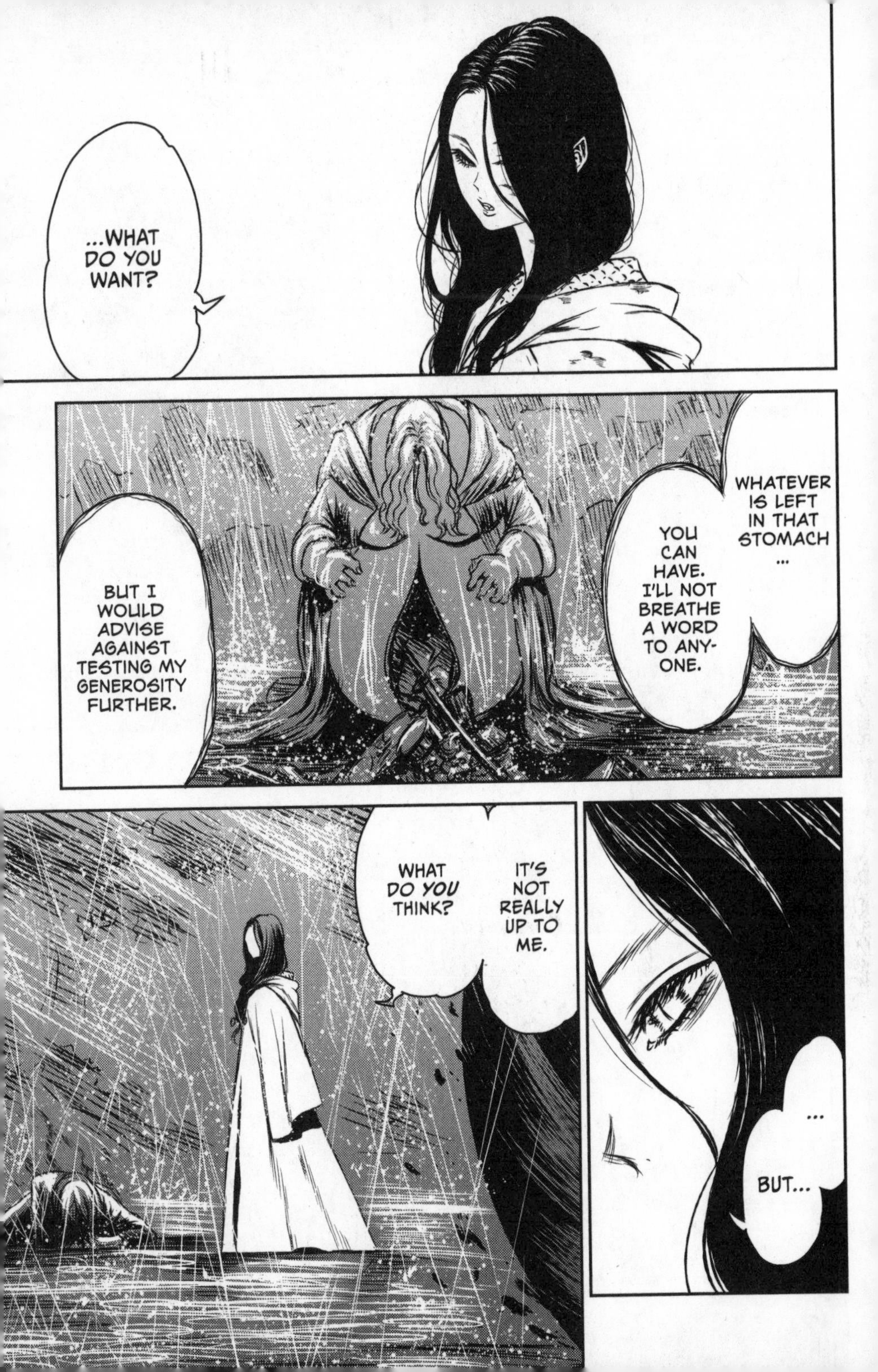
...WHAT DO YOU WANT?
WHATEVER IS LEFT IN THAT STOMACH...
YOU CAN HAVE. I'LL NOT BREATHE A WORD TO ANY-ONE.
BUT I WOULD ADVISE AGAINST TESTING MY GENEROSITY FURTHER.
...
BUT...
IT'S NOT REALLY UP TO ME.
WHAT DO *YOU* THINK?

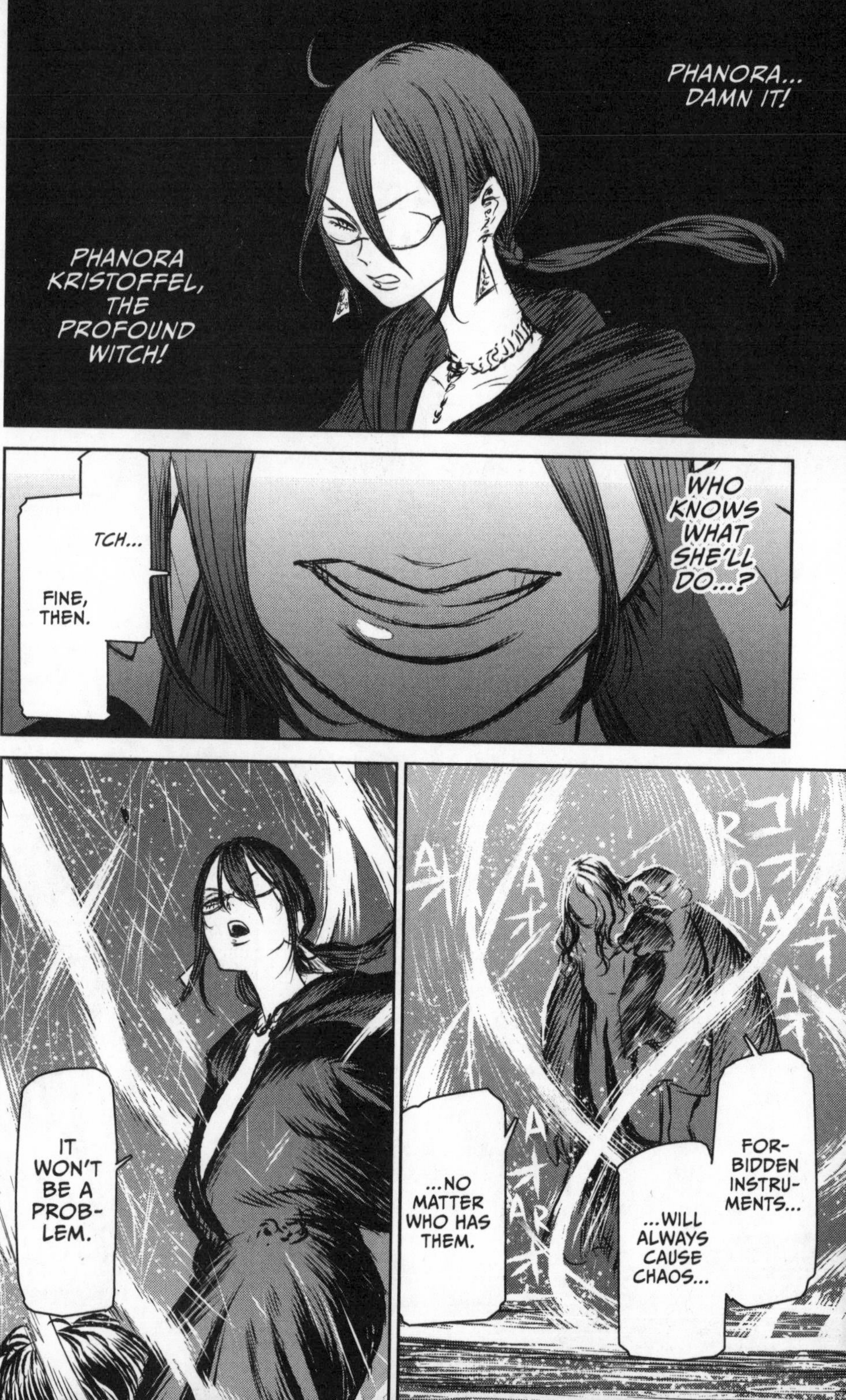
PHANORA... DAMN IT!
PHANORA KRISTOFFEL, THE PROFOUND WITCH!
WHO KNOWS WHAT SHE'LL DO...?
TCH...
FINE, THEN.
ROAR
FOR-BIDDEN INSTRU-MENTS...
...WILL ALWAYS CAUSE CHAOS...
...NO MATTER WHO HAS THEM.
IT WON'T BE A PROB-LEM.

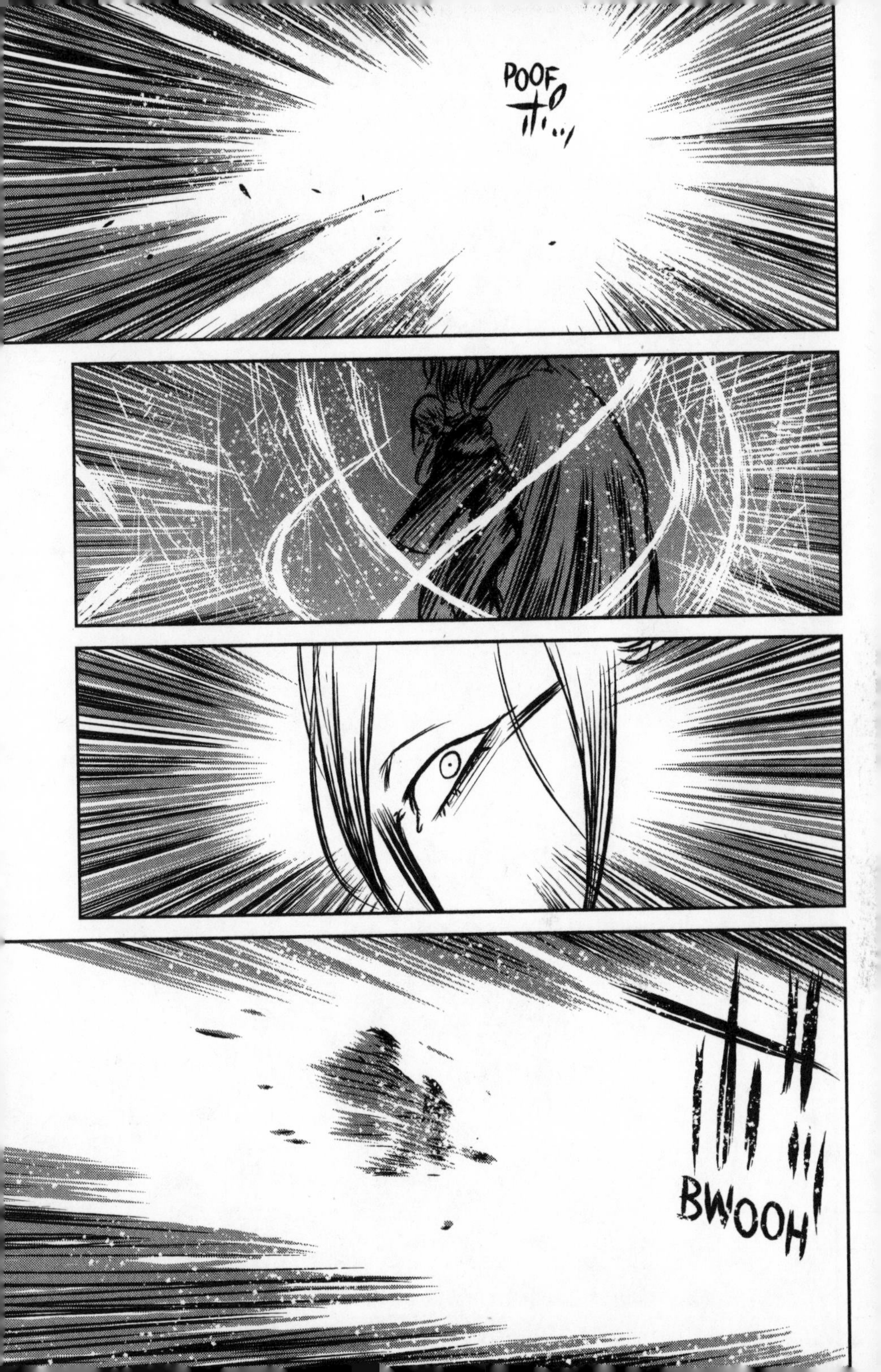
POOF
BWOOH

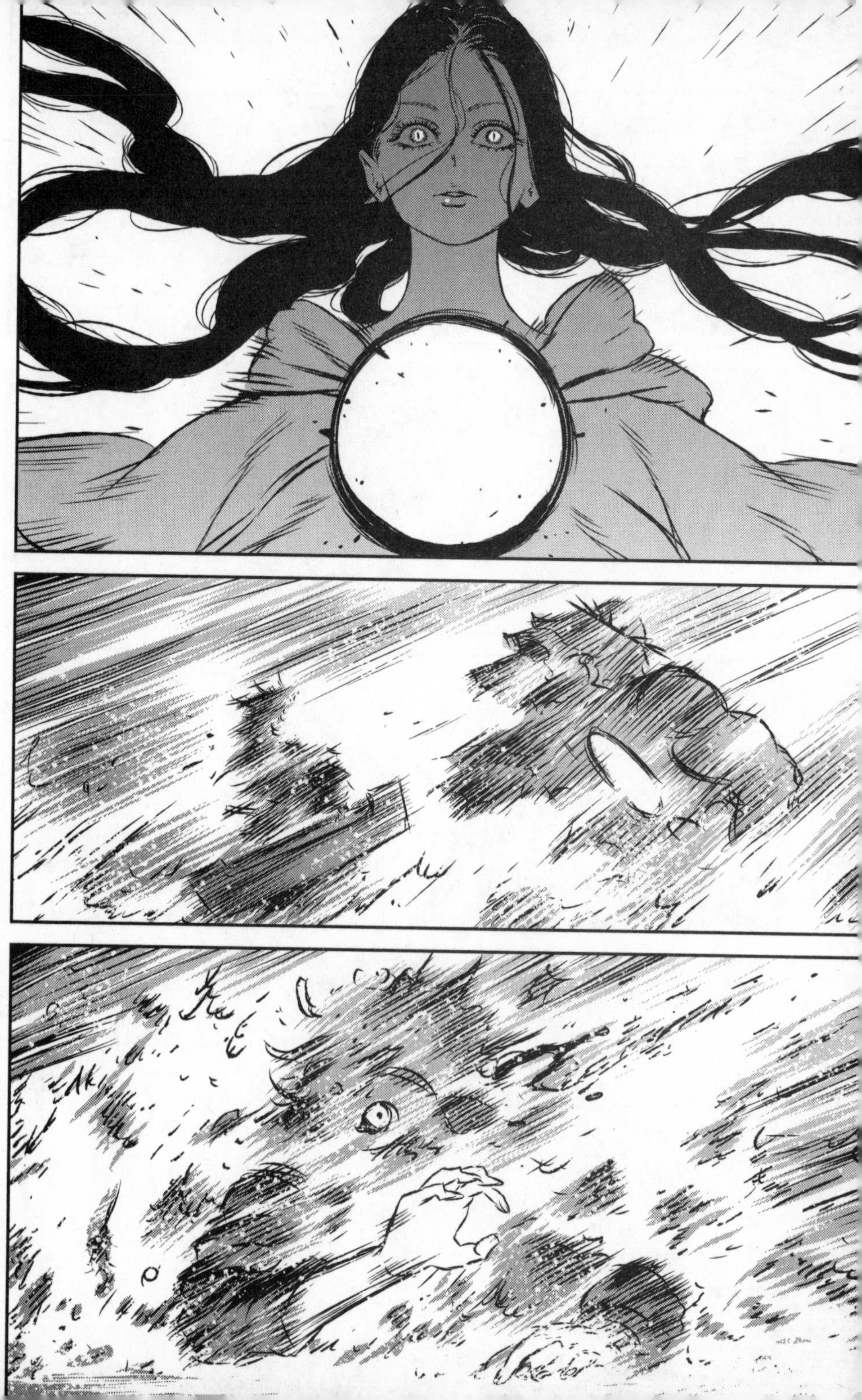

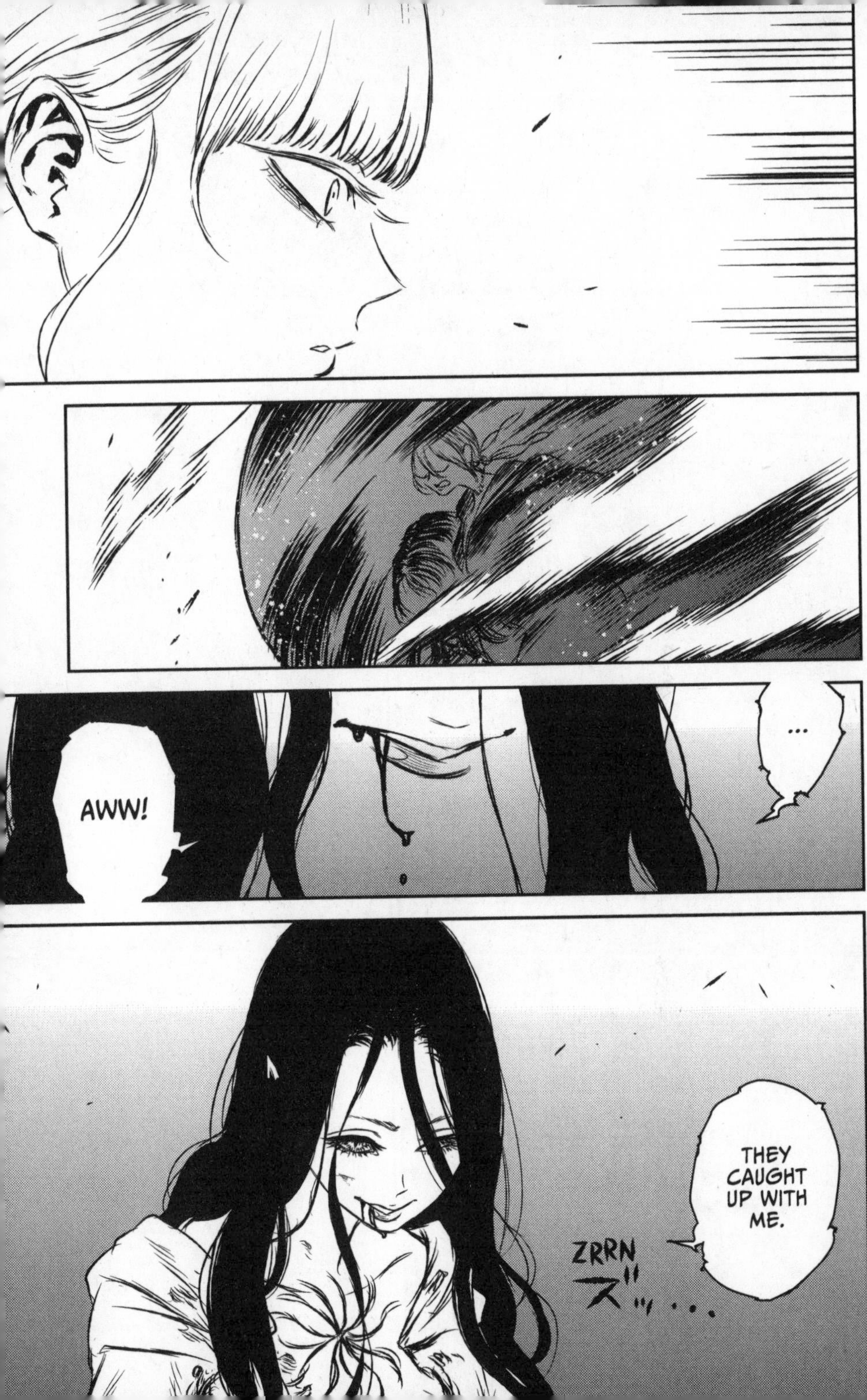
...
AWW!
THEY CAUGHT UP WITH ME.
ZRRN

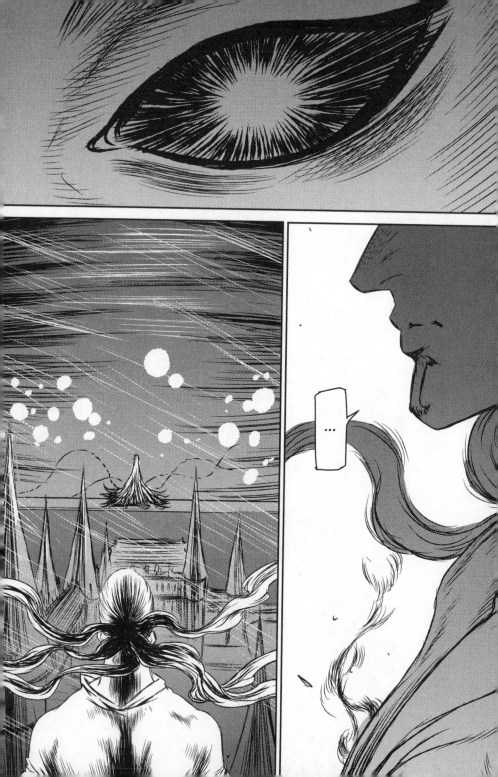

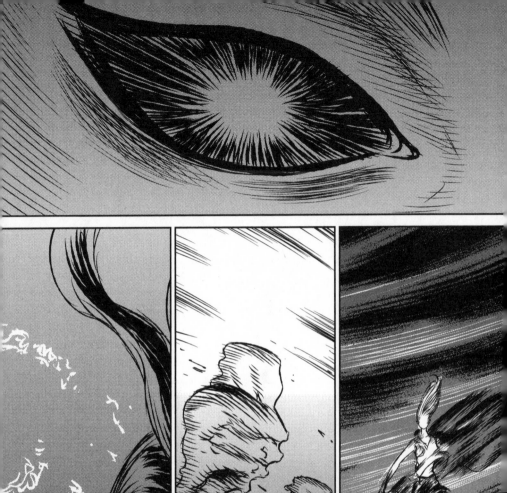

ZRN II
スリ

VR R R R RN
WOO OOM

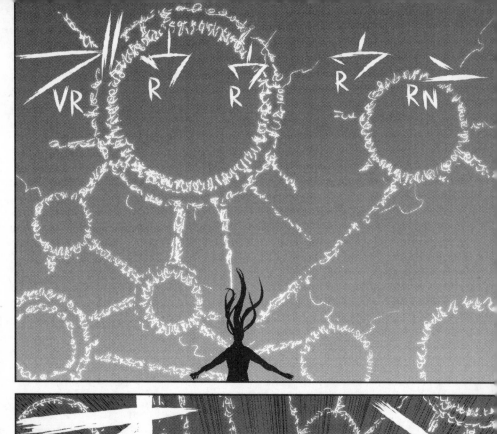

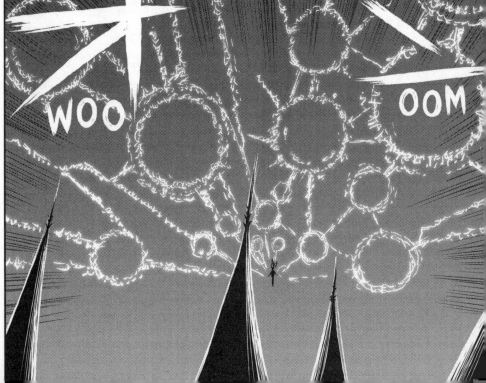

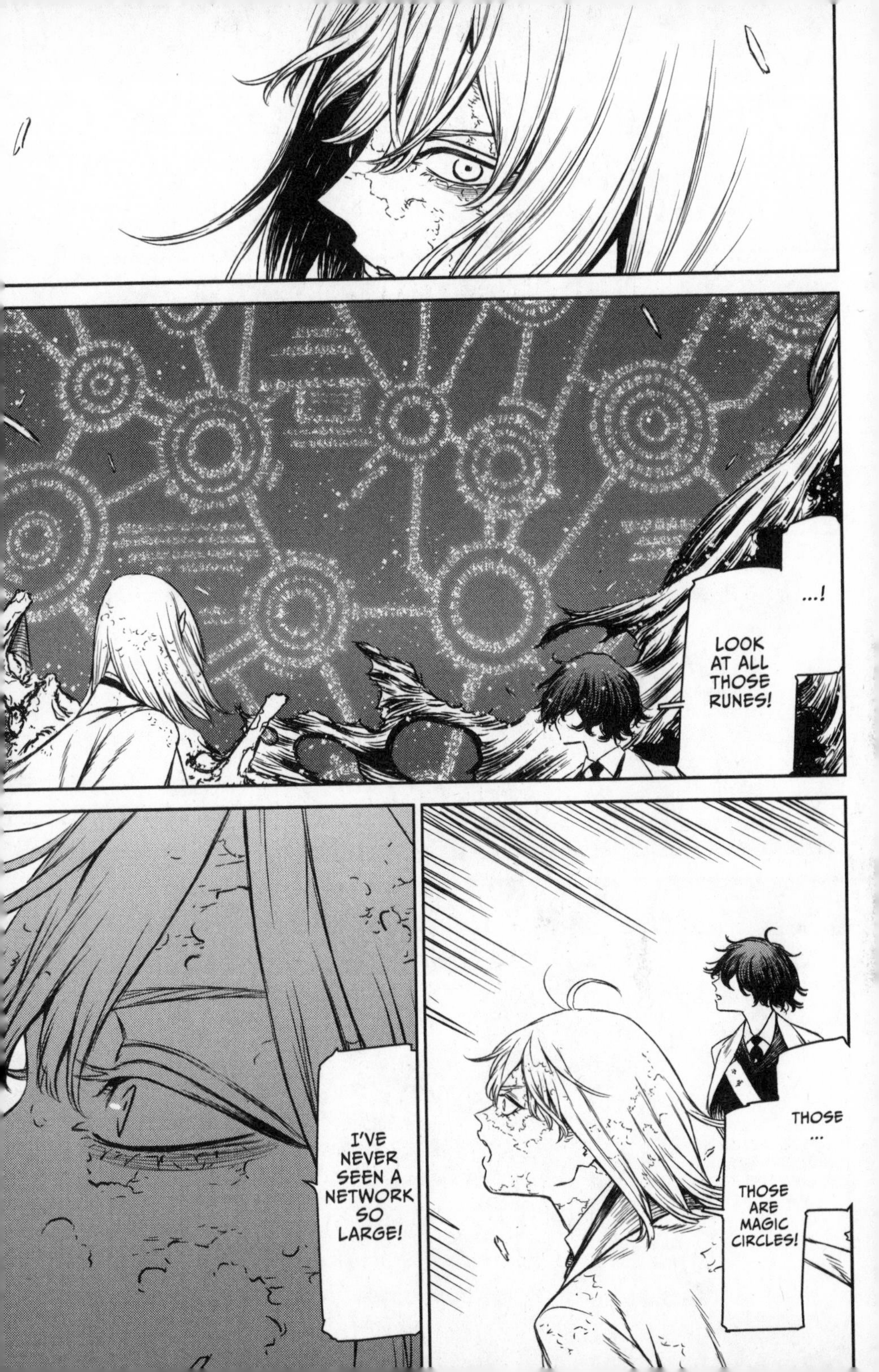
...!
LOOK AT ALL THOSE RUNES!
THOSE ...
THOSE ARE MAGIC CIRCLES!
I'VE NEVER SEEN A NETWORK SO LARGE!

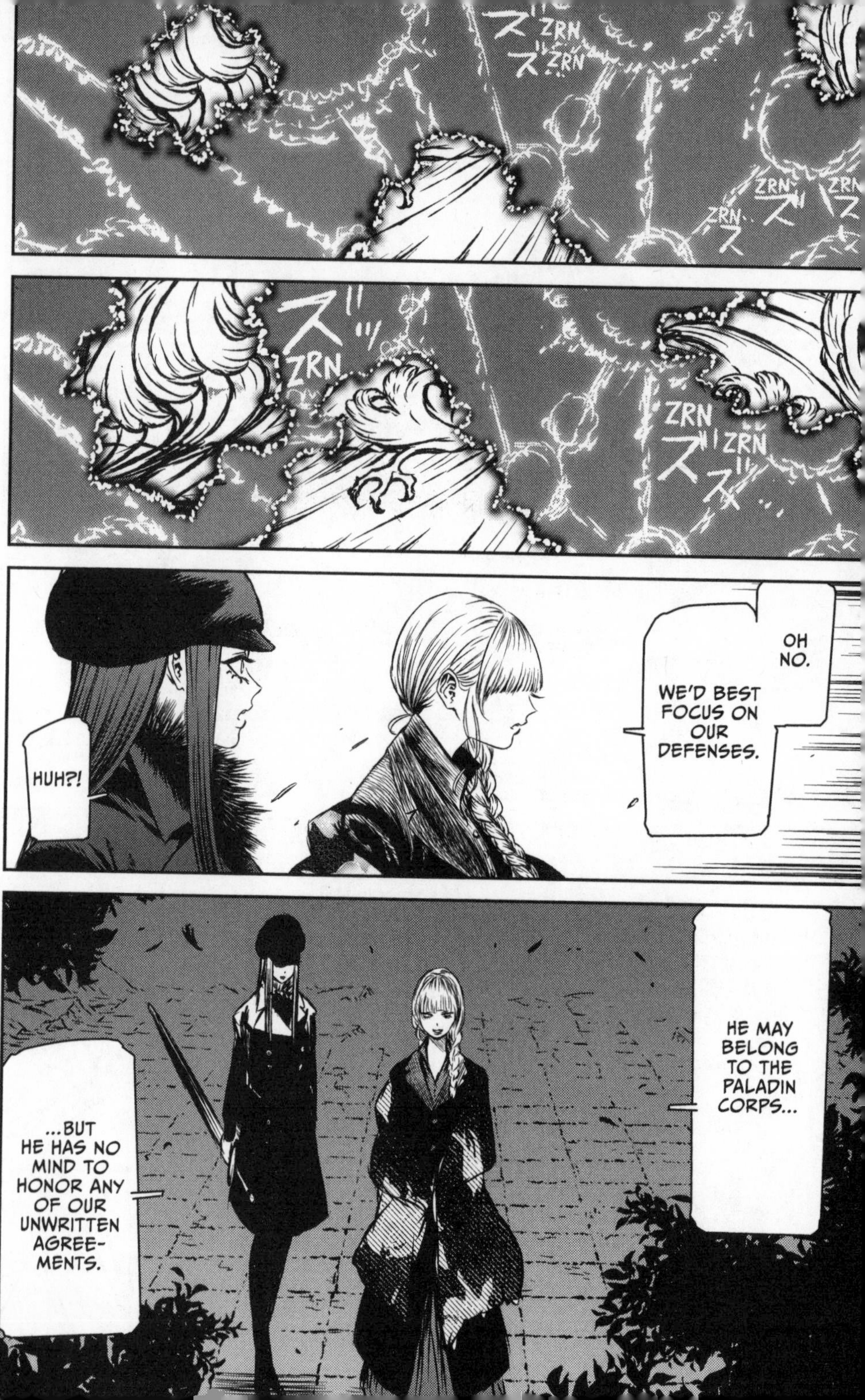
ZRN
ZRN
ZRN
ZRN
ZRN
ZRN
ZRN
ZRN
ZRN
OH NO.
WE'D BEST FOCUS ON OUR DEFENSES.
HUH?!
HE MAY BELONG TO THE PALADIN CORPS...
...BUT HE HAS NO MIND TO HONOR ANY OF OUR UNWRITTEN AGREE-MENTS.

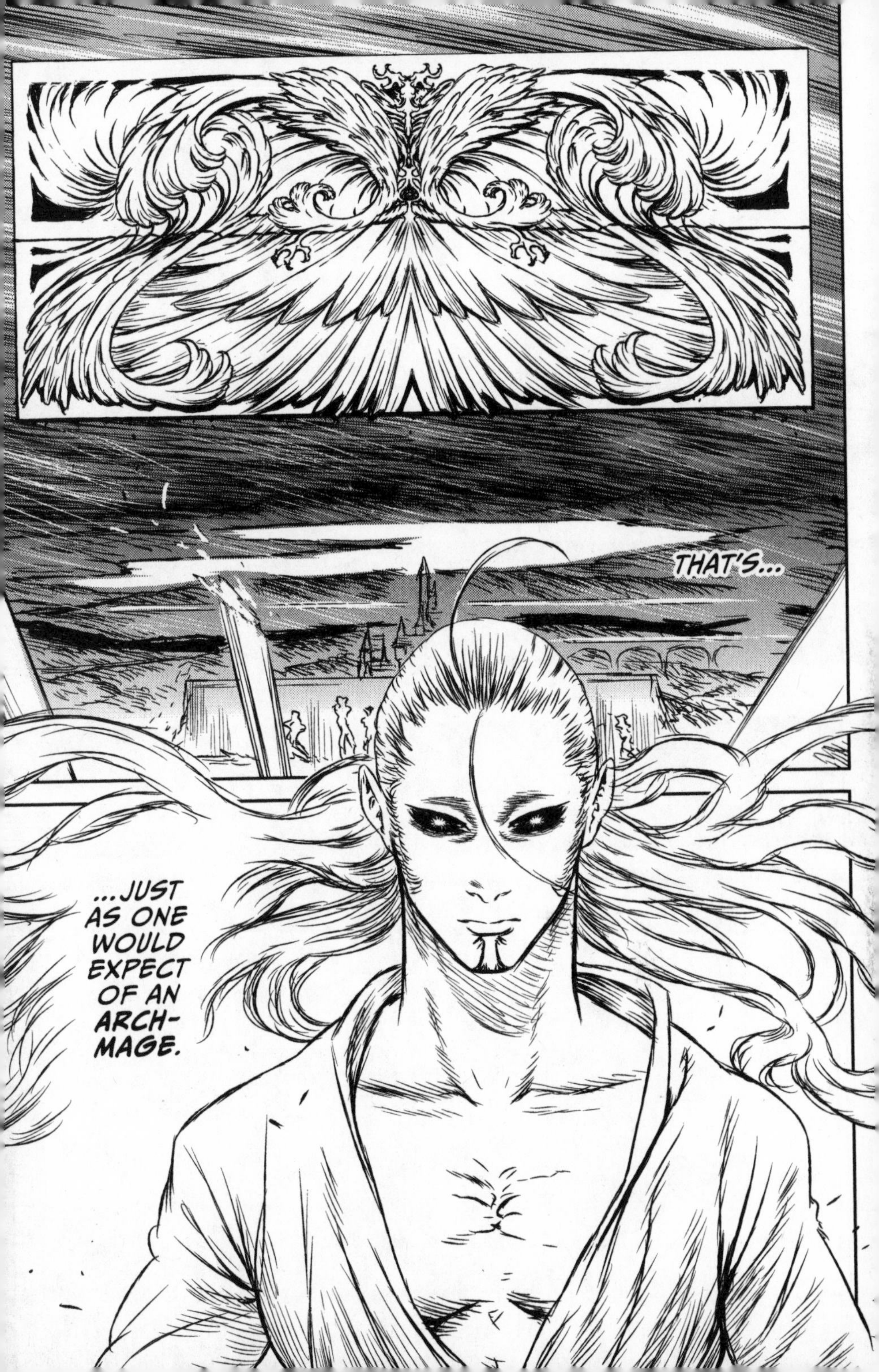
THAT'S...
...JUST AS ONE WOULD EXPECT OF AN ARCH-MAGE.

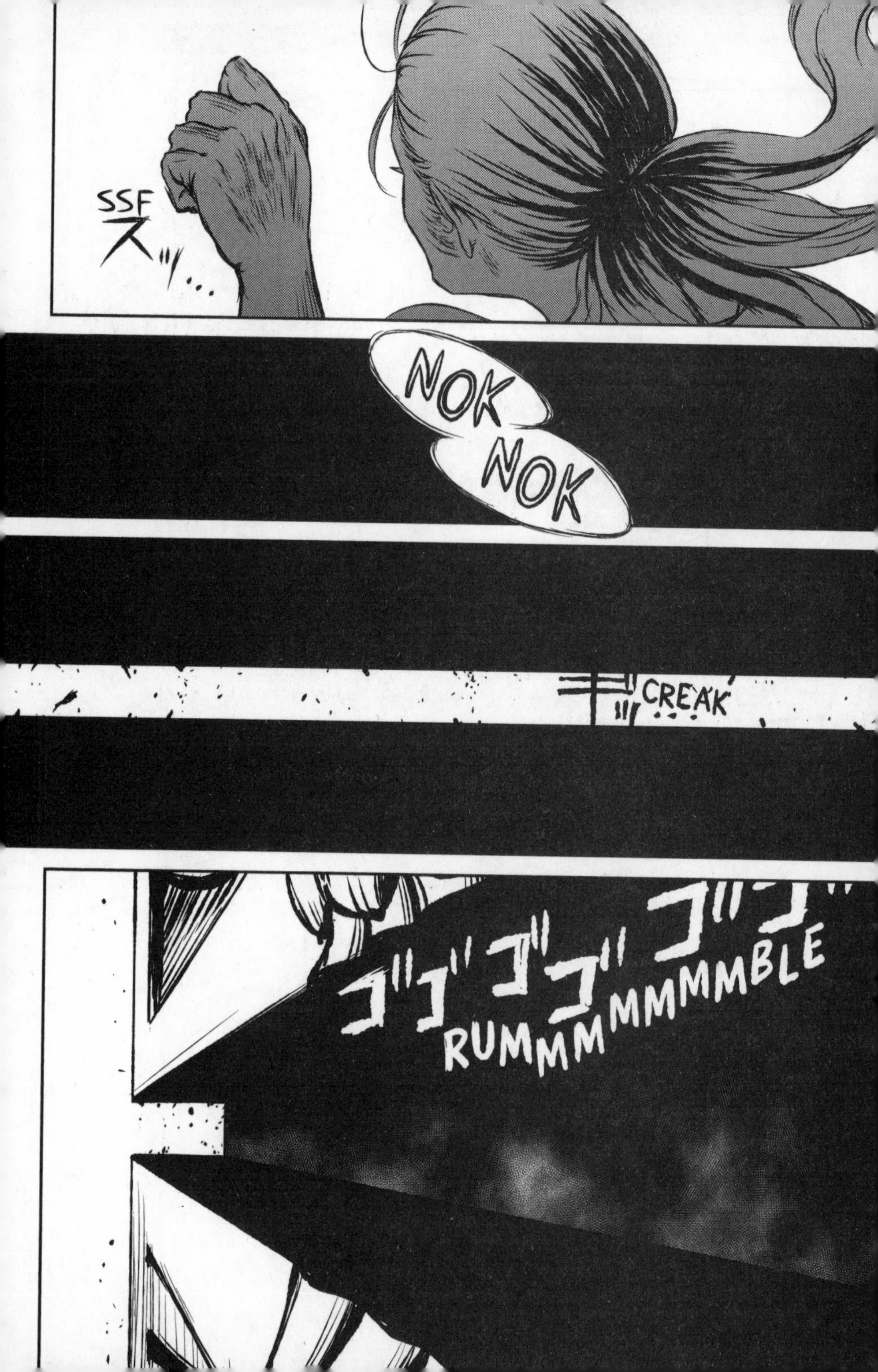
SSF
スッ…
NOK NOK
CREAK
RUMMMMMMMMBLE

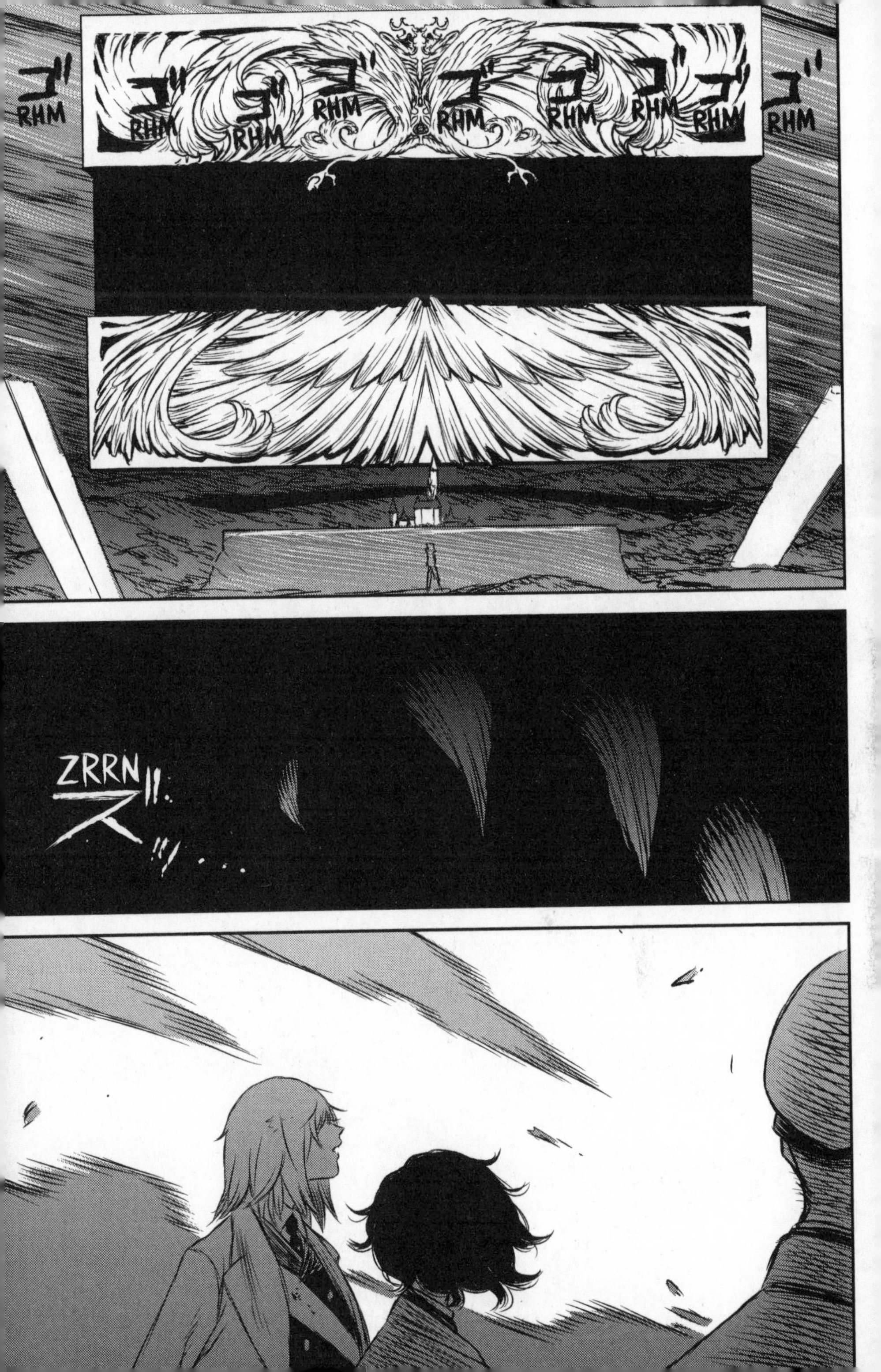
ゴ
RHM
ゴ
RHM
ゴ
RHM
ゴ
RHM
ゴ
RHM
ゴ
RHM
ゴ
RHM
ゴ
RHM
ZRRN
ズ!!…

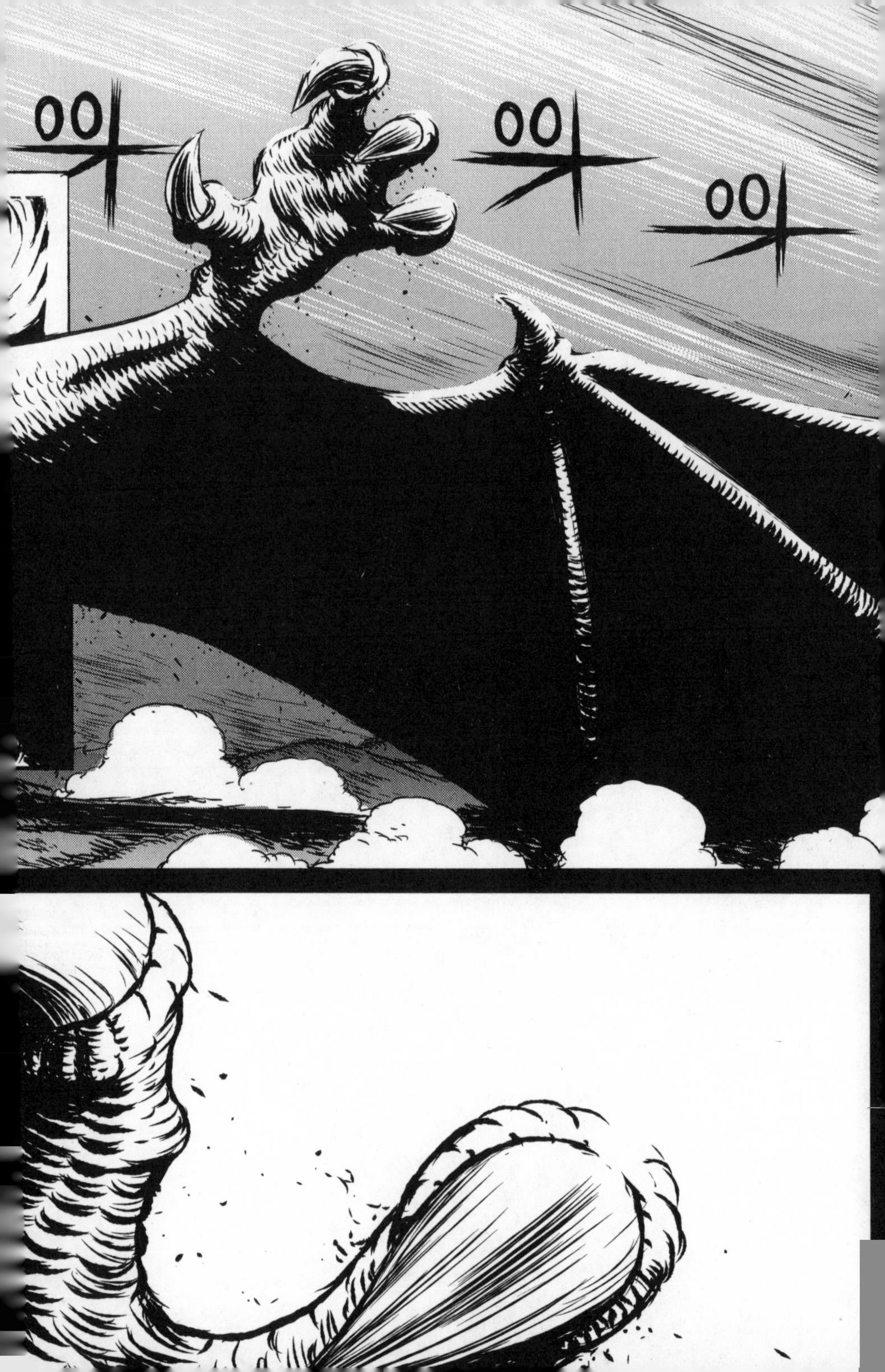

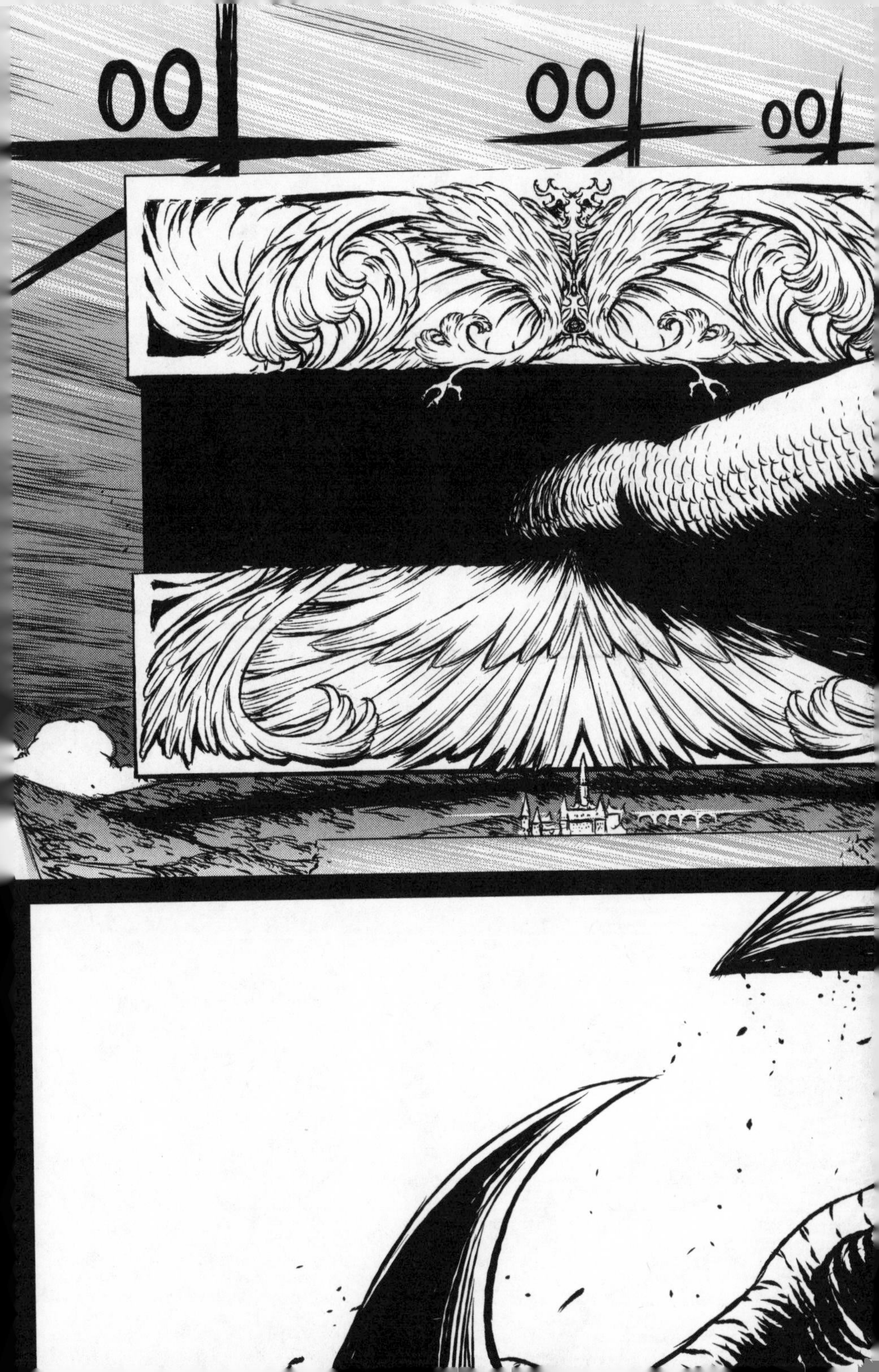
OO
OO
OO

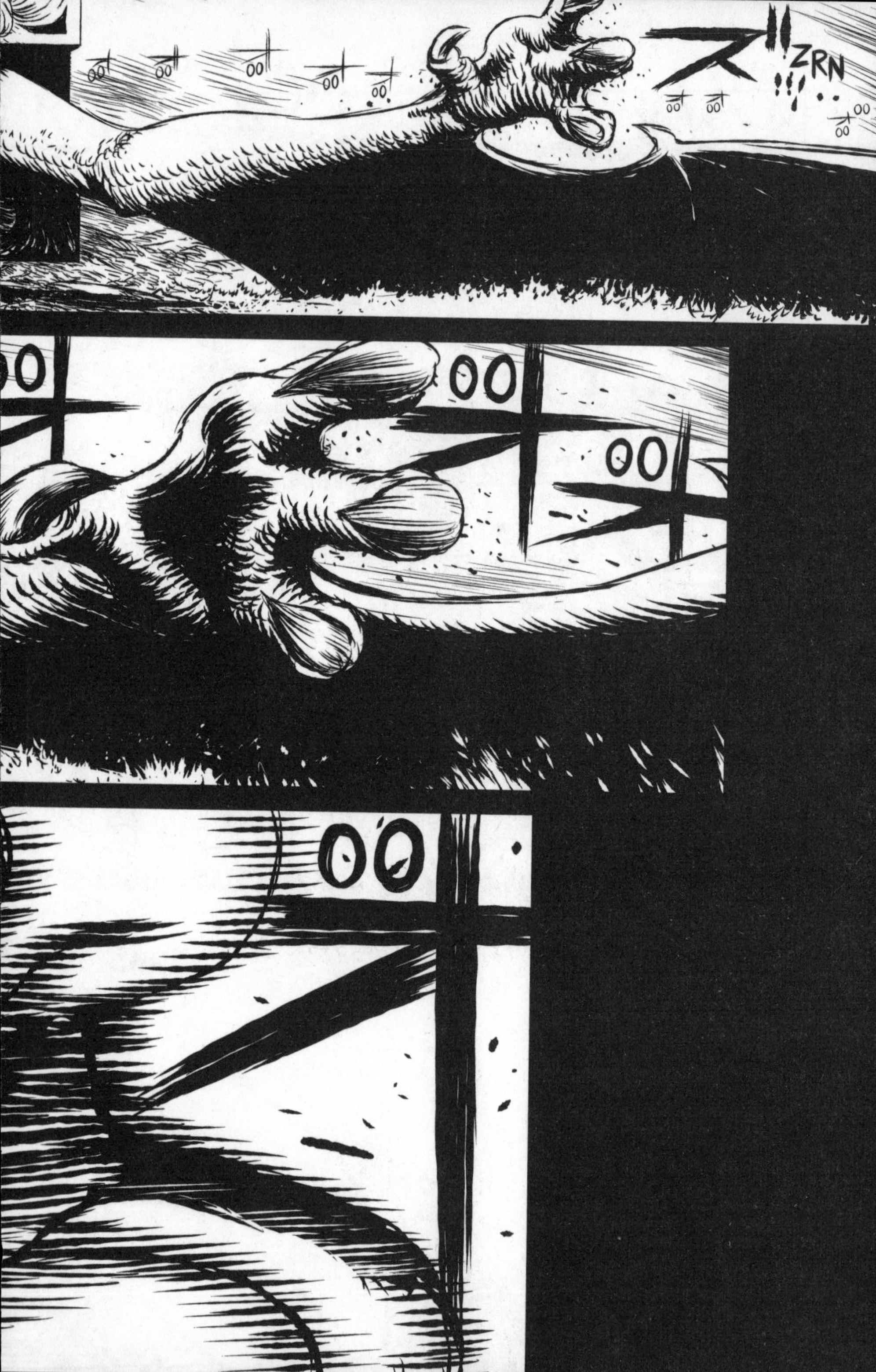
ZRN

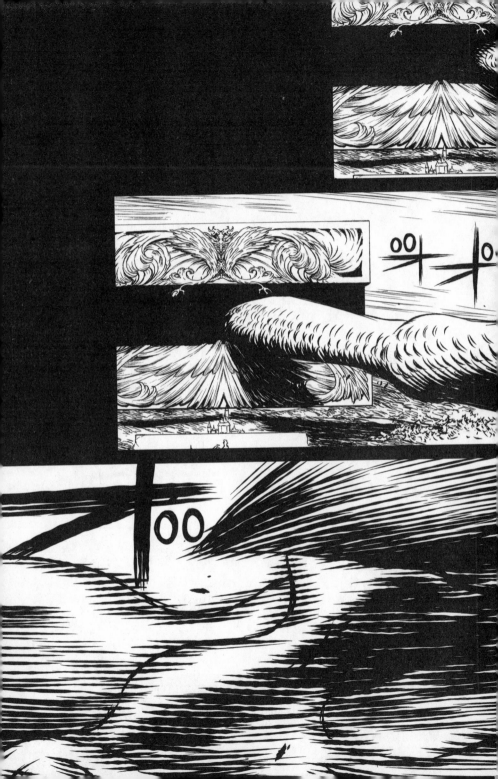

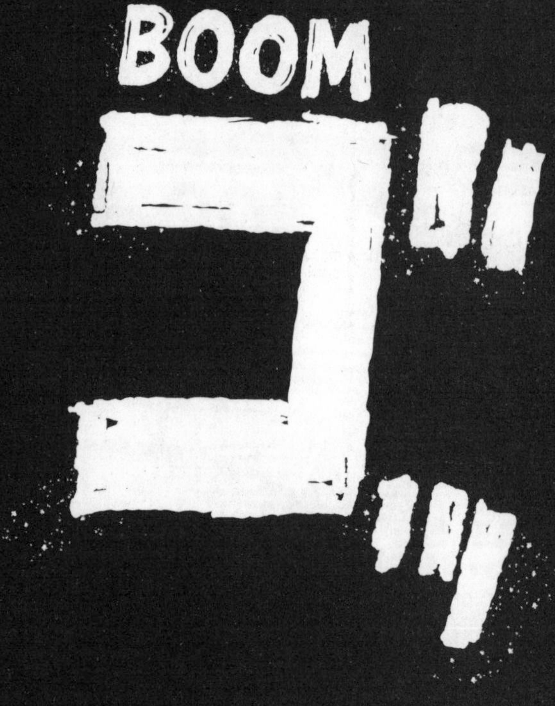
BOOM
ゴ

THE WITCH AND THE BEAST

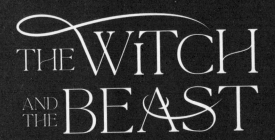

THE WITCH AND THE BEAST

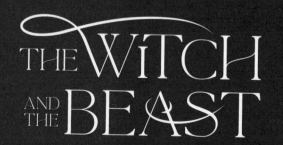

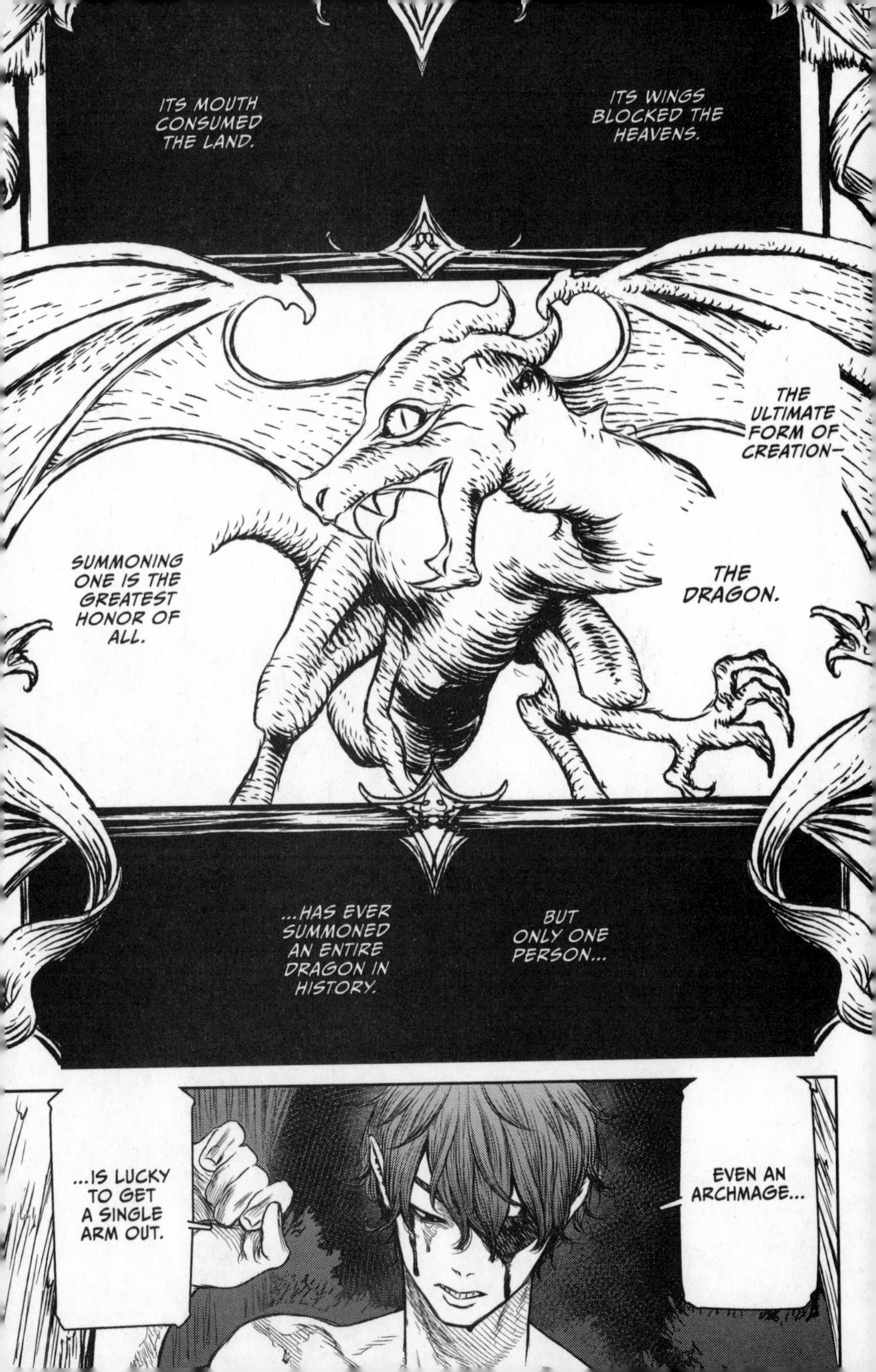
ITS WINGS BLOCKED THE HEAVENS.
ITS MOUTH CONSUMED THE LAND.
THE ULTIMATE FORM OF CREATION—
THE DRAGON.
SUMMONING ONE IS THE GREATEST HONOR OF ALL.
BUT ONLY ONE PERSON...
...HAS EVER SUMMONED AN ENTIRE DRAGON IN HISTORY.
EVEN AN ARCHMAGE...
...IS LUCKY TO GET A SINGLE ARM OUT.

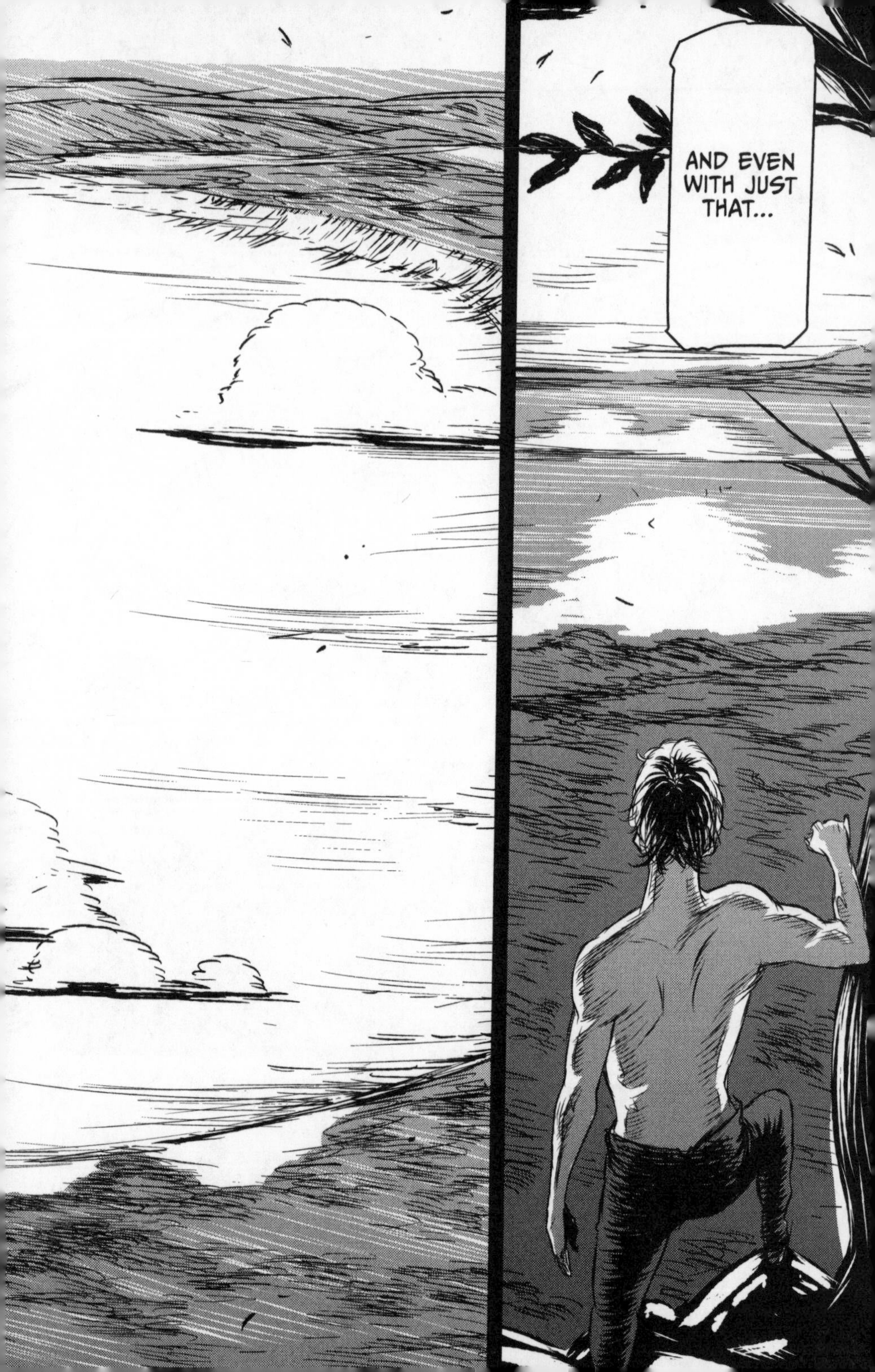
AND EVEN WITH JUST THAT...

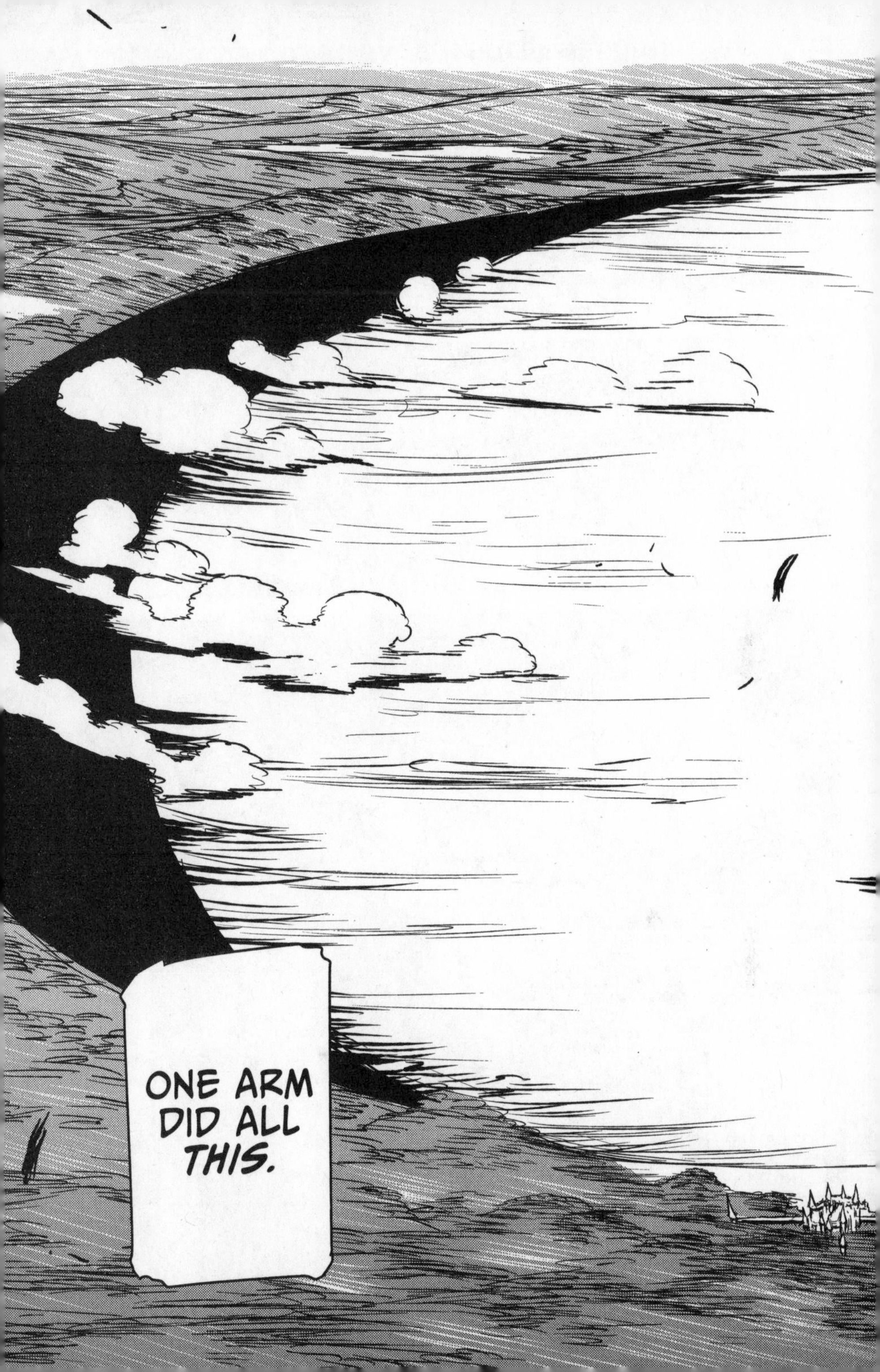
ONE ARM DID ALL THIS.

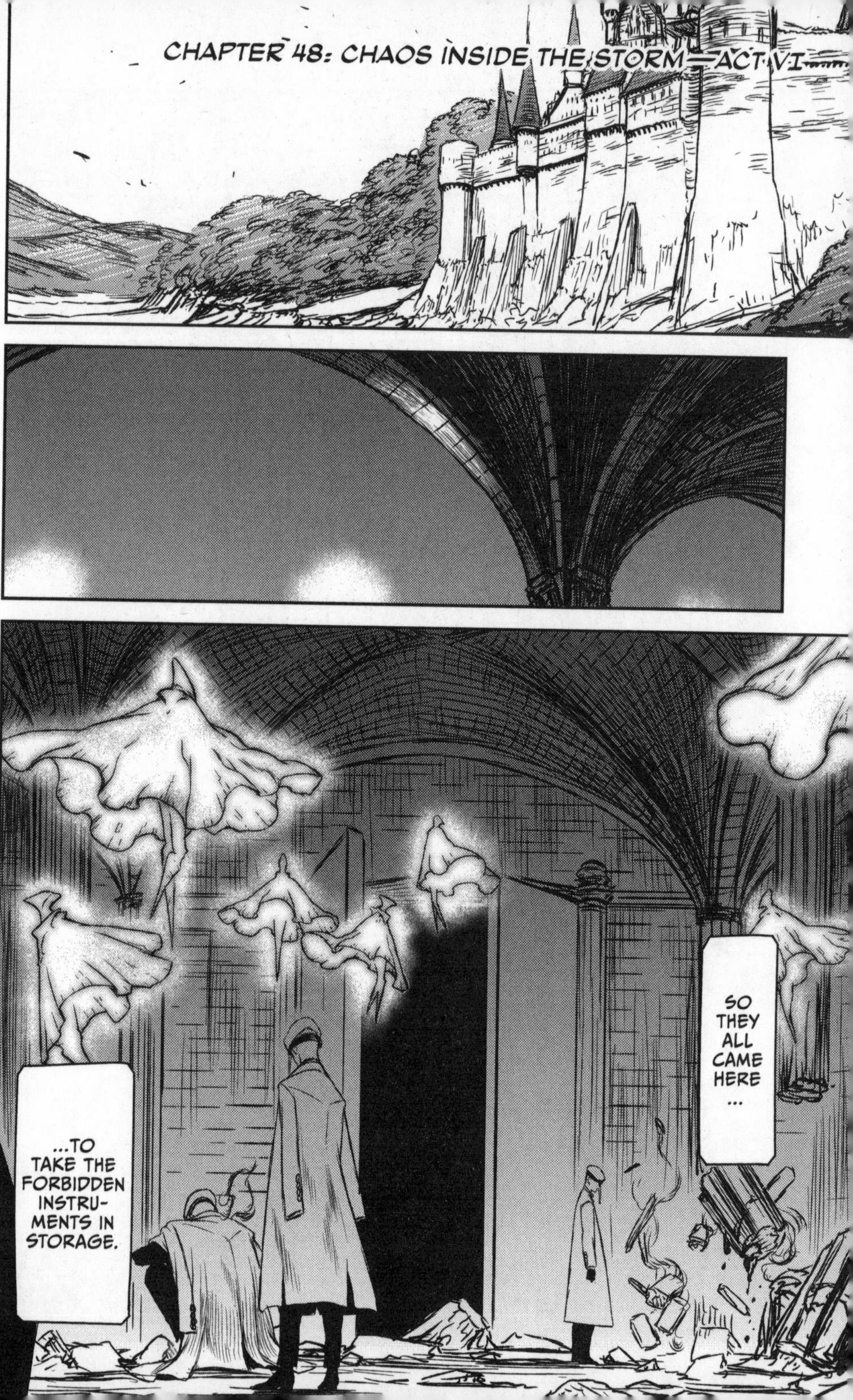
CHAPTER 48: CHAOS INSIDE THE STORM—ACT VI—
SO THEY ALL CAME HERE ...
...TO TAKE THE FORBIDDEN INSTRU-MENTS IN STORAGE.

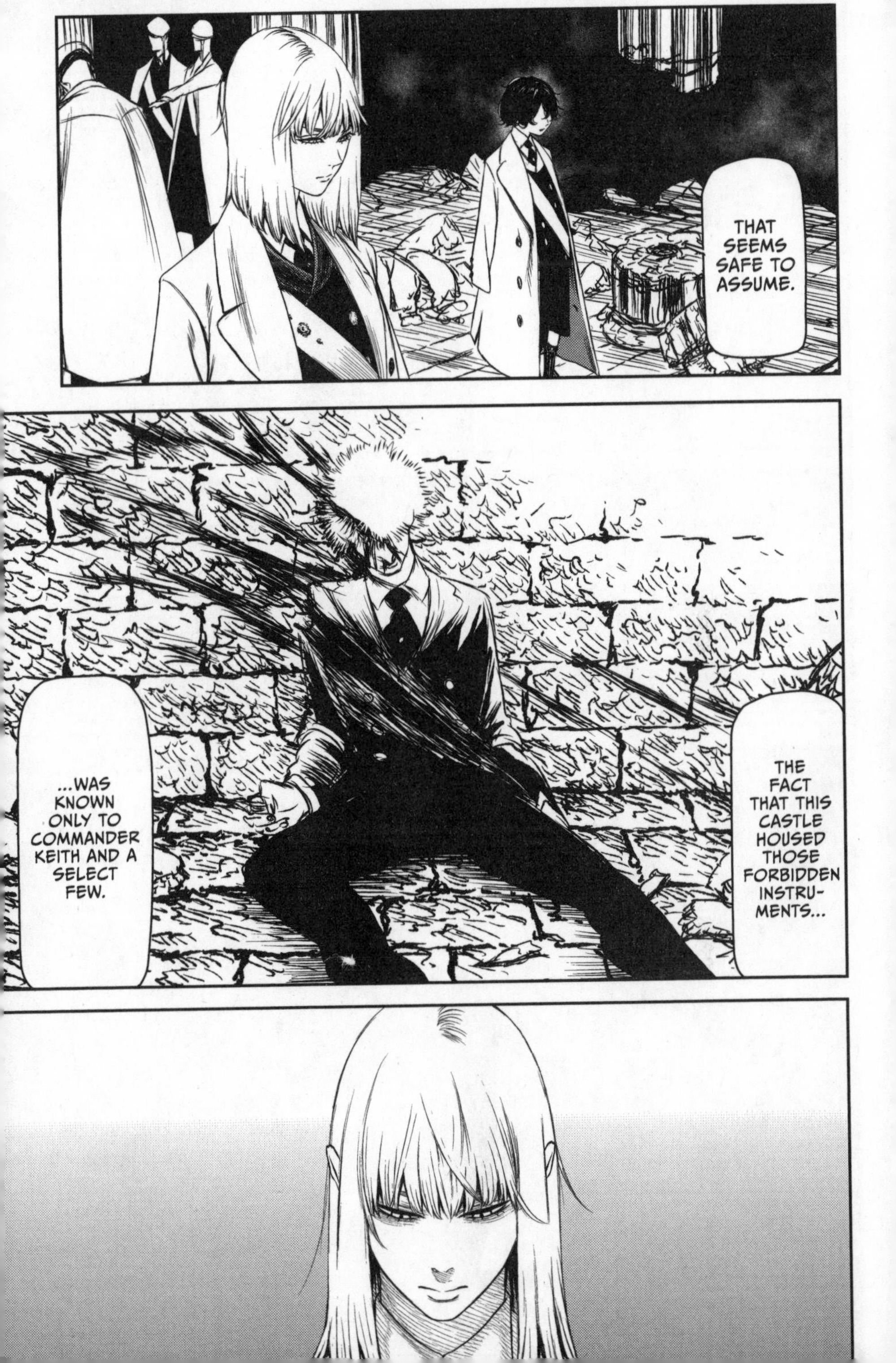
THAT SEEMS SAFE TO ASSUME.
THE FACT THAT THIS CASTLE HOUSED THOSE FORBIDDEN INSTRU-MENTS...
...WAS KNOWN ONLY TO COMMANDER KEITH AND A SELECT FEW.

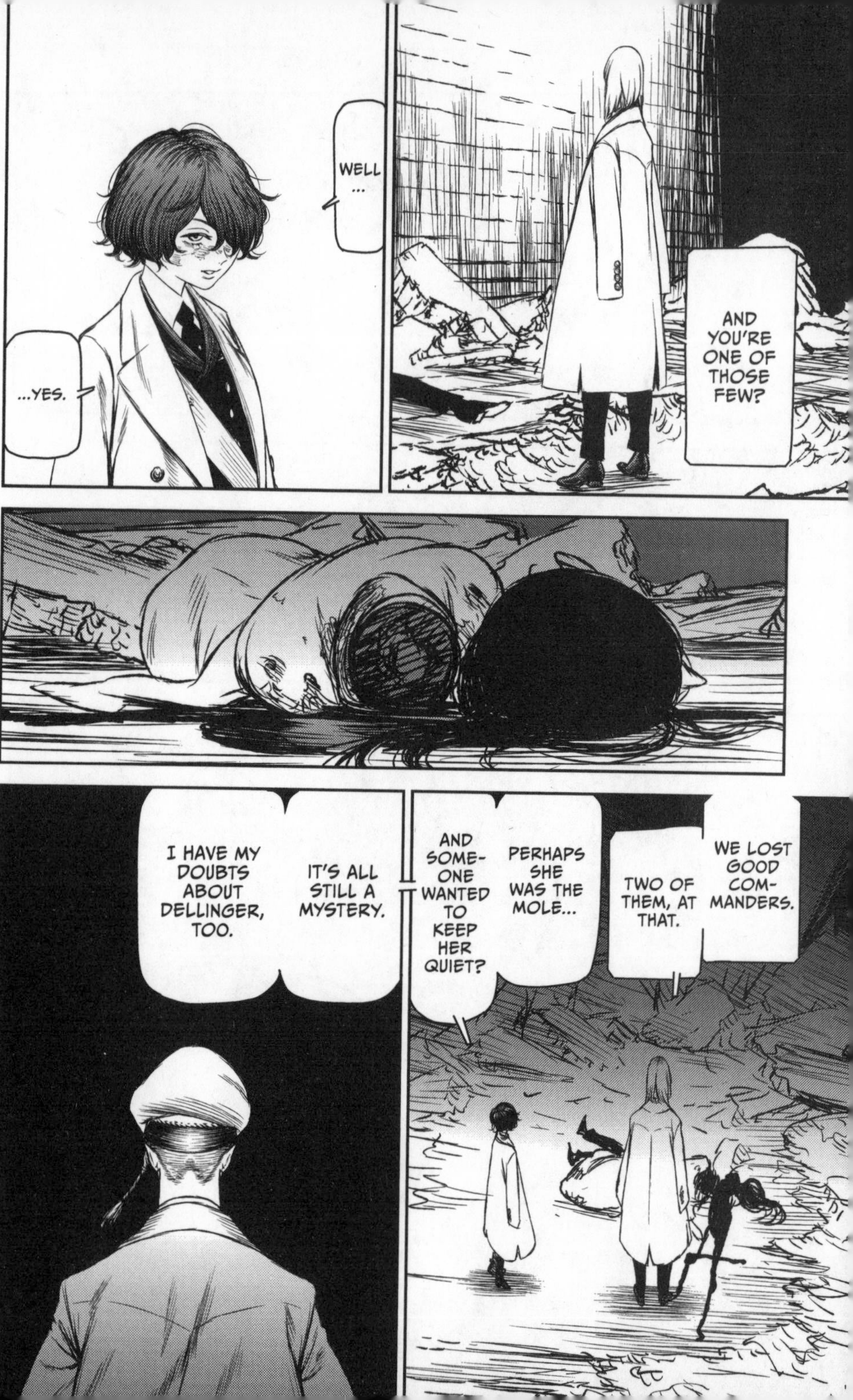
AND YOU'RE ONE OF THOSE FEW?
WELL ...
...YES.
WE LOST GOOD COMMANDERS.
TWO OF THEM, AT THAT.
PERHAPS SHE WAS THE MOLE...
AND SOMEONE WANTED TO KEEP HER QUIET?
IT'S ALL STILL A MYSTERY.
I HAVE MY DOUBTS ABOUT DELLINGER, TOO.

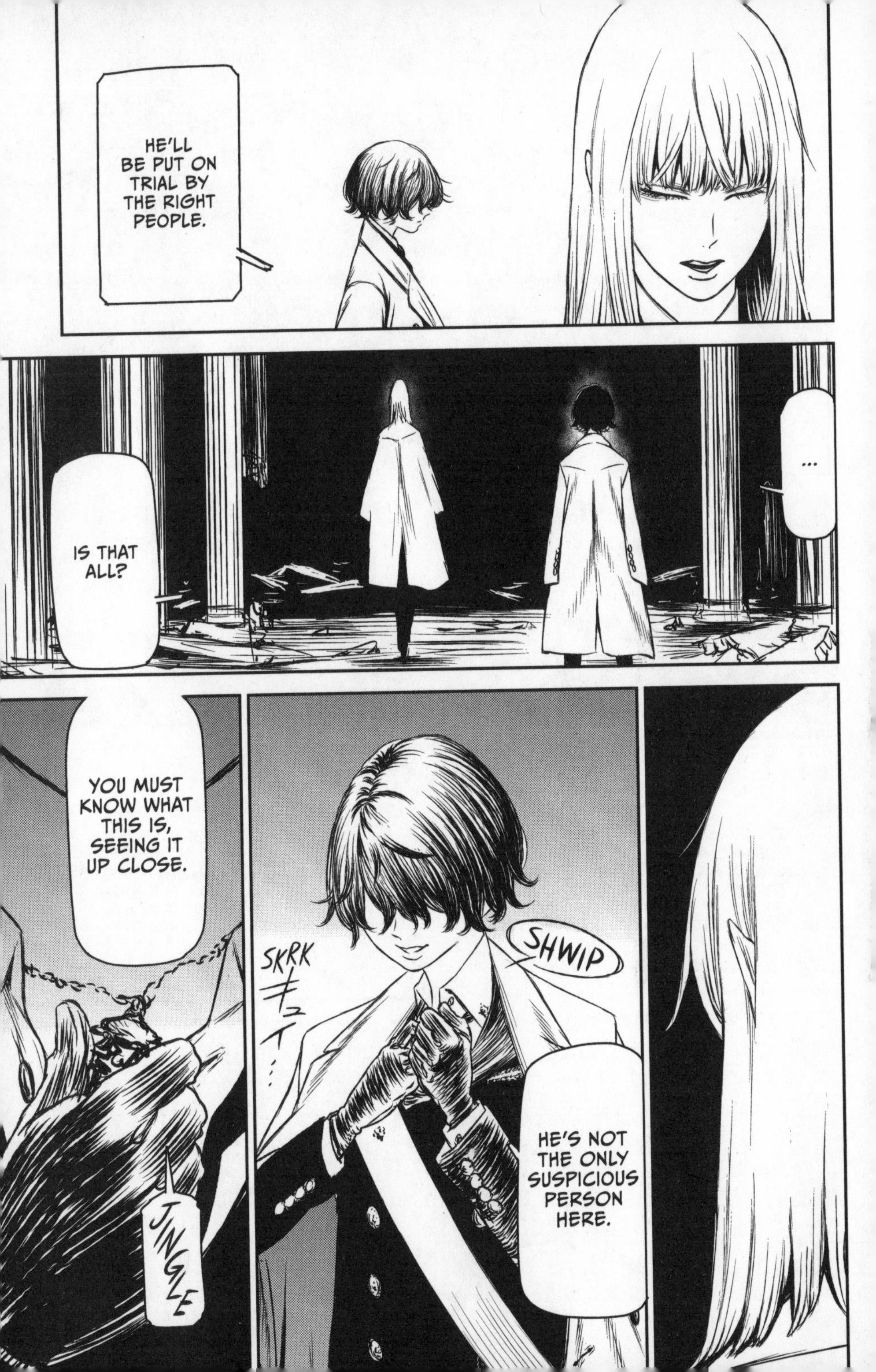
HE'LL BE PUT ON TRIAL BY THE RIGHT PEOPLE.
...
IS THAT ALL?
SHWIP
SKRK
キュイ…
HE'S NOT THE ONLY SUSPICIOUS PERSON HERE.
YOU MUST KNOW WHAT THIS IS, SEEING IT UP CLOSE.
JINGLE

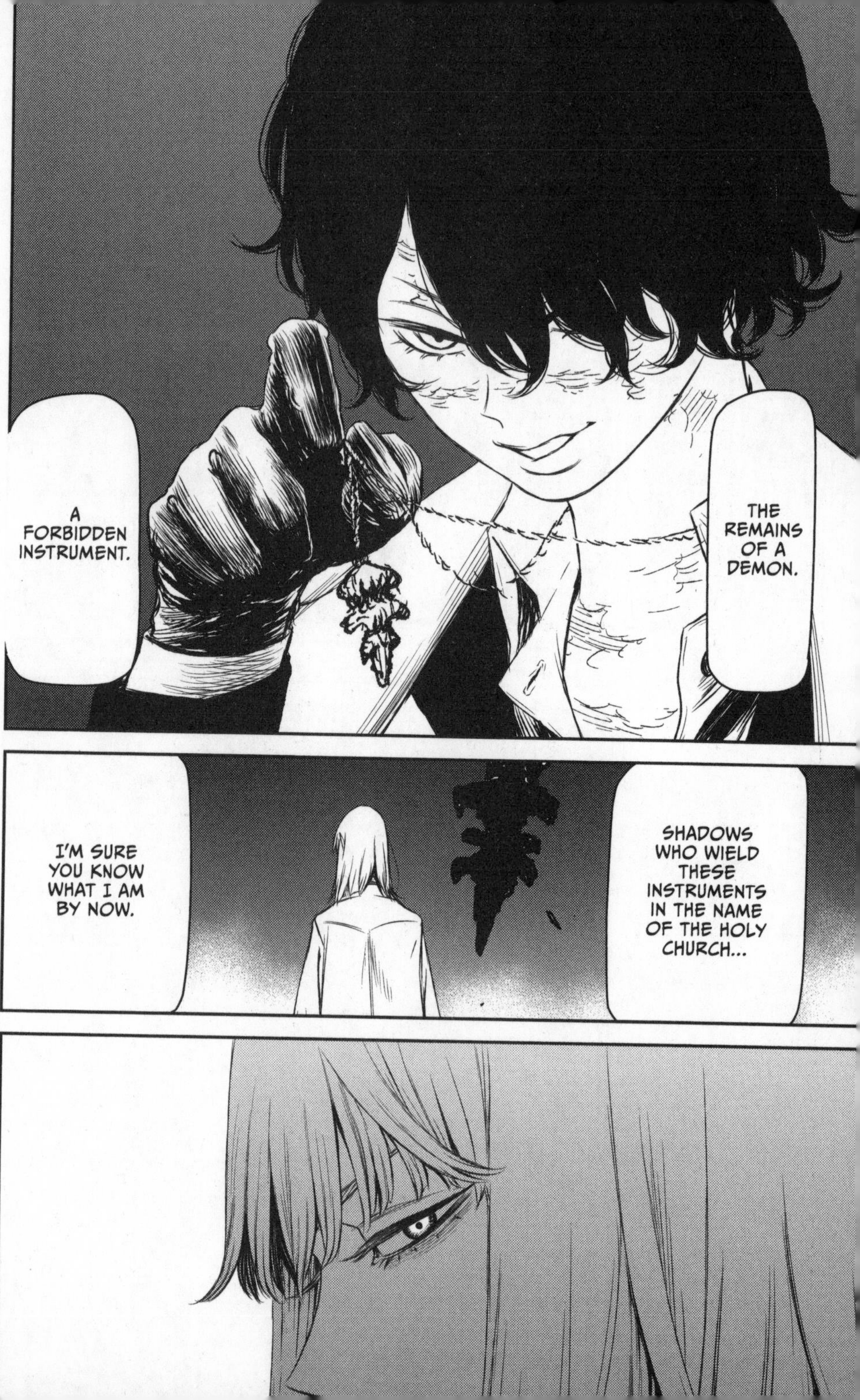
THE REMAINS OF A DEMON.
A FORBIDDEN INSTRUMENT.
SHADOWS WHO WIELD THESE INSTRUMENTS IN THE NAME OF THE HOLY CHURCH...
I'M SURE YOU KNOW WHAT I AM BY NOW.

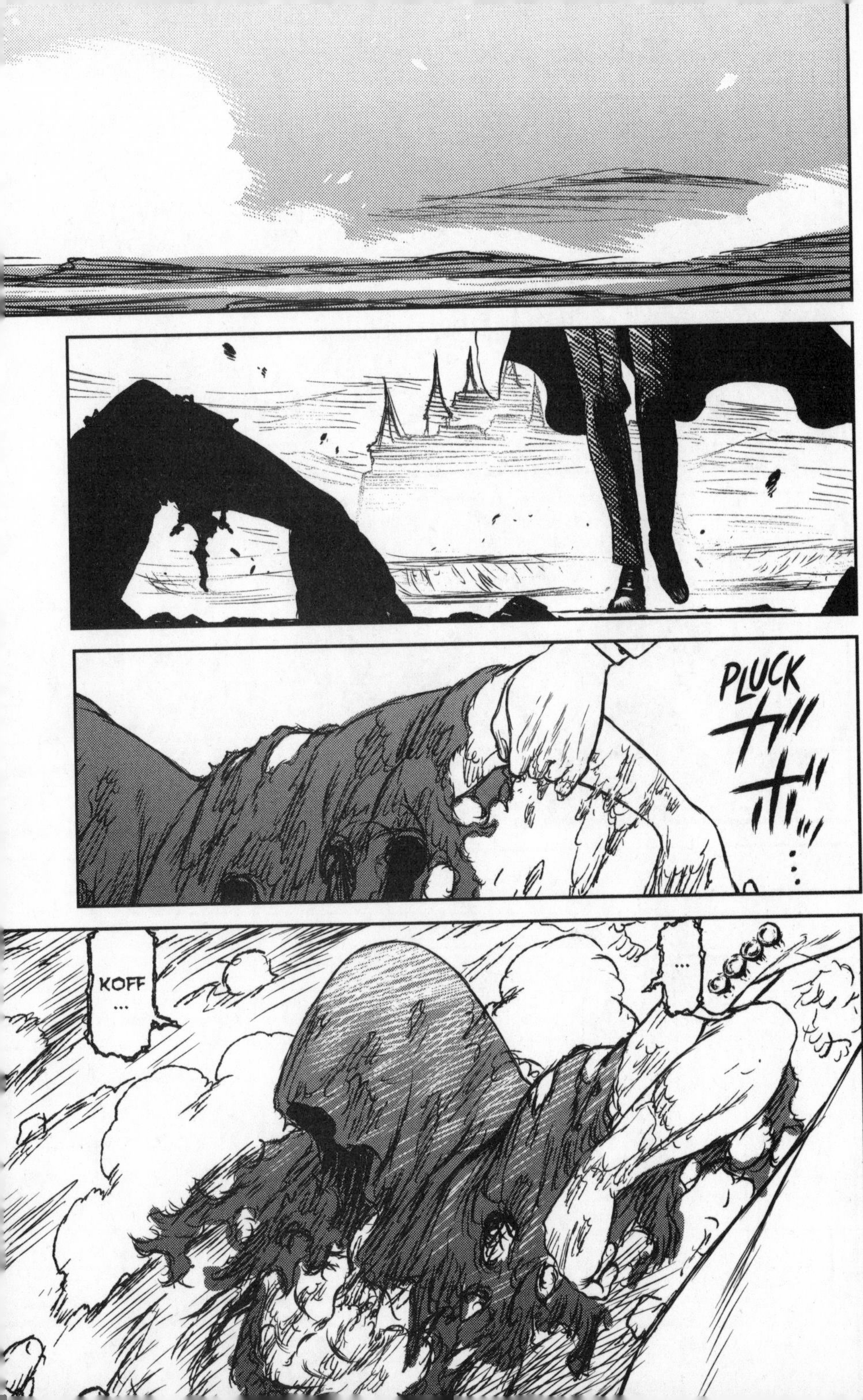
PLUCK
...
KOFF ...

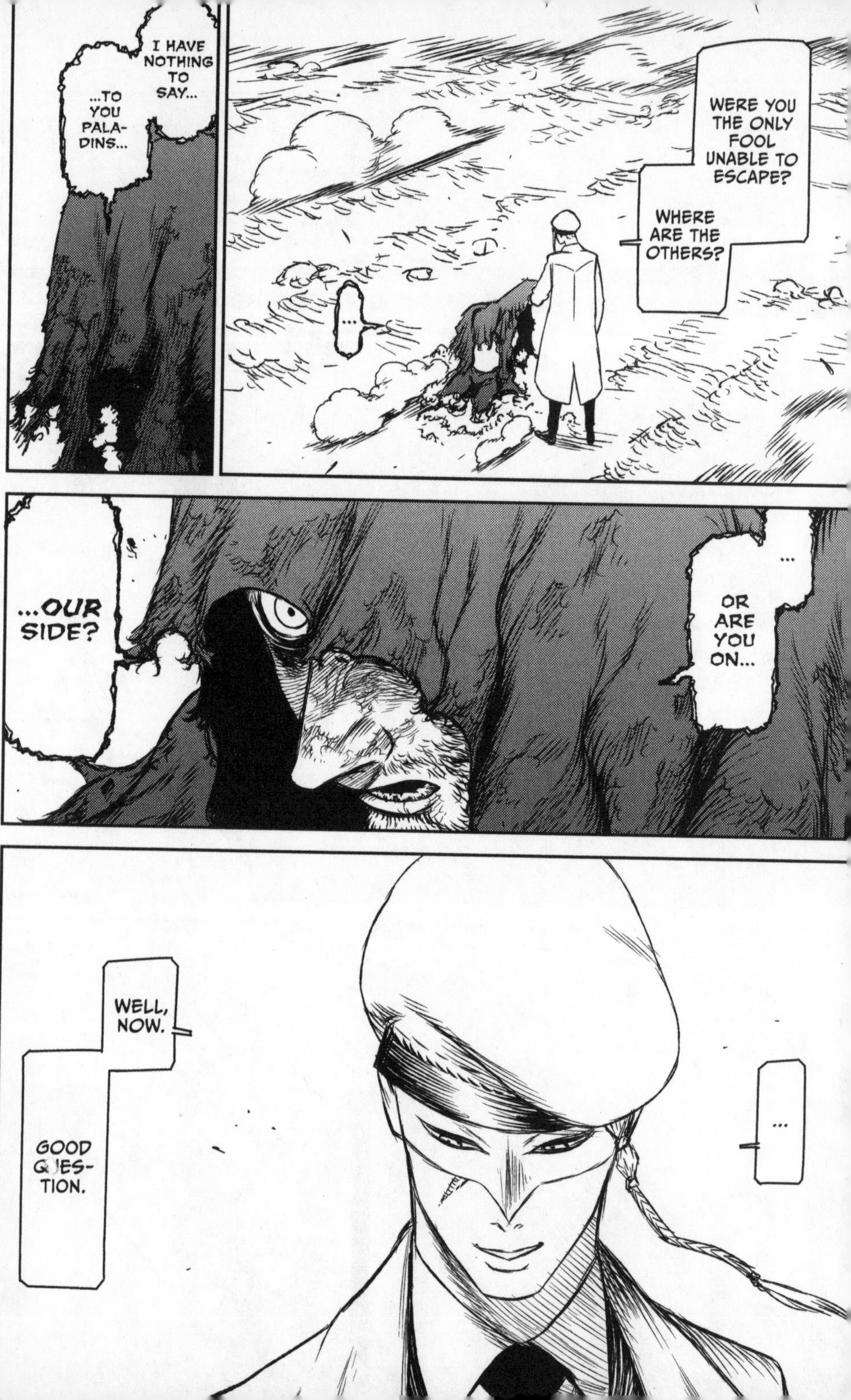
WERE YOU THE ONLY FOOL UNABLE TO ESCAPE?
WHERE ARE THE OTHERS?
...
I HAVE NOTHING TO SAY...
...TO YOU PALADINS...
...
OR ARE YOU ON...
...OUR SIDE?
...
WELL, NOW.
GOOD QUESTION.

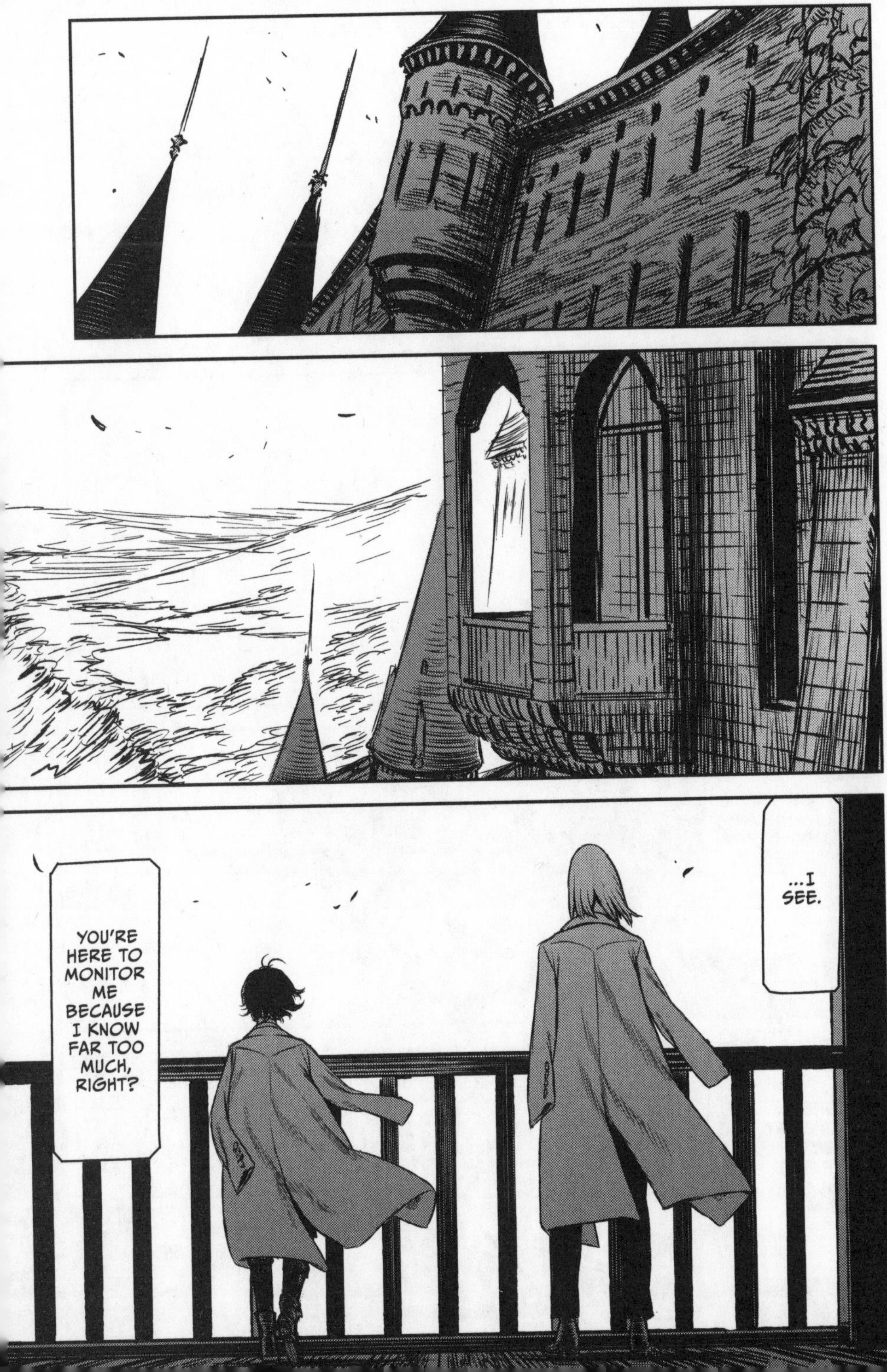
...I SEE.
YOU'RE HERE TO MONITOR ME BECAUSE I KNOW FAR TOO MUCH, RIGHT?

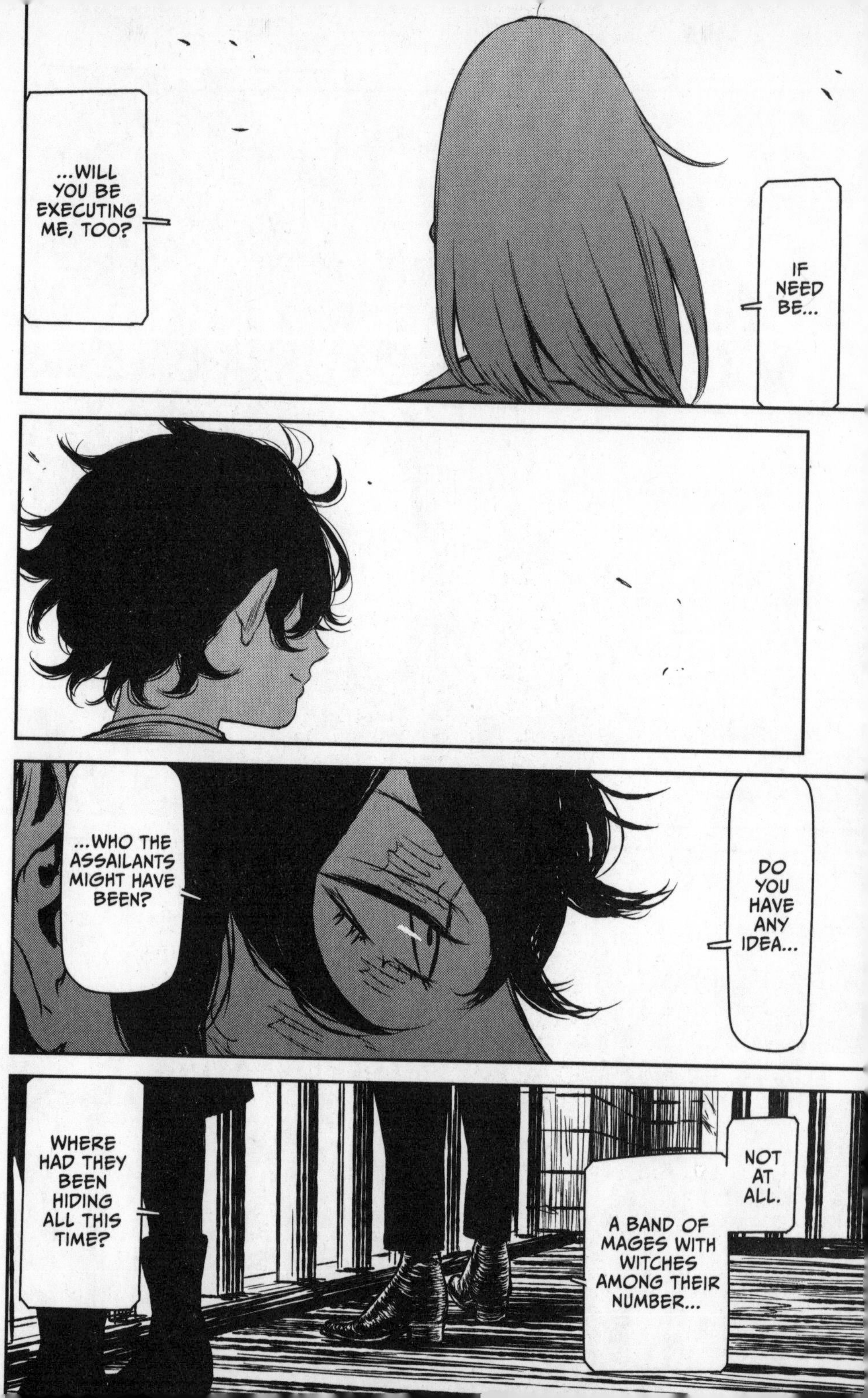
...WILL YOU BE EXECUTING ME, TOO?
IF NEED BE...
DO YOU HAVE ANY IDEA...
...WHO THE ASSAILANTS MIGHT HAVE BEEN?
NOT AT ALL.
A BAND OF MAGES WITH WITCHES AMONG THEIR NUMBER...
WHERE HAD THEY BEEN HIDING ALL THIS TIME?

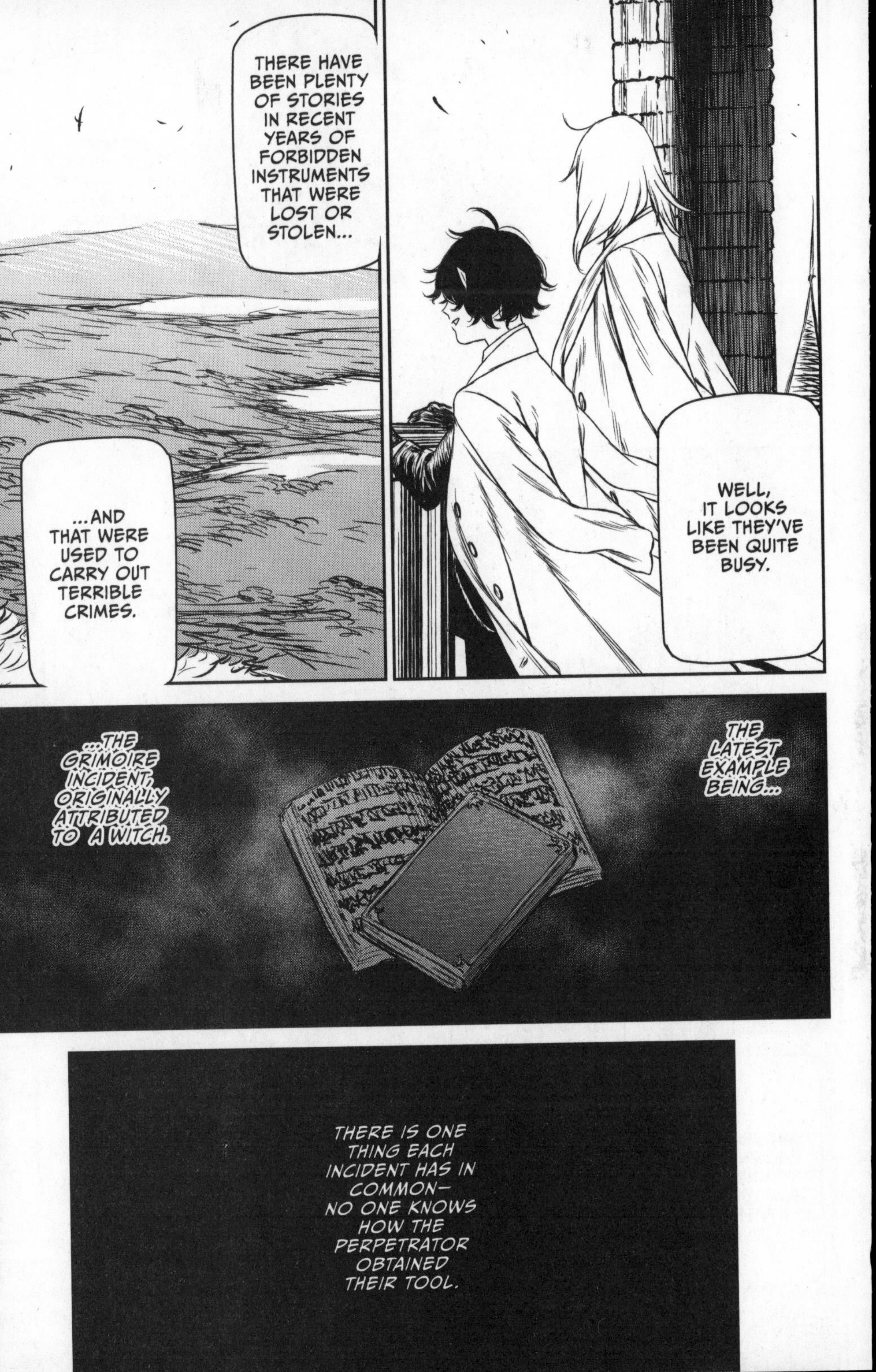
WELL, IT LOOKS LIKE THEY'VE BEEN QUITE BUSY.
THERE HAVE BEEN PLENTY OF STORIES IN RECENT YEARS OF FORBIDDEN INSTRUMENTS THAT WERE LOST OR STOLEN...
...AND THAT WERE USED TO CARRY OUT TERRIBLE CRIMES.
THE LATEST EXAMPLE BEING...
...THE GRIMOIRE INCIDENT, ORIGINALLY ATTRIBUTED TO A WITCH.
THERE IS ONE THING EACH INCIDENT HAS IN COMMON— NO ONE KNOWS HOW THE PERPETRATOR OBTAINED THEIR TOOL.

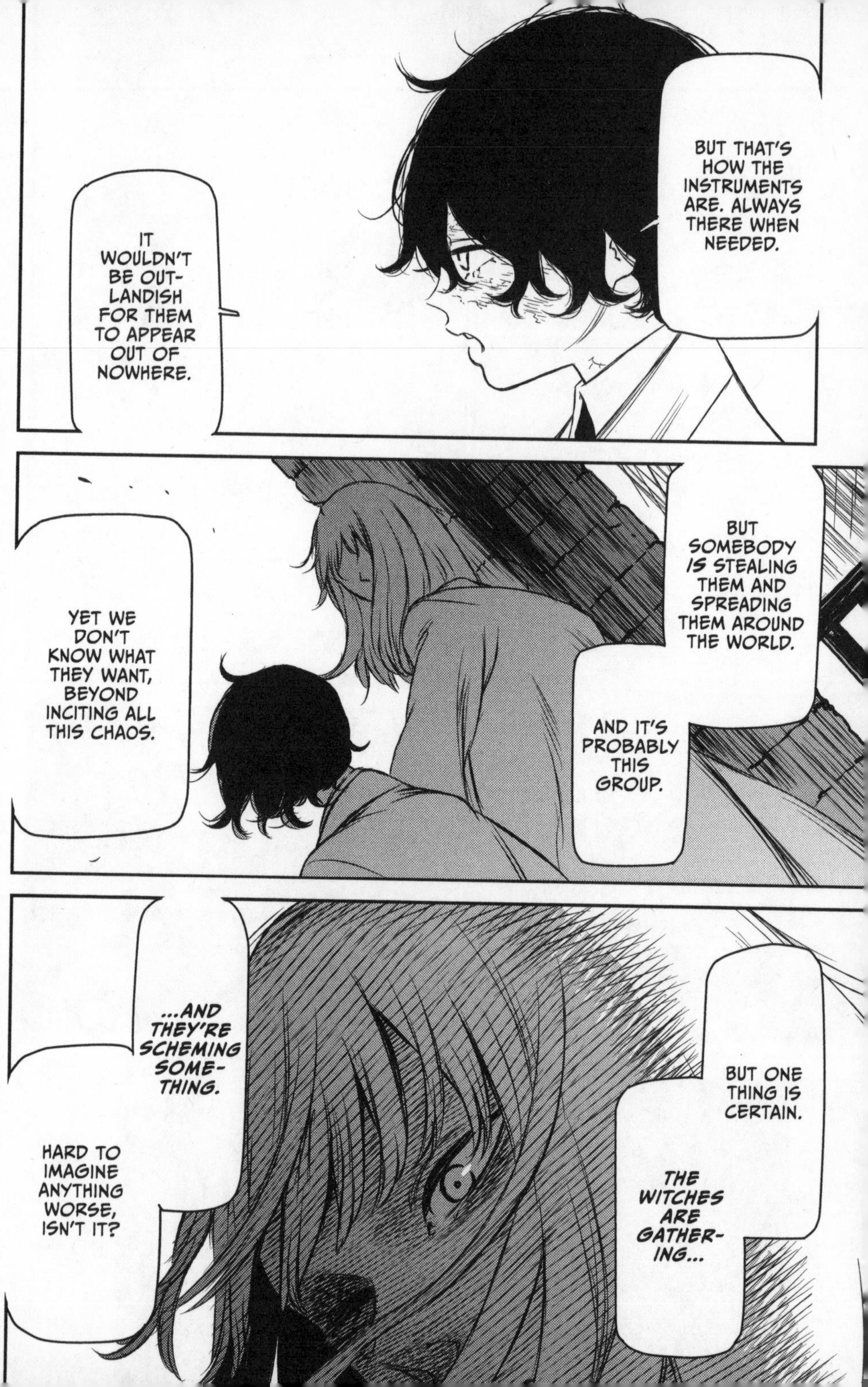
BUT THAT'S HOW THE INSTRUMENTS ARE. ALWAYS THERE WHEN NEEDED.
IT WOULDN'T BE OUT-LANDISH FOR THEM TO APPEAR OUT OF NOWHERE.
BUT SOMEBODY *IS* STEALING THEM AND SPREADING THEM AROUND THE WORLD.
AND IT'S PROBABLY THIS GROUP.
YET WE DON'T KNOW WHAT THEY WANT, BEYOND INCITING ALL THIS CHAOS.
BUT ONE THING IS CERTAIN.
THE WITCHES ARE GATHER-ING...
...AND THEY'RE SCHEMING SOME-THING.
HARD TO IMAGINE ANYTHING WORSE, ISN'T IT?

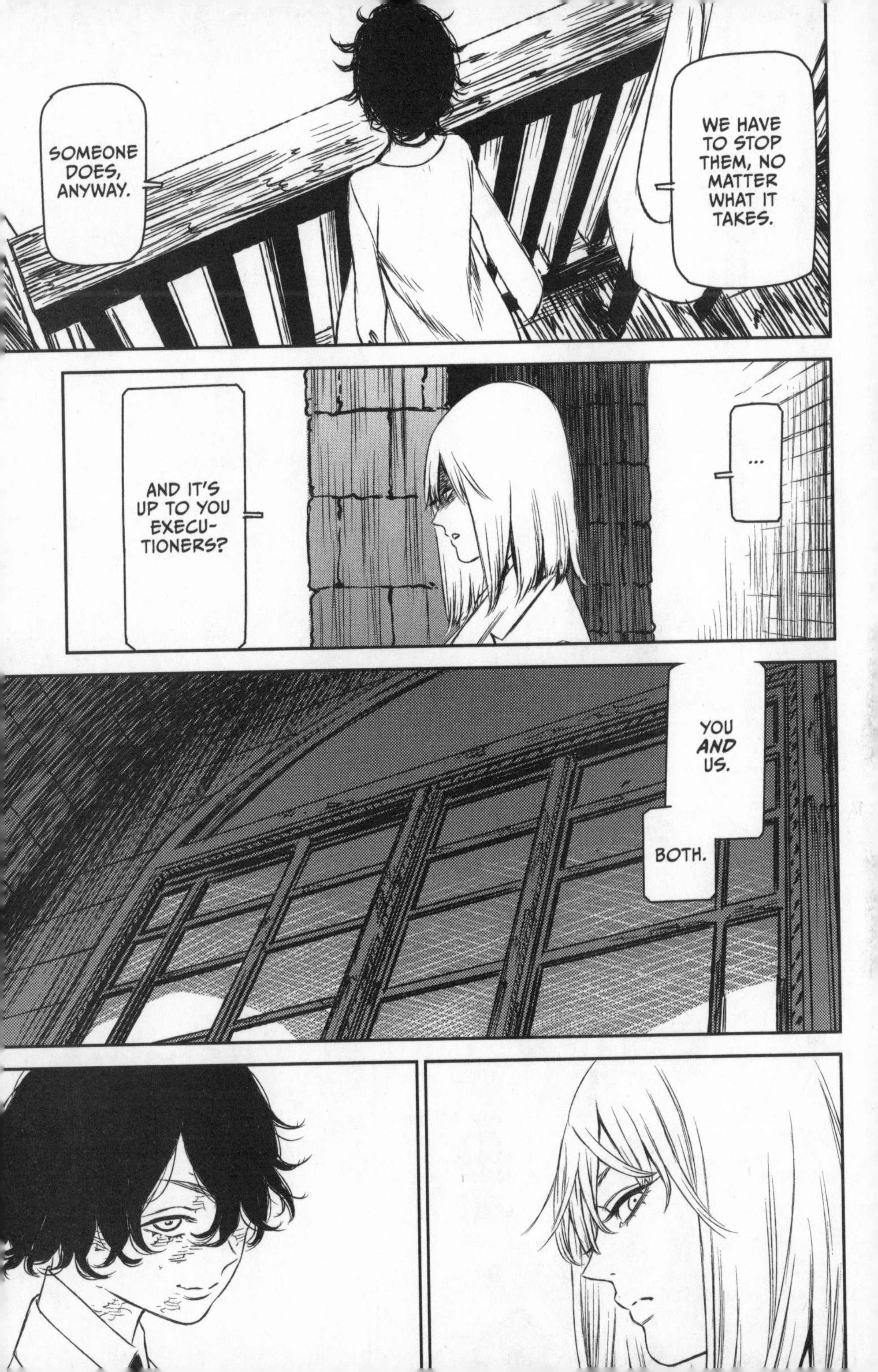
WE HAVE TO STOP THEM, NO MATTER WHAT IT TAKES.
SOMEONE DOES, ANYWAY.
...
AND IT'S UP TO YOU EXECUTIONERS?
YOU AND US.
BOTH.

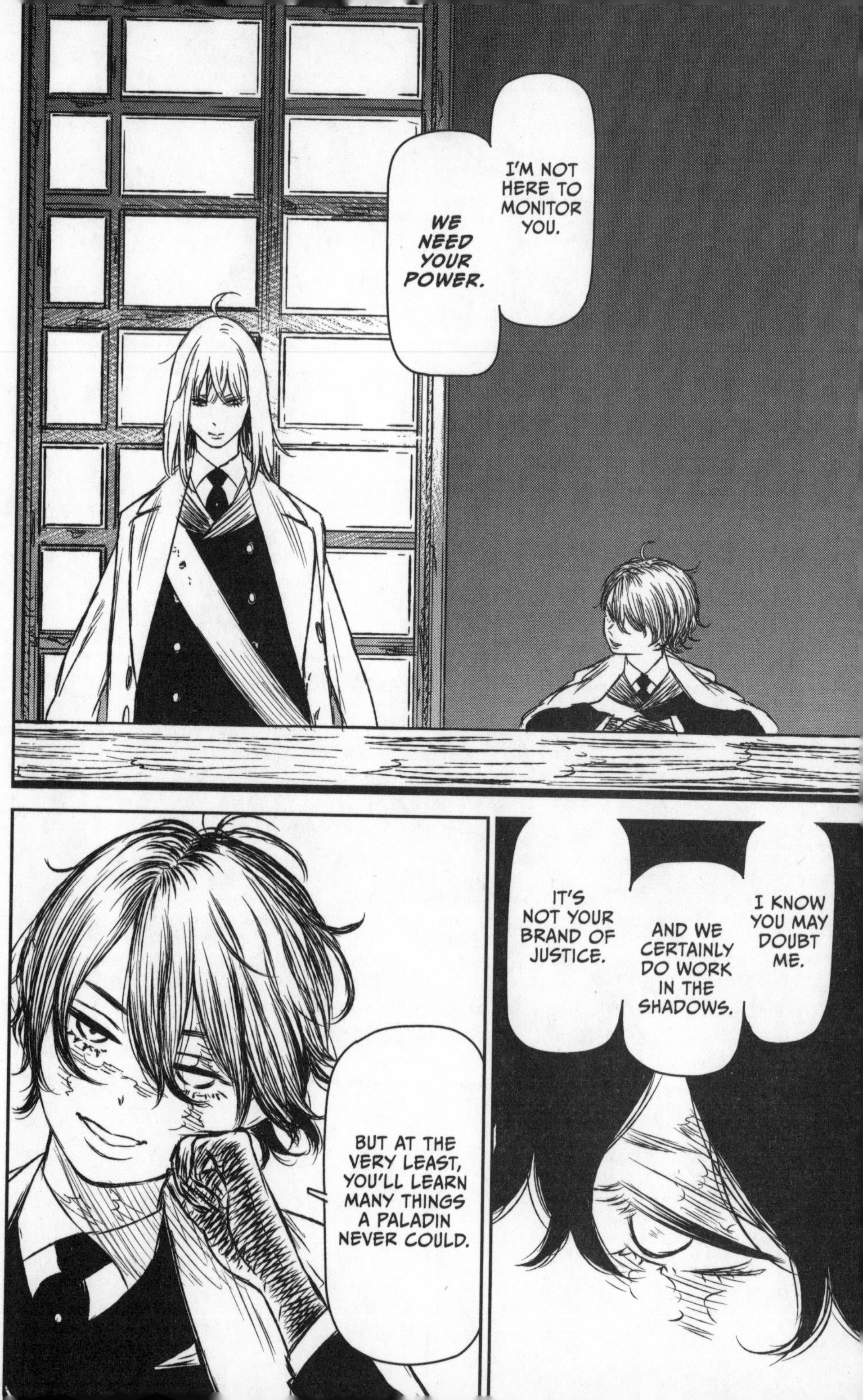
I'M NOT HERE TO MONITOR YOU.
WE NEED YOUR POWER.
I KNOW YOU MAY DOUBT ME.
AND WE CERTAINLY DO WORK IN THE SHADOWS.
IT'S NOT YOUR BRAND OF JUSTICE.
BUT AT THE VERY LEAST, YOU'LL LEARN MANY THINGS A PALADIN NEVER COULD.

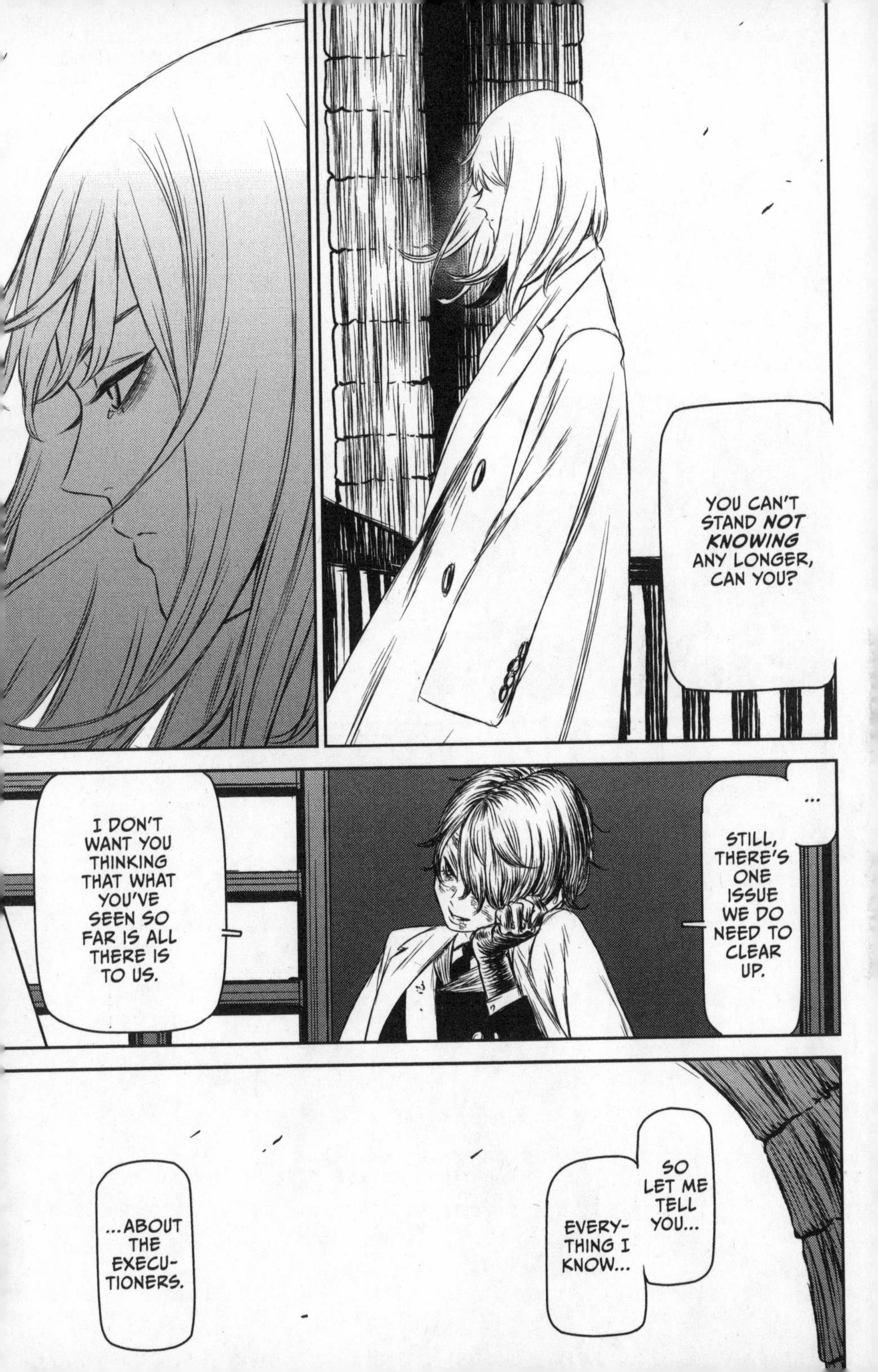
YOU CAN'T STAND *NOT KNOWING* ANY LONGER, CAN YOU?
...
STILL, THERE'S ONE ISSUE WE DO NEED TO CLEAR UP.
I DON'T WANT YOU THINKING THAT WHAT YOU'VE SEEN SO FAR IS ALL THERE IS TO US.
SO LET ME TELL YOU...
EVERY-THING I KNOW...
...ABOUT THE EXECU-TIONERS.

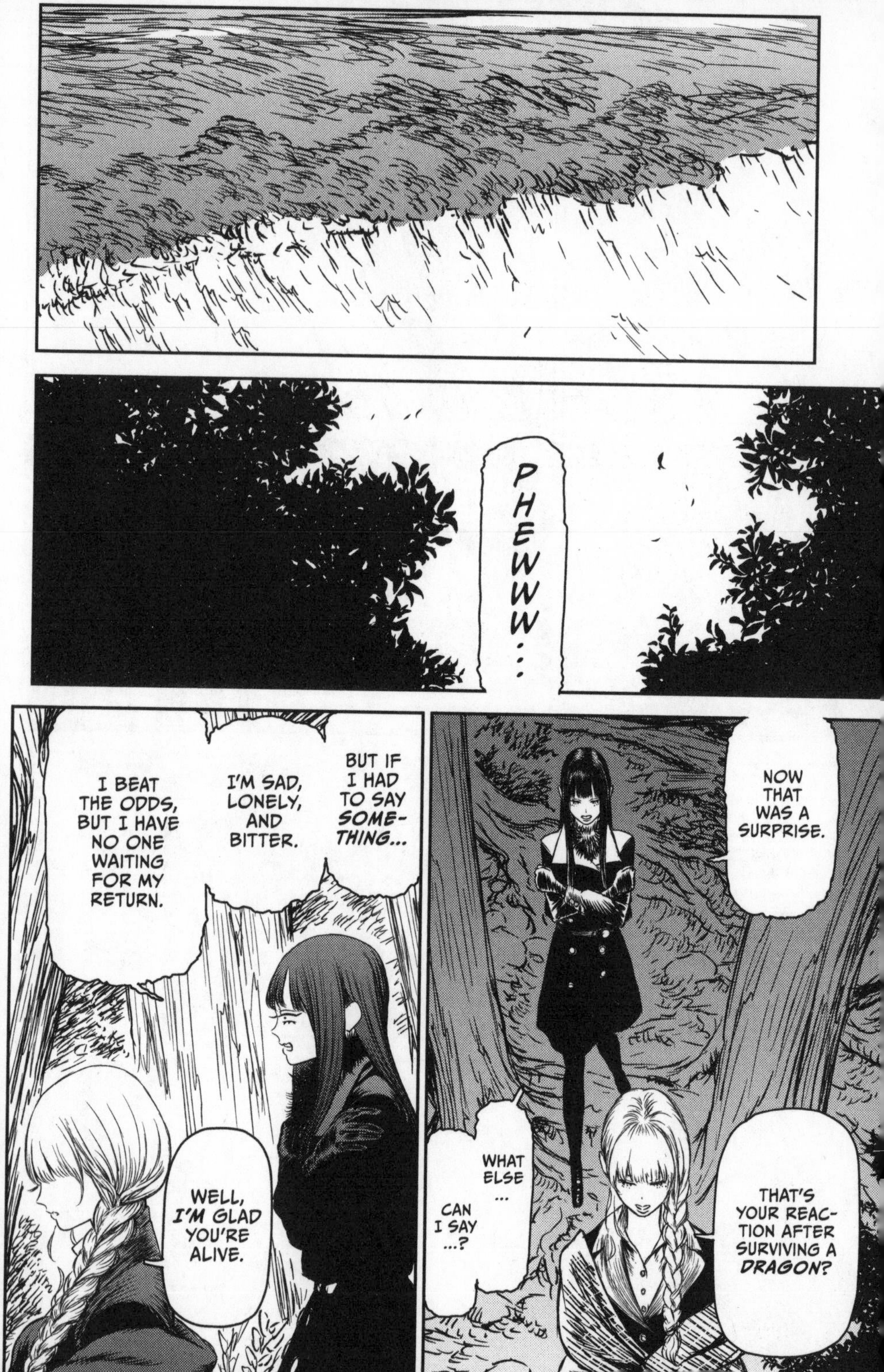
PHEWWW...
NOW THAT WAS A SURPRISE.
THAT'S YOUR REACTION AFTER SURVIVING A *DRAGON*?
WHAT ELSE ...
CAN I SAY ...?
BUT IF I HAD TO SAY *SOMETHING...*
I'M SAD, LONELY, AND BITTER.
I BEAT THE ODDS, BUT I HAVE NO ONE WAITING FOR MY RETURN.
WELL, *I'M* GLAD YOU'RE ALIVE.

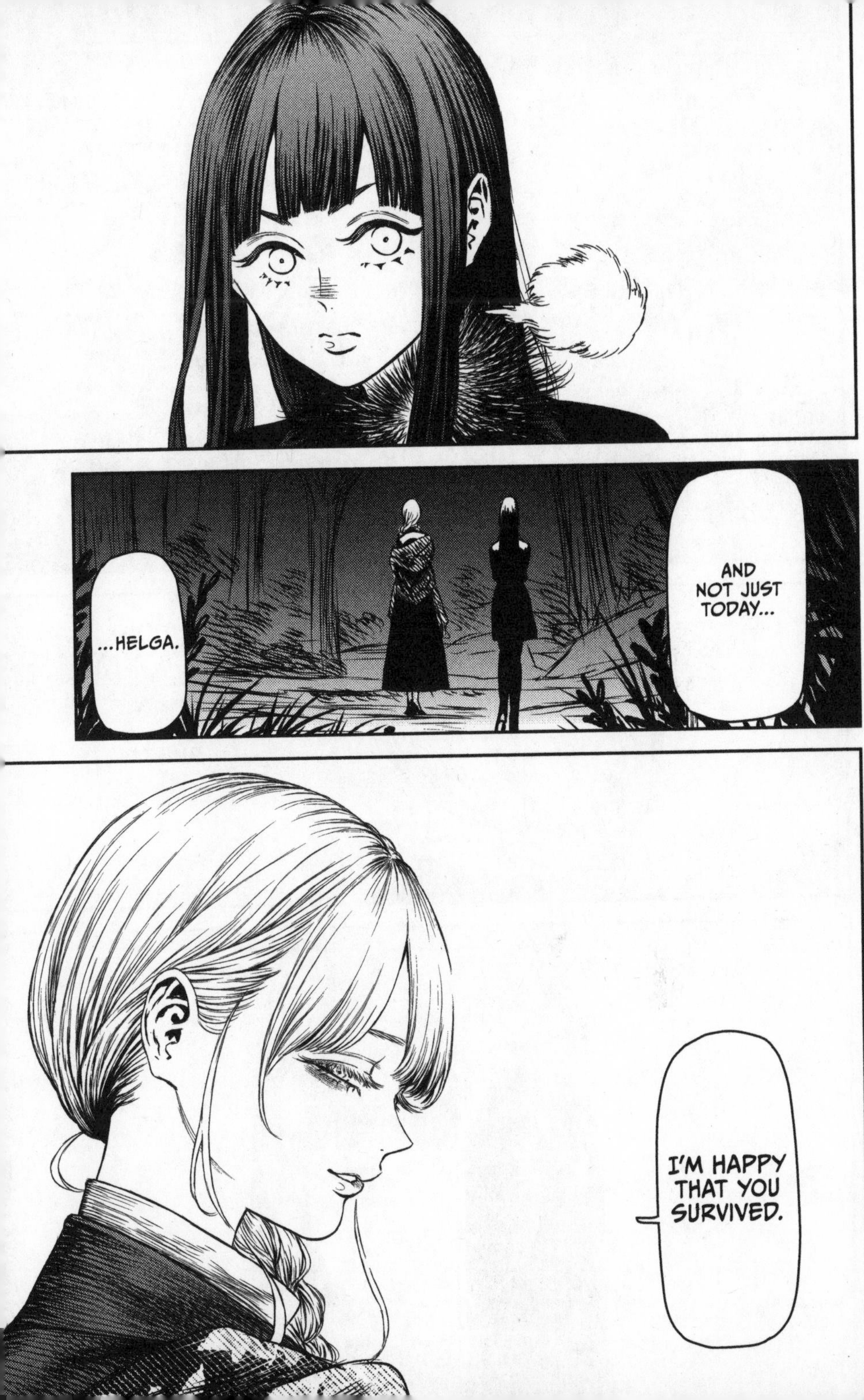
AND NOT JUST TODAY...
...HELGA.
I'M HAPPY THAT YOU SURVIVED.

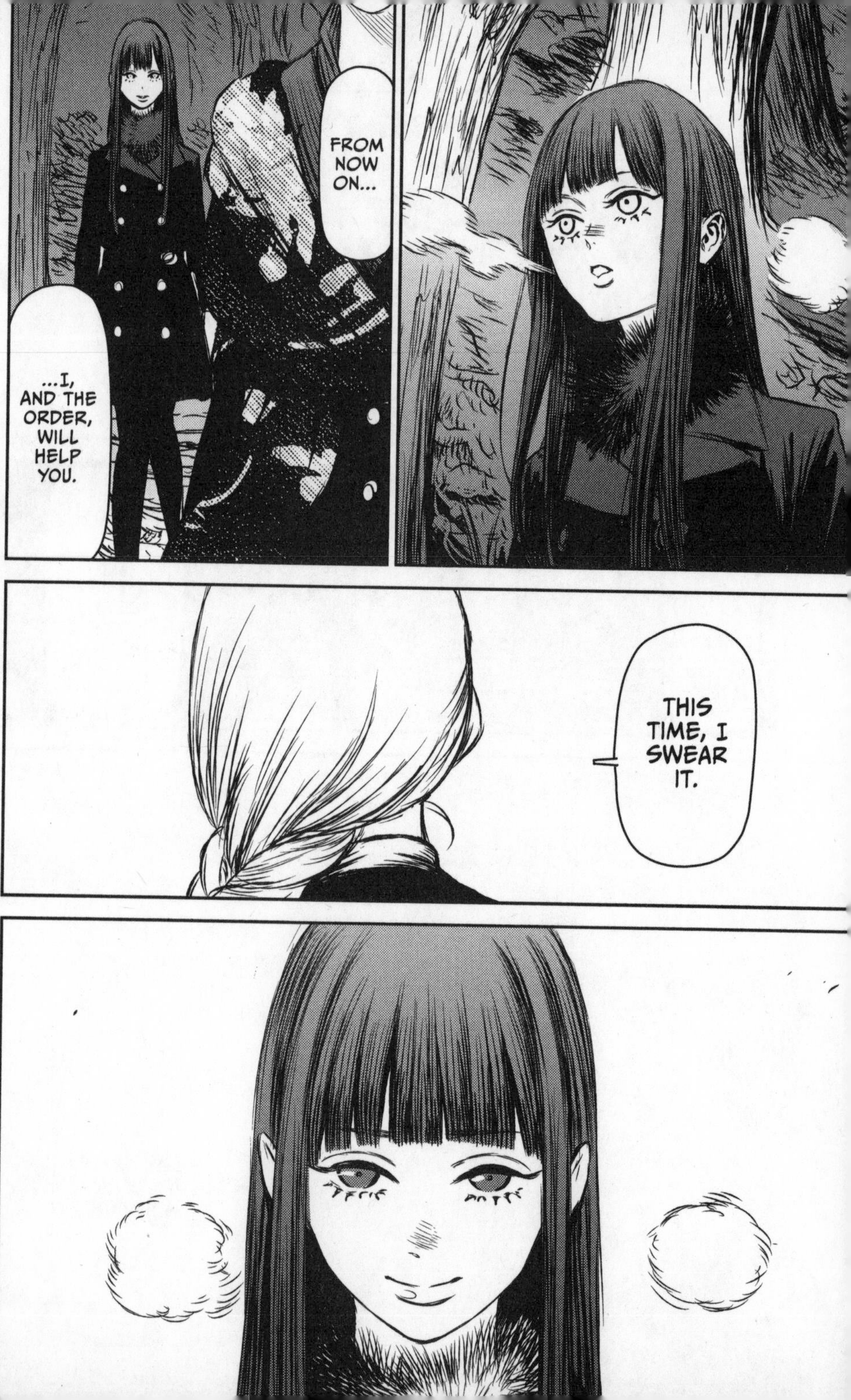
FROM NOW ON...
...I, AND THE ORDER, WILL HELP YOU.
THIS TIME, I SWEAR IT.

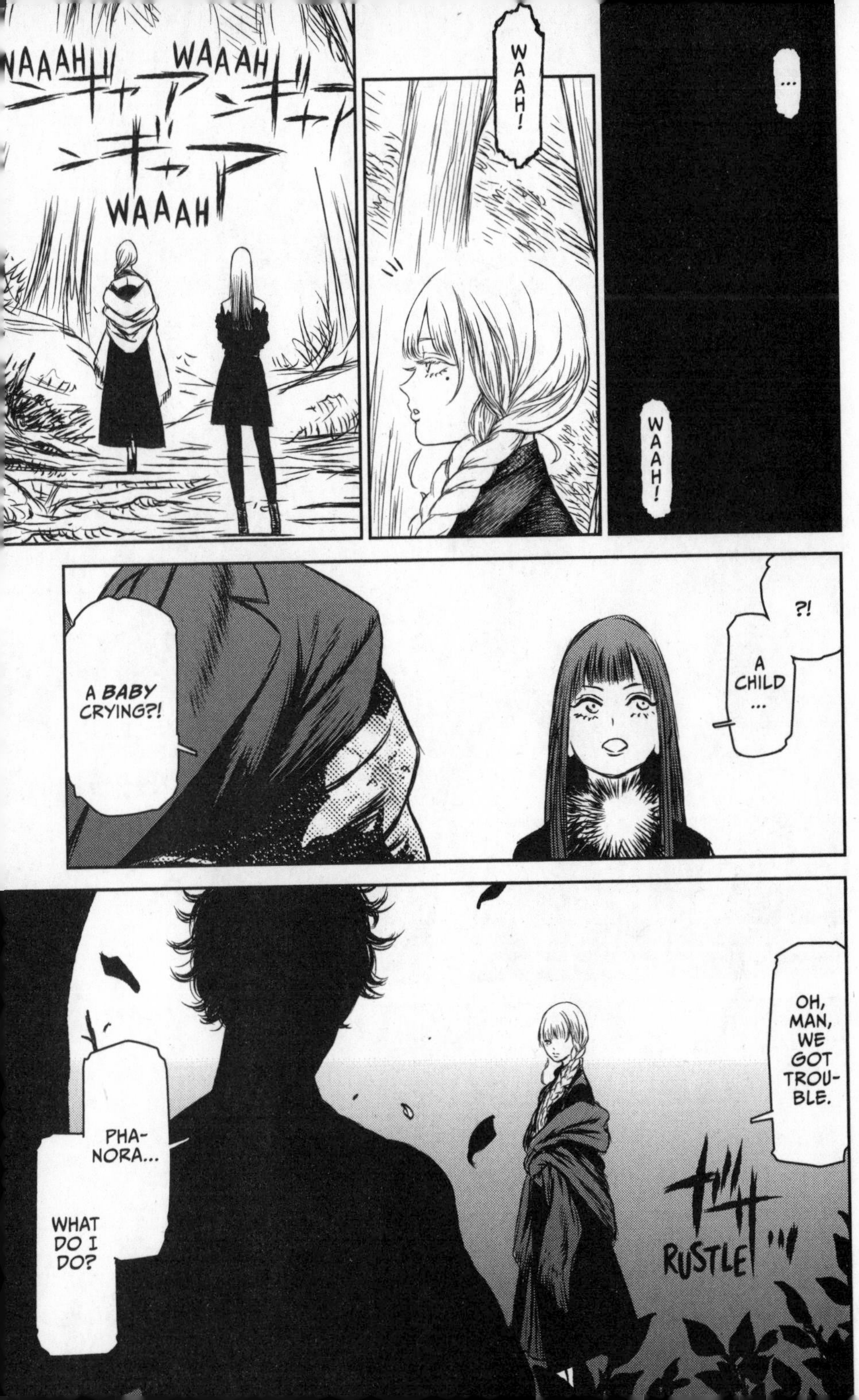
...
WAAAH!
WAAAH!
WAAAH
WAAAH
WAAAH
?!
A CHILD...
A *BABY* CRYING?!
OH, MAN, WE GOT TROUBLE.
RUSTLE
PHANORA...
WHAT DO I DO?

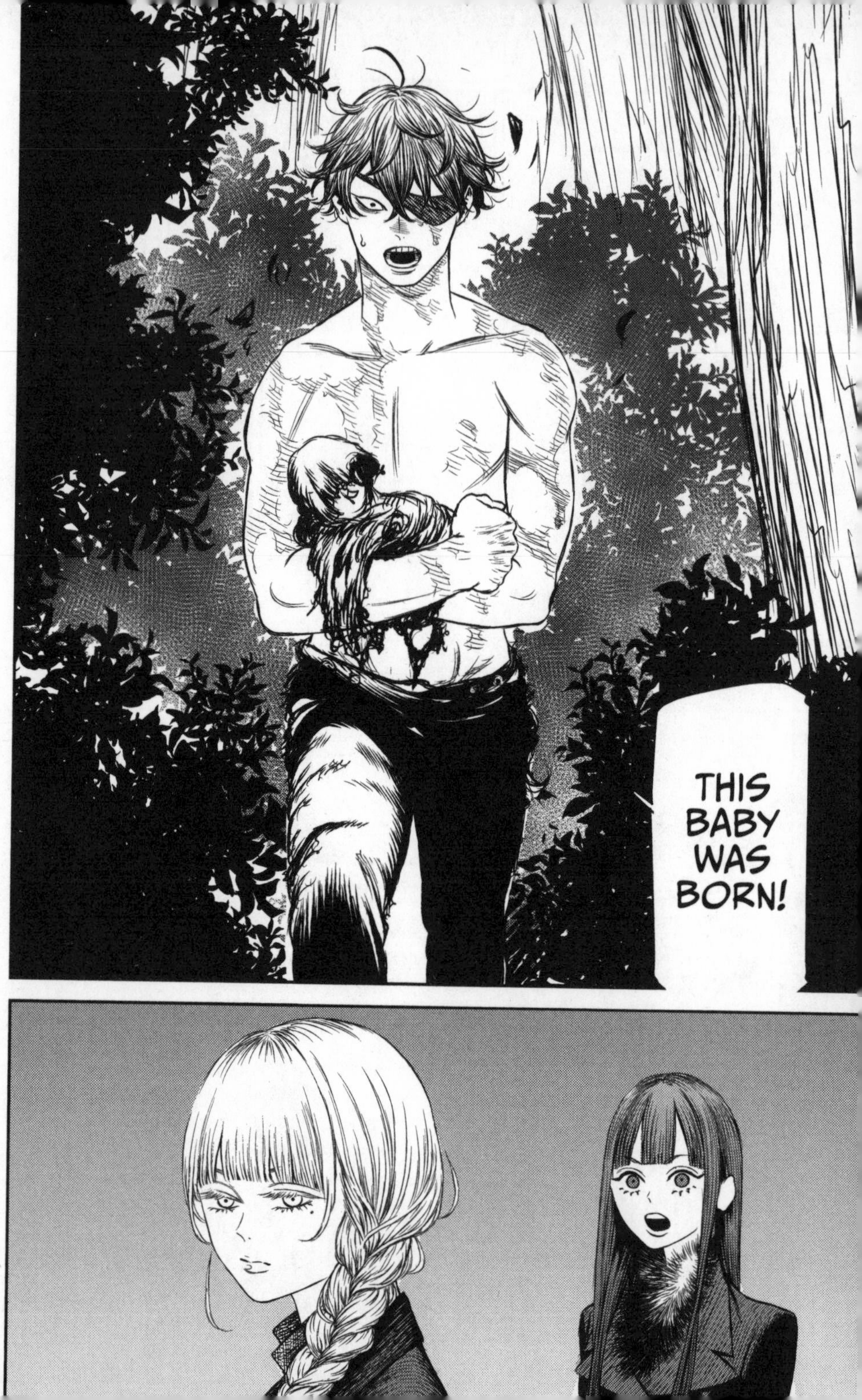
THIS BABY WAS BORN!

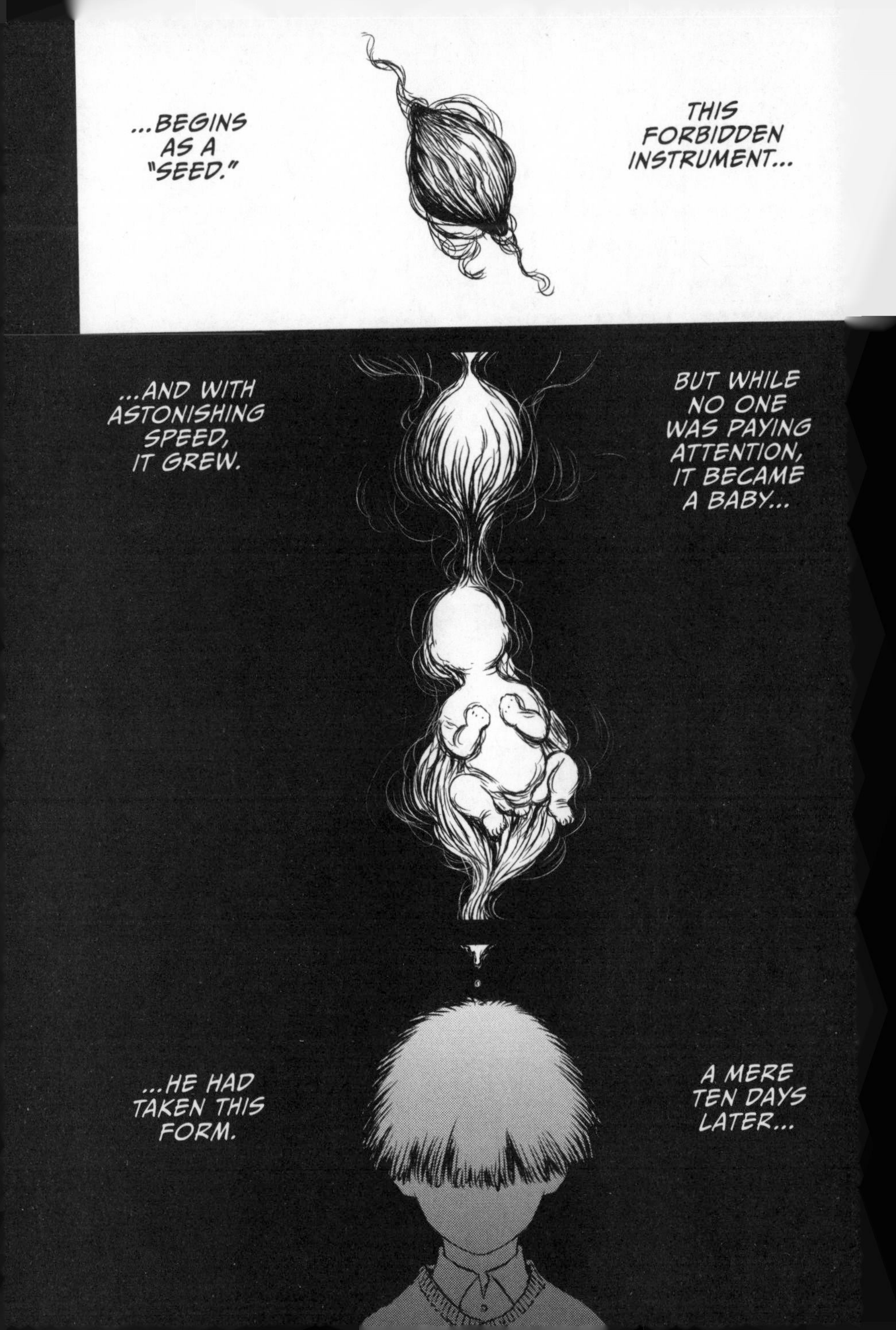
THIS FORBIDDEN INSTRUMENT...
...BEGINS AS A "SEED."
BUT WHILE NO ONE WAS PAYING ATTENTION, IT BECAME A BABY...
...AND WITH ASTONISHING SPEED, IT GREW.
A MERE TEN DAYS LATER...
...HE HAD TAKEN THIS FORM.

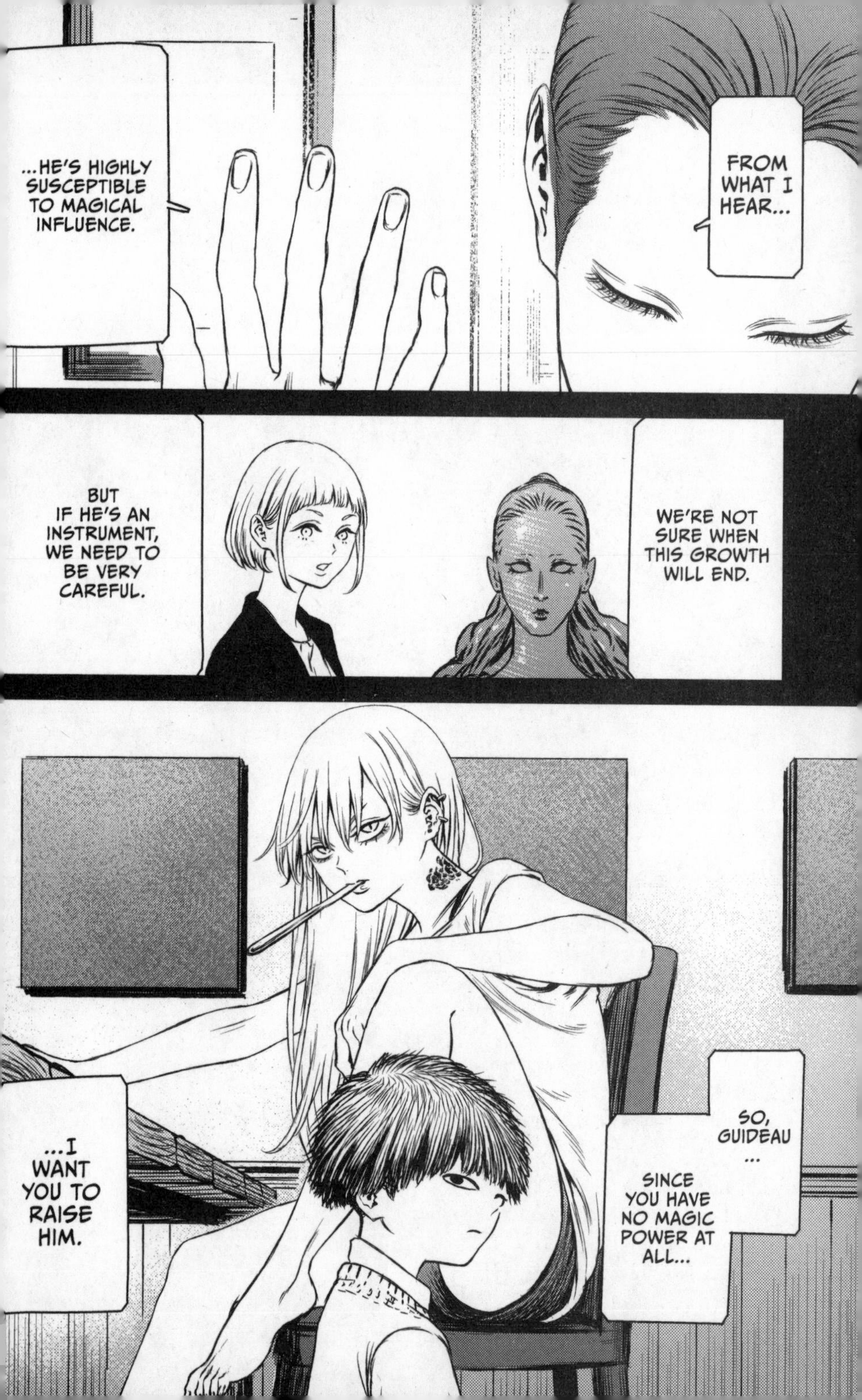
FROM WHAT I HEAR...
...HE'S HIGHLY SUSCEPTIBLE TO MAGICAL INFLUENCE.
WE'RE NOT SURE WHEN THIS GROWTH WILL END.
BUT IF HE'S AN INSTRUMENT, WE NEED TO BE VERY CAREFUL.
SO, GUIDEAU ...
SINCE YOU HAVE NO MAGIC POWER AT ALL...
...I WANT YOU TO RAISE HIM.

THE WITCH AND THE BEAST

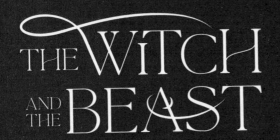

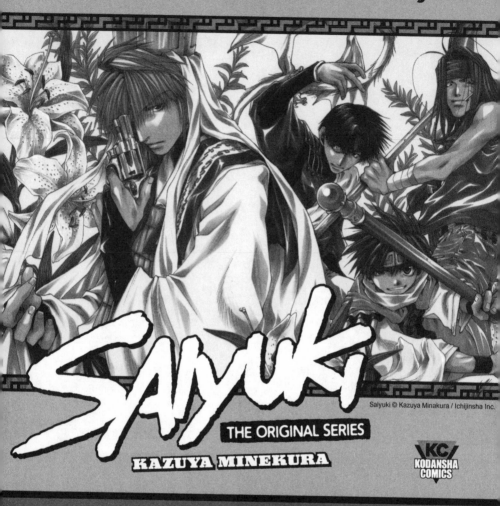

Something's Wrong With Us

NATSUMI ANDO

The dark, psychological, sexy shojo series readers have been waiting for!

A spine-chilling and steamy romance between a Japanese sweets maker and the man who framed her mother for murder!

Following in her mother's footsteps, Nao became a traditional Japanese sweets maker, and with unparalleled artistry and a bright attitude, she gets an offer to work at a world-class confectionary company. But when she meets the young, handsome owner, she recognizes his cold stare...

A Kodansha Comics Trade Paperback Original
The Witch and the Beast 9 copyright © 2022 Kousuke Satake
English translation copyright © 2022 Kousuke Satake

Published in the United States by Kodansha Comics, an imprint of
Kodansha USA Publishing, LLC, New York.

Publication rights for this English edition arranged through
Kodansha Ltd., Tokyo.

First published in Japan in 2022 by Kodansha Ltd., Tokyo
as *Majo to yaju*, volume 9.

ISBN 978-1-64651-391-8

Original cover design by Yusuke Kurachi (Astrorb)

Printed in the United States of America.

www.kodansha.us

1st Printing
Translation: Kevin Gifford
Lettering: Phil Christie
Editing: Vanessa Tenazas
Kodansha Comics edition cover design by My Truong

Publisher: Kiichiro Sugawara

Director of publishing services: Ben Applegate
Director of publishing operations: Dave Barrett
Associate director of publishing operations: Stephen Pakula
Publishing services managing editors: Alanna Ruse, Madison Salters, with Grace Chen
Production manager: Jocelyn O'Dowd
Logo and character art ©Kodansha USA Publishing, LLC